MORE THAN HEROIC

MORE

THAN

HEROIC

*The Spoken Words of Those
Who Served with the
Los Angeles Police Department*

Gary Farmer

BookLocker
St. Petersburg, Florida

MORE THAN HEROIC

Published by BookLocker.com, Inc., St. Petersburg, Florida.

Printed on acid-free paper.

BookLocker.com, Inc.
2017

First Edition

ISBN: 978-1-63492-760-4 (sc)
ISBN: 978-1-63492-780-2 (hc)

Library of Congress Cataloguing in Publication Data
Farmer, Gary
More than Heroic by Gary Farmer
Biography/Autobiography | Law Enforcement | History United States/State & Local/West | True Crime General
Library of Congress Control Number: 2017916834

This book is dedicated to the
families of those
past, present, and future
members of the
Los Angeles Police Department

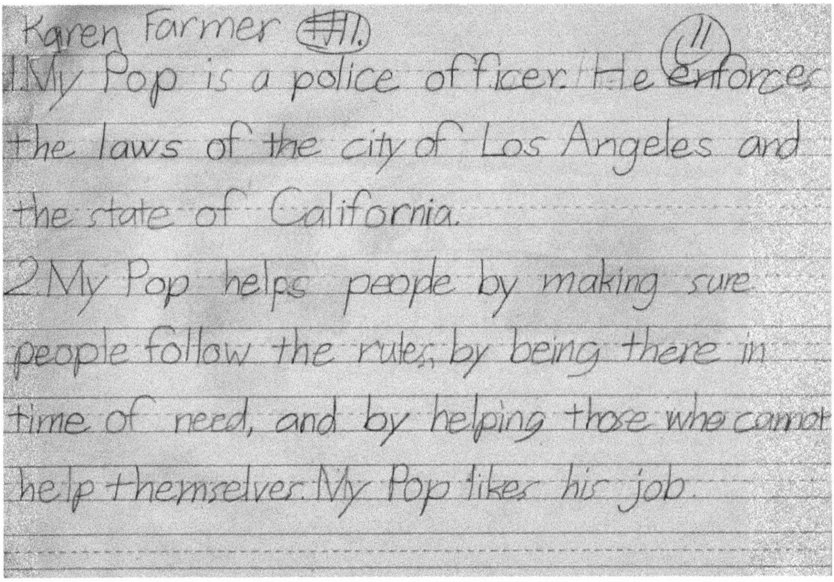

Karen Farmer (#1)
1 My Pop is a police officer. He enforces
the laws of the city of Los Angeles and
the state of California.
2 My Pop helps people by making sure
people follow the rules, by being there in
time of need, and by helping those who cannot
help themselves. My Pop likes his job.

Contents

Front Cover: Center, Bob Drees and John Clapp; top left, Linda Travis; top right, Ken Welty; lower left, John "Jack" Harte; and lower right, Melva Meyers and Margie Collins.

Title page image: Don Stanley and Bob Smitson

Acknowledgments

This book, as with my first book, includes people who came on the Department a long time ago. Thus, there is a natural deadline for getting these books published. For the first book, five have since passed, but fortunately, I was able to get a book into their hands before they left us. Unfortunately, this book has taken much longer to get to the publisher, and two in this book have since passed. The reasons for the delay are not important now. What is important is recognizing the editing effort of Julie Riggott, who came on late in this project, to help me get this book to the publisher. Although she has a family to take care of and job responsibilities, her commitment was total and unwavering.

Gail Carter, a retired policewoman, could write her own book of her experiences with the Los Angeles Police Department. She has been an invaluable resource in tracking down people, locating photographs, and a million other tasks associated with this project.

As with my first book, Kevin Turcotte, a family friend, again put his artistic talents to work. I only had to provide an idea and he designed a cover that truly honors the people within the book. Kevin's schedule does not allow time for side projects, but he made the time for this project and I am forever grateful. Hideki Okuda created the title page illustration. Like Kevin, Hideki listened to an idea and created a wonderful and impressive image of the Los Angeles Police Department.

One last acknowledgement and that is to the families who provided photographs of the officer in their family, who, in most cases, has since passed. The photographs put a face to the words thus completing the story.

On behalf of the officers in this book, and for those who by reading this book gain a sense of what it means to be a police officer, I offer my sincere and heartfelt appreciation to each of you.

From the Author

During our youth, my sister and I would stay with our grandmother for three weeks each summer. During those three weeks, late at night, I would often sit in the kitchen and listen to the police frequency band on my grandmother's 1947 Packard-Bell Model 566 radio. I was captivated by what I heard: the dispatchers from the Los Angeles Police Department sending out radio calls or acknowledging the officers in the field. Although I was hearing only one side of the conversation, I generally understood what was taking place. What was taking place was real life. Only later when I became an officer with the Los Angeles Police Department did my complete understanding of the realities of police work come full circle.

In my first book, *The Streets Are Blue*, and in this book, *More Than Heroic*, I tried to capture the realities of police work through the spoken words of former Los Angeles Police Department officers. Just like listening to the radio, I was fascinated by their stories—even some of which I had been directly involved in. What stood out in listening to the officers as they told their stories was how much those experiences are still a part of them to this day. As they spoke, they were reliving moments in their life that greatly affected them. In some stories, visible emotion was evident. And it wasn't some of the officers; it was most of them. That's why I decided to title this book *More Than Heroic*.

The men and women in the law enforcement profession give of themselves every day knowing that there may be consequences that can cost them their life or stay with them through their lifetime. In my first book, I cited the biblical verse Isaiah 6:8 wherein the Lord asked "Whom shall I send? Who will go for us?" And the response offered was "Here am I. Send Me." A police officer is a simple, ordinary individual that willingly steps forward and says, "Here am I. Send me." Police work is a deadly serious business on which the fate of others depends. For an officer to willingly put themselves in harm's way day in and day out is more than heroic.

As with my first book, the officers in this book include people I worked with or around, people whose reputations I was aware of, people whom others suggested, people whom the officers in the book talked about, or people I contacted purely at random. It didn't matter what their experiences were—the Police Department has had thousands of officers, and each one's career is unique unto itself. When I walked into their homes, I had no idea what stories or experiences were forthcoming. If it was a significant event, I researched as much as I could to ensure the accuracy of the story. More often than not, the story had happened just as it was told to me.

I gave each former officer as much time as he or she was willing to take to share his or her stories. Hence, I acquired pages and pages of material. I omitted a good amount to improve the readability of the book, while still offering a flavor of the individuals' overall careers. Editing was minimal to keep their spoken words intact so that readers can share what I experienced while listening to each individual. As you read the book, hopefully you will appreciate, as I did, the sacrifices these extraordinary individuals made and, through their stories, the sacrifices others have made during their careers with the Los Angeles Police Department.

What Is a Cop?

Los Angeles Times, September 16, 1934

FAST POLICE WORK SAVES BABY'S LIFE

Victim of Ant Paste Rushed to Hospital in Radio Car and Gets Quick Treatment

Prompt action by police and expert treatment of police surgeons yesterday restored Patricia Farmer, 1 year of age, to perfect health after she had become dangerously ill from eating ant paste while playing in the rear yard of her home at 1003 North Figueroa Terrace.

A police radio car arrived on being summoned by neighbors and rushed the child to Georgia-street Receiving Hospital at top speed through downtown traffic.

A message had been relayed to the hospital and preparations were made to care for the sick baby. She was carried to the operating room and after being treated with a stomach pump was fully restored in a few moments.

The one-year-old girl is my aunt, pictured here in the article with my grandmother. My aunt just celebrated her 84th birthday...Author

Harry Lee (full Academy class picture, page 449)

Harry Lee

Birthplace: Los Angeles, California
Career: 1947–1974
Rank at Retirement: Police Officer III
Divisions: Highland Park, Valley, Central

At the start of World War II, I left high school early and became a seagoing Marine aboard the USS Pennsylvania. In '46, a year after I got home from the war, I found myself in a crappy job as an optical technician in downtown Los Angeles.

I was walking home one day feeling sorry for myself when I saw a recruiting billboard for the Los Angeles Police Department. Remembering a neighbor I had when growing up who was a policeman with LAPD, I signed up. Out of six thousand men that took the test, they only picked six hundred. From this group, there were six Academy classes. My class had about seventy. Well, it seemed like everything came at once: I got married, my wife was pregnant, and I was off to be a policeman!

Frankly, the Academy was easy for me. I just enjoyed it. The instructors got mad at me once, though, and it worried me because I thought they were going to dump me. We were on a run, and as we were running up this hill, I thought the instructor said, "Go on."

So I ran right past him. Running was easy for me; I had been a champion sprinter in high school.

He shouted, "Where do you think you're going, home?"

Everything turned out okay, and I graduated from the Academy.

Highland Park was my first division. I was put with an old-timer, a War Emergency Relief guy. Those guys were policemen, but not certified; they were hired because of the manpower shortage from the war. On my first night, he said, "I'm going to give you the keys to drive." I was nervous as hell.

We pulled over a speeder, and my partner said, "You are going to write the ticket." I did, and made all kinds of mistakes. The ticket was later canceled. He was a good guy to work with and more or less took care of me. He said, "Let's get your feet wet, kid." And believe me I got them wet.

At Highland Park, I got in a few pursuits, and I only lost one. Working by myself, I chased a guy down Colorado Boulevard. At the corner of Colorado and Broadway, there were high curbs to control flooding. On one corner was a gas station. The suspect made the turn at the intersection. I misjudged the turn, hit the high curb, and broke the wheels of the police car completely off! The rest of the police car, a '47 Ford, and me, went skidding into the gas station. That was the end of that pursuit.

At night, unless it was a real quiet area, LAPD always had two policemen working together. One time I got a sergeant mad at me, and the next night he put me on a footbeat by myself on Colorado Boulevard. I had never worked a footbeat. I survived it, but the next night I had a little talk with him. I told the sergeant he was dead wrong. I told him, "If you're mad at me, talk to me. Don't stick me out by myself where I can get killed." I got up and walked out, and he never bothered me again.

Valley Division police station

From Highland Park, I went to Valley Division and worked there for four years. There was only one police station for the entire San Fernando Valley. I had two pursuits there that ended up in the deaths of the people that I was chasing. In one, two military servicemen wrapped a car right around a pepper tree and died on impact.

The other pursuit was where Sunland Boulevard meets San Fernando Road. The driver spun out, rolled the car, and hit the trestle at the intersection. That was the end of him. He was a burglar and had all kinds of stolen stuff in the car.

One night a call came out of a robbery in progress at a gas station. We got there quick, but the suspects were gone.

"How long ago?" I asked the attendant.

"Five minutes."

Then he gave us a good description of the robbers.

I said to my partner, "Now, if you just held up a gas station and got some money at two o'clock in the morning, where would you go?"

"I'd go down to San Fernando to that all-night restaurant."

There was nothing open in the area except this restaurant several miles away.

"Let's go."

At the restaurant, we went inside and saw two guys that fit the description beautifully. One of the guys went for his pocket and I grabbed his hand and said, "Don't reach for it." Sure enough, he had a gun in his right front pocket. It was a small semi-automatic. We booked them both for the gas station robbery.

That was a shot in the dark for us, but it turned out good.

Then in 1955, I was off to Central Division. The old Central Station was on First Street, at the corner of First and Hill. My first assignment was a footbeat on Main Street between Third and Fifth Streets. My first day, I heard the old sergeant say, "Let's put Lee down there and see what happens." In Central, on day watch, most of the beats you worked alone. When you work alone, either you make it or you don't. You learn that you have to control the beat. Those two blocks are yours, and it's your job to take care of them.

What a policeman has to have when he walks a beat is a friend on the street to let him know what is going on because the policeman is never going to know by himself. The Department was not particularly fond of informants, but you were out there to solve crime. When you're dealing with people, some can fool you easily or they won't tell you when something happens. Some will give you the wrong information. That's why it was good to have a friend on the beat.

A big, husky guy named John was my best informant. He would tell me about drunks being "rolled," robbed of their money. That was the biggest problem on the beat. You wanted to get the drunks off the street; otherwise, bigger crime came along. The suspects would wait until the drunks were passed out or until they didn't know what was going on, then they'd go through their pockets. John would point out the suspects to me. I watched them, and when they rolled a drunk, I arrested them.

I must have been doing a good job because one day the station received a threatening letter. The letter stated:

> The policeman named Harry Lee is going to die. We are going to shoot him. He is not going to see us, he is not going to know where the bullet comes from, and he won't know when it is going to happen.

The station watch commander called me in, showed me the letter, and asked, "What do you think?"

"I think it is bullshit."

He was going to pull me off the beat, and I said, "No. I know all these buildings. I know where these guys can and can't hide."

We never did find out who wrote the letter, and nothing ever happened.

One tragic thing did happen, though. I was walking the beat when I was told to call the station. It was kind of scary when you're told on the Gamewell, a callbox on a street corner with a telephone for police use, "You need to come to the station right away."

When I got there, the sergeant told me that he had terrible news. My eight-year-old son had been killed. He had ridden his bicycle to the store to return some empty soda bottles for a few cents and was hit by a car. Nothing was done to the guy that killed him, but he really wasn't at fault from what I understood. My wife blamed herself, even though we had always let him go to the store. Everybody on the job was as nice as could be and helped us through it. That was in 1957.

On the street, there was very little in the way of drugs, mostly just marijuana once in a while. Drunks don't believe in that, only in the bottle. Drunks will say, "I'm just a drunk. I drink wine. I don't do drugs." I believed most of them. I think they were afraid of drugs. They knew what the wine would do to them, but they had no idea what the drugs would do.

Louie Rasic and I worked the East Fifth Street beat for about ten years. It was a two-man beat and the area was strictly Skid Row. Fifth Street was more of a drunk area than Main Street.

Each day when Louie and I started, we parked our police car in an alley and then walked the beat. One day after a couple of hours on the beat, we stopped a guy and said, "What's in the bag?" It turned out he had a police radio in it. Well, we walked back to our car to take him to the station, and, sure enough, he had stolen the radio out of our car! We usually left the car unlocked, and people left it alone.

Another time, this guy came up to us, and he was real upset. He said, "The lady I was in bed with is dead." We went up to his room, and, sure enough, the lady was dead.

I asked the guy, "What happened?"

"I gave her ten bucks to go to bed with me, but I was too drunk and I couldn't get it on. When I woke up this morning, I rolled over and she was stiff as a board. I want my money back."

"Well, I think we have got more important things with this now."

We called in the detectives, and they took over the case.

One time a guy pulled a gun on us. We stopped him on Fifth Street, and during my search, I felt the gun. He pushed me away and pulled the gun out of his pocket. He said, "I don't want any trouble. I just want to get away." Louie and I could have shot the man, but we let him back away. He turned and started down the street with his back to us. He was so intent on getting away that we were able to run up behind him and take him down. He still had the gun on him.

Harry Lee, left, and Lou Rasic

Louie eventually made sergeant and did his probation at Seventy-Seventh Division. While he was there, Louie was involved in a big fight between policemen and some suspects. One of the suspects had a knife, got to Louie, and stuck him with the knife in his forehead. After the fight, they could not find the blade to the knife. Louie went to the hospital and was placed off-duty for a few days. He started getting headaches that progressively got worse. Louie was X-rayed and there, plain as day was part of the blade stuck in his skull. He later transferred back to Central and finished his career there. I used to kid Louie, "If you had stayed with me, you wouldn't have had that knife stuck in your forehead."

On the Seventh Street footbeat, I worked by myself. On the beat, there was a guy that got into a fight with me every time he saw me. His name was John, not the same John that was my informant. I got tired of John fighting with me and changed to the Hill Street beat. Well, wouldn't you know it, I find John raising hell in a bar one day on my new beat. I dragged him out of the bar, and we had a big fight on the sidewalk. During the fight, he went down on my leg, and I heard my leg bone pop. I said, "John, I think my leg is broken." He stopped fighting. After that, for whatever reason, I never had a problem with him again. He turned out to be an okay guy, and we became friends.

Most of my good police work was hampered because of something I did that wasn't too good. It was said I was a good cop, but I did not follow the rules. I used to love cigars, and I'd walk a beat smoking a cigar. Over the years, I don't know how many calls came to the station, "Your officer in uniform is smoking a cigar." Then they'd call me in. It was against the rules, and I knew it was against the rules. But if you walked the beat on Skid Row, you had to smoke a cigar to stand the stench.

I retired on the spur of the moment. When the Department told us we could no longer carry .357 magnum handguns, I got up and walked out of roll call. I said, "I'm gone." Years later, I was right. The Department went to using semi-automatic pistols, which were stronger than the .357 handguns and more powerful than the .38 caliber revolvers they required everyone to carry.

Harry Lee

Another change was the baton. The officers now carry a baton called a Monadnock. The worst part about the new baton is that a guy can take it away from you. I still have my old club with a leather strap. I'd wrap the leather strap around my hand, and a guy would have to pull my hand off to take it from me. And they tried. But no one could get it away from me because the strap wouldn't break.

I enjoyed my time on the job. I don't know of a job that has more freedom than being a policeman. Where else could you be on your own for eight hours a day? If your supervisor saw you once a day, he was happy. He'd wave at you and drive on because he could trust you.

I couldn't possibly have worked in a factory where you tighten bolt B on assembly line A. I had the only job that I could handle, and I loved it. For twenty-seven years, it was my salvation, but I just got disgusted toward the end. The job changed, and there were too many rules and regulations. The Department sent me a letter giving me the opportunity to come back, but I told them no.

Once I retired, I was the happiest guy in the world. I was forty-eight years old, healthy, and I could do what I wanted. For nineteen years, I walked the beat, eight to ten miles a day. That is why I am still alive today at ninety-one years old.

Richard "Mick" Meharg

Birthplace: Sommerville, Massachusetts
Career: 1948–1969
Rank at Retirement: Policeman
Divisions: Newton, Seventy-Seventh, Traffic Enforcement

Back home where I grew up in Sommerville, Massachusetts, every kid had a nickname. Mine was "Mick" or "Mickey." When I hear anybody call me "Mick," that means they've known me a long time.

I was working for the Pittsburgh Plate Glass Company here in Los Angeles doing bookwork, accounting-type stuff, and I didn't care for the job. One of the guys I worked with said he was going to go take the police exam for LAPD. Growing up back East, I never gave being a policeman a thought because it's freezing in the winter and too hot to wear the uniform in the summer. But I wanted a more active job, so I went with him and we both applied. I made it, and he did not.

The Academy was a hard six weeks, but I made it. There was a military general from Central America in our class. The first day he showed up in his military uniform, and everyone in the class was asking, "Who is this guy?" He was not there to be a policeman, only to go through the training. He stayed the whole six weeks and did everything we did.

After graduation, I went to Newton Division. My first night at Newton, I worked crowd control for a big event. It was a stage show of some type, but I didn't know anything about it. A crowd of about a hundred people was blocking the sidewalk when I saw this lady dressed in a wedding gown approaching the crowd. I was telling the people to move back and let the lady through. Everybody started laughing. I didn't know what everyone was laughing about until my partner said, "That's a guy, Meharg."

Richard Meharg

I said, "What do you mean?"

He repeated that the person in the wedding gown was a man. I couldn't believe it. I didn't know anything about things like that. My partner said, "We can go backstage when the show starts and you can see." We did, and that convinced me. Yes, she was a he!

That night I was off duty about three thirty in the morning, and I was standing on a corner near the station in uniform, waiting for the streetcar. At the time, I lived at 103rd Street and Broadway. A motor cop pulled up and stopped next to me. He said, "You know there are no streetcars but every hour or two. Do you want a ride?"

It was late, so I jumped on, and then he took off like a rocket. We made it to 103rd and Broadway in what seemed like two minutes. That was a fast ride! My right foot was bothering me when I got off the bike. I looked down and found a silver dollar-sized burn on my new shoes from the muffler.

When I crawled into bed, my wife woke up and asked, "How was your first day?"

"You won't believe it. I'll tell you later."

Newton Division police station

Including Charlie Loust, there were six or seven cadets from my class that went to Newton. One night Charlie was walking a footbeat with Bill Terry. They saw a guy in an alley near Sixth and Central doing something that drew their attention. They went to investigate, and the guy lunged at Bill with an open straight razor, often called a cutthroat razor. Charlie shot and killed the guy. Charlie wasn't on the job over a month and he saved his partner! He did not get the Medal of Valor, but he was a hero as far as we were concerned.

Even though we were still on probation, Charlie and I worked together for a while on a footbeat. Back then walking a beat, you didn't have a handheld radio. When I look back at it now, I realize that other than ourselves, we had no real protection going down dark alleys and such. You had to call in every hour on the Gamewell to let them know, "Meharg and Loust. We're still alive out here."

Sometimes being out on foot had its drawbacks. One night we were out walking a beat, and it was raining like hell. Naturally, we had our rain gear. We had passed a movie theater, and Charlie said,

"Let's go into the movie. There's no point in us getting any more wet."

We went into the movie theater, walked upstairs to the balcony, and lo and behold, there were four more footbeat officers in the seats watching the movie! We were not there long when in came the sergeant. "Okay, you guys, you have raincoats. Get back to work!"

One of the guys said, "We were told policemen don't get wet or go hungry."

The sergeant laughed. He was an old-timer and a good supervisor. No doubt, he once did the same thing.

I had to make a death notification only once when I walked a beat in Newton. Somebody had been shot and he died, and we were told to make the notification to his family. He lived in a house off Central Avenue. It was late when I knocked on the door, and the wife answered, "Who is it?"

"Police officers. We'd like to talk to you for a moment."

We told her, she broke down, and I felt like hell. We stayed there for a little bit, turned, and walked away. I don't remember much about it, but the crying and the feeling bad.

Francis Brokus and I were partners for a long time. He was six feet three inches, a good cop, and well known for his short temper. We called him Fran. We were taking some drunks in the B-wagon to Avenue Nineteen, the Lincoln Heights Jail, when one guy in the back yelled to Fran, "If you didn't have that badge and gun on, I'd take care of you."

Charlie Loust

Fran Brokus

Fran pulled into an alley, stopped, got out, and took off his belt with all of his equipment—gun, handcuffs, etcetera. Then he opened the door to the back of the B-wagon and said to the guy, "Step out." The guy changed his mind. Fran was a good guy, but he had a short temper.

When Fran and I went to Newton Vice together, we worked bookmakers and were initially teamed up with this other officer. We received information on a bookie and went to the location where he was allegedly making book, a doctor's office at Vernon and Central. From down the street, we could see people going in, but nobody coming out.

Finally, we decided that we should go in to see if there was evidence of bookmaking. We opened the door to the doctor's office, and nobody was there in the lobby. The other officer approached another door as Fran and I waited down a hall. He bent down on his knee, signaled us after a few minutes, opened the door, and went in. Fran and I rushed down the hall, and as we approached the open door, we saw that bookmaking had been taking place. The bookie was arrested.

At court, the officer testified that he looked through a keyhole in the door and observed the bookie taking bets. When I testified, I was asked if I saw the officer looking through a keyhole. I said, "From where I was standing in the hall, I saw him bend down. He appeared to be looking through a keyhole."

There was no keyhole. There was a plate, but no keyhole. The officer was recalled to testify, and he tried to backtrack and say he was mistaken, but the damage was done. Ultimately, the defense brought in the door, and there was no keyhole.

The officer was charged with perjury. The case against the bookie was dismissed, although Judge Clement Nye opined bookmaking was going on. It was also uncovered that the officer had been taking $250 a month to provide protection to gamblers and ignore their illegal activities. He was charged with bribery, fired from the job, and went to jail.

After that, Fran's and my name were on many arrest reports for bookmakers. Then one day a bookie unknown to either Fran or me called the office. Fran answered the phone. The bookie wanted to meet and openly made an offer over the phone to Fran asking if he would provide him with protection. We arranged to meet at a bar on Wilshire Boulevard. Prior to the meet, we made sure Fran only had five dollars on him. I went into the bar before the scheduled time and sat on one side of the horseshoe-shaped bar.

A short while later, the bookie came in, sat across from me, and ordered a drink. When Fran came in, the bookie looked at him. I was the only other customer in the bar. Fran nodded at the bookie, and they sat at a table. They had a discussion. Then Fran stood up and said, "Hey, Mick, come over here and check my pockets."

The bookie was startled; he had just given Fran five hundred dollars in exchange for ignoring his bookmaking activities. We arrested the bookmaker, and he went to jail for bribery. We never went to court on him, and that always left me with a bad taste in my mouth. Maybe this guy knew somebody above us and he was used as an informant on a bigger arrest. Maybe he rolled over on somebody. I never heard, not a word.

At the end of our Vice tour, Fran and I left Newton and transferred to Seventy-Seventh Division. It was then that I was called back to the Marine Corps for eighteen months. When I returned in 1953, I applied to motors. The motors class was held at Van Nuys Airport.

We rode Harleys—all junkers, no fenders. And we wore soft hats, no helmets. Helmets did not come along until 1956. In fact, I was one of the guys given helmets to try for a week and then critique them. Everybody said the same thing. They felt safer, but the helmets were very uncomfortable. However, the choice was made for us: we had to wear helmets.

The first week on motors, I was working Sunset Boulevard with Brick Harrison. One day it started to sprinkle, a little rain, and Brick says, "Follow me." He drove to a Gamewell on a corner. He got on the phone and said, "This is Harrison and Meharg. We're out here on Sunset, and it's starting to rain." There was a pause, and then he said, "Okay. Thank you."

He hung up and said to me, "See you tomorrow."

I said, "What do you mean?"

"It's raining. I'm going home. You might as well too."

When I got home, my wife said, "You're home early."

I said to her, "Yeah, they sent me home. It's raining in Hollywood. This is a great job!"

I rode nothing but Harleys on the job, used ones at first. I probably had five or six years on motors before I got a new bike. When I did, we went on a break-in ride. There were about ten guys on new bikes, and we drove all the way up to San Jacinto and back, about a hundred and eighty miles, followed by a mechanic in a truck. It was a one-day ride, and your butt got tired. As time went by, the rides were stopped. I believe it was realized it was not necessary to break a bike in.

My first pursuit on a motorcycle maybe lasted a block or two. Motor officers did not have many pursuits. In those days, to have the siren go off, you had to pull a lever on the handlebar and that pushed part of the siren against the wheel to get a sound. You had to get going like hell to get the siren going. Now, you just push a button. The fastest I went on a bike chasing somebody was probably close to ninety miles per hour. It's not a very good feeling. If you got going too fast, you would get a front wheel wobble. You could feel it, and so you backed off. It wasn't worth getting killed over a traffic ticket. Hopefully, whoever you were chasing would get hung up in traffic, and you could still get him.

Richard Meharg

The bike was also hard to kickstart. If you didn't get the motor going on the first kick, it could take another five minutes of kicking. In the meantime, your ticket has gone down the road. I missed a few tickets that way. Prior to my retiring from the job, they talked about the idea of a button starter. If they had come up with that earlier, I would have probably stayed another couple of years!

I found out quick that some traffic violators try to play games with you. I was working Washington Boulevard at night and saw a guy commit a U-turn. I had to wait for a car to go by, and then I made a U-turn and followed him. The guy made a right turn at the next block just off Central Avenue. I wasn't that far behind him, but when I made the turn, there was no one there. No lights in the distance or anything. I thought *Now where the hell is this guy?* I coasted to the curb, stopped, and turned my radio down. I stayed there for a while looking down the street, but I didn't see anything.

Just when I was about ready to get back on my motor, brake lights came on from a car parked at the curb less than a hundred feet from me.

I walked to the car, and as I approached it, I couldn't readily see anybody inside. I continued up to the driver's side of the car, shined my flashlight in, and there was the violator, lying on the floorboard, leaning against the brake pedal.

I asked him, "What are you doing down there?"

He replied, "Oh! Hi, officer. How are you?" He had traffic warrants, so he went to jail.

I was working Vermont Avenue at Washington Boulevard when I saw a car make a U-turn and I pulled it over. It was one hundred degrees that day, hotter than hell, and with the helmet, it seemed even hotter. I walked up to the car and told the driver to roll down the window. He rolled the window down about two inches and handed me his driver's license through the opening. It was Van Johnson, the actor.

I said, "Roll the window down."

And he did, saying, "I'm sorry. It's so hot to put the window down."

"That's okay. "Do you know why I stopped you?"

"Yeah. For the U-turn."

"What was the reason for the U-turn?"

"I'm going to the Red Cross to donate a pint of blood for one of my college buddies."

That was probably true because the Red Cross building was on the next block. I told him, "I think giving a pint of blood today would be enough." I let him go with a warning, and he was very grateful. He drove off, and naturally, I followed him to make sure he went to the Red Cross, and he did. Everybody that I met of any fame was always very nice.

I was working the Harbor Freeway around seven thirty in the morning one day, and one car drew my attention as it was speeding and making several lane changes. I pulled the car over and told the driver he was speeding. He said, "I'm a professor, and I never speed."

"You were, and I'm going to cite you for it."

"Well, I'll see you in court."

"I'll be there."

About a month later, I received a subpoena. I went to court and testified to what I saw. The professor told his side of the story and emphasized that he never speeds.

The judge asked, "Do you have any witnesses?"

The professor said, "Yes, I do. My wife."

I told the city attorney, "There was nobody in the car except the professor."

He said, "Are you sure?"

"Yes, I know there was nobody in the car." I showed him my notes where I had written only the professor was in the car.

The judge said, "Call your witness."

When the wife finished testifying, the city attorney said, "I only have one question, your honor. I would like to ask the wife where she was when her husband was cited for speeding."

The judge allowed the question, and the wife said, "I was at home when my husband got the ticket. He told me about it when he got home, and my husband is a very careful driver. He never speeds."

The judge said, "Guilty," and the professor had to pay a fine.

When part of the Baldwin Hills Reservoir gave way in December '63, I was right there. At the report of the initial leakage, all motor officers were activated to respond and assist with evacuating residents who lived below the reservoir. I had worked the evacuation, and later I was up in the reservoir with another motor cop and the Wilshire Division captain as he surveyed the situation. We were standing on a crosswalk about twenty to thirty feet from the area of the crack when, all of a sudden, it opened up. We were on solid footing, but the three of us moved back as we watched it go. Then all hell broke loose as the water just poured out of the reservoir. Watching the wall give way and the water gushing out, I was thinking, *Did we get everybody out?* It left you speechless.

The damage was horrific. All these millions of gallons of water flooded homes and businesses. I don't think many of the people who had bought homes there even knew about the reservoir up the hill from them. Several of the motor cops had parked their motorcycles at a curb on one of the main streets. A few were washed away, and the rest were damaged pretty good.

I only had one real fight in all the time I was on the job and that was when I was on motors. I stopped a guy at Adams and Normandie. He had been drinking, and he was nasty. He started to fight, and I wrestled with him. I was having a hell of a time.

Baldwin Hills Reservoir: "It left you speechless."

All of a sudden, I saw these black hands come down on this guy, holding him back. A black citizen had driven by and could see that I needed help. He stopped and helped me. We handcuffed the guy, and I called for a radio car. That's the only time I was in a fight, and a citizen saved me.

At that time, the Police Department had a good reputation with the black community. They were very pro-police. Unfortunately, the '65 Watts riots changed all that.

The second day of the riots, they put a bunch of motor cops in buses and took us down to the police substation on 103rd Street. There were a hundred of us, and some of us were staged in the fire station next door. We stayed there for hours. We were looking out the windows and watching looters carrying stolen stuff walk right by the station. They wouldn't let us go out and arrest them. I couldn't believe it. People were stealing stuff, and we did nothing. We were told to stay where we were.

We all thought it was strange that we were sent there and they did not use us.

The next day I was sent to the intersection of Adams and Normandie and worked with the National Guard. Many of them were just kids. They more or less relied on us to be the adults in the group, to tell them what to do. They didn't have much training.

After the riots, I talked to a storeowner and asked him how things went for him. He told me his store was looted pretty good. He said, "I drove by my store and parked where I could see the front door. I saw my regular customers go in and steal from me. My longtime customers were stealing from me!" And that was the way it was. It's there, I need it, I'll take it.

On motors, we worked escort details for dignitaries, including Presidents Eisenhower, Kennedy, and Nixon. The escort details were a lot of fun, and sometimes you met other famous people besides the person you were escorting. In 1959, Nikita Khrushchev, the premier of the Soviet Union, came to Los Angeles on his tour of the United States. I was part of the escort detail.

We escorted him to Century Fox Studios for a luncheon and performance of dancers from the movie *Can-Can* with Frank Sinatra and Shirley MacLaine. Inside the studio, I was standing next to some bleachers. A number of movie stars were coming into the studio to see Khrushchev, including Clark Gable and Marilyn Monroe. Marilyn Monroe took a seat in the bleachers about four rows up and all the way to one side. I worked my way around to where she was sitting and stood next to her, just off her left shoulder. She turned, looked at me, and said, "Hello, officer."

I said, "Good afternoon." I will always remember that.

They told us at the Academy that we were going to find out, after we had been on a while, that most of our close friends were going to be policemen and their wives. And that is the truth; that is the way it was. Bob Drees is my best friend, and we met while working Seventy-Seventh Division. We have been friends for close to sixty years, and we talk at least twice a week. Bob and his wife Jackie lived down the street from us for over twenty years.

*Richard Meharg, second from left: President Dwight Eisenhower thanking
escort detail, 1958*

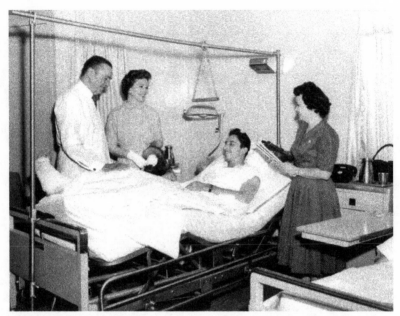

Audrey Meharg, second from left: WOLAPO visit at Central Receiving Hospital

My wife, Audrey, and his wife, Jackie, both belong to WOLAPO, Wives of Los Angeles Police Officers. In addition to other activities, WOLAPO would visit hospitalized officers and firefighters at Central Receiving Hospital. The hospital used to have a ward exclusively for injured policemen and firemen. WOLAPO would bring magazines and food and during the Christmas season sing carols in the ward. A few wives still meet, but the organization is not what it once was.

The day I retired, I went to roll call, and I just didn't feel like going out to work. I went down to my motor, sat on it for a little while, and then said to myself, *No, I'm going in. I'm going to retire.* I called Audrey, and she came and picked me up.

I had worked motors since 1953. I treated the job seriously, and I always felt that I was accomplishing something. I hadn't been feeling well for a few days, and maybe I should have just gone off sick, but you can't look back. There is a saying, "Yesterday is history. Tomorrow is a mystery. Today is a gift. That's why it is called the present."

Robert "Bob" Drees

Birthplace: Los Angeles, California
Career: 1949–1970
Rank at Retirement: Sergeant
Divisions: Parking and Intersection Control, Jail, Seventy-Seventh,
  Narcotics, Special Investigation Section, Intelligence

My dad inspired me to become a policeman. He would tell me all kinds of stories. During World War II, my dad became an auxiliary policeman with the Los Angeles Police Department. He jumped at the opportunity because he always wanted to be a policeman, but my mother was afraid. He worked out of Seventy-Seventh Division, and we lived in the division on Sixtieth Street. My dad patrolled our neighborhood and made sure people's lights were off at night. Everyone had to cover their windows because of fear of air raids. Our windows were covered by cardboard cartons.

While an auxiliary policeman, my dad became friends with George Booker Mogle, a reserve policeman at Seventy-Seventh. In 1946, Mogle was shot and killed by a burglar. I believe his picture is still hanging on the wall in the lobby of Seventy-Seventh Station. It's such a small world; I later worked with Mogle's son, George Ervin Mogle, at Seventh-Seventh.

When I got out of the Navy, Kurt Mauerman, my best friend growing up, read in the paper that the Los Angeles Police Department was having an entrance exam. We went to sign up, but Kurt couldn't take the test because he was only five feet eight-and-a-half inches and the minimum height was five nine. I felt lucky as hell passing the exam. I took the written test at Hollywood High School at the same time as Daryl Gates. He and I would soon be in the same Academy class, and Gates would eventually become chief of police.

There were seven of us at the medical exam conducted by Doctor Vance. One guy was built like a Greek god! He had obviously been a weightlifter, and not many people lifted weights in those days. I was six feet two inches and weighed 172 pounds—I was thin. We were standing there naked, and Doctor Vance came up to me, put his arm around me, and said, "This is what we're looking for at the LAPD." I never saw the Greek god again.

We were the first three-month class at the Academy. We went from eight o'clock in the morning to nine o'clock at night, and we were paid $290 a month. We lined up for inspection every morning. One morning our instructor, Floyd Phillips, said, "Class dismissed. Cadet Drees, stay behind."

As I stood there, Phillips chewed me out with several other instructors surrounding me. He said, "Weren't you told to keep your hair trimmed at all times?"

It was short, but I said, "Yes, sir."

"What happened?"

"I didn't make it to a barbershop. My dad had dog shears so he gave me a haircut."

My dad was not a barber, and it showed. From then on, I was determined not to be called for another infraction. And I wasn't.

Our physical training and self-defense instructor was Sam Posner. Posner professionally wrestled at that time as the "Masked Marvel." We were sitting out on the PT field in our gray sweats one day, listening to Posner instruct us about physical holds. At one point during his instruction, Posner said to Daryl Gates, "Cadet Gates, come here."

Gates, who weighed a little over two hundred pounds, stood up. Posner said to him, "Get on your hands and knees." Then he told the class, "I'm going to show you a hold that can't be broken." Posner put Gates in the hold and said, "Okay, try to get up." Gates did. Posner was surprised and somewhat embarrassed. He said, "The only way you can break that hold is through strength. I guess Cadet Gates is pretty strong."

We graduated in December '49, and they told us we were going to be assigned to Parking and Intersection Control, PIC, directing traffic downtown for the Christmas holidays. Well, that made sense. Later, we found out we had to stay at PIC for an entire year!

Bob Drees, second row from top, fifth from left; Daryl Gates, third row, third from right: Academy class, 1949 (full Academy class picture, page 449)

At PIC, you worked a split watch, peak traffic hours in the morning and evening with a break in between. I worked the intersections at Seventh Street and San Pedro and at Sixth Street and Central Avenue. The "S" and "R" streetcars ran along Seventh Street. At San Pedro, the "S" streetcar would turn south, and the "R" streetcar would continue on Seventh Street.

The streetcars used to have a loader, a guy in charge of loading people on and off the streetcars. On my first day after we were introduced to each other, the loader said, "Bob, see how those tracks turn for the 'S' streetcar?"

"Yeah."

"The 'R' streetcars are not supposed to turn, but once in a while a malfunction occurs or the driver does something wrong, and the 'R' streetcar will turn and go southbound. So don't stand at or in the tracks because you're going to get hit."

"S" streetcar turning from Seventh Street to San Pedro

Well, that went in one ear and out the other. The next day, sure enough, an "R" streetcar came down the street, turned and hit me! It wasn't hard enough to knock me off my feet, but enough to knock off my hat.

It also hit an older gentleman who was in the crosswalk. I went over, picked him up, and asked, "You okay? Do you want an ambulance?"

"Yeah, I'm okay. I'd just like to go on home."

Upon checking him over, I didn't see any broken bones or obvious trauma. He was retired and a nice guy. I took down his information and he left. The Transit Line sent investigators out, and they made a report. The next day I was out directing traffic again when the gentleman from the day before walked over to me and looked like he was hurting.

He said, "You didn't happen to get the information on that streetcar did you?"

"I sure did."

I gave him the information and the address of the Transit Line. They gave him seventy-five dollars. Today, something like that would probably make you a millionaire.

One afternoon I was directing traffic at Sixth and Central when a guy came running up to me and said, "There's a guy down there going to kill a kid!" It was about two blocks away on Kohler Street near Seventh.

I jumped in the police car, and when I got there, I saw a guy in the middle of the street holding a knife to the throat of a five-year-old boy. Of course, I followed my first instinct and pulled out my gun. He tensed up when I did that, so I put my gun away and started talking to him. I talked to him for about five minutes, and then he put down the knife. I hooked him up and called for a Newton Division unit. It was his kid. He had a fight with his wife and he wanted to get even with her, so he said he was going to kill the boy. I don't think he intended to kill the kid. Once I took him into custody, the fifteen or so people watching started clapping. He was taken away, and I never heard anything more about it.

When the year at PIC was up, they told me, "Now you have to do a year at the jail." I did six months at Lincoln Heights Jail and then six months at the old Navy Brig on Terminal Island.

Doctor Vance told me when I came on the job, "You're in perfect physical shape. The only thing is your ears are dirty." That embarrassed me.

I said, "Well, I shower and wash my ears every day."

He laughed and said, "No, it's inner. You have impacted wax." It was so bad I had to go to the doctor four times to get my ears completely clean!

Now I'm working Seventy-Seventh Division, and my partner was Lynn Leeds. Late one night Lynn was driving, and we were on Wilmington Avenue. About 109th Street, there was an old gas station on the southeast corner. We were going slowly, and, all of a sudden, Lynn pulls into the gas station driveway and he bails out of the car. I thought, *What the hell is going on?* Then I saw two guys inside the gas station office and a third running out, with Lynn on his tail chasing him. I quickly grabbed one of the two in the station and handcuffed him to a pole. The other guy had run back into the mechanic's shop and tried to hide, but I found him. As I brought both guys back to the police car, Lynn walked back with the guy he had chased, and Lynn looked mad.

Lynn Leeds, bottom row, second from right: "...a good cop and a great partner, my best partner."

After we had booked all three for burglary, I said to Lynn, "You know, it'd be really nice if you let me know when you see something. Maybe I could help you."

"You son of a bitch! I told you twice, there are three guys in the gas station!" Wax had impacted my ears again so I couldn't hear him. The next day I went to the doctor and had them cleaned.

Lynn Leeds was a good cop and a great partner, my best partner. We worked together at Seventy-Seventh and later at Narcotics Division. He was a big guy and faster than hell—he could really run! He weighed about 210 pounds, but looked like he could have weighed 240. I always kidded him that he was made of marshmallows in his upper body.

I was working morning watch with a new policeman, Rocky Rockwood, when there was a robbery alarm call at the market at 120th Street and Avalon Boulevard. Leroy Lipe and Bill Mockette went to the front, and Rocky and I went to the back. There was a big empty parking lot in back with only a '55 Chevy parked and nobody in it. We checked the hot sheet, and, sure enough, the car was stolen. I touched the hood, and it was warm. I said to Rocky, "Holler around to Leroy and Bill that it's probably a good call."

Right then we heard two shots from the front—it was Bill. Two guys were in the store holding a woman hostage at gunpoint. One of Bill's rounds ricocheted and struck the hostage's ankle, but she was okay. The suspects retreated to the back of the market with the hostage, and we were there waiting for them. The back of the market had big glass windows. We saw the suspects and the hostage, and then they saw us. One suspect had the hostage, and the other suspect had the gun and pointed it at us. I took two shots at the armed suspect through the glass. I didn't hit him.

The suspects ran out the back door with the hostage and headed straight to the '55 Chevy. I shot at the armed suspect again and hit him in the leg. Bill came out the back door and then shot and killed the other suspect. We took the wounded suspect into custody. The hostage, Jeanette Hay, an employee of the market, said there were still two more suspects in the market. They were found hiding upstairs.

We were recommended for the Medal of Valor, but we did not receive it. I always thought it was because the hostage had been wounded.

Sundays, if I was working, I used to eat dinner occasionally with an Italian family, the Smaldinos, who lived in the division. They had six kids, all boys, and I went to school with two of the boys. One night on patrol, there was a call about a fire at Club Mecca, a bar. When we got there, the firemen had already put the fire out and six bodies were laid out across the floor. One of the brothers that I had gone to school with, Tony Smaldino, was among the six dead.

One ex-con and three friends walked into the bar earlier that evening. They eventually caused a disturbance and were kicked out. Upset about having been thrown out of the bar, they drove to a local gas station, bought a five-gallon bucket of gas, returned to the bar, and set it on fire. Two of them received a death sentence, and a third was sentenced to life in prison. The fourth turned state's evidence and testified for the prosecution. Governor Pat Brown later commuted the two death sentences to life without parole. Hell, they got into their car, drove to a gas station, bought some gas, and set the place on fire knowing there were people inside. They should have died in the gas chamber.

Captain Bill Madden had worked Seventy-Seventh and was now in charge of Narcotics Division. He called Lynn and me one day and asked if we would like to work for him. We accepted his offer.

One case we worked was caught up in controversy and made the newspapers. We were going to take down this dope peddler who lived near Western Avenue and Adams Boulevard in the area with the Victorian mansions. His name was Henry, and he came from a bad family. He had several brothers who were all in prison. When we hit the place, Roger Guindon and Lynn caught a gal living there who was also a dope peddler, while Harry Dorrell and I chased the suspect, Henry. He ran down a hallway, and while running, he put a condom containing heroin in his mouth and stopped to swallow it.

As we approached him, it appeared he was having difficulty breathing. Harry asked him, "Can't you breathe?" Henry shook his head no. Harry hit him on his back hoping to dislodge the condom. The dope peddler passed out and fell to the ground. We tried to resuscitate him and remove the condom, but he died there on the hallway floor.

The coroner told us that when Harry hit him on the back, he might have pushed the condom further down his throat. The coroner said the only thing we could have done was a tracheotomy, but then he may have bled to death.

There were articles in the newspapers the following days calling us murderers. There were purported witnesses who claimed we had murdered Henry. Only the female dope peddler was close enough to have witnessed everything, and she said she didn't see anything that we had done wrong. Chief Parker was so upset that he thought we should sue for defamation. It eventually died down, and finally the truth came out about how Henry had died choking on the condom with heroin that he had swallowed.

Soon after that incident, we followed another dope peddler to his home where he kept his stash. He lived in the projects on the east side of Los Angeles. Roger and I went up to his door, and as we entered, the peddler put his package of dope in his mouth. Roger said to him, "Remember Henry?" He immediately spit out the package of dope and gave it to us. We didn't have to do a thing. He knew the story because all those dope peddlers knew each other.

In '65, I was working Narcotics Division when I received a phone call from Inspector Ken McCauley with the Detective Bureau. He said, "We're thinking of starting a surveillance unit. You'll get information on suspects from the various detective bureaus in the different divisions, and you'll sit on them, watch them commit a crime, and arrest them. Would you be interested?"

I said, "Yes sir."

I thought the concept sounded pretty good. A few days later, I got a call to come down for a meeting. I walked in, and Bill Zanone and Chuck Appleton were sitting there. I had worked with Bill at Seventy-Seventh, and we were social friends. I knew Chuck by his reputation for being a hell of a good cop. All three of us had received a call from Inspector McCauley. We would become the first three members of the Special Investigation Section, better known as SIS.

Chuck Appleton: "..a hell of a good cop."

McCauley gave us a list of about twenty guys they were considering for SIS. He wanted to know if we disapproved of anybody on the list. We looked the list over and liked everyone. The three inspectors, McCauley, Jack Collins, and Henry Kerr, picked the next six: Bill Mossman, John Hopkins, Robbie Lee, Monty Madison, John Colella, and Art Van Court.

When the nine of us first started at SIS, Chuck was the natural leader. He had been a sergeant at Metropolitan Division. They would always call me one of one, meaning I was the first one. I'm not one of one, I'm one of nine. Nine of us started SIS.

There was no formal training for SIS. In Narcotics we did a lot of surveillance, so we were asked to do pretty much what we already knew how to do. We had the best damn bunch of cops, so that's what really made it.

In about a month, we were known on the street as the "Execution Squad." It was because we carried shotguns and not because we were executing people. We liked our nickname because you wanted suspects to respect you or be in fear of you, and the nickname did both.

One of our first cases involved suspects doing window smashes at businesses and stealing IBM Selectric Typewriters. The detectives knew that the suspects would send the stolen typewriters to South America, refurbish them, and then sell them back as new in the United States. What the detectives wanted to know was where the suspects took the typewriters before they were taken out of the country. We followed the suspects and watched them commit several burglaries. They window-smashed each business and took the typewriters.

We followed them to an apartment building on Avalon Boulevard at Sixty-Second Street. They stashed the typewriters in a locked storage room underneath a stairway in the apartment building. Then we sat on them, waiting for them to move the typewriters. At some point, the decision was made to arrest them, which we did. When we arrested them, one of them said, "Last night I was wondering what the heck was going on. Every place we went, we'd hear this roar of a car motor." What they heard was Mossman's souped-up Dodge, and it was loud! We never found out who their connection was, but they were all convicted and sent to prison.

Chuck and I were watching an apartment house on Venice Boulevard on this one surveillance. As we were talking, I looked up at another apartment building and saw flames. I said to Chuck, "Jesus Christ, that apartment's on fire!"

We put out a request for the fire department, and then we ran across the street. The door to the building was locked, so we kicked it in. We ran up the stairwell to the apartment and pounded on the door, but there was no answer. We kicked the door in, and the heat from the fire almost blew us away. We both dropped to the floor and in that moment, I gained respect for those officers who were acknowledged for their heroic efforts in similar situations. The guys who say, "All he did was pull a guy out of a fire," have no idea. The apartment was a little studio with a wall bed. The bed was down and was on fire. Chuck crawled toward the bed, and I crawled the other way to see if anybody was there. Fortunately, no one was in the apartment. The Fire Department got there quickly and put out the fire.

One night in San Pedro, we're doing a surveillance on a guy, his wife, and another guy. We had information they were doing stick-ups of liquor stores. The wife would drive a four-door Chevrolet Corvair, and the two guys would do the robbery. We were following them when they stopped near a liquor store on Pacific Coast Highway. They appeared to be interested in the liquor store, until a black-and-white police car that was unaware of our surveillance pulled up. After that, the three took off.

We started following them again, when a broadcast came over the radio, "All units' clear frequency six. There's a disturbance in Watts." The '65 Watts riots had started. We used frequency six, so now we had no radio communication. We stopped our surveillance and went home.

The next morning we reported to police headquarters. Policemen from all over the city were there, and I was teamed up with Walter Burke who I had worked with at Narcotics.

It was hot, there were people all over the streets, and everything was on fire. Everyone was going in the stores and ransacking them. All we could do was run them out of the stores. When anybody was close enough with a TV in their hands, I jammed the shotgun into the glass and broke the TV so they could not use it. Big deal. They would just go back and steal another one. Walt and I arrested thirty-seven people over the course of the riots, but nobody went to prison.

In the next days of the riots, all you could see were military jeeps at each intersection. The National Guard had arrived. If they had not come, the rioters would have burned the city down.

At Thirty-Sixth Street and Central Avenue, I saw three guardsmen holding a fifty-year-old black gentleman at gunpoint. He was up against a brick wall, and I could see the guy was drunk. We stopped, and the guardsmen let me talk to him. He said he lived close by, he had six kids, and he was almost home. He got drunk at home and left, even though his wife did not want him to leave the house. He was in his car approaching the intersection when the National Guard stopped him. There was a sign posted at their checkpoint, "Stop or you'll be shot." If you crossed that line, they shot you. There was no quibbling.

After I had talked to him, I asked the guardsmen, "Did he give you any trouble?"

They said, "No."

"Okay, we'll take him off your hands."

We put him in our car and took him home. Walt followed us in the drunk's car. I went up to the door and said to his wife, "We have your husband out in the car, and he's drunk."

She said, "I know. I didn't want him to leave the house, but he went anyway."

I said, "If he had gone another fifteen feet, you'd be going to his funeral because they'd have shot him. If I bring him in the house, are you going to make sure he doesn't leave?" She pointed to a little hall closet and said, "See that closet there? I'm going to put his ass in that closet, I'm going to close the door, and I'm going to sit on the floor in front of the door. He isn't leaving until he's sober!" We left it at that.

After the riots, I continued to work SIS for about two more years. Most of our work was at night, and I wasn't seeing enough of my two teenagers, so I returned to Narcotics. However, each division now had its own Narcotics unit, so I went to the unit at Seventy-Seventh. And from there, I finished my career at Intelligence Division.

At Intelligence, I worked with Jay Ponce and then Vince Furriel. Vince was a gymnast, "Mr. Muscle." He's in his eighties now, and I bet he's still lifting weights. We worked the harbor area, and our job was to gather information on organized crime. If we met up with hoods out from the East Coast, our job was to strongly encourage them to leave.

Vince and I followed these two Florida mobsters from the airport. We tailed them and watched them walk into a hotel. We knocked on their door, took them downtown, and talked to them. It was a very hot day, and Vince, Mr. Muscle, took off his shirt and tie. These guys were looking at Vince and thought they were going to get beat up, so now they wanted to go back to Florida. We took them to the airport, and one guy said, "Don't worry about me ever coming to California. Even if my daughter were to get married in California, I wouldn't come to the wedding!" So that worked.

Jimmy "The Weasel" Fratianno was a mafia hit man. Among the many murders he committed, he was suspected of killing Tony Brancato and Tony Trombino in Hollywood in a car parked off of Hollywood Boulevard. The case was commonly referred to as the "Two Tony's Murder." The two Tony's were sitting in the front seat of a car, and Fratianno was in the back seat. Both Tony's were found dead in the car with a shot to the back of the head. At the time, Fratianno was suspected, but it could not be proven.

Fratianno knew that Intelligence Division followed him whenever he was in Los Angeles. He called the office one day and spoke to Vince. He said, "Sergeant, I know you follow me whenever I come to Los Angeles. I just wanted to let you know that I'm coming down this weekend to see Jean." Jean was his girlfriend who lived in San Pedro.

We met him in a market parking lot while he was in Los Angeles. It was about six in the evening and starting to get dark. I was sitting in the driver's seat, Vince was in the front passenger seat, and Fratianno was sitting in the back seat. We sat there, had a cup of coffee, and talked for about an hour. Fratianno told us a lot of sea stories about things that had happened to him. We finished talking, and he went to his car.

Vince said to me, "Did you feel kind of funny sitting there?"

"No. What do you mean?"

"He was sitting in the back seat, and we were in the front seat—I got to thinking about the two Tony's."

I believe Fratianno, many years later, admitted to killing the two Tony's. Of course, he's dead now himself.

Jackie Drees with accordion, WOLAPO

My wife, Jackie, was a member of the organization, WOLAPO, Wives of Los Angeles Police Officers. The wives donated time and money to various charities and foundations, like the Sister Elizabeth Kenny Polio Foundation. They also provided support for those policemen and firemen who were injured on the job and hospitalized in the Central Receiving Hospital Police and Fire Ward. Six times a year, the wives would visit the ward bringing gifts such as food and reading materials, and at Christmas, they would sing carols. Jackie provided the music by playing her accordion.

There is a brick embedded in the walk at the Academy that reads:

She Also Serves – WOLAPO – Founded 1953

Bob Drees

When I retired from the Department, I became an attorney and then later a judge. There were times I wished I would have stayed and tried to promote. I don't know if I could have made it, but I would have liked to try to make captain. Many captains were book smart, but a lot of them had never really done police work. I always thought the officers needed somebody that knew what they're going through out on the street.

I really liked working for the Police Department. It was just a great job. Every policeman you've talked to probably says the same thing. They say the same thing because it's true. I've never known or been around a greater group of people. Just really good people. Even today, my best friends are those I worked with, and we still meet twice a week for breakfast or lunch.

John "Jack" Harte

Birthplace: Canton, Ohio
Career: 1949–1978
Rank at Retirement: Policeman
Divisions: Parking and Intersection Control, Central, Jail

One day my cousin Bob Alba showed me a newspaper advertisement for the Los Angeles Police Department and said, "Why don't you become a policeman?" So I did.

My first assignment was Parking and Intersection Control. For a year, I worked at Spring and Temple Streets. The Hall of Justice was on the northwest corner. Not much happened there, but one day I heard yelling coming from the next intersection over, Temple and Broadway, where Eugene Zappey was working traffic control. The yelling only lasted a minute, and I didn't hear anything else.

At end of watch, Eugene told me what had happened. He was standing in the middle of the intersection directing traffic, when a streetcar passed him on his left at the same time a stake bed truck passed him on his right. He saw that the driver's side mirror of the truck was going to hit him, so he jumped and hung onto that mirror. The truck driver did not stop for almost half a block! Eugene was not injured, but that was how close it could get standing in the middle of an intersection directing traffic.

After PIC, I transferred to Central Division, at the old station on First Street. One night my partner, Glen Mozingo, and I responded to a radio call about a guy who was acting strange. Glen was driving, and I was the passenger. When we arrived on the scene, the guy, who was pretty good-sized, seemed calm, but we decided to take him to General Hospital for an evaluation. Because he seemed okay, we did not handcuff him. I sat with him in the back seat.

Temple and Broadway

All of a sudden during the ride, the guy opened the car door and made a move to jump out. I grabbed onto him to keep him from jumping out, but he jumped, carrying me with him out of the car. We landed in the middle of an intersection. Glen stopped and exited the car. As Glen and I were wrestling with the guy, my gun fell out from my holster, but I didn't know it. After we had the guy handcuffed and back in the car, a man came over to me and said, "Here's your gun. You sure had a time of it."

I said, "Yes, indeed!"

Jack Harte (full Academy class picture, page 449)

My holster only had a strap over the gun to hold it in. I don't know what made this guy go off in the car, but we should have handcuffed him. We left him at the hospital.

Late at night one time, there was a broadcast about one bull and three cows that escaped from a truck that had crashed near Alameda Street. We found the bull and the cows on First Street near the Los Angeles Times Building. There were three police cars trying to corral the animals.

Charles Buckland, my partner, was a big Swedish guy with red hair. I don't know where he found a rope, but Buck said, "I'll lasso them." He tried, but one cow jumped up and landed on the hood of one of the police cars. The animals took off, and we pursued them.

At one point, we finally corralled the animals, but then the bull charged one of the policemen and was shot. The sergeant told Buck and me to stay with the dead bull until someone could come and pick it up. The three cows were returned to the owner.

Occasionally, various circuses would come to Los Angeles to do a show. After this one circus arrived, but before any performances, a public radio broadcast announced that a black tiger had escaped from the circus and was on the loose. The announcement was advising people to be on the lookout for the tiger. Well, that generated all kinds of calls. One caller saw the tiger at First and Hill Streets, another at Beverly Boulevard and wherever. The sightings of the tiger were all over the place.

One call brought three or four police cars to a vacant lot just inside Highland Park, a neighboring division. My partner and I responded, and, with other policemen, we surrounded the lot. It was tough to see because there was high brush in the lot. The other cops had their pistols out, but I was holding a two-by-four that I had found on the ground. As we went through the brush, I beat the brush with the two-by-four, but we did not find the tiger.

It turned out that the whole thing was a publicity stunt by the circus to attract people to their show. Because of that stunt, the city did not give the circus a permit to have their show and they had to go elsewhere.

My partner, Ellsworth Haberman, and I were in Central Station when an older man came in and said his son was acting strangely. They lived across from the police station, and he wanted us to go to his house and talk to his son. Ellsworth and I walked across Hill Street and up thirty or forty steps before we reached the house. It was a two-story flophouse, just up from the corner on top of the hill.

The guy's son looked about twenty years old and was in the kitchen. There was a table between him and us, and I took a quick look around for knives and possible weapons. The father said to his son, "I want you to go with these policemen."

The son said, "Just a minute."

First and Hill, two-story flophouse with staircase, far right

Then he turned around, opened the kitchen window, and dove out! We were two stories up, and he jumped without hesitation. Ellsworth and I looked out the window, and the guy was running across the vacant lot next door. We had expected to see him lying on the ground, maybe dead. We ran down the stairs and crossed Hill Street in the direction we last saw him running. At Broadway, we talked to a newsboy who said he saw a guy running down Broadway from Second Street. Unfortunately, we lost him.

Later that night, we were cruising Figueroa in the police car and saw the guy's son again. He saw us too and immediately climbed up a chain-link fence of an impound yard, scaling that fence like a monkey. We searched the yard, but we could not find him, and we never saw him again. I believe he was on drugs.

Tom Davis

Tom Davis and I were partners for about five months. Tom was a class before me, and he was a prince of a guy, a really good partner, but a quiet one. He has since passed. He and his wife had eleven children, and my wife and I had twelve. Our families used to get together a lot.

I don't remember who was driving, but one night we were chasing a trash truck that had run a red light. The truck stopped fast, we were too close, and we hit him. The crash knocked the siren right off the fender, only the wires held it on. In those days, the siren was on the fender of some of the police cars.

Tom and I were driving down Third Street one night, when we saw several people outside on the street. The people were pointing at the St. George Hotel. It was on fire! There were about one hundred people staying at the St. George, which, at the time, was essentially a flophouse. We broadcasted what was happening and then ran inside. The fire was several floors up. Many elderly people were on the floor that was on fire. Tom and I both carried people down the stairs on our shoulders. It was faster than having them try to walk. I do not remember how many trips we made, but we went up and down those stairs a number of times. Six people died in that fire, including one who jumped out of the hotel. The others died from smoke inhalation. Ten people went to the hospital with burns or other injuries.

Tom and I were awarded the Medal of Valor for our efforts. It was the first time since the thirties the Department awarded the Medal of Valor. When Chief William H. Parker presented me with the medal and pinned it to my chest, I felt very proud. Chief Parker was a wonderful man of few words.

After working patrol for about six years, my wife told me she thought the job was getting too dangerous. So I transferred to the jail and stayed there for the rest of my career. I stayed at the jail to honor my wife's wish because I loved her.

In the jail, the drunks would do their time, get out, and invariably within a few days be right back in. We would get to know them pretty well. This one drunk would get out, come back, get out, and come back. One day we were talking, and he asked, "Do you have a job for me?" I told him that he could do odd jobs for me at the house I was building for my growing family. At that time, I would work morning watch until seven o'clock in the morning, go work on the house until about four o'clock in the afternoon, head home for a few hours of sleep, and then return to the jail.

When he got out of jail, I brought him over to the house and he did work for me. I gave him a mattress, food to eat, and the means to cook it. He did various jobs, not anything to do with building the house, but jobs like mowing the yard. He was there for about a month and did not appear to be drinking nor seem drunk during the time he stayed there. Unfortunately, it didn't help him. At one point, he left and a week later was right back in jail. When I saw him, I didn't say anything to him. He was a drunk and stayed a drunk.

During the Watts riots in '65, I was on a bus headed to Watts to work the field jail. As we approached, what I saw reminded me of war—buildings on fire, people running, shots being fired. In World War II, my outfit was the 82nd Airborne. We parachuted into France on D-Day and later fought in the Battle of the Bulge. What I saw in Watts was not exactly the same, but when I went home that night, I told my wife it looked like a war zone.

Jack Harte awarded Medal of Valor by Chief Parker, 1953

Jack Harte and wife Dolores, front left, Tom Davis and wife Helen, right: Medal of Valor Dinner, 1953.

Jack Harte, front row, far left: Academy class reunion, 1969

I retired at twenty-nine-and-a-half years because the pension board was going to change the pension so the longer you worked, the less money you would get. Four hundred and fifty policemen retired, including me. Unfortunately, after we retired, the pension board did not change the pension. Being a policeman was a good job and had there not been the threat of a pension change, I would have stayed longer.

Glen Bachman

Birthplace: Los Angeles, California
Career: 1954–1975
Rank at Retirement: Sergeant / Detective III
Divisions: Jail, Newton, Metropolitan, Wilshire, Narcotics, Rampart

John Misterly, the brother-in-law of a high school buddy of mine, was on the LAPD. John was a high school classmate of Chief Daryl Gates, and they were two years ahead of me at Franklin High School. I had just finished seven years in the military and was looking for a job, and John encouraged me to apply.

The Academy was miserable for me. It was hard, both physically and academically. It was always on your mind that you might be the one called out and never seen again. Bob Smith was the head physical training instructor. He was a runner and a weightlifter. Whenever he entered the classroom, you knew somebody just got the ax. He was the one that escorted you to your locker to empty it out. Because he was a weightlifter, they figured you wouldn't fight with him. Eighty-nine started the Academy in my class, and sixty-nine graduated. In 2004, we had our fifty-year class reunion, and there were nineteen of us left.

Upon graduation from the Academy, they sent me to Lincoln Heights Jail. I was disappointed because I wanted to play cops and robbers. When the Central Jail opened up at Parker Center in '56, they transferred me there. In fact, I booked the first arrestee into Central Jail at three o'clock in the morning, a guy from East Fifth Street who was booked for assault with a deadly weapon. The arresting officers were Gene Grace and Lloyd Eby. Grace and Eby worked a felony car for Central Division, back when we had felony cars.

Glen Bachman, front left: Academy class physical training

Glen Bachman, front left: Academy class self-defense training

Glen Bachman, Lincoln Heights Jail

About a year later, two policemen from Newton Division wanted to work the jail; they were looking for a retirement spot. I traded with one of them and went to Newton.

Warren Sawyer was one of my training officers at Newton, and his son was Blackie Sawyer. Later in my career, I worked Narcotics and then Rampart Detectives. When I was at Rampart, Blackie had an interest in narcotics arrests, so I taught him about working dope. Most policemen, when they made a narcotics arrest, that was the end of it. I taught Blackie how to do a follow-up to get the dope peddler and how to cultivate informants. I encouraged him to go to Narcotics. Tragically, Blackie was murdered working undercover in a narcotics buy/bust operation in '68. The night he was killed, he had a large amount of cash—it was a straight rip-off. The dope dealers who shot Blackie were caught, but unfortunately, acquitted of a murder charge due to conflicting testimony from several witnesses. They did go to prison on narcotics charges.

Tom O'Neal also broke me in as a policeman at Newton. He was a good policeman. On day watch, we worked one-man cars. His unit number was 13L7, and mine was 13L9. Are you familiar with Washington Boulevard east of Santa Fe where it goes around a big gravel pit? That's where Tom crashed my brand-new '56 Interceptor police car. I was on a day off. He was working in my car and on the way to a call, going around that big curve code three, red lights and siren, someone hit him. Tom swerved and put that brand new police car underneath a freight train parked parallel to Washington Boulevard. Peeled the top right off! Tom saw it coming, laid down across the seat, and was knocked unconscious. The next day he and I went and saw the car, and he felt sick and started vomiting. He couldn't figure out how he survived the crash. Tom later made sergeant, worked Metro, and ultimately was promoted to lieutenant. Tom passed away about four years ago. He was a wonderful man, and I really enjoyed working with him.

One night about two o'clock in the morning, Charlie Pierson and I received a radio call of a found child at Fifty-Fifth Street and Central Avenue. On the bus bench was a small, abandoned newborn wrapped in a pink blanket. It was so small that I carried the baby in my police hat. By the time we got to Georgia Street Hospital, all of the news people were there and took a photo of me and the baby. We never did find the mother.

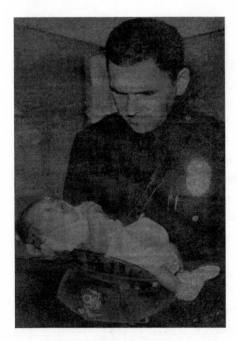

"It was so small that I carried the baby in my police hat."

In '57, I went to Metropolitan Division because I liked police work and Metro was a good place to do it. Metro was like a mobile force used to suppress crime anywhere in the city. At the time, the Department segregated blacks from whites. This was citywide; the Fire Department was the same. The Fire Department had two firehouses for black firemen, one at 113th Street and Central and the other at Florence and Western Avenues.

When I first got to Metro, my boss, Captain Joe Stephens, told us Chief Parker directed that we were going to integrate. Stephens said, "We're going to bring in black officers. Does anybody here know a black officer we should bring into Metro?"

Without exception, everyone said, "BB Martin." His first name was Bertrum, but everyone knew him as "BB." He worked Newton, and he was a good cop. BB came to Metro, and he stayed there until he retired.

Working with David McGill one day down in the south end, we saw two guys in a parked Chevrolet. I ran the plate, and it came back registered to a Ford. They took off. We chased them and pulled them over. The driver had a bunch of marijuana cigarettes on him, and he was on parole. They had just bought the marijuana cigarettes from the place where they were parked when we first saw them. We booked them and went back to where they had bought the marijuana cigarettes. We called for another Metro unit to meet us. Carlo Giufurta and his partner showed up. We door knocked and a young, beautiful lady answered the door. There was a lot of marijuana in the house, and we arrested the lady and her husband.

At court, David was on the stand testifying and made reference to the defendant, the lady. Her attorney said, "Officer, when you say defendant, to whom are you referring?"

"The lady sitting on your right."

"This is the defendant in this matter?"

"That's right."

I was seated at the prosecutor's table and thought, *Her attorney is pulling something.* I leaned back in my chair and looked at the lady who I remembered had a scar on the side of her nose. When I looked over there, this gal did not have a scar on her nose. I told the district attorney, "That's not our defendant. That's another gal that looks like her. That's a lookalike."

Glen Bachman, fifth row from bottom, third from left, David McGill, left of Bachman, Bertrum "BB" Martin, top row, middle: Metropolitan Division, 1959

The district attorney said, "Yes, it is. I have her photograph right here."

I finally convinced him, and the ruse was revealed. It was her twin sister. We didn't know the lady had a twin sister. The twin sister was remanded to the sheriffs. The attorney was convicted of obstructing justice. I don't know whatever happened to him; I never saw him in court again. Both sisters were given immunity to testify. They were champions at testifying against the attorney.

Dave Binstein and I worked a double-stakeout one day. Normally we worked nights, but we were assisting Sid Nuckles and Jim Hillman on their stakeout for the Plaid Bag Bandit. This guy usually hit markets at about six thirty in the morning, so we came in at four o'clock that morning. He was called the "Plaid Bag Bandit" because he carried his gun in a plaid bag. The Plaid Bag Bandit showed up, and Sid and Jim took him down.

That concluded that stakeout, so Dave and I left to work our own case on a group called the "Pants Down Bandits." Of all places, they were sticking up real estate offices in the University Division area. Now, who would rob a real estate office? There was no money in them per se, but the bandits were taking personal money and credit cards from the real estate agents. They would then make the men take their pants off, and the bandits would hide the pants to give themselves a chance to escape.

Frank Beeson and Chuck Appleton, detectives out of University Division, realized they had a problem when a series of real estate offices were being robbed. They called Metro, and Dave and I were assigned the case.

We had a brief description of the suspects and their car, a Pontiac sedan. We saw a Pontiac sedan that was close to the description parked on a residential street. We sat on the car and waited for the bandits to come to us. After a short while, we saw a guy drinking milk out of a Mason jar come walking out of a house and up to the Pontiac. We thought he might be our bandit, and he was! He had stolen credit cards from the real estate agents on him, and he was armed. From our arrest, Beeson and Appleton were able to identify the other bandits and subsequently arrested them.

Dave Binstein

Dave Binstein came on the Department in '46, and his serial number was 3702. He was one of a few Jewish police officers on the Police Department. We were partners for about three years. Nobody worried about me when I was working with Dave. He was a good policeman.

One night the See's Candies at Seventh Street and Broadway was robbed. I heard the broadcast and said to Dave, "Well, I guess we know where we're going to be tomorrow." The candy stores were always good to rob because it was often a lone female working and there were no guns under the counter, like in a liquor store. It was usually good for sixty to eighty dollars.

Sure enough, the next night we were staked out in one of the downtown See's Candies stores. In liquor stores, we always took shotguns, but we were told not to take our shotguns into the candy stores.

Earl Rice and his partner were in an independent candy store near Seventh Street and Broadway. A bandit came in, the robbery went down, and Earl chased the bandit out of the store. He chased the bandit down to Seventh and Spring where Earl got down on one knee, fired, and killed him. The bandit was a white male wearing a blue sweater and gray pants.

The next night we were off the stakeout and working security at the Pan Pacific Auditorium. President Dwight Eisenhower was in town for a fundraiser. Dave and I were sitting in our car when we heard a broadcast of a robbery at the See's Candies at Seventh and Broadway. The suspect was described as a white male wearing a blue sweater and gray pants. I said to Dave, "Can't be. We killed him last night."

Different bandit, same color clothes! Bob Rautert and his partner took him alive. The suspect lived near the candy store in a flophouse. Bob said a pair of dice was on the guy's dresser. The suspect told them he couldn't make up his mind whether to stick up the candy store or not, so he rolled the dice and got a seven. That was a winner, so he pulled the job.

One time we were assigned a uniform detail in Hollywood. I don't remember the reason we were in uniform, but we never made it to Hollywood. We went to the station, checked in, and got our assignment. We were going out Beverly Boulevard and heard a broadcast of a 211 silent, a robbery alarm, at the pharmacy at Beverly and Dillon Street.

The pharmacy was right on the corner, and we were maybe two blocks away. As we were driving up, we saw a motor officer talking to a guy wearing a white pharmacy coat just outside the front door. I got out of the car, and I saw that the guy's pharmacy coat had no business name on it. I approached the motor officer, shoved my gun into the side of the guy with the pharmacy coat, and said, "Get your hands in the air!" He did. The motor officer looked at me funny as I reached into the guy's coat pocket and took out a loaded .38 revolver.

Dave went into the pharmacy and yelled, "I got three people tied up on the floor back here."

I asked the bandit, "Where's your partner?"

"He's around the corner."

"What kind of car is he in?"

"A white Ford."

I told the motor officer to go around the corner and get the other bandit. The motor cop said, "Okay," and jumped on his motorcycle. That was the last we saw of him. The second suspect was arrested three days later. The pharmacist was an older gentleman with white hair. After Dave had untied him, he came out. By that time, I had the suspect on the ground and was handcuffing him. The pharmacist proceeded to put the boots to the bandit. He was really mad.

There was a series of burglaries around Third and Fairfax, primarily Jewish-owned businesses. Dave and I were sent to work the business burglaries. We cruised the area some and then parked on Kilkea Drive just north of Third. We sat and watched. We were in plain clothes, in a plain car, and it was nighttime. We saw a green Studebaker come around the corner and go down the alley in front of us. I said to Dave, "There's our burglar. He's coming to us. I'll go down on foot. Back me up with the car."

I got out on foot and walked into the alley. The green Studebaker was parked at the back of a grocery store next to an old compressor for refrigeration. No one was in the Studebaker. A few minutes later, Dave drove into the alley. He got out, and we could hear the burglar inside the market. We drew our guns and were prepared to do the bandit, right then and there. The back door opened, and out walked a Rabbi with hat and beard. You'll never guess what my partner did. He started talking to the Rabbi in Yiddish. Up to that time, I didn't know Dave could speak Yiddish.

It turned out the grocery store had been converted into a synagogue. It was the Rabbi in the Studebaker. We put our guns away, shook hands, and left.

Dave and I stopped Ernest Carruthers for speeding one night, and we eventually took him to the station. Turned out, he was just released from prison. In '45, he was convicted and sentenced for killing Norbert J. Huseman, but released after serving eight years. Norbert was a reserve officer and the first officer killed in the line of duty from Newton Division. At court for the speeding ticket, Carruthers tried to tell the judge that the only reason he was given a ticket was for the death of Huseman. The judge made him pay the fine.

Dave and I were in uniform working in Wilshire Division, and it was about mid-morning when we heard a traffic car in pursuit of a speeder coming down Pico Boulevard. During the pursuit, the traffic officer said over the radio, "Shots fired. They just shot my windshield." Now that sounded interesting!

Right then, a call came out of a 211 silent, a robbery at a nearby bank. The traffic car was chasing the guys that had just robbed a bank. We joined the pursuit with the traffic officer. At one point, the bandits crashed their new Ford Thunderbird into a big palm tree. It was the only time I have ever seen a palm tree torn completely out of the ground! We captured both bandits, got the money, and handed them over to the downtown robbery detectives.

When we were finished, we drove back to Wilshire Division. It was now the middle of the afternoon, when I saw a column of black smoke just north of Wilshire Boulevard. I said to Dave, "Something's burning. Let's go see what's burning."

A big, beautiful old home in the Hancock Park area of Wilshire was engulfed in flames. People were standing out on the street watching the place burn as the firemen were getting there. I told Dave I was going to check the back of the home because it was burning pretty good. A woman standing at the second-story window of a house next door called out to me. She said, "Officer, I think there is somebody trapped in there."

Upon hearing what she said, I turned and looked and saw part of the roof collapsing. I ran into the back of the home and followed the firemen's hose up the spiral staircase. The hose was all I could see because of the smoke. At the top of the staircase, I found a fireman who was in obvious trouble. He's saying, "Moreno, Moreno," who I later found out was his captain. He passed out.

I also saw that the fire hose was leading into an area of burning roof debris. I thought there must be firemen at the other end of the hose. I grabbed the fireman at the top of the staircase, and I dragged him down the spiral staircase and outside to the front yard. I laid him down on the grass and shouted that there were other firemen upstairs and they were in trouble.

Two firemen were standing in the street, and I yelled at them, "Get me your resuscitator. This fireman needs oxygen!"

They both looked at me and said, "We don't know where it is."

I said, "It's in a cabinet on the other side of the fire truck. It's long with green tanks on it. Get it!"

They found the resuscitator right where I told them it was. I knew the equipment on the fire rigs because I used to drink coffee at firehouses. Once they got the resuscitator, they knew what to do with it. They put a mask on the fireman and started pumping him with oxygen. I'm thinking, *Whoever heard of a fireman that doesn't know where the resuscitator is on a fire truck?* It turned out they were on their ride-along out of the Fire Academy. They were trained in the use of the resuscitator, but they had not received a class on where the equipment was located on a fire truck.

Then I went down with smoke inhalation. Dave took me to Central Receiving Hospital, and I spent the night there. Five of the firemen were also sent to the hospital: the one I brought out, three that were behind the burning roof debris, and a fifth one. Joe Stephens and Paul Trautman came to see me at the hospital. Joe told me, "You might want to call your wife and tell her you're in the hospital before she sees it on the news, because you're going to be a hero on the news tonight." I received the Medal of Valor for saving the firemen.

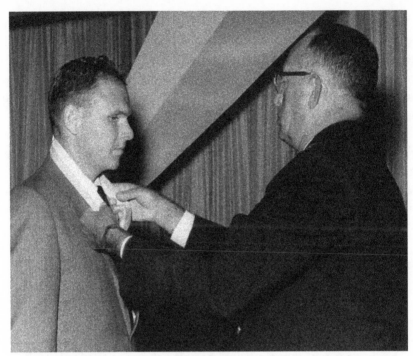

Glen Bachman, awarded Medal of Valor by Chief Parker, 1963

1963Medal of Valor recipients and wives

One day I was working Narcotics out of Rampart Division, when I heard over the radio a broadcast of a robbery suspect walking west on Sixth Street carrying a rifle. The first one at the scene was a motor cop, John Sudicky. John took cover behind a parked truck when he saw the suspect across the street from him. The suspect saw him and fired a round that went through the cab of the truck. I saw John go down and I ran over to him. He looked like somebody had smashed a tomato in his face. His face was full of blood. I asked him if he could run. He told me he could. I said, "Run around the corner. There's a black and white. They will take you to the hospital." The hospital was a block away. As it turned out, he had been hit with a single piece of shrapnel from the truck, but it looked awful.

By now, the suspect had entered what turned out to be his apartment building. He fired again from a second-story window of the building, and now we knew where he was located. An officer from Rampart, Mark Woods, Sergeant Rod Bock from Metro Division, and I went up to the second floor of the apartment building. A young female carrying a baby was looking out her apartment door.

I said, "Somebody's been shooting at us. Do you know where he might be?"

She pointed to the suspect's apartment.

I said, "Get inside with your baby and get on the floor."

Rod was the only one with a bulletproof vest, so he was going to kick the door. Mark was lying on the hallway floor with his shotgun, and I stood to one side of the door. Rod kicked the door, but it didn't open. He kicked it a second time and it opened, but he lost his balance. As he was falling backward, the suspect fired. The round went right over Rod. Mark and I started firing blind into the apartment, and Rod joined us. I don't know how many bullets we put in there, but when the smoke cleared, the suspect was dead. Rod and Mark both received the Medal of Valor. I was told I already had one.

When I promoted to sergeant, I went to Wilshire Division, but I was only there four months and then transferred back to Narcotics. I worked Wilshire morning watch the night Ian Campbell and Karl Hettinger were kidnapped in Hollywood. I was working the field and received a call to come to the station. I was told to take a bullhorn to the command post in

Hollywood, but before I got there, my mission was canceled. They had found Hettinger. I didn't know either officer.

Campbell and Hettinger were working a felony car in plain clothes when they stopped two suspects who got the drop on Campbell. Hettinger gave up his gun at Campbell's direction, and both were taken to Bakersfield, where Campbell was killed and Hettinger escaped. We were told in roll call the next night what had happened.

The night Bobby Kennedy was shot at the Ambassador Hotel; I was working Rampart night watch detectives. I heard the call come out about the shooting—we had a loudspeaker in the squad room. Then I received a call from one of the officers at the scene who told me what had happened. Bill Jordan, my supervisor, said, "I'll call the boss on this one." At that time, the "boss" in charge of Rampart detectives was Charlie Hughes.

Sirhan Sirhan was arrested at the scene and brought to Rampart Station. Bill tried to interview him, but he refused to tell him his name. Sirhan Sirhan was then transported to Parker Center.

I attended Kennedy's autopsy with Bill. Bill was the only guy from Rampart asked to be on the Special Unit Senator Task Force. The unit was tasked with determining whether Sirhan Sirhan acted alone or was part of a conspiracy. Their investigation determined that Sirhan Sirhan had acted alone.

Do I miss the job? Sure, I miss the job every day. That was a good time for me. When I came on the Department, I had a plan to work only twenty years, but I worked twenty-two, and I enjoyed every minute of it.

Francis "Frank" Pfost

Birthplace: Bakersfield, California
Career: 1954–1980
Rank at Retirement: Lieutenant II
Divisions: Newton, Traffic Enforcement, Highland Park, Wilshire, Labor
  Relations

My brother Earl was six years older than me and became a policeman not too long after he returned home from World War II. He was on the Pasadena Police Department and was always telling sea stories about his police work. I was intrigued.

In '50, the Korean War came along and I went in the Navy. In '54, near the end of my tour, I decided to follow in my brother's footsteps, but I applied to LAPD because I thought it was the best police department in the nation. At that time, William H. Parker was the chief of police, and he had a good reputation.

At the Academy, we started with eighty-three cadets, but we lost a few before graduation. I finished seventh in my class. Two of my classmates, Charlie Reece and Bob Vernon, both retired as deputy chiefs.

Ray Ruddell was our law instructor, and he was great. I later worked for him on motors when he was the captain at Traffic Enforcement Division. I thought all the instructors prepared us well for our future.

Marion Hoover was my training officer at Newton Division. He was involved in a few shootings before I worked with him and would be involved in several more over his career. Listening to his stories as a young policeman I thought he was quite the guy. He was respected, ethical, and a well-liked policeman.

Frank Pfost, top row, second from right: Academy class, 1954

During one shooting, Marion chased a suspect who was armed with a handgun into a house. The suspect ran into a bathroom, and Marion followed him. The suspect was standing up on the toilet. He got the drop on Marion, but Marion grabbed the suspect's gun and shot and killed him.

Another time two men and a woman robbed a store on Eighth Street at Westlake Avenue. I don't remember the whole story, but Marion and Ted Gerber confronted them. Marion shot both males who were armed. The girl was about to do something to Marion, I believe to shoot him, and he hit her with his pistol. At the board review of the shooting, Marion was asked why he hit the girl with his gun. He told them he hit her because he was out of bullets!

Marion was a great training officer. You get quite a bit of information in the Academy, but your education really starts when you go out in the field. Marion taught me about being confident as you go about your police work.

I was at Newton about a year when I decided to transfer to motors. My interest in riding motorcycles goes back to my teen years, and since Earl rode motors with the Pasadena Police Department, it was a natural move for me. Our younger brother Larry later joined the California Highway Patrol, and he also rode motors.

Marion Hoover, front row, far left; 1964 Medal of Valor recipients

Earl, Frank, and Larry Pfost, 1966

Forrest Fisher, Earl Dapper, Don Dapper, and Frank Pfost, 1958

On motors, I rode a lot with the Dapper brothers, Don and Earl. One day just before dusk, Don and I were riding north on Figueroa at Avenue Forty-Three when a man came running out of a mom-and-pop grocery store followed by the owner. The owner shouted that the man had just robbed the place and that he had a gun. The man jumped in a car and took off.

We went in pursuit and chased him for quite a distance. I was in front, and Don was behind me working the radio. Just before getting on the Pasadena Freeway off York Boulevard, the suspect stopped. I got him out of the car, patted him down, and handcuffed him. He did not have a gun.

It turned out this poor fellow had lost all his money in a poker game. He couldn't face his wife without a paycheck, so he robbed the market. He wasn't a hardened criminal by any stretch. I don't believe the case went to court, as I don't recall testifying.

Don and I received a call one night about a drunk driver driving south in the northbound lanes of the Pasadena Freeway. First, we stopped the cars traveling north, and then we searched the freeway. We found him. He had stopped in the middle of the freeway and was just sitting in his car. He was definitely intoxicated! We removed him from the car and later booked him for drunk driving. It was amazing that he had not run into anyone.

When you work motors during daylight hours, you usually rode separately from your partner, and then, as it got darker, you teamed up. One day I was working alone, separated from Don in Highland Park, when an armed robbery of a liquor store occurred and the suspect's description was broadcasted over the radio. I came around the corner of a side street, and I saw a guy who fit the suspect's description walk out of an alley. I drove past him, and there was a big old tree fifty feet away. I jumped off the bike, pulled out my service revolver, and took a position behind the tree. He complied with my directions and gave up. He was a seventeen-year-old kid high on drugs. We searched and searched, but could not find the gun. He was booked for the robbery.

I was riding down Riverside Drive one day when a citizen advised me that there had been a traffic accident with people hurt on Riverside at Glendale Boulevard. A car had run a red light and struck a second car. When I got there, there was a lady, not involved in the accident that had stopped and rendered assistance and comfort to both drivers. Once I had everything under control and had requested an ambulance, I thanked the lady for stopping and assisting both drivers. She introduced herself as Helen Parker. It was Chief Parker's wife!

Don Holtz and I were working the Seventy-Seventh Division area when he stopped a car to issue a citation. A speeder passed us by. I went after the speeder and stopped him a short distance away. He immediately exited the car and started walking back toward me. Don was within sight of us. I turned the speeder around and patted him down. Just as I asked him if he had any guns on him, I felt a gun in his front waistband underneath his shirt. I took it from him, cuffed him, and Don and I booked him at Seventy-Seventh for the gun. If Don had not been close by, things might have turned out differently.

In April '58, several storms flooded the Arroyo Seco streambed and the Los Angeles River. The Arroyo Seco parallels the Pasadena Freeway. A radio call came out that a young girl had fallen into the floodwaters of the Arroyo Seco at Avenue Twenty-Six. I responded to an area downriver from where she had fallen in to see if I could rescue her.

I rode through a vacant lot right up to the river. I saw the girl and a policeman who had jumped in further upriver to try to save her. He had his arm around her, and they were coming downriver pretty fast. I went into the river, but not so far that I would lose my footing. I reached out, and the policeman grabbed my hand. I was just about to get him out, but we lost our grip and they were gone again. I climbed out of the water and ran downstream ahead of them, got in again, and this time I was able to pull them both to safety. I was about chest deep in the water, but I was still able to keep my footing. Had I not, they would have wound up in the Los Angeles River about a quarter of a mile away, and one or both may have drowned.

The girl was conscious, and both were okay. Of course, I was all wet, so I went home and changed my uniform. When I returned to work, my sergeant talked to me about what had happened. I didn't think anything more about it, until I was notified later that I was to receive the Medal of Valor. Paul Franey, the officer who jumped in first to rescue the girl, also received the Medal of Valor.

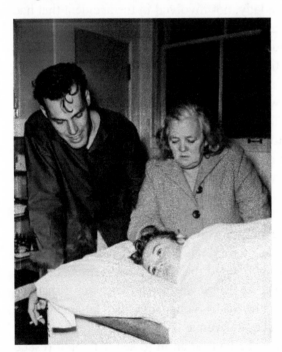

Paul Franey with rescued girl and girl's mother

Frank Pfost, fourth from left: President John F. Kennedy escort detail, 1963

Part of the duties in motors is to provide motorcade escorts for dignitaries like the President of the United States. We escorted President John Kennedy when he visited Los Angeles in June '63, a few months before his assassination. He was here for a fundraiser and attended a few social events. When he was finished with his visit, we escorted him to the airport. We lined up, and he shook our hands. We also escorted President Dwight Eisenhower and President Lyndon Johnson.

At the time of the '65 Watts riots, I was working the freeways. Although I was working days, they kept us on that first night. I wasn't part of it, but at one point Chief Gates, who I believe was an inspector at the time, had a group of motor officers meet him in some dirt field. They were all mad at Gates because to meet him in this field they had to drive through the area where the rioters were, which resulted in getting their bikes beat up pretty good.

The days of the riots were a rough time for most of the men on the Department, although I feel the policemen of today actually have it worse. It was a different world back then. We weren't subjected to the disrespect and negative attitude that happens today. Officers weren't targeted and shot for no reason.

When I made sergeant, I was sent to Highland Park Division where I worked Patrol and Vice. In '67, I was at the major anti-war protest against the Vietnam War at the Century City Plaza Hotel. President Lyndon Johnson was there for a fundraiser. There were estimates that there were at least ten thousand protestors.

My squad of officers and I were on the front line facing the protestors. The protestors were shouting all kinds of vulgarities at us. One policeman in front of me was shaking, so I put my hand on his shoulder and told him to take it easy. He wasn't shaking because he was afraid; he was shaking because he was mad. When the order was given to move the protestors out, boy, did we move them out! The policeman that had been shaking gave this one protestor a big jolt with his nightstick, which the fellow deserved, and we moved on. We pushed them quite a distance to get them completely out of there. That was a long night.

A year after I made lieutenant, Earl Dapper called me from Labor Relations where he was working. He told me there was an opening. I applied and finished my career there.

There were no big labor strikes while I was there, and of the minor strikes that did happen there were no problems. Our job was to handle all crimes citywide connected to organized labor except for bombings, homicides, or kidnappings. Everything else was ours if it was labor-related. It was probably one of the best jobs I had on the Department. Was it better than motors? Well, they're different types of jobs, and I was younger when I rode motors.

I had actually planned to work thirty years. However, because of President Jimmy Carter's policies, inflation was through the roof. In 1980, it was announced that those on the job were going to get a six percent raise, and those who were retired would receive a seventeen percent raise because the cost of living was so high. I thought I would never get an opportunity like that again, and I knew I could go out and get another job, so I retired.

Frank Pfost

I loved the job, though I didn't always care for working the morning watch! After I retired, I missed it for a while, but I later worked with the Pacific Cement Company, and that eased it a little bit. The people I worked with reminded me of the men I worked with on the Department. I made some great friends on the job, and to this day, as we approach our nineties, I stay in contact with some of them, like the Dapper brothers and Don Holtz. I was on the job at a good time.

Bettie Bowden

Birthplace: St. Louis, Missouri
Career: 1956–1968
Rank at Retirement: Policewoman
Divisions: Jail, Harbor

I was working at an aircraft company in production and control, and I liked my job. But I had worked up to the highest level and was told I couldn't go any higher because I was a woman. That didn't sit very well with me.

In a Sunday newspaper, I saw a picture of a policewoman. In the story, it said that she was trying to find young women to be on the Police Department and that they were now hiring.

My friend Ernie Glover was on the Police Department, and I asked him if he thought I could do the job of a policewoman. He knew me pretty well and said, "Of course you can." He told me to go down to City Hall and pay my dollar for an application. And that's exactly what I did.

After submitting my application, I was called and told to go to Hollywood High School for the written exam. There must have been over three hundred women there. I didn't know how many they were going to need, and with that many people I thought, *I don't know about this*. I took the exam, and after finishing the rest of the process, I was hired. I was in a class with five other women, and looking at these other women I thought, *Why would we be chosen out of all that humanity that came to take the first exam?*

The sergeant in charge of our class was Daisy Storms. Daisy was a wonderful person, and we became good friends. She did not have us for very long though—we were only at the Academy for five days.

Bettie Bowden, far left: Academy in-service training, 1957

Bettie Bowden, second from left: Academy shooting instruction, 1957

Earle "Fuzzy" Farrant, seated far right: Los Angeles Police Shooting Team

In those five days, we were overwhelmed with classes, including firearms. I was familiar with guns, having grown up on a farm, but a couple of the girls had never fired a gun before. The shooting instructor was Earle Farrant, and everyone called him "Fuzzy." He was on the Department's shooting exhibition team. He showed us how to handle, shoot, and clean our guns.

Once he had told us all that he was supposed to about firearms, Fuzzy said, "You are all going to be assigned to the jail. Here are some things you need to know." Then he showed us a few control holds, including the chokehold. We were grateful for Fuzzy's added instruction because, believe me, we did use those holds in the jail and that chokehold came in handy many a time.

We did not have a formal graduation. Friday was our last day at the Academy, and the very next night I was working the women's jail at Lincoln Heights.

When I first got to the jail, I was so intent on being careful about not bringing some disease home; I would wash my hands about fourteen times a night. At first, I thought people in jail were really dirty, but I soon learned they weren't any dirtier than the rest of us. Well, maybe a little dirtier. I never washed my hands so much in all my life, but I got over that right away.

One time a policewoman searched an arrestee and didn't find anything on her. The woman was booked and brought back to a cell. Turned out she had a booster bag within her clothes and a five-pound ham in it! The policewoman never lived that one down. I wasn't there for that, but the story got around pretty fast.

Every Friday and Saturday night, the officers would bring in a lot of female drunk drivers. One night a booked drunk driver seriously hurt Marilyn Moon, one of my Academy classmates. Marilyn was trying to take the woman's prints when the woman turned on her. She had been cooperative with Marilyn as she printed her, but then suddenly went crazy. By the time other policewomen could get to the woman and control her, Marilyn had suffered injuries to her head and neck, including a good amount of her hair being pulled out. Marilyn was taken to the hospital and was off for some time.

The hardest thing for me to do was to put someone on what we called the Board." I don't even like to remember doing it. A board was essentially a table with leg and arm restraints. If someone were doing something that was harmful to them, even if they were in a padded cell, we would have to strap them to a board. It was the only way we had of keeping them from killing themselves. That wasn't easy.

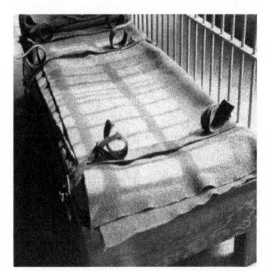

"It was the only way we had of keeping them from killing themselves."

There was a woman one night that did kill herself. She had been arrested for trying to commit suicide. She had been running naked on a major street trying to get cars to hit her. The officers that brought her in had given her a jacket and wrapped a garment around her waist to cover her. That's all she had on. When I searched her, I felt something like a very thin belt within the lining of the wrap she had been given. But because it was sewn in, I didn't go further with it.

That night she was found hanging in her cell. She had removed the item I had felt and used it to hang herself. I had to cut her down. You could say it was my fault, or you could say she was determined to kill herself. That was her intent, and she was going to do it one way or another. That stayed with me a long time.

Did anybody try to escape? One tried. She had been booked for narcotics, and two detectives talked to her in an interview room. The room had a large window that cantilevered out to allow in air. When the detectives had finished their interview, they left her alone in the room, and they did not tell anyone that they were leaving. She climbed out the window looking to drop into a garbage truck that was directly below. We were on the fifth floor! One of the policewomen heard her yell, went into the room, and saw her holding on to the window. She was pulled back in, thus saving her life. It was a good ending, but, of course, there was a lot of explaining that had to be done.

Six months was probation. Once you're off probation, the other policewomen treated you like a real person. Up until then, you were just a person there to do something for them if they needed it done. They wouldn't let you get involved in anything. They would be planning parties or to meet up after work, and they wouldn't let us go out with them. At first, our feelings were hurt. Then we finally found out: they were waiting for us to pass probation so that we wouldn't get into trouble and jeopardize our career. That showed you how much they really cared about you. They were wonderful.

I worked the jail for a year, and then I was transferred to Harbor Division working the Juvenile unit as a leader in DAPS, the Deputy Auxiliary Police Service program. Harbor Station was in San Pedro City Hall. Police and Fire had the main floor, there were courts on several floors, and the women's jail was on the top floor. In fact, not too long ago, I went down to City Hall, and it was being rejuvenated.

San Pedro City Hall

The building was built in 1929. It's still there and beautiful. In 1962, we moved to a new police station near the freeway. That station has since been torn down and a new police station built, but the City Hall building is still working. There's something wrong somewhere.

My partner in DAPS was Morris Gilmore, we called him "Gil." He was a policeman of the highest degree, and he and his wife, Chloe, a policewoman, became lifelong family friends. We had a big group of kids in DAPS, almost seventy-five in the senior group and an even larger junior group. There was a movie house at Sixth and Beacon Street with a large basement that Gil finagled to get as our meeting place. You learned to finagle in DAPS because we did not get funds from the city.

We held fundraisers, including selling Christmas trees. We had a Christmas tree lot, and no one in San Pedro bought their tree anyplace else. With the money we raised, we built an archery range in our meeting place and held dances once a week. We took them on trips like half-day fishing on a boat and Disneyland. It was up to us to figure out what to do to take care of these children and try to teach them good morals and a good way of life.

Gil was a Marine and had been in WWII. He was a prisoner of the Japanese for four years. He taught the kids how to march, and we would practice marching at Fort MacArthur up on the hill overlooking the harbor. They marched in various parades. Gil was very considerate, and he loved the kids, although being a former tough Marine, he wouldn't let them know that.

Some of the kids had no transportation to our meeting place, so Gil and I would pick them up in the station paddy wagon. We put as many kids in there as we could. I used to remind Gil not to go around the corners too fast or the back doors may fly open and we could lose a few! For the kids, riding in the paddy wagon was part of the fun.

We had kids from all over the harbor area, including the projects in Wilmington. One was Peter Gravitt. Other boys from the projects would make fun of him because he belonged to DAPS. Peter went anyway and once told me it changed his whole life. He later became a police officer for twenty years and rose to the rank of general in the U.S. Army Reserve. He also became Secretary of the California Department of Veterans Affairs.

Morris "Gil" and Chloe Gilmore

Ezequiel Encinas, second from left, Vietnam: "We called him "Zeke.""

Another kid from the projects was Ezequiel Encinas. We called him "Zeke." Zeke grew up to be a military pilot in the U.S. Air Force with the rank of major. Unfortunately, he was killed in Vietnam on a mission over Laos.

I was in DAPS a year when the program was brought to an end in June 1958. That was one of the worst decisions the Police Department ever made. The reason given was that men were needed back in the field. That was the saddest thing. I mean really sad. DAPS was a great program. A number of kids went on to become officers, but more importantly, they became positive role models within the community, some in leadership roles. Zeke was in charge of his flight crew and an ace pilot. You don't get there unless you're paying attention. As a kid, he lived in the projects with drugs and everything else available to him, and he said, "No." I would like to think our program had something to do with that.

When DAPS was shut down, I was reassigned to the women's jail upstairs on the seventh floor. Rita Eberhardt was my sergeant.

At Harbor, there was one policeman, Frank Haley, who had to have been 110 years old. He was a character, and we all loved him. His job was serving arrest warrants. One day he came up to the jail and asked Rita if he could have a policewoman go with him for a warrant on a woman. Rita asked me, and I said, "Sure." Just as Frank and I were walking out the door of the building, I asked him what the warrant was for, and he told me murder. I then asked who the person was, and he told me her name. I knew her. She was one of the girls that were always in and out of jail. She had a drinking problem, and when she drank, she became mean.

One time when she was in the drunk tank, something set her off and she ripped out the toilet and washbasin with her bare hands! This time, she had been arrested because she had apparently got in a fight with some gal while drunk and tried to put a pair of scissors through the gal's head. She bailed out, but failed to appear in court, hence the warrant.

Frank and I went to her house, and she was not there. We could see something cooking on the stove, so we knew that she was not far away. I told Frank she might have gone to a market that was down the block. We knew she did not have a car. We went to the market, and there she was, getting ready to buy some groceries. She saw me, and I told her she had a warrant. She said she was expecting it.

I said, "Well, you understand we need to take you over to the jail."

"I understand, Miss Bowden."

She cooperated fully. If I hadn't known her from previous times, I'm sure it would have been different. I don't know what the outcome of her case was.

After we moved to the new station, one day I had four prisoners ready to take to court, but there were no cars. Getting a police vehicle in the morning was tough. The courtroom was about five miles away and Judge Benz was not one to take being late to court too kindly. At the last minute, a car came in, and I grabbed it. I loaded the four girls in, and off we went. About four blocks from court the car started sputtering, and soon I realized we were out of gas.

I got the girls out of the car and said, "Okay, girls. You see City Hall. We are going to walk over there. Now listen. I just cleaned my gun, and I don't want to have to do it again. So let's everybody pay attention."

They all replied, "Yes, Miss Bowden, we will."

We started walking toward City Hall, and at Fifth and Beacon Street one of the girls turned to me and said, "Miss Bowden, I can't walk by that bar. My friends are in there. They'll see you marching me around, and I'll be so ashamed."

I knew what her arrest record was, and I told her, "You got a lot more to be ashamed of than that, girl."

We marched right to City Hall and up into the court. We made it on time! I called the station and told Rita to send somebody from the garage with some gas to pick up the car.

Rita asked, "Well, how did you get them from there to the court?"

I said, "Never mind, Rita. You don't want to know."

Policewomen were often loaned to Vice or Narcotics for investigations requiring the presence of a female officer. One day Gil and I were cleaning up the DAP meeting place. I was in jeans, a sweatshirt, and old shoes. A couple of the guys from Vice came in and asked if I could work a detail with them.

I asked, "When?"

"Today."

"This is the way I'm dressed."

"That's the way we want you."

They were going to take down a bar for bookmaking. All that the officers wanted me to do was when they came in, to take the bookmaker, a woman, into custody. The sergeant and I went in early and sat at the bar. The woman bookmaker was behind the bar. When the officers came in, she grabbed a big old hockey stick. I jumped over the bar and said to her, "We're just going to put that down, and we're going to go over here and stand still. That's all you have to do, but you're going to do it. Do you understand?" She understood. She put her hockey stick down.

The guys were searching all over the place for betting markers, and they couldn't find any. The sergeant told me to take the bookmaker into the women's restroom and shake her down. I took her in there and told her to take her clothes off. She said, "Take my clothes off?" They were always like that, all of a sudden modest. She took off her clothes and out dropped a marker. That was it, the only marker.

About two or three days later, I asked one of the officers what happened after the raid. The officer said, "Oh, you didn't hear? We lost the marker on the way back to the station." One marker for the whole raid, and it was lost!

Corine "Guzzie" Guzzetta and I went on loan to detectives for their investigation of a fortune-telling gypsy family. The father in the family had died, and the officers thought his death was suspicious, that his sons may have killed him. Guzzie and I were to get our fortunes told and try to develop a relationship that may give the family confidence in us, so that we may learn how the father died.

The mother told my fortune, and I asked her if she would tell my friend her fortune. She said she would. Guzzie and I went back a day or two later in a very expensive-looking car that the officers had borrowed. We were really putting it on. Guzzie had her fortune told, and we went back about three more times. This was around Christmas time, and the family invited Guzzie and me to their Christmas party.

Policewomen Nancy Lukes, Sydney Rester, and Corine "Guzzie" Guzzetta

We went to the party and met the rest of the family: brothers, cousins, all of them. These were bad people, mean people. When we left, the detectives felt we had given them enough information for them to work with. Eventually, a murder warrant was obtained for two of the sons. The case went to court. I never had to go, and I don't know what the outcome was.

What was my fortune? I was told I was going to get money. I'm still waiting!

I mentioned Frank Haley being a character. We had a number of characters at Harbor, and I just loved them all. Caraway Weems was one-of-a-kind. He had been on the Department a long time when I came on. Caraway was our sharpshooter, and one time he had to take a guy out with his rifle.

A call came into the station that a man was holding hostages in an apartment building and threatening to kill them. The officers responded, and after several hours, it was decided to take this guy out. Caraway was tasked with taking the shot. The guy walked back and forth a few times in front of a window, and finally Caraway got a bead on him and knocked him down. The people were very thankful, let me tell you. They knew this guy was going to kill some of them, maybe all of them.

I was working the front desk that night, and the news people were all over the station. Finally, when things settled down, I walked back to the coffee room, and Caraway was sitting there all by himself. He looked in deep thought. When I asked him how he was, he said, "You know." He wouldn't comment anymore.

I said, "Yeah, I do. Let me talk to the watch commander and get somebody to take over the desk, and I'll drive you home."

He looked at me and said, "You are the sweetest thing."

"No, I'm not. I'm just going to drive you home. This isn't any long-time romance." I knew his wife.

He laughed and said, "No."

"Okay, then it's time for you to go home if you think you can drive yourself. But I would be happy to go with you."

"No, no," he said, "I can drive."

"Okay," I said, "Get in your car and drive on home. Get some sleep."

Caraway said he was okay, and he drove home. He was in deep thought because he had just killed a man. You don't kill a man and not give it a lot of thought before and after. To me, it doesn't matter the lives you're saving, you're really thinking about the life you're taking. All of us were pretty close, and, of course, everybody loved Caraway. He was such a nice, big old bear, a great big guy. He was just as sweet as he could be. After that, I never knew him to have any problems from the shooting.

I was assigned to the front desk because I had been injured while working the jail. I was booking a prisoner who was very, very drunk, big, and heavy. I was going through the prisoner's purse and recording the contents when, all of a sudden, she came swinging a left and then a right hand to hit me. She was so drunk that she couldn't keep her equilibrium, and we both went down. She came down right on top of me, and it injured some vertebrae in my lower back. I could not walk straight and eventually had to have two surgeries. I was worse off after the first surgery, and the doctor fused the vertebrae in my lower back in the second surgery. I still wasn't able to walk very good, and eventually I medically pensioned off the job.

When Chief Parker died, I was on medical leave for my first surgery. I drove to St. Vibiana's Cathedral in a full-body cast. It was a hot day, and I shouldn't have been there, but I went anyway. I started to walk up to where the crowds were, and I realized I wasn't going to make it. I felt that I was going to pass out. I didn't want to make a fool of myself and disparage Chief Parker's name, so I went back to the car. I sat in the car until it was all over.

My goal was not to retire the way I did with an injury. I wanted to put in my full time, a full twenty years. I thought I was doing good work. I really felt like I was accomplishing something because I could work with the public very well. I recognized that when people had problems they could do some dumb things. I felt I could look through a situation and help them. I thought that was worthwhile.

Recently, I was given the Connie Speck Award by the Policewomen's Association. Connie was a policewoman who was the first woman to achieve the rank of lieutenant and then captain on the Department. She was a role model for the rest of us. Out of respect for her accomplishments, an annual award was established in her name.

Bettie Bowden

It was an honor for me to receive it. I appreciated being honored by my own people. That really meant something. And to my complete surprise, Peter Gravitt, the kid teased for being in the DAPS program, came up from behind and sat next to me at my table. I just about passed out.

Deputy Chief Sandy Jo MacArthur gave a speech to honor me, and she came to my table at the conclusion of the ceremony. She took her stars off her collar and gave them to me. I cried. She didn't know me on the Department, but she was honoring me for my faithful work. That was a touching thing to do.

I think about the different personalities of all the people I worked with over the course of my career. Everybody is a little different from each other, but they're the same when it comes to the Police Department. You're glad you are a police officer, and you're glad your partner is who he is or who she is. You depend on your partner totally, so you have to care for them as they do for you.

Sidney "Sid" Nuckles

Birthplace: Jamaica, New York
Career: 1956–1989
Rank at Retirement: Detective III
Divisions: Jail, Highland Park, Metropolitan, University, Southwest,
  Robbery-Homicide, Officer-Involved Shooting Team

Tom Scebbi, my Academy classmate, was killed in '58. When you are a young officer and someone you know is killed, it really makes an impression on you. We only had two years on the job.

Tom was working with Ray Espinoza in Wilshire Division. At about three o 'clock in the morning, they had received a prowler call around Third Street and Kingsley Drive. They saw a guy walking on the sidewalk and stopped him. Ray was in front of the suspect, and Tom stood behind him. The suspect, James Eugene Hooten, had a gun under his shirt. He could see Ray's hands, but not Tom's. He pulled the gun and turned, shot Tom first, and then shot Ray. Tom was hit in the heart, or close to it, and Ray was shot in the stomach. Tom fired back and hit Hooten on the heel of his left foot as he ran off. Tom went back to the car on the driver's side, grabbed the mic, and broadcasted a help call. He died on the seat holding the mic.

A picture of him lying on the front seat of the police car was on the front page of the newspaper the next day. Will Gartland told me what happened. He and his partner was the first unit to respond to the help call. They found Hooten hiding nearby and took him into custody. Hooten was executed in the gas chamber at San Quentin Prison in '60.

What made me become a policeman? Across from the hotel where I lived, there was a bowling alley. It had a lunch counter, and I ate there all the time. One waitress had a son, a big guy, who worked LAPD Central Division. He liked me and said one day, "You know, you ought to be a cop."

Sid Nuckles

"Sure, yeah. I bet they'd laugh."

"No, no kidding. They are always looking for cadets."

That weekend he took me up to the Academy, and we ran the obstacle course. We did that a few weekends, and I got good at it. I applied, made it, and entered the Academy.

In our first month at the Academy, we had a pay raise. We went from $375 to $440 a month. The way everyone was celebrating, you would have thought we had gotten ten thousand dollars. My first ride-along was at Central Division, and I worked with the waitress' son who suggested the LAPD to me.

When I graduated from the Academy, I was assigned to Lincoln Heights Jail. I found out one day that the Department fired the waitress' son. Apparently, he and his regular partner were taking money from a liquor storeowner in exchange for providing protection. He was caught in a sting. He worked with a new guy one day, not his regular partner. After he collected the money from the storeowner, he said to the new guy, "My partner's not here, so we'll split it." The "new guy" was actually from Internal Affairs Division. The liquor storeowner had made a complaint. A couple of guys from Central thought I had turned him in. They said, "He told us about you, and now all of a sudden he gets fired." I said, "What? I didn't know about any of this. I wasn't even there." It took them a couple of years before they finally got over it.

After a year, I transferred to Highland Park Division, and I was assigned to morning watch. My first partner was Bob Kraus. The sergeant said, "You'll like him. He used to be a Chicago cop." I was thinking, *I've got to watch the store with this guy from Chicago.* Bob told me later that when he was told he would be working with a guy from New York, he thought, *What did I do?*

We ended up having the best time. Bob was a great cop. He could speak Spanish fluently. We would pick up suspects who conversed in Spanish thinking we could not understand them. He would let them talk, and when they essentially confessed to doing the crime, he would say in Spanish, "You dummies, you just put yourselves in jail."

One night at roll call, we were told to be on the lookout for a lion running loose. During our watch, a lady saw the lion in her yard and called the police. Stan Modic, our sergeant, got there and captured the lion. The lion was a cub, but of good size. Modic had Bob and I take the lion to the animal shelter.

I was driving, and the lion was in the back seat, and it smelled to high heaven. As we were driving to the animal shelter, the lion saw a cat on a sidewalk and let out a big roar. I almost had a heart attack! When we entered the animal shelter, all the dogs were barking. The lion let out another roar, and you could hear a pin drop. Everything went quiet.

Bob eventually went to Metropolitan Division. He told me, "You've got to come to Metro." I only had two years on the job, but I tried anyway. They looked at me as if I had lost my head.

They said, "Two years? You know this is a high-class outfit."

Bob later made sergeant, went to Wilshire, and came back as a sergeant at Metro. He called me again, and this time I applied and made it.

Bob Kraus

My first night in Metro, I worked with Joe Nelson. We heard an "F" car, a felony car, put out a call for assistance in Seventy-Seventh Division. Bob Flanagan and Rich Irwin stopped a guy that resembled a wanted burglary suspect in front of his residence. When they opened the door to his residence to retrieve his identification, they could see a gal inside with a needle stuck in her arm. Her boyfriend was also there doing narcotics. Bob and Rich detained the three and called for assistance.

We responded to the call, and when we got there, I was told, "We're going to search the place. You search the closet." Being the new guy, I was given the smallest place to search I pushed back the curtain covering the closet. I looked down, and there was a trunk. I opened it up, and lo and behold, there was a bag with $100,000 worth of heroin inside! I said, "You can stop now. I found it." That amount of heroin would be worth around a million dollars today. It was my first night at Metro, and I found $100,000 worth of heroin. All the Metro supervisors were asking Bob "Is this guy like this all the time?"

Trio Jailed, $100,000 in Dope Seized

Jim Hillman became my regular Metro partner. He was very intelligent and always kept himself in great shape. Jim was quiet with a good sense of humor. If anyone got combative, he would always be ready to join in the melee. Jim was great.

Jim and I rolled on a burglary one night in Wilshire Division. The responding officers had missed the suspect. My experience with burglars was they usually left the key in the car so they did not have to fumble around in their pocket when they were leaving the scene of the crime. Get in, turn it on, and go.

We looked around and found a car with a key in the ignition. We staked out the car, and after twenty minutes, the burglar popped out and was looking around as he walked toward his car.

We were in uniform, so we crouched down in the front seat of our plain Ford. I said, "It's got to be him." We waited, he approached the car and got in, and we got him.

We called the patrol unit that had originally responded to the burglary and gave them the suspect. Then we thought, *Maybe he has someone else with him?* We looked around, and on the main boulevard just up the street, we saw a guy sitting on the bus bench looking around nervously. Jim said, "That's got to be his partner."

Jim Hillman   *Sid Nuckles*

I walked over to the guy on the bench and said, "Hey, your friend is looking for you. Get in." Then I pointed to our police car. The guy had stuff from the burglary on him, and we booked him for the burglary, but not until after he told us the location of the main burglar's drop place for his stolen stuff.

Jim went to the drop place, a house, with other officers, and I stayed at the station with our arrestee. Jim called me and said, "You should see this place. It looks like a store. He's got everything in it." Everything in the house was stolen. We got a truck and recovered the property.

There was a robber dubbed the "Plaid Bag Bandit." Robbery Division had been looking for him, and Metro was asked to do some stakeouts. The Plaid Bag Bandit would rob markets in the early morning hours when the markets were just opening or in the late hours when the markets were closing. His pattern was to break into the market's delivery van that typically had no back windows because it was used to transport groceries. He would wait for an employee to come out to the van, and then pull a gun on him or her. While holding a gun to the employee, he would walk back in and rob the market. He carried a gun in a plaid bag, thus the nickname, the Plaid Bag Bandit.

Jim and I were staked on this one market in Wilshire Division early in the morning, along with two other Metro units, Ray Inglin and Gordon Palmer, and Glen Bachman and Dave Binstein. It was about six in the morning when we saw a guy walk toward the market carrying a plaid bag. I said, "Jim, there he is. Look at the bag he's carrying. I'll get out, and he will think I'm just another guy living around here." We were in plainclothes.

I got out of the car and walked on the sidewalk. He looked at me, but didn't pay me much attention and continued walking. He walked up to the market and peeked in through the window, then walked over to the delivery van. As he got in the van, I put my gun on him and said, "You move, and I'll blow you right out of your socks."

Jim came over, and we handcuffed him. We searched his plaid bag and inside was a gun, fully loaded. The bandit confessed to seventeen armed robberies, pled guilty to two robberies, and was sent to prison.

About six years later, I was working Southwest Homicide, and my fellow detectives were out to lunch. I was reading the teletypes and saw one about a guy robbing markets in the morning and at night. I thought, *Jeez that sounds familiar*. I called the detective handling the case.

He said, "What have you got?"

"I had a guy a couple of years back, and he's probably out of prison by now. He was doing market robberies the same way the guy you are looking for does them."

I gave him the information on the guy, and he said, "I'll check it out." About twenty minutes later, he called me back and said, "It's him." I got the Plaid Bag Bandit twice!

The guys came back from lunch and said, "Did you do anything?"

I said, "Yeah. I captured a bandit for robbery."

Chief Parker was big on stakeouts, and because Metro Division was a citywide crime suppression unit, we did a lot. One time officers were staked out at two different liquor stores on the same block. One store was robbed, and the robber was shot. Another suspect saw a bunch of policemen at the liquor store where the suspect was shot, so he robbed the second liquor store. Policemen were still staked out at the second store, so that robber was shot too.

There was a rash of robberies at many of the downtown See's Candies stores. Metro staked out all the stores, plus some independent ones, with two policemen in each store. Ed Meckle and I were staked out in one of the See's Candies when we heard gunshots outside. A guy robbed the independent candy store across the street where two other policemen, Earl Rice and his partner, were staked out.

Earl chased the robber, and Ed went after them. I did not see the second policeman come out of the candy store, so I went into the store to make sure he and the employee were okay. Usually, when we did a stakeout inside a store, one policeman would be high and the other low. When I came in, Earl's partner was coming down from his position. Earl shot and killed the armed suspect.

On one stakeout, a policeman chased a suspect who was armed with a magnum revolver. At one point, the suspect turned, shot the policeman in the foot, and got away. The suspect was later identified, and Jim and I went and sat on his house. Right after we had been relieved, the suspect came home, and the relieving officers arrested him. At the court trial, after the guy was convicted, the judge commented on the newness of magnum revolvers. He called the officer up who had been shot and said, "Do you have a magnum revolver?"

He said, "No, sir."

The judge said, "You do now. Bailiff, give him the gun."

When Marilyn Monroe died, a big crowd was expected at her funeral. Metro was brought in for crowd control. It was hot, and we were in uniform. When the service was over, Joe DiMaggio, who had been previously married to Monroe, was walking away when a reporter came up with a microphone and said, "Joe, how do you feel?"

Joe was walking with another guy, a big guy, who told the reporter to get lost. The reporter kept at it, and we could tell Joe was getting upset. We're watching this from the bus. Joe started to turn, and I thought he was going to knock the reporter flat. Instead, the big guy stepped in and knocked the reporter down. The reporter got up, but we jumped out of the police bus and intervened. The reporter said to us, "Did you see what happened there?"

We said, "We didn't see anything. Get out of here, or else you'll get dumped again." He left. Joe did not need that harassment.

I went on loan to Homicide Division from Metro. On the second day I was there, Ian Campbell and Karl Hettinger, two officers working a felony car in Hollywood, were kidnapped and taken to Bakersfield. Ian was killed, and Karl escaped from the suspects. Inspector John Powers and Sergeant Pierce Brooks brought Karl back to Los Angeles.

*Karl Hettinger and
Inspector John Powers:
"I felt so sorry for him."*

I saw Karl as he walked through the office, and you could see his eyes were wide open like someone that was in shock. I thought, *My God!* I felt so sorry for him.

The next day, my partner and I went over to the Coroner's Office for an autopsy on an unrelated homicide. There was a big guy lying on a gurney being prepared for an autopsy. He was so big he took up the whole gurney. He had bullet holes in him. I asked the deputy coroner who the guy was, and he said, "Ian Campbell." I had not known Ian, but looking at him that day, I thought that if Gregory Powell and Jimmy Lee Smith had not got the jump on him, Ian could have taken either one of them.

After five years at Metro, I made sergeant and went to University Division. I did a year as a supervisor and three years with University Detectives before I finally got into Robbery-Homicide. It was Homicide Division when I started, and the next year Homicide and Robbery merged. I stayed at Robbery-Homicide until I retired in 1989.

When the Charles Manson murders went down in 1969, the whole division was involved in the investigation. Gary Broda and I assisted on the murder investigation of Leno and Rosemary La Bianca, two of Manson's victims. We attended the autopsies for both La Bianca's. During the autopsy of Leno La Bianca, the coroner discovered a kitchen knife nearly five inches long inside his throat. Even the coroner was shocked when he found it. The suspects had placed a pillowcase over Leno La Bianca's head when he was killed, and it was not removed until the autopsy.

We did not know who committed the murders until Susan Atkins, one of Manson's girls, spilled her guts out. I was not involved in her interview, but we were told, "Don't go home."

Eventually, I went on an extradition to New Hampshire with Policewoman Joan Simpson, and we brought Linda Kasabian, another Manson girl, back to Los Angeles. She had turned herself in to the police, and although facing several counts of murder, she testified about the murders. She was the best witness for the whole case. She did two weeks on the witness stand with five attorneys going at her, and she beat them all.

Sid Nuckles, Linda Kasabian, and Joan Simpson arriving from New Hampshire

For eighteen years, I was assigned to the Officer-Involved Shooting Team working for Lieutenant Chuck Higbie. On one case, I responded to investigate an officer-involved shooting in Newton Division. John Puis and his partner, Ken Yerkes, received a radio call about a violent male. They were met by the sister of the male who told them her brother was mentally ill and had attacked their mother earlier in the day. He was now alone inside their house. John and Ken, along with other officers, went to the back of the house. John entered the house and was shot twice by the brother. As other officers were coming in, John was yelling, "Don't come in. You'll get shot like I did!" The brother escaped out the front door and ran over to a nearby school. SWAT responded and found him hiding in some bleacher seats, still armed. He was shot when he pointed his rifle at two of the SWAT officers.

I went to the hospital to interview John. I was there with his captain and my partner, and this kid is hurting. John told the doctor he could not breathe. His lung was filling up. The doctor took a needle and stuck it right in, and it sucked out the liquid that was filling his lung. John survived.

When John was in better condition, I went back to interview him regarding the shooting. Before I went I thought, *What could I do for this officer?* I had a picture of the suspect after he had been shot. I had it enlarged, and I gave it to him. I said, "Don't tell anybody. You just take that home, and whenever you start hurting, you look at that picture and you'll feel better." He stayed on the job and received two Medals of Valor, one for his actions in this shooting.

Gary Broda and I were the lead investigators on the murder of Officer Michael Edwards in 1974. Deputy Chief Gates asked Lieutenant Higbie who he wanted to handle the case. Higbie told him, "Sid and Gary." I received that call while I was managing a little league baseball game. I was told, "You're working it."

Michael was assigned to Seventy-Seventh Division. The night he was killed, Michael went off duty and made several stops after leaving the station, including one at the Academy. In the early morning hours, Michael was found in a small building shot several times. Whoever shot him tried to burn down the building, but was unsuccessful. When I retired, the case was still unsolved. Sadly, it is still unsolved today.

For most of the shootings, I was very impressed with the tactics and actions of the officers, especially considering the highly stressful situations they were confronted with. On one officer-involved shooting in Hollywood, I was really impressed with the officer who did the shooting. Two guys, one with an ax, were smashing the glass of the advertisement boxes outside a movie theater. When the two officers got there, one suspect fled, and the other suspect came at one of the officers with the ax. He had it raised over his head and was going to ax this officer. The officer who was about to be struck shot him with a shotgun.

During our investigation, I asked the officer, "Show me how far away he was when you shot him." He took a step that was about two to three feet from me. I said, "Why didn't you shoot sooner?"

He said, "I didn't want anybody to second-guess why I shot." I thought, *Here is one calm dude.* I could never have waited until he was that close.

Not a month went by, and we got another call of an officer-involved shooting in Hollywood. It turned out to be the suspect who had fled in the earlier shooting of the guy with the ax. This guy also had an ax and wanted to get to his neighbor by axing through a common wall where they lived. The police responded, the guy charged an officer with his ax in hand, and he was shot.

Elmer "Bruno" Pellegrino also worked the shooting team. He called me at home one night and told me James Pagliotti, an officer working Metro Division, had been shot and I was needed to assist with the investigation. James was working a detail looking for a burglar. He was in plainclothes and driving a rental car.

Another officer on the detail saw two guys involved in a drug transaction and believed both were armed with handguns. Over the radio, the officer gave the direction the suspects were walking.

James saw the suspects. He pulled over, parked on an incline, and got out of his car with the motor still running. He took cover behind the car, and during an exchange of gunfire, James' car rolled, exposing him to one of the suspects. One of that suspects rounds hit James in the chest, but he was still able to wound the suspect. James ultimately died. Both suspects were captured, and the one who shot James was sentenced to life in prison.

By the time I got to the scene, James was already at the hospital. Several years before, I had handled his first officer-involved shooting. It was a good shooting. Now, I was investigating his death. James was a good officer, and I went to his funeral.

Robbery Division was investigating several robberies at one market by a lone, armed bandit. He would rob all the checkout stands and then flee the market. Higbie said they needed more detectives for stakeouts and looked at me. I said, "All right."

Inside the market, they put me on a ladder that had to be fifteen feet high. I was looking through a small hole with a view of all the checkout stands when I saw a guy go from the first checkout stand to a second one and knew it was the robber. I told my partner, "It's going down."

My partner was an older detective. He went into the main store area without the shotgun he was supposed to carry. He left it leaning against the wall, and I later learned he had left his handgun in the car. He was wearing a light blue coat. It was the same color and type worn by the store manager. The suspect saw my partner, thought he was the manager, grabbed a cashier hostage, and fired a round into the ceiling. Everybody went to the floor.

As I was coming down the ladder, I heard the shot. I thought he had just shot my partner. I did a crouched walk behind the counters while the customers and employees were looking at me. The suspect released the girl he was holding and fled, but stumbled as he ran out the door. I jumped the counter, grabbed the girl, and told her to roll out of the way. I ran just outside the store, took a shot at the suspect, and missed. He turned and fired a round at me, and he missed. He took off running, and I chased after him.

The bandit ran in the direction of a barbershop with its glass door propped open. He ran around the door, took a position of cover, and sited up his gun on me. I stepped in to avoid being shot. He fired one round, then I fired two rounds. As I fired, he leaned out from the door, and my two shots went right through the glass door where he had been. He rolled on the sidewalk and dropped some money. He got up, ran, dropped some more money, and then jumped a fence into someone's yard. A dog started barking, and he took a shot at the dog.

The bandit got away, but dropped most of the remaining money in the yard. As I continued to search for the bandit, I yelled at my partner,

"Get the dough!" My partner was a ways behind me, but he recovered the money. Convinced that the bandit had escaped, I was returning to the market when I saw a man seated in a truck that would have had a front row seat to the shooting.

I asked, "You have a driver's license?"

"Yeah," and he gave it to me.

"Somebody is going to interview you."

The man turned out to be a good witness for me. The barber, however, was madder than a wet hen because of the two bullet holes in his glass door. I told the barber, "The city will take care of that." I had previously given up smoking, and the first thing I did on my way back to the market was stop at a cigarette machine. I bought a pack and smoked the whole pack, right then and there.

All my friends were retiring, and I got to thinking, who do I know now? Then I got an opportunity to be chief of investigations for the Los Angeles County Coroner's Office. Lieutenant Higbie was talking with the Coroner who told him that the chief of investigations for the Coroner's Office was retiring. The Coroner offered the position to Higbie, but Higbie said no. Higbie told him that he knew someone who would be good for the job, and he called me. He said, "I'm putting the word in for you. You should apply for this job."

Chuck Higbie

I applied, was accepted, and went to the Coroner's Office. I had no second thoughts. I always said I would know when I was ready to leave the Department. It was a good and timely move for me.

Chuck Higbie was probably my best friend both on and off the job. We could argue over a report, I mean have a heated disagreement in front of everyone in the office, and then later just the two of us would go out for drinks after work. We would both laugh and wonder, *Do those guys really think we're mad at each other?* You rarely won an argument with him. Chuck answered to one man and one man only, Chief Gates.

When Chuck died, there was very little written about him, about his impact on the Department and the hundreds of officers' lives he helped, especially during his tenure as the Officer-in-Charge of the Shooting Team. Commanding that unit was a very difficult job, and after he retired, no one, and I mean no one, could ever fill his shoes and run it as well as he did. I'm here to tell you that his impact on the reputation of this Department was absolute.

Kenneth "Ken" Risen

Birthplace: Bell, California
Career: 1959–1979
Rank at Retirement: Sergeant I
Divisions: Central, Accident Investigation, Wilshire, Hollenbeck

Being a policeman taught me things I would have never learned about people and the law. It made me what I am today. That background is still a part of me, and I rely on it daily.

After graduating from college, I was certified to work on airplane engines and airframes, but I could not find a job in the airline industry. Married and needing a good job, I wondered what I could do that I could still do when I was old. I applied and was accepted to LAPD. Big mistake. Try being a policeman when you're old.

I couldn't start right away. I had to wait because I was not yet twenty-one years old. When I did turn twenty-one, I had to wait six more months until the next class started in May '59.

On the first morning at the Academy, we were all milling around waiting for whoever was in charge to show up. Then somebody yelled "Atten-hut!" and we were told to march. I had never been in the military, and I said to myself, *Oh, no, I joined the Army!* We marched throughout our time at the Academy, and I was a very poor marcher. Whenever we did an about face and turn around, invariably I would step on some guy's shoes and mess up his shine. There was one guy worse than I was, so thankfully, they were always on him.

Roy Bean was our primary physical training and self-defense instructor. He was like a machine. When he took us running through the hills the first week, that killed my feet. In those days, people did not run cross-country. They generally ran around a track or on the street. Nobody ran in the hills. But we did.

Ken Risen

There were about seventy guys in my class, and I think we lost ten by graduation. One guy had been a policeman in Chicago, and he was fired for theft because one day he found a pair of handcuffs on a bench in the locker room and he did not turn them in right away. Another guy committed suicide. He went to a movie theater and shot himself inside the theater. Supposedly, he got a girl, not his wife, pregnant.

The Academy was located in Elysian Park, in a small area called Chavez Ravine. At the time, people were being evicted from their homes in the Chavez Ravine area. The reason for the evictions was to make space for the new Dodger Stadium. I came in one morning and saw Los Angeles County Sheriffs evicting families out of the last five or six homes still standing. Once the families were out, the hill was cut and construction started.

In the Academy, we went on ride-alongs, and the first policeman I ever worked with was Frank Gallant. Frank was a very good policeman. We were driving down a street in Newton Division and saw a guy chasing about twenty people and swinging at them with a seven-foot-long two-by-four. The guy was drunk, and he was almost as tall as the two-by-four. We had to fight with the guy to take him into custody.

Ken Risen, fourth row, second from right: Academy class, 1959

I asked Frank, "Do we have to do this on every arrest?"

"Oh, no, it's not like this."

I thought, *Good.* It was my first arrest, and I didn't want to have to go through that for the next twenty years!

To be honest with you, I disliked the Academy immensely because we were treated rough. I could see why they hired former military because they fit right in. Around fifteen cadets in my class had been in the military. Although I had never experienced anything like that, I was determined to make it. I just tried to blend in. Chief Parker spoke at our graduation, but I don't think any of the graduates understood what he said. He talked about the future, and here we were, brand new policemen. Parker was a good chief and perfect for the job, but he was very firm and strict.

When I was a kid, I recall hearing that the Department had a lot of dishonesty. Chief Parker cleaned it up. After I was on the job for a little bit, if someone had told me a policeman was dishonest, I would not have believed him. If someone had told me, a policeman punched a guy too many times, though, that I could have believed. But if a policeman was dishonest, he was fired. In fact, a classmate on a ride- along went into a large department store on a burglary call at night. After he had finished searching the store, he changed his flashlight batteries with ones from the store. He was terminated.

Central Division was my first assignment upon graduation, and I worked footbeats and drove the B-wagon. We dealt mostly with drunks. Most of them were good people; they just had a drinking problem. There were some sad situations though. There was a young guy, about a year younger than me, that I arrested for public drunkenness. He also loved to fight and invariably lost teeth due to his fighting. Over a year's period, I could see him physically deteriorating. He became like an old man. It was really just a tragic, tragic thing.

There were some burlesque places on Main Street. I was just twenty-one, so I had not really been in bars or places like that. We walked into one burlesque theater, and there was this gal, a dancer, sitting there half-naked. She was smoking. She saw my partner and me, and she yelled, "Oh, no, the Fire Department. We're busted!" She took off running out into the alley behind the place. I'm not sure what fire codes she was worried about, but she certainly didn't know the difference between a policeman and a fireman. We never really stayed for any of the shows, but we did see a few acts now and then, including Lili St. Cyr, then a famous dancer.

Follies Burlesque Theater, Main Street

Karl Hettinger was in the Academy class after me. He came to Central Division after he graduated, and we worked together on footbeats and the B-wagon. His primary training officer was Bob Burke. Karl had been in the Marine Corps. He was a blond kid, and he was sharp. He was about my age, and we got along well. He was a good guy and a great policeman, even as a probationer.

About five years later, I was working Wilshire Vice the night Karl and Ian Campbell were kidnapped in Hollywood while working a felony car. Two guys got the drop on them. The officers gave up their guns and were taken to Bakersfield. Campbell was murdered, and Karl managed to escape as they shot at him. The two suspects, Gregory Powell and Jimmy Lee Smith, were caught, convicted, and sent to prison.

After the incident, Inspector John Powers came around to all the divisions and told us what had happened. As I sat in roll call listening to him, I was thinking, *What would I have done under the circumstances?* From working with Karl, I knew he did the best he could at the time because, to me, he was a top-notch cop.

Afterwards, there was a lot of stress on Karl from the way the Department treated him for giving up his gun. And seeing how Karl deteriorated emotionally was very disturbing. I talked with Karl at the Academy about a year later. We had to qualify with our weapons every month, and he was there qualifying. He was not the same guy. Karl looked like he had aged thirty years.

From Central, I went to Accident Investigation Division. We handled traffic accidents and such for all of metropolitan Los Angeles, but not the San Fernando Valley. We also handled the freeways, which we later gave up to the California Highway Patrol. A number of accidents on the freeway were head-on collisions. Originally, the freeways had no center barriers and cars would cross the center median into oncoming traffic. Posts were tried and then cables, but nothing worked until what they have today, the cement K-rails.

John Smith and I worked together quite a bit at AI before he went to motors. One night after John had gone to motors, he was sitting on his motorcycle watching freeway traffic from the City Terrace onramp of the 10 Freeway. The onramp actually starts over the freeway lanes. As he was sitting there, a drunk driver crashed right into him, knocking him down onto the freeway lanes where he was killed.

"Originally, the freeways had no center barriers and cars would cross the center median into oncoming traffic."

Ken Risen, right, administering field sobriety test

John was twenty-four, about my age. When I went to his funeral, his wife was a girl I knew from junior high school. I had not seen her since then, and I did not know she was John's wife. I thoroughly enjoyed working with John, and his death was a very personal loss.

I worked AI a little under two years, and then I got to pick where I wanted to work. I asked for Wilshire Division. Wilshire had a nice, wealthy area, a high-crime area and businesses. You had everything, including radio calls that were not always police work. One call was a woman who told us her husband was an invalid and that she had a woman there to help her give him a bath. She said, "I can't get him in the bathtub. Could you guys lift him and put him in the bathtub?" He was about 250 pounds.

I asked her, "How are you going to get him out?"

She said, "I'll get him out, just get him in." We put him in the bathtub, and we left. Surprisingly, we got calls like that quite a bit.

At some point, most everybody wants out of patrol and I was no different. I went to Wilshire Vice. Marion Johnson, Jim Gibson, David Gonda, and Joe Wambaugh were my partners. Larry Nolan was our sergeant.

Joe went on to become a famous author. His first book, *The New Centurions*, included an incident I was involved in. When we worked prostitutes, we would be in separate cars. One night I was driving by myself when a prostitute driving her car made eye contact with me. She motioned for me to pull to the curb, and I did, stopping behind her. We were stopped on Vermont near a construction site for a portion of the new 10 Freeway. I walked up to the car, and she was by herself. She made me an offer of sex for money, then quickly reached up and placed her hand on my waist area as she said, "I want to search you to see if you're a cop." Before I could step back, she felt my gun, which was under my shirt. She said, "You're a cop."

I told her to get out of the car. It was my intent to arrest her for the prostitution violation. But she put the car, an Oldsmobile, in low gear and started to take off. The window was down, and I tried to reach in and turn the ignition off, but it was on the other side of the steering wheel. I grabbed onto the door as she was hitting me with her elbow, trying to knock me off. When she accelerated, it was too late for me to let go, and we crashed through a wooden barricade on one side of the

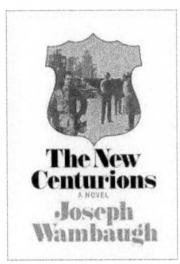

construction site and then through a wooden barrier on the other side of the site.

The emergency brake handle was within reach, and I pulled it. The car started fishtailing. It slowed enough for me to let go and jump off. She drove off and disappeared. I was not hurt, but it did scrape off the heels of my brand new Hush Puppies shoes. I walked back to my car more embarrassed than anything. I was a young cop. I didn't have five years on, and I was new to the Vice unit, so I decided not to say anything.

About a week later, Joe and I were staked on this motel watching for prostitution activity. We saw two prostitutes with their trick, a customer, entering the motel. I immediately recognized one of the prostitutes. It was then I told Joe the story. We approached the motel room and tried to overhear the conversation between the prostitutes and the trick. At one point, one of the girls threatened the trick, and we kicked in the door. When we entered, the prostitute recognized me. Joe said, "My partner says you tried to kill him." She readily admitted to what had happened a week prior, but denied she was trying to kill me, only that she was trying to keep from being arrested.

We took her and the other prostitute to the station. I told the sergeant what had happened, but he said it would be a problem trying to prosecute her because of the lapse in time. We let it pass and never filed on her.

How could I have taken her into custody that night? My partner was in a different car, and I don't remember how we got separated. If I had arrested her, I would have handcuffed her, and we would have walked to a payphone where I could have called for another unit to meet me. To be honest, I was not thinking that far ahead.

I was working Vice the night Bob Endler and Charles Monaghan were shot and killed at the Sears Department Store next door to Wilshire Station. Because we were in Vice, we were not involved in the search for the killer, Leamon Russell Smith. Both Bob and Charles were night watch detectives. They received a call from Sears that Smith and his girlfriend had been detained for forgery. They walked over to Sears, and another officer, Endel Jurman, who was off duty, went with them.

As the officers entered the security office, Smith pulled a gun and shot five times, killing Bob and Charles and wounding three others, including Endel. The girlfriend gave up Smith's name, and he was caught several days later in Chicago. I knew Bob well. We had worked both patrol and off-duty jobs together. I didn't know Charles as well. I went to both funerals, and that was tough.

When I left Vice, I worked Wilshire Detectives for a little bit, and then I made sergeant. I went to Hollenbeck Division and then to Hollenbeck Detectives. In those days, Hollenbeck was a unique division. The people who lived there, the East Los Angeles area, were generally very good people. They were not criminals. If there was a criminal, it was more often than not a wild kid in the family. People there did not have much, so there was not much to steal.

I can tell you a sad story. I was working Hollenbeck Juvenile when a little boy, a fourth grader, was brought in for purse snatching. I interviewed him without his parents, and he told me what had happened. His school had a fundraiser selling cookies. He sold all the cookies that were given to him. But his family had very little money, barely enough for food, so his mother took the money from his cookie sales and bought food for the family.

The school kept pressuring the boy to turn in the money from the sale of the cookies. He loved his mother and did not want to tell the school why he did not have the money. He decided he was going to steal to pay back the cookie money, and he took a woman's purse.

The mother and his father came in, and when I told them what had happened, the mother started crying. She admitted to taking the money. I counseled and released the boy. The father made arrangements with the school, and the money was eventually paid back. That was the first and only time the boy was arrested. These were poor, poor people.

I was working Hollenbeck Detectives night watch when Jerry Maddox, a policeman just off probation, was killed. He and his partner, Frank Benavidez, who was still on probation, responded to a disturbance call in the Pico Gardens Projects at Fourth Street and Gless. One suspect took off running. The officers had separated from each other, and Jerry chased and caught the suspect, but the suspect, disarmed and shot Jerry. A search was conducted for the suspect, and he was confronted several blocks away by a motor officer. They exchanged shots, and the suspect was hit, but survived.

I rode in the ambulance with the suspect to the hospital and stayed there as the doctors treated him. Once the doctors were finished, I tried to interview the suspect, but he would not talk. He later admitted in court that he killed Jerry. Jerry was going to be an outstanding policeman.

At Hollenbeck, I worked Robbery for a number of years with Bob Suter. I was very lucky in my career to have had two tenacious partners, Bob at Hollenbeck and, later, Sherman Oakes at Wilshire.

A market on First Street was robbed one day. When the suspect left, a box boy from the market followed him. The suspect saw the box boy following him, turned and shot the boy, killing him. Bob took the case and stayed with it until he identified the suspect. I do not know how many people he interviewed, but it was a lot. His tenaciousness really showed, and he did not stop until the suspect was caught and convicted.

Bob Suter

Most of the time Bob and I handled robberies, but once I was given a rape case. A radio call was broadcasted of a man holding a rape suspect at gunpoint. Bobby Wheelis and his partner responded to the call and through a window observed a man pointing a gun at another man inside a house. Bobby went inside, convinced the guy to put the gun down, and took the rape suspect into custody.

I interviewed the rape suspect first, and he told me that he and this man's wife worked together as janitors. She had invited him over to her house, and the husband caught them having sex. I then talked to the husband, and he told me he had suspected his wife of having an affair and then caught them in the act. I asked him why he did not shoot the suspect. He said that in Texas he was convicted of voluntary manslaughter when he shot and killed the guy his first wife was having an affair with, so he knew better than to shoot this guy.

Then I talked to the woman. She said that the suspect was her boss and that he had forced himself on her several times in the past at work. He went to where she lived and again forced himself on her. That is when her husband found them. She never reported it because she did not want her children to know she had sex with someone other than their father. She was very upset. I took the case to the District Attorney, but he chose not to file the case. He couldn't see how that was going to be seen as rape after so long. This was before people's concept of rape had changed. The suspect was released.

A few months later, I was going through crime reports and saw a report on this same woman that said she had attempted suicide. A couple of months after that, there was another report, a death report. The woman had killed herself. She felt so much anguish over what had happened that she committed suicide.

When I went to Wilshire Detectives, I teamed up with Sherman Oakes working robberies. He was a great partner, and we had a lot of fun working together. One case, two guys had rode the bus from Hollywood and got off at Western and Eighth near their home when a guy robbed them at gunpoint. Once he had their money, he shot one, killing him, and wounded the other. The wounded victim was taken to the hospital and stayed there for several days.

We received a panicked phone call from the victim while he was still in the hospital. He said we needed to get over to the hospital right away because he had just seen the suspect who had robbed and shot him. The suspect was still there when we got to the hospital, and we took him into custody. The suspect found out through the newspaper that one of the victims had survived the shooting, and he went to the hospital to kill him. The suspect did not have a gun on him, but he did have a knife. We went to trial, and the guy was convicted. He got life without the possibility of parole.

Sherman and I got a call from Detective Lalo Ortiz with the El Paso Police Department in Texas. He said he had information that two murder suspects he was looking for were in a hotel on La Cienega Boulevard and asked us if we would arrest the suspects for him. We went to the hotel and arrested both suspects. Ortiz wanted us to talk to them, and we got confessions from both of them.

l to r: Chief Daryl Gates, Detective Sherman Oakes, and Detective Dudley Varney at Hillside Strangler murder scene, 1978.

A few months later, we went to El Paso for the first defendant's trial. About four months after that, we went back to El Paso for the second defendant's trial. On this visit, LAPD narcotics detectives requested that we look for a suspect who was wanted in Los Angeles. The suspect escaped from custody in El Paso before he could be brought back to Los Angeles for trial. We were given his picture.

In Texas that first night, Ortiz and his wife took Sherman and me to a restaurant in Juarez, Mexico. The Rio Grande River separated Juarez and El Paso. The four of us were inside the bar area of this restaurant, when in walked a guy that looked very much like the narcotics suspect we were looking for. Ortiz knew the Juarez chief of police and called him. Within minutes, the bar was filled with Mexican police. They grabbed this guy and took him to their police station. At the station, we walked into the interview room where the suspect was being held. He refused to cooperate with us, shouting he was going to sue us and call the FBI. The Juarez chief of police vaulted over the table, stood in front of the suspect, and told him to shut up, that he was the chief's prisoner. The chief then told us to leave and that he would call us later.

A day later, Ortiz received a call from the chief telling him he was going to leave the suspect on a bridge between the two cities, and if we wanted him, we could take him. Sure enough, the suspect was on the bridge, just lying there. We picked him up, and he could hardly walk. I asked him what happened. He said they took all his clothes off, put him in a box with holes in it, squirted him with water, and electrocuted him with electric cattle prods. It was a pretty wild story and we didn't see any injuries consistent with what he said. We flew him back to Los Angeles. The guy pled guilty to the narcotics charge, and again disappeared into the dust.

Only once on the job did I fire my gun. We were chasing a burglar during the daytime. He went between some houses, and as I got close, he came out from behind a garage. I yelled, "Stop, or I'll shoot!" He took off running, and I fired, but missed. Then I heard a whole bunch of shots coming from the direction he ran. Somehow, all of the other officers missed him as well. He kept running and dropped what he had stolen on a corner near Adams Boulevard. Claude Ferguson, a bookmaker, walked to the corner and stood over the evidence so no one would take it. The burglar was eventually caught. I recognized Claude from my time in Vice. I did not work bookmaking, but everyone in the unit knew him. Claude didn't consider himself a crook because he did not steal.

Sherman's wife worked at the Los Angeles Police Protective League, and one day she talked to me about how there was so much dissent among the policemen. They felt the league directors were not representing the interest of the officers in their negotiations with Department management. She said, "Why don't you run?"

It had always been my plan to leave the job at twenty years, so I ran for a director position at the league, won, and spent my last couple of years there. It was not as bad as everyone had thought. The directors really were working for the officers. While I was there, I had a role in the development and passage of the Policeman's Bill of Rights.

I finished my career working Hollenbeck Homicide. When I first got there, John Curiel, the lieutenant, said to me, "Ken, can you go to this autopsy for me? We need the bullet for court." I went to the coroner's office, and when I walked in, there was a body on every autopsy table. There were bodies lined up and down the hallway. Even the icebox was full. Long before, when I first went to an autopsy, there were maybe two people on the tables. That was how much things had changed.

I had not seen an autopsy in several years, and I had forgotten how horrendous it was. It can be a gruesome sight to see a body cut up to determine what killed them. However, the coroners do a good job. They do treat the dead with honor and dignity.

When I worked Robbery at Wilshire, Dick Sullivan and Dwight Stevens were two of the detectives also working Robbery. They both had gone to law school and had passed the bar exam to become attorneys. Dick introduced me to the owner of a law school, I went to the school, and I eventually became an attorney.

When I did retire, I served on the Board of Prison Terms conducting parole hearings. I worked there for about a year, but I didn't like being around the prisons and dealing with inmates. I left and went into private law practice. I feel bad for police officers today because they work their hearts and souls to catch criminals to keep the community safe, but the criminals spend a shorter time in prison and then are out again and doing the same thing. The sentences are so short that there is no deterrent to committing a crime.

Bill, Ken, and Bob Risen

Both my brothers followed in my law enforcement footsteps. Bob, my youngest brother, was on LAPD. Unfortunately, we never had the opportunity to work with each other. My other brother Bill retired as a lieutenant from the Monterey Park Police Department.

Charles "Chuck" Teague

Birthplace: Inglewood, California
Career: 1959–1982
Rank at Retirement: Sergeant I + II
Divisions: Wilshire, Seventy-Seventh, Central, Administrative Vice,
    Accident Investigation, Traffic Enforcement, South Traffic

After I left the Marine Corps, I returned home and went back to
school at a local college. An LAPD sergeant was a student in one
of my classes. During a class break, we talked about his job, and he said
I should consider taking some police science classes. I signed up for a
couple, and I really enjoyed them. Most of the guys in the classes were
policemen. One was a motor cop with the California Highway Patrol,
and we became good friends. He taught me how to ride a motorcycle
and encouraged me to become a policeman.

For me, the Academy was a piece of cake, although there was one
moment I thought I might not graduate. While in the Academy, you're
sent on ride-alongs at a division. My first ride-along was in Seventy-
Seventh Division, and I rode with a sergeant. We were cruising around
when a radio call came out about a family dispute. We were only a few
blocks away, so the sergeant decided to roll on it.

At the house, we were confronted by a drunk who was the subject of
the call and definitely not cooperative. He proceeded to direct a battery
of expletives at us. Then he charged the sergeant, knocking him off the
porch and onto the front lawn. He jumped on the sergeant and started
punching him. I didn't have a sap, and I didn't want to shoot the drunk,
so I took my baton, the old hickory stick, put the baton across the front
of his neck, and placed my knee in his back. I pulled back and was
having some success, when the officers that were assigned the call
arrived.

Ted Bach, Chuck Teague, and Don Tudor: Academy graduation,
1959

We overpowered the drunk, and he was taken into custody and booked for assault on a police officer. The sergeant was treated for injuries at Morningside Hospital, but he remained on duty, and we spent the rest of the night doing paperwork. I quickly learned that a family dispute call should not be taken lightly.

A week or so later during one of our classes at the Academy, Sergeant Griffin McKay called me out. He did not tell me to bring my hat and books, a sign that your time at the Academy was over, so that was good. He told me that two sergeants from Internal Affairs were there to interview me about the family dispute incident on my ride-along.

The Internal Affairs sergeants told me they were investigating an allegation against me for excessive force with my baton. They asked where I had learned the tactic of placing my baton around a suspect's neck. I told them that in the Marine Corps during advanced combat training we were taught the tactic using our M-1 rifle. I never heard another word about it. Sergeant McKay and our physical training instructor, Roy Bean, said they could not recall a cadet being bounced out of the Academy after a ride-along. I was glad not to be the first, but I was sweating it for a while.

Karl Hettinger was the valedictorian of our class. We were both former Marines, and we got along great. We used to kid each other when the physical training got tough, "Remind you of boot camp?" Then we would both laugh. I finished number one in the class in physical training, and Karl was right there with me. For our graduation, Karl and I were both selected and honored to be part of the four-man color guard.

Later, Karl would become widely known in the much-publicized Onion Field incident, where he and his partner, Ian Campbell, were kidnapped while on duty working a felony car in Hollywood Division. The two suspects, Gregory Powell and Jimmy Lee Smith, took the officers' guns and drove them to Bakersfield, California, where they killed Ian and shot at Karl as he fled to safety.

Chuck Teague, fourth row from bottom, far right; Karl Hettinger, top row, middle white hat; Academy class, 1959

A few evenings prior to that night, I visited with Karl when I was at Hollywood Station. I was working Administrative Vice Division. We sat in the coffee room reminiscing about our days in the Marine Corps. We were talking about the training we had received, and Karl mentioned the zigzag training. Zigzagging was what you did when advancing on the enemy so the enemy could not draw a bead on you.

I met up with Karl at Parker Center sometime after the incident. I was careful not to bring up what had happened, and I was surprised when Karl mentioned it. He asked me if I remembered our conversation in the coffee room about running in a zigzag pattern. I said I did, and he told me that training probably saved his life after Campbell was shot. He knew he was next to die, but he instinctively took off running in a zigzag fashion while they were shooting at him. He said he could hear bullets whizzing by.

Months later, I met with Karl again, and when I asked him how he was doing, he said things were terrible and he could not sleep. He felt the Department held him responsible for Campbell's death. He said Inspector John Powers made him attend numerous roll calls to talk about what happened that night. You could tell Karl reliving it over and over was taking a toll on him. He eventually left the Department.

Sometime later, Karl was getting off the elevator at Parker Center as I was getting on it, and we talked for a few minutes. That was the last time I saw him. He looked disheveled. He did not look like the Karl I had known. Powell and Smith were found guilty and received the death penalty, but their sentences were commuted to life in prison. Smith ultimately was paroled.

We graduated from the Academy in October 1959, and I was sent to Wilshire Division. On my first night, I went into the locker room and set my stuff down on the bench in front of my assigned locker. A policeman came into the locker room, knocked my stuff on the floor, and said, "Never put your stuff here. This is my locker."

My locker was the one next to his. I said, "You don't have to be so damn mad about it." Then I caught myself. It was my first night. If I had an altercation, I would be fired. I told him, "If I had known, I would not have done it. I won't do it again, but don't be giving me any problem." He was good about it after that.

Joe Rieth

Turned out it was Joe Rieth. Later on, my first watch commander, Lieutenant Tom Bradley, assigned me to walk a footbeat with Joe. Lieutenant Bradley told me that Joe had asked for me. Some old-timers said Joe had asked for me because I stood up to him. Joe was a great partner and taught me how to walk a beat. He treated everybody on the street well, and, as a result, he got a lot of respect.

We were walking a beat one night, and as we came around the corner at Vermont and Wilshire, there were several guys harassing a man selling newspapers on the corner. The man was about forty years old, missing his arm at the elbow, and wearing a watch cap and a Navy pea coat. We chased the guys off, and I took the occasion to talk to him. Before when I would pass by him, we traded hellos but not much more.

The man had graduated from college with an engineering degree and lost part of his arm in WWII. He had attained the rank of commander in the Navy. I asked him why he sold newspapers. He said he did not need the money, he was getting a disability pension, but it gave him something to do. He had a little apartment nearby. On that day, I learned that often times you never know about the person who you are saying hello to.

At the urging of Don Peterson, one of my training officers, I approached Lieutenant Bradley to request a few days off to get married to a student nurse I had met at Central Receiving Hospital. When Lieutenant Bradley asked me why I was getting married, I told him, "I guess I'm in love!" Lieutenant Bradley started laughing so hard that as he leaned back in his swivel chair, he fell over backwards. He picked himself up and said he hadn't laughed so hard in quite a while. He gave me the days off, and everyone saw another side of him. He had a reputation for not smiling or laughing.

I got a chance to work with my classmate John German on morning watch. One night we were really tired because we had both been in court all day. It was about four thirty in the morning, and I was driving. I stopped for the red light on Wilton Place at Wilshire. The next thing I knew, somebody was knocking on my window. I opened my eyes, and it was the milkman.

I cranked the window down—no electric windows in those days— and I said, "May I help you?"

"I came by here about forty-five minutes ago, and you were sitting here waiting for the light."

John and I had fallen asleep at the intersection! We went straight to Wilshire Station and told Lieutenant Bradley. He said, "Put yourselves out to the station. That's where we finished our tour of duty.

The If Club was a lesbian bar on Vermont at Eighth Street. When I had walked the beat with Joe Rieth, we made bar checks there, and I got to know Harry, the proprietor, and his employees. One employee, Valerie, had a young daughter about five years old. Sometimes during the day, the little girl would be in the bar, but nobody minded. When I came in, I would say hello and talk to her.

One Christmas I was shopping with my wife and told her about this little girl. We bought her a doll and had the store wrap it up, and I brought it to work. I had arranged for another unit to bring me the gift when I reached the club. I walked my beat as usual, and they met me with the doll. I gave it to Valerie and said, "This is for your daughter." She got teary eyed.

Not too long after that, there were a slew of liquor store robberies. The robbers would take money and shoot the owners or the clerks. I worked one stakeout in plain clothes and hid in a liquor store waiting for the robbers to hit. But no luck. One day I got a call from Valerie. I met her, and she told me that she had heard about the robberies and that she knew the robbers and their home address. I did not ask how she knew.

I called the station and gave the information to Lieutenant Bradley. He called Captain Ed Jokisch who came into the station and called in other detectives. They interviewed me, and I repeated what Valerie had said to me. It was decided to hit the robbers' residence, and Captain Jokisch asked me if I wanted to be a part of it. I said, "Yes, sir."

Their place was an apartment off New Hampshire Avenue. We hit it, caught the guys, got their guns, and found evidence of the robberies. They were ultimately convicted. I thought, *Look what the rewards could be with just a little bit of kindness*. I had given a true gift of friendship and did not expect anything in return.

In the early '60s, I was transferred to Seventy-Seventh Division on the wheel. I had not been there long when I was told to be at Parker Center for a meeting. Until then, white officers worked with white officers, and black officers worked with black officers. The Department was integrating, and I was selected to be a part of the integration program.

My new partner was Richard Johnson. We got along great. Rich was great to work with because he did not like to drive and I did. He had a degree in chemistry from the University of Chicago. One day we were eating at a barbeque place on Wilmington at 111th Street, and I asked him, "Why are you working as a policeman when you have a chemistry degree?"

He said, "Chuck, I'll tell you. You don't know what it is to be black. And you don't know what it is trying to get a job being black." Rich did not have to say any more. I understood.

We had answered a family dispute call one day and knocked on the door of the residence. I stood off to one side of the door, and Rich was on the other side. A black lady opened the door and immediately looked at Rich. She said, "I want the white law." She wanted to talk to me, not Rich. It was as if she did not trust a black officer even though she was black. Rich was a gentleman about it, and we handled the call. He sure was a great partner.

Bill Davis: "Mr. Cigar"

I worked with Bill Davis for a while. He was a sharp policeman. Everyone called him "Mr. Cigar." He used to hold a cigar in his left hand as he drove the police car. One day we got a call for him to call Homicide Division. We drove to a Gamewell, and he made the call. He was standing there, and I was listening. He said, "Yeah. Yeah. Yeah. Give me about an hour, and I'll get back to you." We left, and he told me that Homicide Division was looking for a murder suspect and that we were going to find this person's location. He told Communications not to assign us any radio calls until further notice.

We made a couple of stops, and then we went to a place where a bunch of big-as-a-house, half-drunk guys hung out. Bill walked right through them and then talked to one guy off to the side. We went back to a Gamewell, and he called Homicide. He said, "This is the name of your suspect, and this is where you can find him right now." Bill was phenomenal.

Bill Davis taught me that you treat everybody with respect until things dictated otherwise. That was his philosophy. He was given a tremendous amount of respect from everybody in Watts. I never saw him heavy-handed with anybody.

I was on day watch working a one-man unit, when I received a call of a disturbance at a pool hall. On the way there, the call was upgraded to an assault. When I entered the pool hall, the bartender pointed to the very back of the hall. There was a bunch of pool tables, and a guy was lying on his back on one of them with a pool cue stuck in his chest. He was dead, and the suspect was right there drinking a beer. I requested an ambulance and detectives.

The suspect told me what had happened. The deceased bet the suspect a twenty-five-cent bottle of beer that the suspect could not make a shot during their game. The suspect made the shot and wanted the beer. The guy would not pay up, so the suspect stabbed him with the pool cue. While he was telling me this, everybody was still drinking and shooting pool. It was no big deal, like this happens every day. There was obviously no value of life with these guys.

The wheel hit again, and I was off to Central Division. I was now walking a beat on East Fifth Street, Skid Row, with all the drunks and homeless people. It was a world of difference from walking a beat in Wilshire Division. I was only at Central for a short time when I got the opportunity to go to Administrative Vice Division, which everyone called "Ad Vice." I got another chance to work with a classmate, John Polakovic. Our other partner was Earl Nishimura.

One of the first cases I worked was a high-dollar prostitute operating out of her home. I posed as a dairy worker and made the telephone call, and she answered. She was comfortable with my cover story and gave me her address. It was a second-story apartment on Leimert Boulevard. My job was to try to get a prostitution violation, and if I did, to signal my partners by whistling. She invited me in, and as I entered, I saw a closed door to a room on my left, and I started that way. She grabbed my arm and led me to a room to the right.

Once in the room, my shirt came off. My t-shirt came off. My shoes came off. My trousers came off. I'm down to my shorts! Then she stripped her clothes down to her underwear and gave me a violation. I said, "I'm sorry, honey, but you're under arrest. I'm a police officer." She screamed and ran down the hallway toward the room with the closed door. She opened the door and ran in, and I was right behind her.

There was a guy sitting on a couch in front of a window, and I saw a .45 automatic on the table in front of him. He started to get up and reach for the gun, and I hit him as hard as I could. He went right out the open window and fell to the ground. She was screaming. I grabbed the gun and was trying to whistle, but I couldn't. I started yelling to John and Earl, and they kicked in the front door.

We arrested the girl and found all kinds of narcotics upon searching the apartment. The guy I knocked through the window was a big-time dope dealer. He survived the fall without any serious injury. It was a good arrest, and I got a lot of ribbing after that: "Hey, Teague, you going to put anybody through a window today?"

Ad Vice was hit with a corruption scandal. This one detective worked bookmakers, and when Joe Gunn came to Ad Vice, he was assigned to work with him. One day, the detective gave money to Joe and told him it was protection money from the bookmakers. Joe thought his integrity was being tested so he went into the captain's office and challenged the captain. An investigation ensued, and Joe was asked to play along with the detective until there was sufficient evidence he was in fact receiving protection money. The investigation established that the detective was not the only one taking money. A Vice sergeant from another division was also on the take. Both were convicted and sent to jail.

Unfortunately, a wide shadow was cast over the rest of us working bookmakers. I was interviewed to help further the investigation and was not accused of anything. Most of the division was transferred out, including me and even the captain, so the division could start anew. Fortunately, it never affected my career. The new captain asked me where I would like to work. I told him AI, Accident Investigation, and I was on the next transfer.

One very rainy night I received a call about a traffic accident on the Hollywood Freeway at Barham. A drunk driver had collided with another car. That portion of the freeway is a hill between Hollywood and the San Fernando Valley. When I arrived, the ambulance was already there, and the attendants were putting one of the victims in the ambulance. I immediately started to place a flare pattern back up the hill as a warning to oncoming drivers who were blind to the accident until they reached the crest of the hill.

I was about halfway up the hill when a car came over the crest right at me. It was traveling way too fast and went right through the flare pattern. I jumped out of the way, and the car crashed into the back of the ambulance, hitting one of the attendants. He survived, but I believe he lost a leg. The momentum of the car caused the ambulance to hit my police car and my police car to hit the two cars that had been in the first accident. Now I had a secondary accident on my hands. It just mushroomed. I remember standing in the rain looking at that mess and thinking sarcastically, *I'm sure glad I came to AI.*

At AI, I learned that when things seem overwhelming, especially at the scene of a tragic accident, you have to take a moment, calm down, and do what needs to be done. Just take one thing at a time. I had once been assigned a traffic accident where four juveniles in a stolen car had crashed into another car, killing the other driver. I had never investigated an accident before that, and it took me six hours to get through it. But I did.

The other half of investigating an accident with fatalities is making a death notification. I must have made fifteen in my career. They were never the same. On Western Avenue in Harbor Division, an eleven-year-old boy riding his bike was run over by the rear wheels of a semi-truck, an eighteen-wheeler.

I was able to identify him because in his bike rack was a book that had his home address. Kids that age usually just had a baseball glove on the handlebars. I went to the address and knocked, and a girl maybe thirteen years old came to the door. I used the last name I found in the boy's book and asked if the house was the residence of that family. It was. I asked her to go get her father.

The father came to the front door. I said, "Sir, please step out here and shut the door." He knew whatever I was about to tell him was not good. Through the window, I could see that the family had dinner on the table and were probably wondering about the boy. I told the father what had happened. He tried to gather himself at probably the most emotional moment in his life. His wife came out, and then I told her. She went into the arms of her husband. That part of the job is really, really hard, but it is something you have to do. That is the human aspect of being a policeman.

When the Watts riots hit, I was assigned to the Seventy-Seventh area. Dennis Darger and I were partners. The second night of the riots, Sergeant Marty Harabedian was near the Mosque on Broadway at Fifty-

Eighth Street. Shots were fired at him as he was driving by, and he believed the shots came from the Mosque. He put out a help call, and a number of units responded.

We took a bunch of guys out of the Mosque, lined them up, and searched them. They were not armed. We looked inside, and I found spent shell casings by a window on the second floor, but we did not find a gun. I turned in the shell casings for evidence, and the guys were put on a bus and taken to the station. I don't know what became of the investigation.

During the riots, the National Guard had a checkpoint at the intersection of Vermont and Slauson. There was a jeep positioned there with a .30 caliber machine gun on the back of it. Dennis and I were talking with the guardsmen when a car driving northbound on Vermont caught our attention. It was driving fast with no headlights on. We shined our flashlights to get the driver's attention, but the car kept going. As it passed us, the guardsman on the jeep opened up with the .30 caliber machine gun. He stayed with the car as it drove into the intersection. You could see the tracer rounds hit the car.

The car stopped, and the driver, a female, fell out. We ran up to the car, and she was dead. The rear seat and trunk of the car were full of Pyrex plastic bottles filled with gasoline along with wicks to make Molotov cocktails. We could not understand how the bottles did not ignite from the machine gun's rounds. Officers a quarter mile up Vermont called and said they were under fire. Those were the bullets from that machine gun.

Dennis and I were driving down San Pedro Street, and there was a bunch of looters inside a liquor store at Sixty-Eighth Street. When we stopped, most of them ran. As I approached the store, a looter inside saw me and threw something, breaking the plate glass window and causing some glass to go into one of my eyes. I was momentarily blinded in that eye, but I saw the looter as he ran out of the store. I followed and tackled him, and then we wrestled in the middle of the street.

The looters that had run away started coming back. Dennis put out a help call while I was still wrestling in the street. I lost my badge, but I did not know it at the time. In the distance, I could hear a police siren, the sweetest sound you can hear. Dennis and I finally subdued the looter and handcuffed him. He was booked for assault on a police officer.

Dennis Darger

Chuck Teague, left: Watts Riots, 1965

Dennis took me to Morningside Hospital, and the doctor took pieces of glass out of my eye. He gave me a doctor's note that put me off duty, but I never turned it in. They needed policemen with the riots going on. About three months later, I got my badge back! Somebody had found it and dropped it in a mailbox.

After two years at AI, I was off to motors. We did a lot of escort details on motors. President Lyndon Johnson came to Los Angeles in 1967 for a fundraiser at the Century City Plaza Hotel. We met his plane at the Los Angeles Airport and provided the escort to the hotel. Thousands of demonstrators were at the hotel to protest the Vietnam War. We escorted the limo safely into the hotel's subterranean parking lot.

A few minutes later, we heard the sound of a helicopter. We were thinking, *The president is here and a helicopter was allowed over the hotel?* That surprised us. What surprised us more was that President Johnson was in the helicopter. We had escorted a decoy! Of my many escort details, this was the only one where the person we were supposed to escort was not present.

President Johnson, white jacket, exiting helicopter, Century City Plaza Hotel, 1967

I was working the 110 Freeway when a radio call was broadcasted about a jumper on top of the Biltmore Hotel. I was close, so I took the next off-ramp and pulled up on the south curb of the hotel on Fifth Street. I looked up and saw the jumper. I could tell it was a woman. I grabbed my mic and started to advise Communications that I was there, when she jumped. She landed about ten feet from me, half of her on the sidewalk and the other half in the gutter. I could not even distinguish her face. I called for an ambulance, and I stopped traffic. I never found out why she jumped.

Chuck Teague, center, with white helmet, Biltmore Hotel: "...she landed about ten feet from me..."

*Chuck Teague, center, Frank Albert, center right, commended by Fire
Department for rescuing disabled man from apartment building fire, 1969*

On April 23, 1970, my partner, Frank Albert, and I were working
the midday watch. After roll call, Frank and I headed to a coffee spot on
Manchester. On our way there, we heard a broadcast about a robbery
where a brown '68 Pontiac Firebird was taken. I joked with Frank,
saying, "Let's go have coffee and then catch that suspect." When we got
to the coffee spot, two police cars were there. Two were too many, so
we decided to make a run of our beat and then return for coffee.

We were traveling northbound on Western, crossing Seventieth
Street, when suddenly a brown Pontiac Firebird quickly exited the
parking lot of the Security Pacific Bank. It stopped in the northbound
lane to try to make a left turn to go southbound. I had to apply my
brakes hard to avoid a collision, but the front wheel of my motorcycle
did touch the driver's door. The driver's window was down, and the
driver pointed to the bank parking lot and yelled, "There's a man in the
parking lot that's sick or hurt." I turned my head and observed the man

on the ground. There were people standing around him, but nobody was saying anything or trying to get our attention.

As I started to back up my motor, I looked back at the Pontiac now merging into southbound traffic, and I saw bullet holes in the rear window. I yelled to Frank, who was a little behind me, "Stop that car!" The Pontiac took off and quickly made a right turn at Seventieth Street, with Frank in pursuit. I was behind and had to play catch up. As I came to the end of Seventieth, a "T" intersection at Horace Mann Middle School, I saw Frank on the corner to my left. His motor had stopped with engine trouble. He was waving me on, and I could see the Pontiac two blocks away southbound on St. Andrews Place. The suspect had to be going at least eighty miles per hour. He was going so fast that when he hit a road bump, the car lifted up and I could see the undercarriage. I was doing sixty miles per hour just trying to keep up with him. At one point, I lost him. A woman and her son flagged me down. The woman said the driver of the Pontiac had stopped, jumped out of his car, and ran down an alley off Seventy-Third Street carrying a gun and a black bag. I broadcasted what the woman told me.

Knowing the guy was on foot, I drove east on Seventy-Third Street to Budlong Avenue. I did not see him and turned back to retrace my route. Another woman standing in front of a house in the nine hundred block of West Seventy-Third Street shouted to me that a man with a gun ran down the side of her house to the back yard. I drove up onto her front lawn and put the kickstand down, but the ground was soft and the bike went over. I cautiously walked down the side of her house, with her house on my left and a six-foot wall on my right, but I did not see the suspect.

There was an alley behind her yard, and as I entered the alley, I took a position next to a power pole. All of a sudden, I heard gunshots to my right. I saw two plainclothes detectives from Seventy-Seventh shooting at the suspect who was under a boat that was on a trailer. The boat was on the other side of the wall that I had just walked along. The shooting was over quickly. As the detectives and I approached the suspect, I immediately recognized him as the driver of the Pontiac. He had a .38 caliber revolver in his hand and a black bag containing a large amount of money on the ground next to him. He was dead.

The suspect was Charles Henry Mack. He had committed a robbery at the Security Pacific Bank, and as he left the bank, shot and killed the security guard. Earl Riddick, an off-duty LAPD officer, followed Mack out to the parking lot and tried to take him into custody. Mack shot him, and Earl fired several rounds through the back window of the Pontiac as Mack entered the vehicle. Earl died at the scene. Neither Frank nor I heard any shots as we rode northbound on Western Avenue, and none of the people in the immediate area tried to get our attention. During the pursuit, I never connected the earlier robbery broadcast where the brown Pontiac had been taken with the brown Pontiac I was now chasing.

Mack had been released from San Quentin Prison six months prior to this incident. In the six months since his release by the state parole board, he had murdered five people and wounded two in several robberies. All were shot with the same stolen .38 caliber revolver he used to kill Earl Riddick.

At Seventy-Seventh Station, Inspector Charlie Reese spoke with me. He said, "Somebody up there likes you. It just wasn't your day to buy the farm." At that instant, the image of Mack looking at me as he was trying to leave the bank parking lot came into my mind. His left hand was on the steering wheel and he pointed back with his right at Earl. The gun may have been in his lap or within easy reach. The only thing between him and me was the windshield of my bike. That image remained in my mind for several months.

Do you believe in divine intervention? I believe it happened twice in my career, the first being the Mack incident. The second happened after I had met Alex Ilnicky. When I was first assigned to Seventy-Seventh Division, I worked the jail with Alex who was the main jailer. We became good friends. When the Department started the helicopter program, Alex became a pilot. He had been a combat pilot in World War II. In those days, the helicopters were assigned to Traffic Enforcement Division, and their responsibility was to monitor the freeway traffic conditions. The helicopters were based in Glendale. The helicopter observers were all volunteers from TED.

In roll call when the supervisors would ask for volunteers, I would always raise my hand. One day they asked, and I volunteered for the next day. But the next day, I had traffic court. When it was getting close to start of watch and my case had not been called yet, I telephoned the office and told a sergeant my situation. I said that my partner, Larry Amberg, was working alone since I had volunteered to be an observer and that Larry could go in my place. Larry had worked as an observer before, and he really liked it.

My case was finally called, and I testified. When I got back to Parker Center, the place was utter chaos. My lieutenant said to me, "You don't know what happened?"

I said, "No, sir. I just got back from court."

"Alex and Larry were flying over Dodger Stadium, and they collided with a news helicopter. Both Alex and Larry are dead." I was devastated. Both were good friends. Divine intervention? Maybe. I don't know.

I liked being in the field, but it cost me physically. By the time I retired I had two pins in each shoulder, three herniated disks, three neck procedures, surgery on both elbows and shoulders, and my hearing was bad, which was common for motor officers. Eventually, I would get a stent in my heart.

At the Academy, I had set a goal for myself. I wanted at least ten years on the street before I took a sergeant's exam. I figured if I had ten years of field time, I could tell someone else to do something that more than likely I had already done myself. It was not an easy transition, but I achieved the only goal I had set for myself.

When the Ambassador Hotel on Wilshire Boulevard closed, various things in the hotel were up for auction. I went into the old coffee shop. A reporter happened to be there along with two of the waitresses that had worked in the coffee shop for a long time. I told the reporter that I had walked a footbeat at night in front of the hotel when I first started my career. I would come into the coffee shop, and columnist Walter Winchell would sit in the first seat at the counter. That was his seat. I would sit next to him, and we would talk over coffee. The two waitresses remembered me and said, "That's right! Only Walter would sit there, and you were just a kid!"

Walter would stay at the hotel whenever he was in Los Angeles, and I think he lived there the last couple of years of his life. The reporter took my picture, and it was published in the paper the next day. I enjoyed one last chance to be where I started.

Dorothy Pathe

Birthplace: Glendale, California
Career: 1961–1990
Rank at Retirement: Sergeant / Detective III
Divisions: Juvenile, Jail, Business Office, Public Affairs, Robbery, Bunco-
  Forgery

When my first husband was discharged from the military, we came back to California where I had grown up. I went to work because we knew he had to go back to college. I had some flunky little job at the time.

My dad called and asked me, "What do you think you would like to do?"

"I don't know, Dad."

"Well, the Los Angeles Police Department is hiring."

My dad was an insurance investigator for traffic accidents, and he often went into police stations and spoke with clerks to review files. That was how he learned about some job openings.

I went down to City Hall, and the openings were for the position of policewoman. I took the test and passed. When my dad found out I had taken the test for policewoman, he about died. He had told me about the openings because he thought the Department was looking for clerks.

There was a written test and then an oral interview. When I went in to take my oral interview, Daisy Storms was scheduled to be on the board. Daisy and Albert Storms, both on the Department, were the mother and father of Connie, one of my high school girlfriends who was killed in a traffic accident the year prior. I had not seen much of Daisy since Connie's death. Daisy asked me if I was okay with her on the board because she thought it might be uncomfortable for me. I told her that it was fine with me and I appreciated her thoughtfulness.

*Daisy Storms and John Locker, 1963, with new police
motto "to protect and serve"*

Nine women were in my Academy class, and Margie Collins was in charge of our class. She was a great example of what a policewoman should be and had a tremendous influence on us.

Part of our training was learning how to shoot. I had never shot a gun before. On our first day on the target range, we were instructed to shoot at specific targets. All I heard was "number six." When we were told to shoot, it was, "Ready on the right, ready on the left, commence firing."

When we had finished firing, two shooting instructors approached me, and one of them asked, "What were you shooting at?"

"The number six."

"Well, you sure shot the hell out of the number six!"

I had shot at the actual number six up in the corner of the target. He corrected me, and on our next round of shooting, I hit what I was supposed to hit. I did pretty well once I knew where I needed to shoot.

Policewoman Francis Sumner on target range with numbered targets

I was always athletic, and I never had any trouble with the physical training. In fact, later in my career I played tennis in three California Police Olympics and won in both singles and doubles.

Chief William H. Parker gave us our diplomas when we graduated. I did not get a choice of where I wanted to work after graduation. I was assigned to Juvenile Division at Georgia Street Station for six months. That station and the street segment it was on no longer exist. In the late '80s, numerous buildings, including the station, were demolished, and several streets were absorbed to expand the Los Angeles Convention Center. The South Exhibit Hall now stands where the station once stood.

At Juvenile, I worked out in the field with male partners. We would primarily look for juvenile runaways and ones out past curfew. If we found a lost kid, we would try to find the parents. There were many times we came across sad situations. We got a call one time in Hollywood after a teenage girl had overdosed on drugs. I looked at her and thought, *What a waste to be so young.* It was a shame. We called the homicide detectives from Hollywood Division, and they took over the case.

Dorothy Pathe, second from left, Margie Collins, far left: Academy class, 1961

For the next two-and-a-half years, I worked the female section at Lincoln Heights Jail. Working the jail did not bother me, as I needed to get the experience. No matter where I worked, I always thought what I was doing was worthwhile.

Some of the prisoners were characters. One day I was talking with a prisoner, and I mentioned I was going to go out to dinner with my husband that night. She asked me what the occasion was. I told her it was our wedding anniversary. She asked, "How many years?"

"Five."

She looked at me with a straight face and said, "Five years! To the same man?" She could not believe it.

I have never forgotten this one young girl. I should say woman, but she was closer to being a girl. When she was brought in, it may have been for narcotics, she was verbally abusive to the policewomen. I thought, *If only her parents could see and hear what she was saying.* To me, she did not belong there. She was well dressed and seemed educated. I had seen so many repeaters come in, and I did not want her to do anything that would make her come back to jail.

I gave her some cleaning stuff, and I took her over to this small utility room for water pipes. I told her to clean the pipes, and I locked her in the room. I came back several hours later, opened the door, and the pipes were clean. She was very calm and nice. Her mouth had cleaned up, and her attitude changed. She was respectful. That was the only time I did something like that, but I am glad I did it. I would like to believe it helped her. I never saw her in the jail again.

Policewoman Lomie Hall came in one day to book an arrestee. I had not met Lomie before, but we started talking during the booking process. She asked me how long I had been at the jail and if I was planning to leave. I said "sure," but I didn't really know where I wanted to go. She said there was an opening where she worked at the Business Office, which today I believe is called Detective Headquarters. Lomie spoke with the captain in charge of the Business Office. The captain interviewed me, and I got the job.

Lomie Hall

In the jail, I used to tell the prisoners that were griping or were grumpy about something, "You have a release date. I don't!" That would usually make them laugh. Whenever I saw Lomie after I went to work at the Business Office, I would always tell her, "Thank you for getting me out of jail!" She was a wonderful person.

During August of 1965, I was on a day off at the beach with some girlfriends listening to the radio when all of a sudden there was an announcement that all Los Angeles Police Department officers were being ordered to return to work. The Watts riots had started.

Because of my jail experience, I was sent to the Seventy-Seventh Division men's jail to be a booking officer. I had to drive in my own car by myself, and I was pretty nervous driving through Watts with all that fire, smoke, and looters everywhere. I was just hoping to make it to the station and back home each day.

After the riots, I went to Public Affairs. One of my duties was to represent the Department at various functions. Once I was sent to appear in uniform on *Art Linkletter's House Party* television show. Art interviewed me during the show and asked me about my duties.

Dorothy Pathe, far right: Boy Scouts tour of Parker Center, 1966

Dorothy Pathe, seated center: Rampart Division dedication, 1966

At one point, he excused himself, and his son Jack took over the interview. As Jack and I were standing on the stage, someone came up behind me and grabbed me. Reacting instinctively, I twisted his arm and flipped him over onto the floor of the stage. It was Art Linkletter!

He just laid there, looked up at me, and said, "I'll never do that again!" The audience laughed. Art Linkletter did not hurt me, and I was hoping I had not hurt him.

When Chief Parker died, I was asked to accompany his wife, Helen, during the funeral services. I had not met Mrs. Parker before then, but I sat with her all through the service and stayed with her until the funeral was over. She was quiet. I thought she handled it very well.

When the Charles Manson murders occurred, I was working Robbery-Homicide Division. At the time of Manson's trial, detectives from Robbery-Homicide, including me, were sent to Inyo County to bring back several witnesses. I rode in the back seat with one of Manson's girls. Metropolitan Division officers drove our vehicles to provide security. On the way back, this girl talked about the murder of Sharon Tate, how the baby was cut out of Tate's stomach. She told me the girls who did the killing were laughing about how they were trying to feed it with their breasts. There was no sound of remorse from her; she was not sorry at all about the murders.

ROBBERY
DIVISION
1969

CAPT. R.C. PERRY
1-14-68

LT. C. APPLETON
5-19-68

LT. R.C. BARRON
8-17-64

LT. C.A. HIGBIE
6-16-68

V.V. BRASHER
9-26-47

S. BROADHURST
11-5-67

C.F. BUCKLAND
9-18-58

F. ESTRADA
12-12-50

J. FARRELL
2-25-68

A.C. FUENTES
5-13-62

J.A. GIROUD
6-10-62

J. LEON
1-26-52

S.R. McCALEB
8-26-50

G.L. MOON
1-20-63

W.P. PAILING
6-24-59

D.A. PATHE
12-27-68

R.W. REED
8-15-55

K.L. SCHWARZ
12-10-58

H.E. SERET
3-3-60

I.T. SMITH
12-27-68

S.J. STRIEGEL
12-5-65

J.A. VIETTI
7-11-53

S.T. WAPATO
2-25-68

F.M. WHEELING
7-17-67

J.H. WILLIAMS
5-12-60

R.E. BARE
3-10-69

E.F. BENSON
8-17-53

W. BRAY
4-14-63

C.B. DAVENPORT
3-13-66

J.S. DEIRO
2-19-61

R.D. JOHNSON
12-24-61

D.P. MAHONEY
3-9-69

B.J. RAUTERT
2-26-64

W.K. STEWART
3-9-69

C.B. THOMPSON
3-9-69

D.B. WELD
5-19-68

S.J. MURDOCK
8-26-68

I finished my career working Bunco-Forgery Division. Connie Speck was my first partner, and then Fanchon Blake was my partner for several years. Fanchon was a character. When the Sylmar earthquake hit in 1971, we were sent to a gymnasium where people who had lost their homes were being evacuated. Our job was to help them in any way we could. On the way to the gymnasium, there was a big traffic jam, and we were right in the middle of it. Fanchon jumped out of the car, and just like General George Patton in the movie, she started directing traffic. In no time, we were on our way again! Fanchon was in the military during World War II and then rose to the rank of major in the military reserves.

One day in 1971, all of the policewomen were directed to be in the auditorium at Parker Center to hear from Chief Ed Davis. Chief Davis essentially said there was no place in police work for women. He was not going to get rid of us, but he was going to eliminate the policewoman position. Instead, we would be placed throughout the city as clerks. I was listening to him and thinking, *How can he do this?*

Fanchon Blake

When he finished, Fanchon and I left the auditorium and entered the elevator on our way back to the office. Fanchon said emphatically, "We'll see about this!" She contacted the American Civil Liberties Union, and they were instrumental in putting a stop to Chief Davis' plan.

Fanchon did not stop there. After she had promoted to sergeant, she knew the policy was that policewomen could not promote higher. She initiated a lawsuit against the Department that ultimately paved the way for women to promote and opened the door for more women to be on the job. There is a good chance none of these changes would have happened when they did if not for Fanchon Blake.

Working forgery, I had this one case where a doctor scammed three women out of their money through phony investments. Their losses were hundreds of thousands of dollars. When each woman found out what he was doing, she filed a crime report. None of the women had met each other until they came to court.

At the preliminary hearing, all three testified, and the doctor was held to answer to the charges. The case was sent to Superior Court for trial. The first day of that trial, all three women walked into court at the same time wearing T-shirts printed with, "Trust Me. I'm a Doctor." He was convicted and sent to prison.

Only once in my career did I pull a gun on someone. We were serving an arrest warrant on a guy for forgery. My partners went to the front of the residence, and I went to the rear in case our suspect came out the back. They hit the front door, and the suspect ran out the back, intending to jump over the porch railing right where I was standing. I pulled my gun and said, "Freeze!" He stopped and looked at me, and this big look of fright came over his face. I guess he had never had a woman pointing a gun at him before! The guys came through the house and handcuffed him.

I used to get Christmas cards from people I put in prison. They didn't write "Wish you were here!" type of sentiments or anything like that. They genuinely wished me a Merry Christmas.

One day I was walking back to the office after court when someone shouted, "Detective Pathe! Detective Pathe!" I looked around and running towards me was a forger I had sent to prison. He served his time, and now he was out. He said, "I've wanted to thank you so much.

I turned a new leaf in prison." He had found religion and felt that had he not gone to prison he would still be committing crimes. We stood there talking for a little while. I thought it was very nice of him to stop me and tell me that.

Pope John Paul came to Los Angeles in 1987, and he stayed at St. Vibiana's Cathedral downtown. On the last day of his visit, our lieutenant told us, "We need a couple of people to go down to St. Vibiana's and help guard the Pope."

I immediately raised my hand and said, "I'll go."

At St. Vibiana's, uniformed personnel were lined up around the church. My partner, Art Ramirez, and I were stationed at the driveway. Art was on one side, and I was on the other, amongst uniformed officers. We were the only two in plain clothes. The limo carrying the Pope came out the driveway. The limo paused, and Pope John Paul, who was seated on my side of the limo, looked right at me. He made the sign of the cross as he looked at me. I got his blessing! At that moment, I thought of how fortunate I was to receive his blessing. I am Catholic, and I fully believe it made a difference in the rest of my life.

I feel the same about my career. I loved my career. It was a blessing and made a difference in my life. The people I worked with were wonderful. I did not want to retire, but I did. Everyone talked about retiring and traveling, something I had never really done. I decided that before I got too old I wanted to do some of those things. I said to myself, "I earned a retirement. I guess I'll use it!"

Richard Kalk

Birthplace: Watertown, New York
Career: 1961–1991
Rank at Retirement: Sergeant / Detective III
Divisions: University, Hollywood, Seventy-Seventh, Metropolitan,
    Southwest, Hollenbeck, Rampart

I was born and raised in Watertown, New York, and for whatever reason I decided to join the Marine Corps. When I was ready to be discharged, I called my brother in Watertown, and he said home was a ghost town and there were no jobs. As I was waiting for my discharge at Camp Pendleton in Oceanside, California, I saw a hiring advertisement for the Los Angeles Police Department.

Growing up, I had cut my eyeteeth on the television show *Dragnet*, a cop series about the LAPD. I applied and was in the next class. To think, there I was a farm kid in New York watching *Dragnet*, never imagining that someday I would not only get to California and be on the LAPD, but I would actually meet Jack Webb, the creator and star of *Dragnet*.

During my time at the Academy, my first ride-along was at Highland Park Division. As soon as we left the station, my partner saw a car blow through a boulevard stop. We had a short pursuit with red lights and siren. They turned a corner and had to stop. Once out of the police car, my knees were shaking so bad I could hardly stand up. I was so excited; I had to lean on the car. What an adrenaline rush! It was a bunch of teenagers in the car. My partner cited the driver, and that was it.

Richard Kalk, front row, second from right: Academy class, 1961

When we came back from our ride-alongs, the instructors asked each of us, "Well, what happened to you?" I really had nothing to tell, but one of my classmates did. He said they chased a guy on foot who had a rifle. The guy they were chasing reached the middle of the street, stopped, turned, and put the rifle to his mouth. He pulled the trigger and blew his brains out, right in front of my classmate! As I heard his story, I thought, *Holy cow! Is that what's coming?*

After graduation, University Division was my first assignment. The station was at Jefferson and Hoover, but it has since been torn down. The land is now part of the University of Southern California campus. The old station was so small that the locker room and the roll call room were the same room. It was a busy division.

After a year, I was transferred to Hollywood Division and put on the felony car practically right away. My partners were Ian Campbell, Danny Stewart and Clyde Brand.

Ian was a good partner. The most memorable arrest I made in Hollywood was with Ian. One night at roll call, the robbery detectives told us about a suspect they were looking for who was robbing gas stations. They dubbed him the "Gas Can Bandit." They said, "We believe he lives in the Hollywood area because he has not robbed a gas station here. Here's a description of the car we believe he is in and the partial license number." It was a silver-gray Cadillac.

Later that night, Ian and I were checking an alley behind a liquor store on Sunset Boulevard. Recently, there had been several robberies of liquor stores. We didn't see anything in the alley, so we came out onto a side street and turned toward Sunset Boulevard. We pulled up behind a car waiting to make a left turn. We saw that the car was a silver-gray Cadillac, but we were too close to see the license plate. I told Ian to hold back, and as the driver turned, we saw the license plate and realized it was the car wanted by the detectives. There were two guys in the Cadillac, and they pulled into the Tiny Naylor's Restaurant parking lot at La Brea and Sunset. We stopped them and took the Gas Can Bandit into custody. The guy with him was not involved in the robberies. That was a great arrest.

Tiny Naylors Restaurant

After working the felony car for six months, my wife wanted me to work day watch, so I returned to uniform patrol. About two months later, I was getting on the Pasadena Freeway at the Fair Oaks onramp heading to work when there was an interruption in the program on the radio. The announcer said that Ian Campbell and Karl Hettinger had been kidnapped the night before, and that Ian had been killed. I pulled to the shoulder and sat there in total shock. That was devastating to hear. When I got to Hollywood Station, the place was mass confusion. They were just getting ready to bring Karl back.

Ian and Karl were working the felony car when they stopped two suspects in a car. At one point, suspect Gregory Powell got the drop on Ian and disarmed him. Powell then told Karl to give up his gun. At Ian's direction, Karl complied. Both were taken to a field in Bakersfield where Ian was shot and Karl escaped. Knowing Ian as I did, that incident was the most traumatic thing I experienced as a cop.

Ian played the bagpipes, and he used to practice down in the basement of the station. Did you know he was going to be a doctor? He went to medical school, but had to drop out because he got married and needed money, so he joined the LAPD. After I retired, I was chatting with a doctor, and he asked me what kind of work I did. I told him I was retired from the LAPD. He said he had known someone that had been on the Department. I asked him who it was, and he said, "Ian Campbell." He and Ian were roommates in medical school. Can you believe how small the world can be?

In those days, during your first three years you changed divisions every year. After University and Hollywood, I was transferred to Seventy-Seventh Division. I was designated as a training officer for new officers and recruits on their ride-alongs.

One day Sid Renfro, a recruit from the Academy, was on his ride-along, and we were working the Watts car. We were cruising down 103rd Street just east of Central when we saw a car bust a stop sign. We pulled him over, and when he got out of the car, we were looking at a guy the size of a giant and very muscular. He had an expired driver's license, which in those days meant he had a warrant. A check with Communications Division confirmed that.

I said to him, "Sir, there are warrants for your arrest. You're going to have to go with us."

"I'm not going."

"Sir, you don't understand. There are warrants for your arrest, and you're going to have to go with us."

"No, you don't understand. I'm not going with you."

I don't know what possessed me, probably looking at his size and what it would take to get him to the station, but I walked over to our police car and picked up the mic, but I didn't push the button.

I said, "Twelve-A-seventy-eight requesting an ambulance."

He looked around and asked, "Who is the ambulance for?"

"You, if you don't get in that car."

Surprisingly enough, he walked over, opened up the back door, and got in the police car. Sid got in the back seat with him, and on the way to the station, Sid asked me, "Don't you think you ought to cancel the ambulance?"

"What ambulance?"

In the booking cage at the station, the guy started laughing and then shook my hand. He said, "This is the first time I've ever gone to jail laughing."

At the time of the '65 Watts riots, I was now working Metro Division. During the riots, there was a curfew from ten o'clock at night to six o'clock in the morning. Anybody on the street could go to jail.

One of the nights, we saw an elderly black gentleman walking down the street behind the Watts Substation. We could tell he was upset. We asked him what was wrong. He said, "This makes me so mad! I got to get to work, and there are no buses running because of the curfew."

We gave him a ride to 120th Street at Vermont Avenue where the buses were still running. We picked him up again the next night and did the same thing. Many of the people that lived in Watts were not involved in the riots, but the riots impacted their daily lives.

At Metro, we worked a variety of details, including stakeouts and loans to specialized divisions. One stakeout was for the "Remorseful Rapist." This guy used a toy gun and was responsible for a number of rapes of young women in the Wilshire area. After he raped a woman, he would pray and ask for forgiveness from the victim. We even worked it for a while in plain clothes on bicycles.

A patrol unit, Carl Kuehn and his partner caught the Remorseful Rapist during a traffic stop. They found evidence in his car, including a toy gun and tape, linking him to the rapes. He was convicted of multiple rapes, I believe twelve, and went to prison. The detectives believed he was responsible for a lot more rapes, including some in the outlying cities. He was paroled in '72 and committed more rapes once he was out. He was caught again and returned to prison.

There was a pair of bandits who robbed banks with shotguns and wore fake beards as a disguise. Because of the beards, we called them the "Castro Brothers." We had a bunch of banks staked out. Richard Anderson and Edward Orias staked the bank on Adams just west of Crenshaw Boulevard. A guy came in and saw Ed look at him. I don't know if he thought Ed was the police, but he drew his shotgun and fired at Ed, wounding him. Rich killed the second suspect, then he and Ed both shot the first suspect, paralyzing him. It was the Castro Brothers. Nobody else in the bank was hurt. As usual, I was one bank up the street. Both Ed and Richard received the Medal of Valor.

When I made sergeant, I was sent to University Division, and that's when the Black Panthers were big. Norm Roberge and Rudy Limas were on my watch. After roll call one day, they went out on patrol and saw a car that drew their attention. They followed the car to Ham's Gas Station at Adams and Montclair. There were four black militants in the car, all Black Panthers. The suspects got out of the car and put the hood up. Norm and Rudy pulled in behind them and directed the suspects to the front of the police car. They complied and placed their hands on the hood of the police car.

At some point, one of them pulled a gun and shot Rudy in the stomach. A gunfight ensued between three of the suspects and the officers. Rudy and Norm were each shot several times, but they killed the three-armed suspects. The fourth took off running and was later identified through fingerprints he had left on the hood of the police car. He was the brother of one of the suspects that was killed and later turned himself in. The shooting was over by the time I got there.

Paramedics took Rudy and Norm to the hospital, and both survived. I supervised the crime scene until the detectives got there. It was one hell of a shooting. Both officers received the Medal of Valor.

One day I received a call from Lieutenant Carl Schumacher. Carl was older than mud—his badge number was Number Five. Carl was in charge of Hollenbeck Detectives and asked me to come and work

Hollenbeck. I had almost two years as a field sergeant and always
wanted to work the detective bureau. I transferred to Hollenbeck in '69
and teamed up with Joseph Wambaugh. We worked burglaries together
for about four years until he quit after writing the book, *The New
Centurions*. *The New Centurions* was about the Los Angeles Police
Department.

Joe handed me a crime report one day and said, "Read this." I read it
and didn't catch what it was he wanted me to see. He said, "Read it
again." It was a burglary report, and a witness listed on the report told
the police he had seen a burglary and watched the suspects hide the
stolen property in a storm drain. The stolen property was recovered, and
a lead on the identity of the suspects was generated because of the
witness' information. The witness to the burglary was named Preston
Tingle. Preston Tingle? Well, what a name just before Christmas!

Joe had this idea that it would be a good Christmas story, so he
called the press and arranged to meet them the next morning where
Preston Tingle lived. Tingle was a hobo that stayed under the Seventh
Street Bridge. In the summers, he rode the rails to the East Coast, and
then he would ride the rails back to Los Angeles for the winters. We
went out and talked with Tingle, and he was fine with meeting the press.

Now, where Tingle actually stayed was unique. The bridge was over
the Los Angeles River. He had a ten-foot pole with a hook on the end
hidden underneath a stack of railroad rails. To get to his place Tingle
would reach up with the pole, hook an eyelet attached to a rope ladder,
and pull the ladder down. Then he would climb the rope ladder to a loft
under the bridge, unlock a gate, enter, and then pull the rope ladder up.
Tingle had a mattress, a chest of drawers, and other home-type
conveniences in his loft. When he wanted to leave, he kept the rope
ladder in place and used another rope tied to a steel cable to lower
himself. Tingle would swing out over the riverbed on the rope to a
fence. When he would let go of the rope, the cable would snap back and
pull the rope with it. Now mind you, when he was swinging over the
riverbed, he was about sixty feet above the riverbed.

The next morning when we got there, Tingle was already answering
questions from the reporters. He was up in his loft, and the reporters
were on the ground. Joe and I were watching Tingle, and we concluded
that he was drunk. When a reporter asked how he got down from his

loft, Tingle said he would show them. We were yelling at Tingle, "No! No!" But he insisted. He lowered himself on the rope and started swinging, but kept missing the fence. Joe and I were both thinking our careers as we knew them were over should Tingle fall.

After three times of missing the fence, he caught it and stepped to the ground. The news media asked us why we had given him booze. We didn't. Tingle later told us that some reporters had talked to him the night before and gave him a bottle of good whiskey.

One day Joe asked me to take a picture of him. I said sure and asked him why. He said he needed a picture for a book he had just written, *The New Centurions*. If you will notice, I got credit for taking his picture in his first three books: *The New Centurions, The Blue Knight*, and *The Onion Field*.

Preston Tingle accepting reward from Jim Hammett, manager of nearby freight terminal

*Joseph Wambaugh, Richard Kalk, and actor William Holden on the
television movie set* The Blue Knight

Columbia Pictures contacted Joe and told him that Robert Chartoff
wanted to produce a movie based on *The New Centurions*. Joe came to
me and said, "Richard, what are you doing for lunch?"

"Nothing. Why?"

Joe told me Robert Chartoff invited him to lunch. We went to a
restaurant in Burbank and had lunch with Chartoff and the screenwriter
Stirling Silliphant. During lunch Silliphant asked me, "Has anything
funny ever happened to you on the job?"

I told him the story about pretending to call the ambulance while
working Seventy-Seventh Division. They both laughed and wrote it into
the movie even though the story was not in Joe's book. George C. Scott
uttered the line in the movie.

Once Joe's books were out, life for him as a policeman changed. He
could not really function as a detective because of the constraints put on
him being a famous author. In fact, we were interviewing a guy for
robbery, and during the interview, the guy was looking at Joe. He said,
"Are you that author?" There were times we would get a call that the
press was in the station lobby. Joe would have to take circuitous routes
through the station to avoid them. He told me he couldn't work and be
effective anymore. The day he quit I picked up his badge and police

identification card from his home and turned it into Personnel Division for him.

After Joe left, I went to Hollenbeck Homicide, working with Nick Romero, Ernie Valenzuela, and John Collella, and our boss was John Curiel. In those days, we handled everything, including gang homicides. The problem with a gang homicide was your witnesses were always afraid to go to court. Usually two or three days before court, gangsters would show up at a witness' house and just stand in front of the house or sit on the curb to intimidate the witness. If we sent officers to chase them off, the defense attorneys would claim harassment.

We had one case where a gang member, Mario, confronted a kid who was simply walking through the area the gang thought they controlled. Mario asked the kid, "Where you from?" When the kid tried to answer, Mario shot him. Gang shootings were as simple as that. We identified Mario through two witnesses and filed a murder case on him. However, when we got to court, our witnesses now could not identify Mario, and the case was dismissed.

Maybe a month later I was sitting in the office, and John Collella came in and asked, "Didn't you have a case on a guy named Mario and lost it at trial?"

"Yeah."

"Well, I have a case on him that we aren't going to lose."

He dropped the report on my desk. Mario had killed himself playing Russian roulette. So, there is justice.

In Hollenbeck Division in '69, Jerry Maddox and his partner responded to a gang party. Jerry chased a suspect who had run from them and got into a fight with him. The suspect wrestled Jerry's gun away from him and shot Jerry in the neck and then several times in the back. He was convicted and sent to the California Youth Authority. The suspect was sixteen or seventeen at the time of the shooting, and when he turned twenty-five years of age he was released.

After his release, another gang shot his brother. The suspect retaliated for the shooting of his brother by firing several shots into a group of guys standing by a trash can at Hollenbeck Park, killing a fourteen-year-old kid. That was the mentality of a gang member. Later that evening officers saw the suspect driving a car, went in pursuit, and captured him. We filed a case on him, and he was convicted.

One day Nick Romero and I did a follow-up with a witness in Pasadena on an unsolved homicide. On our way back, I asked Nick to stop at a bank so I could withdraw some money. We pulled into the back parking lot of the bank. Nick stayed in the car, and I walked in through the back door. It was a very small bank. From the back door, the administrative desks were to my left, and the two teller positions were to my right. Straight ahead was the front door and I saw about eight people standing at a bus bench in front of the door. There was nobody at the administrative desks, and no customers in the bank. There were two tellers working.

I walked over to the farthest teller, who was next to the bank sidewall, and I told the teller I wanted to withdraw some money out of my savings account. I heard the teller at the next position say, "Can I help you?" I realized that another person had entered the bank. He approached the counter and laid a brown paper bag on it.

I sensed something wrong and knew what it was. He opened up his jacket, and I could tell from the reaction of the teller that he had a gun. You know how a cop's mind works. It was too late to take a day off or call in sick. I was hoping the teller helping me would take her time so the guy would get his money and walk out of the bank.

As luck would have it, my teller returned and started to hand me my money. To stall, I told her she must have made a mistake. Then the guy turned toward me and showed me his gun, a .38 revolver, in the waistband of his pants. He said, "Be cool." Then he told the teller to get the money from my teller's position. The other teller walked over to my teller's position as the guy walked around me to follow her. We were face-to-face as he passed me.

When he reached up to receive the money from the teller, I did an old high school wrestling hold and brushed my hand up in his face, distracting him enough to move in behind him. I grabbed his wrists as he was reaching for the gun. He then tried to get away from me as I held onto him. As we reached the front door, I tackled him and tried to hold him down with my body weight.

I yelled to the teller to go get my partner. She did. And when Nick came into the bank, we handcuffed the suspect. The guy was convicted and went to prison. I was awarded the Medal of Valor and met Jack Webb when he hosted the ceremony.

Richard Kalk awarded Medal of Valor by Chief Daryl Gates, 1979

"As we reached the front door, I tackled him...."

Nick and I responded to a call one day that uniforms found a dead body in an alley. That day it was raining like hell. The water runoff from the rain was so heavy that it was running around the body that was lying on its back. The dead person was clothed in a heavy jacket and hat, and we couldn't tell if it was a man or woman.

After door knocking several places nearby, we were unable to locate any witnesses. The coroner came and took the body. During the autopsy, we determined that the person was a female and had been shot three times in the back and once in the back of the head. We opened her wallet and removed her identification. I recognized the name. I knew the girl and her family. She had a younger brother, maybe twelve years younger, the same age as my daughter. They went to school together, and that was how I knew the family.

Now I had to make a death notification to people I knew very well. I went to the house, and the wife was at home. There was no easy way to break the news. I just said, "Your daughter is dead." She telephoned her husband, and I told him over the phone. That homicide was as close as you ever want to come to being personally involved. Making the death notification was very tough. We identified the shooter, and although we never truly confirmed why she was killed, he was convicted and sent to prison.

That was it for Hollenbeck, and I transferred to Rampart Detectives and worked Homicide there for about six years. One day I had just got into the station when I was told, "Richard, we got a dead body behind a business down off Pico." When we got there, the uniformed officers were already canvassing the area to see if anybody had seen what had happened. No witnesses, nothing. The body was a male in his late-forties or early-fifties and well dressed in a sport coat and slacks. He had been strangled. We could not find identification on him, but later identified him through his fingerprints because of a drunk driving arrest a few years prior. Through the family, we found out he owned a Porsche and was driving it the night of his death. We found no Porsche at the scene.

We put out a want on the car, and a few days later a fireman on his way to work found it parked on the side of the road near Las Vegas, Nevada. He noted smoke inside of it. A burning cigarette had been dropped on the rear seat and was left smoldering. The interior burned to some degree before the fire was extinguished.

We searched the car and found a hotel receipt underneath the front seat. The hotel was in Los Angeles, not far from where the body was found. There were also two cigarette butts in the ashtray. We took them for saliva and secretor analysis.

At the hotel, we got the names of a man and a woman who had rented a room the night the man was killed. We came up with an address of a friend of theirs who they had stayed with for a while. We talked to the friend, and he said he hadn't seen the two for a few days, but offered that some of their stuff was still at his house. He told us he would call us if he heard from them. The friend called a short time later and said the two suspects called him from Oregon. We had enough for arrest warrants and brought them back to Los Angeles.

They had met the victim in a bar. The victim had been drinking heavily, and the woman lured him to the hotel room. Once there, the man strangled him, and they took his money and jewelry. They put him in the Porsche, drove to the alley, and dumped him. They were driving the Porsche to Las Vegas, ran out of gas, and abandoned the car.

Our male suspect smoked the brand of cigarettes we found in the car, and he was a secretor. You very rarely have an eyeball witness to a murder. Usually the case is circumstantial where one or two things may not mean much, but five or six pieces of evidence and you can put together a good case. The male was convicted of murder, and if I remember right, the gal pled to a lesser charge.

It is important to maintain a sense of humor in police work. When chatting with other officers, often the conversation will get around to how old you are. As a response, and depending on my age at the time, I would tell them I was forty-six years old, but I would have been forty-seven had I not been sick a year.

One day I was working with John Shambra. We brought in a suspect, and we interviewed him. During the interview, I asked him how old he was. He said he was seventeen. I told him his driver's license showed he was eighteen. He looked at me straight in the eye and said, "I flunked a year." I looked up at John, and he was just about to bust a gut. This guy had pulled my own joke on me!

Toward the end of my career, I was in charge of the Auto Theft Section of Rampart Division. I was sitting at my desk one day thinking about retiring and how it's absolutely ridiculous that when you retire there is nothing to say you were here. That was the moment when I had the idea for a police museum, a place to maintain the history of the Police Department.

I started talking to various officers and asked them what they thought about having a museum dedicated to the Los Angeles Police Department. They were all for it. I approached Chief Gates with my idea, and he blessed it. He was on board from day one.

In '89, I formed a charity corporation that became a repository for all kinds of memorabilia from all over the Department for the museum. We learned that the old Highland Park Police Station had been sold, but fell out of escrow. The building was built in '25 and opened as a police station in '26. With the help of officers Richard Ledesma and Karen Klobuchar, we campaigned to get the building for the museum. Councilman Richard Alatorre was instrumental in helping us secure the building on a thirty-year lease for a dollar a year.

Highland Park police station, now the Los Angeles Police Museum

One day I called Chief Gates' office and said, "I have Joseph Wambaugh's badge number. Would it be possible for the Department to locate the badge and donate it to the museum?"

Chief Gates said, "Sure."

Within a few days, I received a call that the badge had been reissued to another policeman, Robert Risen, the brother of Ken Risen who I had worked with at Hollenbeck. I contacted Robert and told him that he was wearing Joseph Wambaugh's original badge and asked him if he would be willing to give it up. He did, and the badge is currently at the museum.

After I retired, I dedicated the next eleven years to the Los Angeles Police Museum. It became what I envisioned, a place for everyone to see the history of the Los Angeles Police Department. Today I'm no longer involved with the museum, but I volunteer at the American Legion Police Post and on the World War II ship, the S.S. Lane Victory, anchored in San Pedro. You should come down for a visit.

Elmer "Bruno" Pellegrino

Birthplace: Weed, California
Career: 1965–1991
Rank at Retirement: Detective III
Divisions: Harbor, Southwest, Training, Hollywood, Special Investigation
    Section, Internal Affairs, Robbery-Homicide, Officer-Involved Shooting
    Team

B runo was my nickname on the Department. When I started, I worked with Rudy De Leon and Caraway Weems in Harbor Division. Rudy said, "You're not an Elmer. I'm going to start calling you Bruno," and it stuck for the rest of my time on the job.

How did I get to the Police Department? I met my future wife while we were both students at college. Her father, Karl Lee, was a captain on LAPD in charge of Harbor Division, and he encouraged me to apply.

At the oral interview, when they asked me why I wanted to be a policeman, I told them so I could help people. I didn't pass. They told me maybe I should be a sociologist.

Fortunately, I passed my oral interview on my second attempt and entered the Academy in August 1965. The first day of our class was also the first full day of the Watts riots. I remember driving up the Harbor Freeway through the Watts area with two of my classmates. There were buildings on fire on both sides of the freeway. We arrived at the Academy, and we were told that the riots had started. Half of the Academy staff went to the riots, and the other half stayed at the Academy. After a week, the staffs switched. The class before us went to the riots, but not us.

Elmer Pellegrino, Academy graduation, 1965

There was discussion of using us, but it was decided that we weren't ready for that type of involvement. I'll never forget my mom calling me and asking me what kind of job I took because they could see on the television the city was burning down. My parents were immigrants from Italy and lived up in Northern California.

While I was in the Academy, my girlfriend and I got engaged. Her father was now the rank of inspector, but nobody knew that I was engaged to his daughter. At least I thought nobody knew. In the last month of the Academy, Bob Smitson, our physical training and self-defense instructor, called me into his office. He and some other instructors started asking me who I knew on the Department. At first, I played dumb. Then they gave me the "now don't lie to me" routine. They asked me if I knew Karl Lee, and I had to fess up. I said, "Yes, sir. I'm engaged to his daughter."

"Do you think you're going to get special privileges?"

"No, sir."

Bob Smitson, front center left, Academy Staff: "He's never told me how he knew."

They gave me a little extra running and a little more of this and that, just to see how I would handle it. Smitson and I are very good friends to this day, and we always laugh about that. He's never told me how he knew.

After the Academy, I went to Harbor Division, and it was probably the best thing that happened to me. I walked a footbeat on Beacon Street in San Pedro with Caraway Weems. Caraway was a World War II veteran. We were mid-watch, so we would go out and answer radio calls until ten-thirty or eleven o'clock at night, and then we parked our car and walked the beat along Beacon Street until the bars closed.

If you go to Beacon Street now, it's completely different. At that time, there were sleazy bars on both sides of the street. The longshoremen from the shipping yards would go to the bars, and there were fights every night.

On my third night, I was walking with Caraway, and we went into this bar. He pointed to a guy sitting at the bar with his back to us and told me to see who he was. Unbeknownst to me this was my "trial under fire." In those days, you could do that. The guy at the bar was a fighter, and he didn't like to be touched. As I walked over to him, the other people in the bar moved away from me. I approached the guy, touched him on the shoulder, and said, "Sir." That's all I said.

The next thing I knew I was flying backward. He hit me, knocked me backward, and the fight was on. We were rolling around on the floor, and as we were rolling, I saw a few more policemen standing with Caraway. I finally got the guy subdued. Caraway came over, and we handcuffed him. The other policemen said they'd take it from there. I'm sure they walked him outside, said, "Hey, thanks," dusted him off, and sent him on his way. They now knew I was not afraid to mix it up and I could handle myself. Beacon Street was a tough beat, and the policemen needed to know they could trust you during a fight.

Then the training started. Caraway taught me about police work and how to talk to people. When he showed me how to write reports, he used to tell me, "Never lie, just write exactly what happened, because ninety-nine percent of the time we're right in what we do. If you fall in that one percent, then actions have consequences, and you alone have to deal with the consequences." If I was a good policeman on the job, his training was what made me one.

Beacon Street

Caraway Weems, second from left: "If I was a good policeman on the job, his training was what made me one."

When my probation ended, I stayed in Harbor Division and worked the Wilmington area. One day I was working a one-man car, and I saw a hole in the fence of a lumberyard and a gangbanger-type inside. I stopped and climbed through the opening in the fence. I grabbed the guy, then two others came at me, and the fight was on. One of them tried to grab my gun.

We did not have handheld radios in those days. If you got away from your car, your umbilical cord was only as long as you could take the mic with you. Luckily, there was a convent next to the lumberyard, and one of the nuns saw me fighting with the guys and called the police. Guess who was the first policeman to come help me? My father-in-law, Karl Lee. He and his driver were in the area and heard the radio call. When they arrived, I had one guy down, and they helped me get the other two into custody. All three were booked for burglary.

On another day, I was working by myself, and it was near end of day watch. It was wintertime so it got darker earlier. I was on my way to the station, passing an old hotel that had been converted into apartments, when I heard yelling and saw a woman backpedaling out onto the balcony of a second-story apartment. A guy holding a gun followed her onto the balcony.

I stopped, grabbed my shotgun, and stepped out of the car. I yelled at him to stop and to drop the gun, but he didn't respond to my direction. As the woman reached the end of the balcony and was unable to backpedal anymore, I made a decision to shoot. My light shined on the gun, and I realized it was a water pistol. I pulled the shotgun up, but it went off, and the round hit an archway above them. The guy dropped the water pistol and screamed for me not to kill him. They were just playing. Thank God, I didn't hit him.

I must have stood there for twenty minutes waiting for the sergeant to arrive. As I waited, I had thoughts of losing my job or, worse yet, going to jail. A sergeant came and asked me why my finger was on the trigger. I told him the image in my mind was that he had a gun, and I was going to shoot him. As I pulled up the shotgun, I didn't get my finger off the trigger quick enough.

I ended up with an admonishment for having an accidental discharge. It was called an accidental discharge, although I was intentionally going to pull the trigger. I still tell that story when I teach tactics training today. There was an officer-involved shooting once where an officer actually shot someone holding a water pistol, believing it was a gun. It caused some controversy, and I know I could have been in the same predicament as that officer.

After a six-month stint in the Army reserves, I came back and was transferred to University Division. I worked uniform patrol for a month or two, and then I went to the Special Operations Squad. Bob Smitson was our supervisor. Captain Charlie Reece asked Smitson to put together the SOS unit for crime suppression. Bob was given the latitude to pick the guys he wanted, and I was one of them. Eddie Brown was my partner.

One night Eddie was off, and I was working with Terry Speer. We were in plain clothes, but in a black-and-white police car. It was really foggy and hard to see anything, but we saw a stolen car and went in pursuit. Terry was driving, and he was a good driver. At one point, I thought we had lost him, and Terry was still driving as if we were right behind him.

I asked him, "Where you going?"

"I'm still chasing him."

We made our way up into the Baldwin Hills area above the fog level where it was clear, and there he was. How Terry found him, the Lord only knows. We stopped the suspect and took him into custody.

In 1967, President Lyndon Johnson attended a fundraiser at the Century City Plaza Hotel. It was the height of the Vietnam War, and an estimated ten thousand anti-war demonstrators were there. I was on the front line. We were spit at and called various names, even by three nuns. I was born to an Italian Catholic family, and upon seeing these nuns, it rather changed my whole view of life.

Pretty soon, a sergeant was walking along behind us. I don't know who he was, but he told us to take off our ties. We took them off and put them in our pocket. You could tell the crowd was watching and wondering what was going to happen as we did this. Then we got word to push the demonstrators back. That was the first time I was involved in that type of situation. My brother at the time was in Vietnam, and I was thinking of him while I was pushing this crowd.

I was a member of the SWAT unit from 1966 to 1971. It wasn't called SWAT when I first became part of the unit, which was comprised of sixty officers from across the Department, four of whom were from University Division. Our biggest mission was the service of search warrants at the Black Panthers' headquarters on Central at Forty-First Street in December 1969. Jerry Woempner and I had the responsibility of capturing the lookout on the roof of the two story building and putting tear gas through the skylight if need be.

We snuck up onto the roof at the rear of the building and took down the lookout while he was concentrating on the front of the building. He didn't hear us coming. We handcuffed him and placed him away from the skylight. We heard Dave McGill announce, "Police," and when we heard shooting at the front of the building, we broke the glass on the skylight and started pouring in tear gas.

The Panthers inside started shooting at us through the roof, trying to keep us back. Jerry and I fired at them through the skylight and then would retreat as the bullets came through the roof. At one point, Pat McKinley came up on the roof with a charge given to him by the Fire Department. Pat set the charge and it blew a hole in the roof.

That scared the people inside the building, and they pretty much gave up. Jerry and I were on the roof for about eight hours. It was a huge shootout, and we were prepared, but I don't think anyone thought it would take that long. huge shootout, and we were prepared, but I don't think anyone thought it would take that long.

Reality set in as we debriefed at the Georgia Street Station. As we were talking, I was thinking, *That was scary. We all could have been hurt.* You don't think about it at the time because you're focused on doing your job.

When I returned to the Academy later to change my clothes, I saw that the pants leg of my uniform had been torn from either a round fired through the roof or shrapnel. When it had happened, I didn't realize it because the adrenaline was pumping and I was doing whatever I thought I needed to do for the situation. Neither Jerry nor I were injured, but some guys were shot as they entered the building. I think one Panther was shot. We were awarded the Medal of Valor.

Black Panther building rooftop

Elmer Pellegrino awarded Medal of Valor by Chief Ed Davis, Jerry Woempner, right, 1972

SWAT never fired a shot before the shootout at Forty-First and Central. We were involved in some hostage rescues, barricaded suspects, and similar incidents, but never fired a shot. I think that was why SWAT was established. If SWAT had been in a bunch of shootouts, there wouldn't be a SWAT team in Los Angeles. It was incredible that you could go that long dealing with those types of situations and never have to fire a shot.

I'm not a big funeral guy, but when Gary Murakami was killed, I went to his funeral. Gary was only out of the Academy a few days when he and his partner answered a radio call of a nude man knocking on doors at an apartment building on Sixtieth Street. As they approached the building, Gary's partner saw a man pointing a shotgun at them from inside his residence. The partner hollered to Gary just as the man fired hitting Gary. When we got there, Gary had just been pulled to safety, but later died at the hospital. This old-time policeman had a sniper rifle, drew a bead on the suspect standing inside his apartment, and shot him. Gary had a little son who shook our hands at the funeral. It was very sad.

When Bob Smitson transferred to the Academy, he asked me and Terry Speer to go with him as physical training instructors. I worked training for about a year and a half. In those days, they broke the classes into squads, and I had seven or eight recruits to evaluate. I had a recruit once who was just a zero. He was smart enough book-wise, but physically he was terrible, and he never tried to get any better. We tried all the techniques to try to help him, but eventually we fired him.

Almost twenty years later, I was working the Officer-Involved Shooting Team at Robbery-Homicide Division. There was an off-duty LAPD officer involved in a shooting in an outside city. We rolled, and officers from that city's police department were at the scene. We were doing our investigation, and a lieutenant from the outside city walked over to me.

I said, "Can I help you?"

"You don't remember me, do you?"

"No, I don't."

"You are the biggest asshole I've ever known. You got me fired from the Academy when I was in training."

"Well, that's too bad."

I went back to the crime scene. I told my boss Charlie Higbie, and we laughed. It had to be almost twenty years that this guy carried a grudge. We did put a lot of pressure on him, so maybe it was a lasting thing, but it must have helped him because he ended up being a lieutenant with another police department.

At the Academy, I was the guy designated to tell a recruit to bring his hat and books with him to Room Nine. These recruits were going to be fired. Unlike in the past, we waited until a break and privately told the recruit to report to Room Nine. Of course, when they heard Room Nine, they knew. When I was a recruit in the Academy, a recruit was called out in front of his classmates and told to bring his hat and books. We sat four to a table in class, and at one point, I was the only one sitting at my table. Three chairs were empty—those guys were gone.

When I promoted to sergeant, I went to Hollywood, where I met
Tom Dixon, another sergeant. We would later be partners at SIS,
Special Investigation Section. When SIS had openings, they asked us
both to apply. We were accepted, and Danny Bowser was our lieutenant.
Tom and I replaced Eddie Watkins and Ted Breckenridge.

At SIS, we followed career criminals around waiting for them to
commit crimes, and sometimes we were given special assignments. One
time Johnny Carson, a celebrity television talk show host, was being
extorted. Carson was building a house up in the Hollywood Hills, and a
guy left a note telling Carson that he was going to kill him unless he
paid him money. He left a grenade to emphasize the threat. Lieutenant
Higbie from Robbery-Homicide Division was in charge of the
investigation and requested SIS surveil Carson until the extortionist
provided directions for a money drop.

We followed Carson and his wife for weeks. Finally, the suspect
communicated what he wanted and where to make the money drop.
Carson was in his own car with the money, and we were following him.
It was a forty-five minute drive, and Carson was wired so we could hear
him. He was nervous, so he was telling jokes. He had us laughing so
hard, we finally had to tell him to shut up.

Carson dropped the money, and while we were setting up, a car
came by. One guy got out of the car and took the money. The driver of
the car got spooked, and he took off. Tom and I got the driver, and
another unit got the guy with the money, although it was not really
money. The grenade was a training grenade painted to look authentic,
and the suspect was one of the construction guys working on Carson's
house.

We only had one shooting during my time at SIS, and the bullet
only grazed the suspect. We were following a robbery suspect who
stopped at a liquor store. One unit had eyes on the liquor store, while the
rest of us waited. Tom and I stopped on a street behind a gas service
station, while another unit pulled into the service station. Suddenly, a
guy, unrelated to our surveillance, ran out of the service station
minimart with a bag of money in one hand and a gun in the other. He
had just committed a robbery. He jumped into his car and took off.

The unit in the service station went in pursuit, and we followed.
During the pursuit, the suspect stuck his gun out of his car and fired a

round at the unit in front of us. The unit fired a round back and hit the suspect in his arm. He crashed his car, and they made the arrest. That was the only shooting in the two years I was there. I enjoyed my time at SIS, but after two years, I thought it was time to move on.

After a stint at Internal Affairs, I returned to the Academy. Part of my duties at the Academy was teaching use of force and patrol tactics to recruits, at in-service classes and at sergeant's school.

Lieutenant Higbie would teach officer-involved-shooting investigations to the recruits, and I would substitute for him when he couldn't be there. Lieutenant Higbie and I developed a wonderful relationship, and he eventually asked me if I would like to come to Robbery-Homicide Division to work the Officer-Involved Shooting Team. I told him that I had no homicide investigative experience and that the only detective experience I had was at SIS. He teamed me up with Otis Marlowe, whom we called "Odie." Odie was a legend of a homicide investigator and he taught me a lot.

I worked the Officer-Involved Shooting Team from 1983 to 1991. Sid Nuckles was the assistant officer-in-charge of the unit. Did you know Sid was responsible for the requirement that officers on the Department have a California driver's license? He was from New York, and in New York, it was either a bus or the subway. They asked Sid for his driver's license when he applied to the Department in 1956, and he said he didn't have one.

They asked him, "How are you going to be a policeman without a driver's license?"

"I don't have to drive. I'll just let my partner drive."

They told him to go get a driver's license. We used to tease him about that quite a bit.

I investigated the murders of nine policemen. Paul Verna was my first one. Verna was a motor officer working the Lakeview Terrace area of the San Fernando Valley. Although I did not know him, that was a tough one. Verna was watching an intersection for stop sign violations. A car drove through the stop sign, and Verna pulled the car over. The female driver got out of the car, and there was a conversation between Verna and her. She told him the two guys in the car were her husband, and her cousin. She did not have a driver's license, but gave Verna a check-cashing card with her name on it. Verna filled out a field interview card.

Unbeknownst to Verna, the car was stolen with cold plates on it, and the suspects had been involved in several robberies. Verna was shot when he returned to the car and had approached the driver's side. He fell backward, and according to witnesses, one of the men got out of the car and shot Verna several more times. The man then dropped his gun and took Verna's.

The suspects got in their car and left, but they returned to grab the murder weapon and the female's check-cashing card. Verna had a death grip on the field interview card when we got there. The card gave us information to follow up on, and we identified an address for one of the suspects. The suspects were later caught and convicted.

This was my first autopsy of an officer. You can look at a suspect, but this was an officer. There would be eight others before I retired.

Tina Kerbrat was the first female officer killed on duty, and I was involved in that investigation as well. She had been out of the Academy about four months. She and her training officer, Earl Valladeras, saw a couple guys drinking beer on the sidewalk. They pulled over and stopped near the two guys. One of the guys immediately approached the police car and shot Kerbrat as she was getting out of the car. She fell back on the seat and died. Her partner engaged the suspect and killed him.

I received a call one night that an officer and a suspect were down. Stacy Lim worked Hollenbeck Division, and she was off this particular evening, but stopped by the station. Unbeknownst to Stacy, she was followed when she left the station. Stacy drove a Ford Bronco with special rims, and when she got home, she parked in front of her residence. Then a car pulled up behind her with two guys and two gals intent on taking her car for the rims. She exited her car, saw them, and immediately realized something was up.

The driver got out of his car and Stacy armed herself as the driver showed a gun. He shot her right in the chest, and the round struck the bottom of her heart, then went through her liver and intestine, destroyed her spleen, and exited through her back. She returned fire and killed the suspect. The second male suspect and one of the females split in the car. The second female took off running down the street.

Stacy Lim

Stacy's roommate heard the shooting and came to her aid. The police arrived, and they captured the second female hiding in some bushes. Through her, we identified the other two suspects and captured them. About six weeks later, Stacy was out of the hospital and walking around. She had been given an hour to live, but she refused to die and survived three cardiac arrests. For her to return fire and drill the suspect after being seriously wounded was incredible. Eight months later Stacy returned to the job full duty. She is one tough gal.

It was about two o'clock in the afternoon when two uniform gang units and homicide detectives from Southeast Division arrived at the scene of a gang-related homicide. They discovered the shooters' identities and an address where they might be. The two gang units went to the house where they believed the shooters were, kicked in the door, and found two other gang members inside. They told the officers that the suspects had just left and that one of them had a girlfriend living in Seventy-Seventh Division. The officers and detectives went to the girlfriend's house.

When the officers pulled up, two girls came running out of the house screaming, which was later determined to be a diversion. The officers heard a crash and ran to the back of the house. The two suspects had jumped out of a second-story window. As the officers came around the corner of the house, the suspects fired at them. The officers returned fire, but both suspects fled into an alley. In the alley, the suspects fired again at the pursuing officers and then hid behind a dumpster. The officers shot one suspect, and he went down. The second suspect ran further down the alley and into a backyard. He kicked in the back door of a residence and ran inside. Two officers stayed at the back, and two others went to the front. This was now about ten o'clock at night.

The officers in the front could see an older gentleman inside the residence, and fearing for his life, kicked in the front door. When the older gentleman saw the officers, he dropped to the floor exposing the gunman, and the officers put him down.

We conducted the shooting investigation. The officers were criticized for their aggressive, self-initiated police work, but luckily, the Use of Force Board consisted of some pretty standup deputy chiefs who found the shooting within policy. The officers received a Police Star for their actions, but should have received a Medal of Valor.

In the nine years I was with the OIS team, Higbie took very few vacations. At a crime scene, he was the only lieutenant on the job that captains and deputy chiefs never interfered with during an investigation.

One time there had been an officer-involved shooting in Seventy-Seventh Division. The shooting was in a parking lot off an alley. It was during the daytime, and Higbie was in charge. Two commanders were standing and talking just outside the crime scene tape. As their conversation continued, it became louder and included laughter. I watched Charlie walk over to them. He went under the tape and put his arms around the shoulders of each commander. He walked them down the alley a ways and then left them. He didn't say anything to them. They left shortly thereafter.

I was at a luncheon a few days after this, and both commanders were there. I overheard their conversation, and both were obviously upset with what happened.

One said to the other, "Are you going to let him do that?"

"Are you going to say something?"

Neither commander did anything. It couldn't have happened to two nicer commanders. When you were at Higbie's crime scene, he wanted respect shown for the involved officers.

After twenty-six years, I felt like I had had enough. Higbie had left, Chief Gates was on the verge of retiring, and the style in which I was trained was going to the wayside. In the nine years I was on the OIS team, we never had an attorney or a representative sit in on an interview with an officer. Now the officers have attorneys or representatives. We used to work shooting investigations straight through until we were finished. Sometimes we would work thirty hours straight.

I understand that now an officer may get several days off prior to their interview for them to "come down" from a horrific shooting. Higbie used to say, "You can never create what an officer went through. You can't put the officer back in the same exact position. You can't put the suspect in the exact same position. You can't speculate. You have to rely on physical evidence and the officer's testimony, and his testimony is best at the time of the shooting." I'm still good with that.

Ronald "Ron" Treutlein

Birthplace: Hollywood, California
Career: 1965–1992
Rank at Retirement: Police Officer III + I
Divisions: Wilshire, West Los Angeles

After I got out of the Navy in '65, I was working the graveyard shift as a switchman with the railroad. One morning when I came home from work, my three roommates and their two friends were getting ready to go somewhere.

I asked, "Where're you going?"

"We're going down to join the Police Department."

"Good luck."

"No, we're all going."

They grabbed me and threw me in the car, and we all went together. I thought we were all going to make it after the testing process, but one guy was colorblind, and the police psychiatrist rejected the other four. He told them they were too keyed-up from serving in Vietnam and they needed time to calm down. It was their idea to be policemen, so I was shocked to be the only one who made it. My railroad job paid exactly what the Police Department was paying, about $600 a month, so I became a cop.

Wilshire Division was my first division after graduation. Wilshire was an active division, and we would race from call to call. One night my partner and I saw some guys stealing tires in a car lot near Hoover and Olympic, right on the border with Central Division. Rampart Division did not exist yet. I had only been out in the field for about a month and a half and was working with a guy that had about twelve years on.

Ron Treutlein, second row from top, far right: Academy class, 1965

The suspects had taken two tires off a car and were removing a third when we saw them. My partner drove into the lot, we jumped out of the car, and my partner said, "Freeze!" One guy put his hands up, and the other took off running. My partner said, "It looks like mine surrendered. Yours is running!"

I ran after the suspect and chased him for what seemed like a mile and a half. He crossed Hoover and then ran about three blocks north of Olympic into Central Division territory. He ran behind an apartment building, and I had lost him, but I could hear a dog barking. I followed the sound of the dog, and I found the suspect hiding behind a trash can. I made him lie flat on the ground and then handcuffed him.

As I was walking the suspect back, several police cars showed up. The officers were from Central Division, and I did not know any of them. They gave the guy a few punches and even hit me a few times. Then the officers left. Evidently, if you run from the police and get caught, you wind up with a few hurts to let you know that you shouldn't have run.

A few minutes later, my partner drove up and said, "You caught him!"

"Yeah, he finally gave up. He ran out of energy."

"I see you fell down too."

"That's not what happened."

"Don't worry about it. I'm writing the report."

During the Watts riots, some of us were sent to Seventy-Seventh Division. I was not familiar with the streets and did not know where I was most of the time. At one point, the National Guard was brought in. One night we were about six blocks south of a posted National Guard unit, and someone shot at the unit from a building. The guardsmen opened up with their machine guns. The bullets ricocheted off the building near us and over our heads. It scared the hell out of me, and we were six blocks away! We dropped to the deck, and when the bullets stopped, we got in our car and got out of there.

I remember being in an alley with three other policemen when a bunch of rioters looked like they were going to come right at us. One of the policemen fired a shotgun round over their heads. The rioters all turned around and took off.

Initially, I was not scared because I was new on the job and I was with senior guys. I was sure they would know what to do. However, a couple of times they seemed worried, and I realized this was all new to them. I began to wonder if we really had a handle on it. When the riots ended, I went back to Wilshire.

In October 1966, I was working morning watch with Keith Du Puis. One night at about four o'clock in the morning, we saw two guys in front of us on Pico Boulevard in a new beige Ford Thunderbird with Ohio license plates. At Crenshaw Boulevard, they entered the right-hand turn lane, but did not turn. When they did it a second time at another intersection, Keith said, "Why don't you run that car."

Communications advised us there was no want on the car. Because they were driving erratically, Keith decided we should stop them. We stopped them about a block from Wilshire Station. I was the passenger officer, but Keith wanted me to handle the stop.

Watts riots, 1965: "...I realized this was all new to them."

As I cut between the cars and approached the driver's side, the driver, Gilbert Durham, got out of the car and started to walk back to me. He was dressed in a coat and tie. He handed me the vehicle registration and an Ohio driver's license that looked like a credit card. I had never seen anything like it. Durham told me, "Well, that's what they use in Ohio. They can write tickets faster. They have a machine in their car, and they swipe the license in the machine, and then they finish writing the ticket."

I showed Keith the license, and he was not familiar with it either. Keith decided to get the passenger, Edgar Robinson, out of the vehicle. Keith walked up to the passenger side of the car and directed Robinson out. Robinson got out of the car and was also dressed in a coat and tie. Keith walked Robinson back toward our car. As they reached the rear of their car, Keith said to him, "Raise your hands. I want to check you for a weapon."

Robinson raised his hands and quickly stepped into the street between the two cars. He had what we called a "secret agent" holster, an upside-down holster in the small of his back. The gun hangs so a shooter can pull it down, bring it out, and fire in one motion. Robinson reached under his coat, pulled out a handgun, and pointed it at me. When he saw Keith had already started for his gun, Robinson turned away from me and shot Keith in the mouth.

Keith continued to bring his gun up and fired a shot at him as Robinson was turning back toward me. I fired a round, and Robinson fell back in the middle of the street as Keith fell back onto the sidewalk. I was not sure if Keith's round had hit him, but I thought mine did by the way Robinson fell backwards. I was later told a single bullet hit Robinson through his arm, went into his chest, and then out his side. Our rounds were not recovered.

Robinson was lying in the street on his back with the gun in his hand. Durham disappeared when the shooting had started, but then I saw him at the rear of our police car, crouched on one knee with his hands partially raised. I grabbed the mic and told Communications that shots were fired, my partner was down, and we needed an ambulance. Then I told Durham to crawl out from behind the car and get in front of me. I didn't know if he had a gun, and I didn't want to get shot from behind.

Durham had started crawling out when I looked over at Robinson in the street bringing his gun up. I screamed at him, "Drop the gun!" Robinson did not drop his gun, so I fired a round, which hit the pavement right next to his cheek. He dropped the gun. I now had one suspect lying in the street, and the other kneeling on the sidewalk close to where Keith lay. I thought Keith was dead because when his head hit the sidewalk, a huge spray of blood shot out from his mouth and ears.

A sergeant arrived first. I told him there was a suspect on the street that I thought had been shot and his gun was on the ground off to his side. I told him there was another suspect that had not been checked for weapons. The sergeant searched Durham and found a throwing dagger that was flat like a Malayan throwing dagger. An ambulance and what seemed like twenty police cars came. One sergeant took my gun from me, and another drove me back to the station.

Keith lived for about two weeks. Robinson's bullet hit the base of Keith's skull and then ricocheted down against his spinal cord. If Keith had lived, the doctors said he would have likely been paralyzed from the neck down. Keith was a fantastic officer, and I really liked working with him. I believe this was his fourth or fifth shooting.

Robinson and Durham were cousins and parole violators from Ohio. They had left Ohio and committed a robbery in Omaha, Nebraska, at a market. Robinson and Durham tied up the manager, but he got loose. As they were leaving, the manager was able to get a description of their car, but not the license plate number. They ditched that car in Lincoln, Nebraska, stole a brand new Oldsmobile Toronado, and drove to Texas. No one had seen a new Toronado, and everyone was asking them about it. Robinson and Durham became nervous, so they ran the Toronado into an irrigation ditch and then flew to San Francisco. There the cousins stole a brand new Ford Thunderbird, the car we stopped. They altered the vehicle registration and put license plates on the Thunderbird that they had from a Ford in Ohio.

Robinson and Durham were both charged with multiple felony crimes, including murder of a police officer. I testified at the grand jury hearing. As I finished my testimony and got up to leave, the entire grand jury stood up and applauded me. I was shocked because I had never expected that reaction. It was very different from what had happened at the station after Keith died. Some of the old-timers asked me how many bullets I had left. My gun was a six-shot revolver, and when I told them four, they said, "Your partner is dead. Why are they alive?" Anything I tried to say did not seem to make a difference. A couple of years later one of them apologized to me for his and the other officers' conduct.

Both Robinson and Durham were convicted of murder. Robinson's gas chamber sentence was reduced to life in prison, and he later died there. Durham received life in prison.

The next month my probation was over, and I was on the transfer to West Los Angeles Division. West L.A. was a slower division than Wilshire. However, one night my partner and I were driving down Santa Monica Boulevard when we saw a guy drive through a red light at Avenue of the Stars. We stopped him for the traffic violation, and I got his driver's license and registration. The car was registered to the Los Angeles City Employees Credit Union, and he had a Los Angeles City identification card indicating he was a director with Urban Affairs.

We got him out of the car, and I talked with him while my partner wrote the ticket. He asked if it was okay for him to put the vehicle registration back in the glove box. The guy was a city employee and he had been cooperative, so I said, "Sure, go ahead." I thought he was going to walk down the passenger side of the vehicle, but instead he went to the driver's side. I walked down the passenger side and around the front of his car. The driver's door was open, and I was standing on the other side of it. He never saw me and didn't know I was there.

West Los Angeles Division police station, circa 1936

Instead of going to the glove box, he reached under the front seat and grabbed a .357 revolver. He held it above the seat and looked back at my partner, and then he looked as if he was wondering where I went. I put my gun to his ear and said, "Drop it." He dropped the gun. I handcuffed him and walked him back to our car.

We had checked for warrants when we first stopped him, but the return from Communications was slow. When I brought him back to the police car, the return had come back, and we were advised he was wanted for murder in Washington, D.C. We took him into custody and booked the gun. I never found out what happened on the murder case.

I later went to West L.A. Vice. One night my partner and I were investigating a complaint about possible prostitution at a big hotel. Sergeant Don Barnett was with us. We found no evidence of prostitution activity at the hotel, and we left to check two other locations with complaints of illegal activity.

We split up. Don and I went to a restaurant having trouble with prostitution activity. My partner went to a bar in a steakhouse restaurant where someone had complained the bartender had cheated in a bar-sponsored gambling game. Don and I finished our check at the restaurant and went to the bar to assist my partner.

As we parked in the parking lot at the bar, Don asked Communications for a time check. We were told 2:11 a.m. That should have indicated to us what was about to transpire: two-eleven being the penal code section for robbery. Unbeknownst to us, my partner was in the restaurant's meat cooler locked up with other customers. Don and I walked in the front door and stood in the vestibule, which was about six feet long and about as wide as a hallway. We did not see anyone immediately, and Don hollered out, "Hey, anybody home in this bar?"

Right then a guy came around the corner with a gun in his hand, shoved it into my stomach, and said, "Hold it!" I grabbed his gun, a lightweight snub-nose five-shot revolver, and stepped off to the side. His finger was on the trigger as the gun caught on my sport coat and a round went off. The bullet hit my right hand and ricocheted into the ceiling. At the time, I didn't know my hand was injured.

As I shoved the gun backward toward him bending his forearm. the suspect started yelling for his buddy. A second suspect appeared. Don went after the second suspect, while I continued to bend the gun back toward the first suspect. His finger was still on the trigger, and a second round went off striking him in the chest, barely missing his heart. He dropped the gun and ran out through the front door into the parking lot. I heard Don shouting commands, so I figured he had the second suspect under control.

I followed the first suspect out into the parking lot, and he was down on the ground behind a parked car. I took a wide turn in the parking lot looking for a getaway car. I didn't see anyone in any of the cars and came up behind the suspect. He said, "You shot me! You shot me! I'm dying!" I asked him if he was shot in the head because as I touched him, there was blood all over his head. He said, "No, in the chest."

It was then I realized that the blood was coming from my hand. Before this moment, I had not felt it at all. There was no indication to me that I had been shot. Then I heard police sirens and figured someone inside the bar must have called the police.

The two suspects had come into the bar and took wallets from six patrons, the bartender, and my partner, all at gunpoint. My partner did not have his gun on him, which was not an uncommon practice at the time. They took money from the cash register and then locked everyone up in the meat cooler.

When Don and I entered the bar, the bigger suspect was raping the pianist, a girl about twenty-four years of age. When he heard us, he grabbed some money and tried to pull up his pants while he ran to the back door. Don chased him, and as the suspect reached to pull the back door open, his pants fell down. The guy fell to the floor, but still had a gun in his hand. Don took him into custody.

Both suspects were on parole for robbery, and both were convicted of rape, robbery, and attempted murder. They each got life in prison, although the suspect who shot himself later died from the gunshot wound. I was awarded the Medal of Valor for my actions.

For several years, I was a member of the Department's dive team. I had been a diver in the Navy, and I always enjoyed scuba diving. Arleigh McCree was also on the dive team, and his regular job was on the bomb squad. For some of our training, Arleigh devised explosive-looking devices and placed them on the bottom of boats or ships. When we located the device, we drew a picture of it and then took it to him. He rigged the device so if you messed with it, a little light would flash indicating the device had exploded.

We were usually called out to find guns or evidence of a crime under investigation. One search was for license plates in a water canal in Venice Division. A thief had been arrested, and he told the investigators about a group stealing motorcycles. The group would switch the license plate from a wrecked motorcycle onto a stolen motorcycle. The thief said the suspects would then throw the license plates from the stolen motorcycles into a particular canal.

We made the dive and recovered several plates. Even though the canal was only about ten feet deep, we had to use our scuba gear because the water visibility was terrible and required a longer dive. We also found some stolen motorcycle frames along with the license plates.

Another time we were tasked with searching for a jewelry box that had been thrown off a pier. The jewelry box was taken during a big heist, and the suspect told the detectives where he threw it. We were able to locate it. We also found a gun thrown off a pier in a similar situation.

Ron Treutlein awarded Medal of Valor by Chief Ed Davis, 1971

Ron Treutlein, front row, center: Medal of Valor recipients, 1971

There was a system for finding small stuff. We had a large, square, plastic pipe frame with multiple ropes spaced apart equally across the frame. Each diver followed a rope to stay in a line as we swept our hands back and forth across the bottom. The frame was about ten feet long, and once you reached the end of it, you flipped it over and continued on the search, guided by the ropes. We would slowly sift through the silt and the mud feeling for objects. Occasionally we would come across something and think, *What is this?* We would find chains, cables, automobile fenders, just about anything.

A couple times, we worked with the lifeguards looking for people that had drowned in the Venice Beach area. The lifeguard boat towed a bar that we held onto at a lower depth. We never found any bodies. Sharks? No, we never had a problem with any sharks.

I dove for lobster one night right after a short rainstorm. I was outside the breakwater, and water visibility was good. I was using a snorkel, and at one point, I tasted something terribly bitter. The next day, all of a sudden I had terrible chest pains and thought I might be having a heart attack. My wife took me to the hospital, they checked me over, and my heart was fine.

The doctor said, "You don't happen to do diving by any chance?"

"Yes, I do."

"When was the last time you went diving?"

"The night before."

The doctor surmised I might have swallowed some poisonous solvents used for boat cleaning to kill sea life such as barnacles. Later when I started spitting up half-dollar-size clots of blood, the doctor was totally convinced that was what happened. He told me the solvent burnt the outside lining of my lungs causing an infection and bleeding. The doctor had me keep my arms upright for two days and I could not take anything for the severe pain. After the two days passed, I was getting better, but that put an end to my diving with the dive team.

One time a shooting went down right in front of me and my partner. We heard it, but we did not see it. We were driving in a police car just south of Santa Monica Boulevard on Federal Avenue. All of a sudden, the cars in front of us stopped, and we heard a couple shots. We saw a guy carrying an Uzi submachine gun take off running from the middle of the street in front of the stopped cars into an apartment complex.

We pulled over and ran after the suspect. We did not see him when we reached the alley to the rear of the complex. Then we heard another shot. We went in the direction of the sound of the shot and found a big guy, about six feet four, who had been shot in the chest. We set up a perimeter and requested an ambulance. Because we did not know where the shooter was, we did not want the ambulance to come directly to our location. A sergeant drove down the alley in a police car, we loaded the wounded gentleman into it, and the sergeant took him to the awaiting ambulance.

We were sure the shooter was still contained within our perimeter. Turned out the shooter lived in the complex. He had reached his apartment and called his parents in China. His parents contacted their attorney who was here in Los Angeles. The attorney contacted the shooter and then notified the Police Department that the shooter wanted to surrender, which he did.

The shooter's apartment building manager had warned him several times about loud music coming from his apartment and about his friend and him running naked around the apartment building. That day the manager warned him again about the loud music, and the shooter just lost it. He chased the apartment manager down to the street and shot her, where she fell in front of a car. That was the initial shots we heard. Then he shot the big guy who was the manager of an apartment complex across the alley from the shooter's apartment building. Ultimately, that manager died as well. The suspect surrendered, and he was taken into custody.

Dennis Capitain and I were partners for about seven years. When we got off work in the mornings, we would go surfing if we did not have court. Dennis was a good guy to work with, very easy-going, just a great partner.

One night about three o'clock in the morning, Dennis said, "Let's get some coffee. I need a cup."

There was a coffee shop he liked called Arlene's on Santa Monica Boulevard at Bundy Drive. We were headed that way when I saw a car come up behind us fast and then slow down right away when he saw us. I said, "We've got a stolen."

"I need my coffee."

Ron Treutlein

"Dennis, let me run the plates, and if it's not stolen, we'll get your coffee."

I ran the plate, and the car came back stolen.

He said, "I don't get my coffee?"

"I'll buy you one at the station."

We arrested and booked all four suspects, and Dennis got his coffee.

I retired because the 1992 riots put me on edge. The riots were in response to the not-guilty verdicts of four LAPD officers accused of excessive force against Rodney King. During the riots, I had a headache that would not go away. I went to the doctor, and he said I had high blood pressure caused by stress. I thought, *If I didn't have the job anymore, then I wouldn't have the stress anymore.* That was an easy decision to make, and I retired after twenty-seven years on the job.

Clifford "Cliff" Wong

Birthplace: Honolulu, Hawaii
Career: 1966–1992
Rank at Retirement: Sergeant II + III
Divisions: Wilshire, Metropolitan, Rampart, Hollenbeck, Recruitment,
Northeast, Jail, Air Support

A friend and I were scuba diving instructors, but we both wanted to be police officers. Just before the '65 Watts riots, he became a police officer with the Vernon Police Department. When the riots started, he called me and said, "Cliff, I need you to go to my house, pick up my clean uniform, and bring it to me at the Vernon Police Station."

I went to his house, got the uniform, and drove right through the rioters to get to the city of Vernon. This was about eleven o'clock at night. I made it to the Vernon Police Station, gave him his uniform, and drove back the same way, right to the Los Angeles Police Department Central Police Station. I entered the lobby and approached the front desk officer. I said, "I want to be a police officer right now."

"Well, I'm sorry, sir. It's going to take longer than that to be a police officer."

I applied and was hired in January 1966. My first day at the Academy, I parked my car and walked through the parking lot to the stairs of the main building. I had my blue suit on, and as I approached the stairs, someone at the top of the stairs yelled, "Get up here! Run!" I looked up, and it was Bob Koga, whom I would very quickly find out was an instructor at the Academy.

I looked at him and said, "Me?"

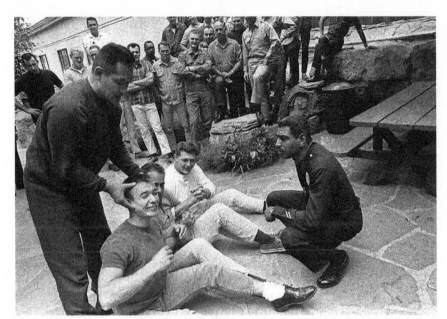

Self-defense instructor Bob Koga, front left: Police Academy training, 1966

Yes, you! Get up here!"

I scrambled to the top of the stairs, and he said, "What are you doing here?" I answered, and then he asked me a couple more questions. From then on, for my entire time in the Academy, he was on me as if he was going to break me. He just wore me out. At first, I had a bad feeling for the guy, but I really grew to love him. He made me do the things that needed to be done for me to become a good police officer. Later, after I left the Academy, we became good friends and worked out regularly together for physical fitness and self-defense. I respected him very much.

At the time of our graduation, it was believed that I was the first Chinese officer on the Department. Later, someone offered that his father was Chinese and had been on the Department during the 1920s. I don't know if that was ever proven.

My first assignment was Wilshire Division. One day my partner and I pulled a guy over for a traffic violation. The driver was very irate with me. At one point I said, "No speaky English. Driver's license, please." He never said a word after that. He gave me his driver's license, I wrote him a ticket, and we left.

Cliff Wong, Wilshire Division police station open house, 1967

When we returned to the station, the watch commander, Sergeant Marty Schwartz, said to me, "Wong, get in here right now!" He proceeded to tell me that our traffic violator called and told him what I had said to him. He asked me if that was true, and I told him it was. He said, "Don't you know you're on probation?" After he chewed me out a little bit more, he said, "Don't let that happen again."

In May '66, a controversial shooting occurred in Seventy-Seventh Division. Leonard Deadwyler was speeding while driving his pregnant wife to the hospital because they thought she was in labor. Officers pursued him, and he eventually stopped. One of the officers leaned in through the car window to turn off the ignition. Deadwyler was still in the driver's seat. According to some witnesses, the officer had his gun in his hand, the car lurched forward, and a round went off, killing

Deadwyler. When the case went to court, there had already been major protests for weeks.

Officers from other divisions, including myself, were sent to Seventy-Seventh to fill in for Seventy-Seventh officers who had gone to the court hearing. I worked with Armando Hernando. During our shift, we received a call of a robbery in progress at a fast food restaurant on Central Avenue at 103rd Street. As we approached the location, we saw the suspect running out of the restaurant. He stopped and turned toward us with gun in hand. We were now on foot. Hernando yelled, "He's got a gun." We fired along with another pair of officers who also had just arrived. The suspect went down. He survived, we took him into custody, and he was later convicted of robbery.

The community was upset over that shooting, claiming it was racial. When they learned that Armando was Filipino, I was Chinese, and one of the other officers who had shot at the suspect was black, the protestors didn't have much to go on. The only reason the suspect was there at the time we arrived was because he had robbed the restaurant, left, then returned to demand more money. It was deemed a good shooting.

In July '66, Chief Parker died. I stood guard along with some other officers over Chief Parker's casket for a few days, a couple of hours each day. Tom Reddin was eventually selected as Chief Parker's replacement.

One day before I came on the job, my roommate's girlfriend was visiting, and they were swimming in the apartment building pool. I was inside the apartment and heard his girlfriend yelling from outside. I rushed out and saw my roommate at the bottom of the pool. He had lost consciousness. I jumped in, pulled him out, and gave him mouth-to-mouth artificial resuscitation. After a few minutes, he started coughing up water. The Fire Department arrived and took him to the hospital. He survived.

The National Red Cross gave me an award for saving the life of my roommate, and Chief Reddin presented me with the award. At the time, there were no regulations for wearing a national award pin on our uniform. Chief Reddin authorized wearing such a pin because of the award I was given.

*Cliff Wong receives
lifesaving award from
Red Cross Chairman
Cecil Zaun and Chief
Tom Reddin, 1967*

When President Lyndon Johnson was holding a fundraiser at the Century City Plaza Hotel, I was assigned there along with hundreds of other policemen. We were there because thousands of protestors were demonstrating against the Vietnam War. I was with a squad of officers positioned directly in front of the hotel. As I looked at the crowd, I wondered how we were going to block ten thousand people from charging the hotel. There was a line of policemen in front of us, about fifty to a hundred yards, positioned between the protestors and us. When the order was given, the line of policemen pushed the protestors back. I remember seeing one policeman hit with a cinder block on his chest. Eventually, the protestors were dispersed.

After a couple years in patrol, I worked Wilshire Vice with Dale Ostrum and John Grogan. We were responsible for enforcement against bookmaking. One bookmaker that had been around a long time was Claude Ferguson. Claude was a horse bookmaker. When he took wagers over the phone or in person, he recorded the wagers on a Formica board, easily erasable if necessary, like in a police raid. After he had recorded four or five wagers, he would call them in to his back office for permanent recording in books. The back office was at another location.

The hard part was raiding the cash room where Claude was and capturing the recorded wagers, evidence of the illegal activity, before they were erased or destroyed, and the money. If you were successful, you had the bookmaker and the evidence all in the same place. Most bookmakers had some type of warning system to alert them that the police were coming. Claude had a guy working as a lookout. Claude's cash room was on the second floor of a building on Adams Boulevard and the lookout was positioned at the top of the stairs leading to Claude's room.

It was my second day in the unit, and they were going to try to take down Claude. Dale and John put together a package containing empty Chinese food boxes. They handed me the package and said, "What you're going to do is run up this flight of stairs. At the top of the stairs will be Claude's lookout. You carry this and ask, 'Who ordered the Chinese food?'" The purpose was to distract the lookout long enough for Dale and John to enter the building.

We went to the location, and I started up the stairway. I don't remember what the lookout said, but he looked at me and then yelled to Claude. John and Dale ran up the stairway and right over me. But it was too late, Claude had erased the wagers. Dale told Claude, "Okay, we don't have enough evidence on you, so we're not going to take you to jail today, but we are going to close you down."

Once we sent everybody away, Dale said to Claude, "Now you're going to take the rest of the day, and you're going to teach Officer Wong everything you know about bookmaking." We stayed there for over four hours, and Claude told me everything about how bookmakers operate. It was a priceless education. I arrested him a few times after that. He always understood what it was about. He was a big guy and one of the nicest.

Once I left Vice, I had about four years on. Sergeant Jim Beal, who I had worked for in patrol, encouraged me to apply to Metropolitan Division. He even called them on my behalf and told them they ought to consider taking me, and they did.

In Metro, we did mostly stakeouts or crime suppression across the city. We were also loaned on occasion to different detective divisions as investigative support. One of my loans was to Rampart Division Detectives, and I did that for about seven months.

Frank Beeson, who was in charge of Rampart Detectives, called me into his office one day and said, "I have good news and good news for you, but you have to pick the better of the good news." He liked my work in Detectives and offered me an investigative position on a permanent basis. He said, "But before you answer me, let me tell you this. I just got a call from Jim Beal at Air Support Division, and he wants you up there on Monday. What would you like to do?"

I chose Air Support and was very fortunate to get it. I had a strong interest in flying and a commercial pilot's license, but I had less than five years on the job. Even with the license, they normally wouldn't consider you with less than five years. Luckily, Jim Beal really liked the way I worked. Jim played a big part in my career.

While at Wilshire, I brought in an arrestee to the station one day. As we got out of the car, my arrestee laughed at something I said to him. I noticed that Jim and another sergeant were standing in the parking lot watching me. At one point, the other sergeant took out his wallet, removed a five-dollar bill and handed it to Jim. Later on, I found out that when I had put myself out to the station, the sergeants heard it over the radio in the watch commander's office. Jim bet the other sergeant that my arrestee would be laughing by the time he got to the station. So they came out and stood in the archway, and that was when I saw the other sergeant hand Jim money.

Jim has since passed away. When he died, there was a large obituary with his picture in the *Los Angeles Times*. He promoted the air support program from one helicopter, maybe two, and built it up to become the biggest civilian air force in the world.

At Air Support, I flew the Bell 47 helicopter. I loved that helicopter. It was a glass bubble type. We did have one Jet Ranger helicopter, different design, a little faster. But you could not fly the Jet Ranger unless you had five hundred hours of flight time and you were an instructor pilot.

One night my observer, Phil Calamia, and I landed at the Post Office Annex in downtown to take a break. We were sitting in the helicopter talking when we saw this airplane flying really low over Los Angeles County Jail. The pilot did about three dives down to within a couple hundred feet over the jail. We lifted off to investigate, and we followed him toward Pasadena. In Pasadena, he did a couple more low dives over a building. We advised the control tower at Burbank Airport of our observations, and they advised us they saw him on their radar. Burbank is the regional airport for the area that includes Pasadena.

Jim Beal, standing, far left, Cliff Wong, next to Beal, Phil Calamia, bottom row, third from left.

We followed him to a smaller airport just north of Burbank, where he landed. However, as soon as he was on the ground, he turned around to take off again. I landed the helicopter on the runway to block him from taking off, but he accelerated down the runway toward us. I pulled up, and he went right under us. We continued to follow him, and he landed at Burbank Airport. We also landed, blocking him from taking off again. Phil jumped out of the helicopter and took this guy into custody. He apparently dropped rocks from his airplane onto the jail and the Pasadena Library. We could see the striations on the side of his plane where the rocks had hit it. I can't remember why he did what he did, but we booked him.

Phil and I were working one night flying over Southwest Division, when we heard a very loud bang coming from the area of the helicopter engine. The helicopter was still flying okay, but we landed in the parking lot of the Los Angeles Coliseum and visually checked for what may have caused the noise. We didn't find anything, so we lifted off and headed to the heliport in Glendale.

A few minutes later, we're over downtown, and all of a sudden, there was another bang, much louder than the first time. The helicopter started swaying side to side and became erratic. I told Phil to put out a help call. We had to make an emergency landing.

I did some emergency procedures to keep control of the helicopter, and we landed hard, but safely, on San Pedro Street at about Eighth Street. That was my first emergency landing. When it was happening, it was happening so fast. All I wanted to do was set it on the ground before something worst happened.

The mechanics came to the scene, put the helicopter on a truck, and took it back to the heliport. We found out the first noise were the fan belts breaking, and the second noise was when the fan had actually broken. When a fan breaks, the helicopter is still flyable, but only for a brief period of time. The fan belts turn the fan, which cools the engine. Without the fan, the engine will overheat very fast, as it takes a huge amount of air to cool the engine. Fortunately, we were able to land safely.

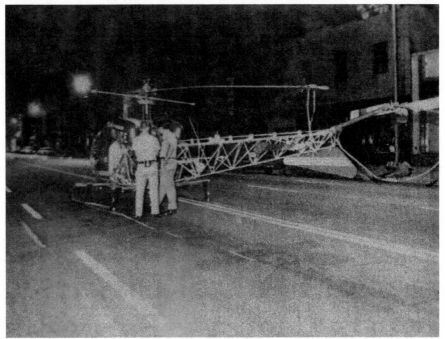

"All I wanted to do was set it on the ground before something worse happened."

The next day Jim Beal said, "I want you to get in a car and drive down there where you landed." I went to the location and looked, and even to this day, I don't know how we missed all those wires and power lines crisscrossing the streets. I made an emergency landing only one other time, at Slauson and Crenshaw. Same thing, broken fan belts.

One night at 108th Street and Western Avenue, my observer and I were circling overhead following an armed suspect running between houses, trying to get away from officers on the ground. We were directing the ground units, trying to get them closer to the suspect. All of a sudden, he stopped, turned his gun toward us, and started shooting at us. We saw the muzzle flashes, and we could actually hear the shots. We were about three hundred feet above him and we had headsets on, and we could still hear the shots! He fired three rounds at us, but we did not feel any of the rounds hit us. After he was in custody, we landed right away to check the helicopter. We didn't find any damage from the gunshots.

The tall buildings of downtown presented some unique challenges for flying. Of course, there were not nearly as many tall buildings back when I was flying as there are now. I remember my first time flying through the high-rises. It was one of those times, you're on patrol and nothing was going on, so you say, *Let's try this.* You aim for a center point between two buildings, hold your breath, and go. That's basically it. Once you went through the buildings like that, you had no reason to go again.

The toughest challenge was taking off from the top of a tall building, although it was a simple technique. As you lift off, you always look at the horizon—you don't look down. As you lift off, you're about ten feet above the building. Once you clear it and if you're looking down, you're immediately looking down about five hundred feet and your perception goes crazy. You try not to do that.

One day Joe Sela, a pilot, said to me, "I want you to come along as my observer on an operation with Narcotics." This was a chance for me to learn surveillance and watch Joe operate the Jet Ranger!

The surveillance continued into Riverside County, and the narcotics officers became involved in a shooting. We landed at Thermal Airport, and Joe was needed out at the location. Someone picked him up, and I remained with the helicopter at the airport. Jim Beal, now a captain, called flight service at the airport. Someone came and told me, "Your boss wants to talk to you."

Jim said, "Where's Joe?"

I told him, and Jim said, "I want you to get in that helicopter, bring it back to Parker Center, pick up the Officer-Involved Shooting Team, and take them back out there."

"Captain, I've never flown the Jet Ranger before."

"Does it have a checklist in it?"

"Yes, sir."

"Well, read it!"

He hung up, and my heart was really pumping. I went out to the helicopter and started it up, following Joe's steps, which I had watched. Next challenge, there were only fifteen gallons of fuel left, not enough to get to Parker Center. Thermal Airport did not have the right fuel, so I flew to Palm Springs Airport. You're not supposed to put in fuel when the engines were running, but since I was pressed for time, I told the attendant to hot fuel it. At first, he said he couldn't do it, but when I explained my situation, he filled it up for me. I made it to Parker Center, landed on the roof, and picked up the three detectives. Just as I took off, I received a call from base, and they said to return to base, that Bob Gray was going to fly the helicopter. I was relieved to be relieved.

When I went back to work the next morning, I saw my name on the scheduling board: "Cliff Wong and Joe Clarence, Jet Ranger Training." That was my start with the Jet Ranger. That specific Jet Ranger is now at the Los Angeles Police Museum.

Eventually, I decided to promote to sergeant, but I felt I needed more field time, so I left Air Support, went to Hollenbeck Division, worked on loan to Recruitment for a little bit, and then transferred to Northeast Division.

I was working by myself one day when I got an unknown trouble radio call on Cliff Drive, up in the hills of Mount Washington. When I arrived, some people directed my attention to the side of the roadway where the nude body of a teenage girl was lying. She had obviously been murdered. Her name was Lauren Wagner, and she was the tenth victim of the Hillside Strangler. I called the detectives and protected the crime scene until they got there. To this day, I can still vividly see her lying there.

Cliff Wong with Jet Ranger helicopter

Commander George Morrison was into scuba diving and knew that I was a diver. He called me one day and asked me to meet him at the Rowena Reservoir. Story goes, about three o'clock in the morning of the day he called me, witnesses had heard someone run past their house and then they heard a splash, like the sound of someone throwing something into the reservoir. That was the night that Leno and Rosemary La Bianca were killed by the Manson family on Waverly Drive, a block from the reservoir. The investigators wanted divers to check the area of the reservoir where the splash was heard.

The Department did not have a dive team at the time, hence George's involvement and his call to me. I met George and the investigators with all my gear. One investigator took a rock and threw it as far as he could. He said, "That's how far out you will search." You know, real scientific. We spent about four hours diving, just going through the mud, kind of feeling our way through, looking for a possible weapon. We found a lot of junk, but nothing to further the investigation. The water was about fifteen to twenty feet deep.

When I promoted to sergeant I was sent to Jail Division. I was only there for four months when I heard there was a sergeant position opening at Air Support. I applied, and within a few weeks, I was back flying helicopters, but now as a sergeant. I spent the rest of my career there.

When I was in college, there was an opportunity to take a test to determine where your interests were to help you with career choices. I took the test, which was very involved and lasted several days. My two highest identified interests were aviation and law enforcement. At that time, I didn't think I had the aptitude or the capabilities of a pilot, but I had always wanted to be a policeman. Thinking about it now, I am very fortunate to have achieved both.

Dalton "Dick" Postma

Birthplace: Lewiston, Idaho
Career: 1967–1989
Rank at Retirement: Police Officer III
Divisions: North Hollywood, Jail, Wilshire, Van Nuys, Valley Field Unit,
    Narcotics

In 1967, my wife and I were living in the San Fernando Valley. One day we're shopping at a nearby market, and I see this young guy running around in the store with no shirt on. As we're checking out, he went through a closed checkout stand, but now he's wearing a brand new shirt! He doesn't buy anything, just goes right on through.

I told the clerk, "That guy just stole that shirt. He shoplifted."

"Well, yeah."

"Aren't you going to do anything?"

"There's not a lot we can do."

"Well, that's a shame."

When we got home, I called the LAPD Van Nuys station and related what happened. I was talking to this policeman for probably five minutes when he said, "Have you ever thought about becoming a policeman?"

"No. I have a good job, and it pays well."

As the conversation continued, he said, "Well, we're giving a test this weekend down at City Hall. Why don't you come down and take it?"

I thought about it, and I did. I passed the written test, and on the same day, we were sent over to the Academy for the physical agility test. I did everything, including the obstacle course. Then we had to do pull-ups, perfect pull-ups. Unfortunately, I kicked my feet on the last pull-up, and that didn't count. I had to do it again. From then on, I couldn't do the last one. I went home bummed out.

The next Monday I went to a local gym and started working out until I could do more pull-ups. I went back in a few weeks, did my required number of pull-ups, and then just a few months later I was in the Academy.

I was twenty-seven years old when I went in, which was a little older than the other guys. I had been out of school for a long time, so the academic part was tough for me. And I really wasn't in shape like some of the younger guys. On the runs, I was never last, but I was never first either.

In our first month at the Academy, Roger Warren, out of the Academy for a couple of weeks, was shot and killed in Van Nuys Division. Warren and his training officer saw someone hiding behind a barbeque pit in a park directly across from a market. As they were getting out of the car, a shot from a rifle was fired, and Warren was hit with a bullet. He died at the hospital. The suspect, the one hiding in the park, who was sixteen years of age, was killed by Warren's partner.

Dick Postma

Dick Postma, top row, third from right: Academy class, 1967

The next day our class was sent to the park to look for evidence, like shell casings. We formed lines and went slowly across the grounds, but I don't recall us finding anything. Turned out, I did some glasswork for the suspect's father. The father was in construction, and before I came on the job, I was a glazer installing glass mirrors. I believe the suspect's friend had been arrested for shoplifting at the market, and the suspect was going to take some type of revenge against the storeowner when Warren and his training officer stopped at the park. It stuck in my mind how dangerous the job could be. We all realized that this was what we were in for, that this kind of thing was going to be part of our life once we left the Academy.

At the time I was in the Academy, protests against the Vietnam War were occurring across the country. On the day, President Lyndon Johnson came to Los Angeles for a fundraiser at the Century City Plaza Hotel; our class was sent to help other officers with crowd control for a large anti-war demonstration in front of the hotel. There were thousands of protestors.

Half of our class, including my squad, was sent down to the front line to face the protestors. I was looking at this crowd, and they're yelling and screaming right in my face. They had placards, and they're yelling obscenities at the government and at us.

Century City protest, 1967: "...we were told to push them back and we did."

At one point, we were told to push these guys back, and we did. We were physically fighting with these protestors using our batons. It was something I had never experienced before. Eventually, it subsided, and we went home. That was my first encounter with an unruly mob, and it was truly an unruly mob.

Upon graduation, I went to North Hollywood Division. After a few months, I was assigned to morning watch. My first night on morning watch, I worked a one-man car. Vance Procter, my Academy classmate, was also working a one-man car. We're out there following each other around all night, backing each other up, but, believe me; neither Vance nor I knew what we were doing.

One night I was working a one-man unit, and I saw this old, beat-up car going down Victory Boulevard near Lankershim Boulevard. There were four people in the car, and the trunk was open enough that I could see a bunch of new tires in the back almost falling out. I thought, *These guys just ripped off a tire store!* I called for backup, and Communications told me there was no one available. That got my attention real quick.

Fortunately, I was following them in the direction of the North Hollywood Station, which at the time was on Tiara near Oxnard Street. The North Hollywood watch commander heard my backup request over the radio and emptied the station of officers to come help me. The suspects stopped, and I waited to get them out of the car until the other officers arrived. The suspects cooperated, and we took them into custody with no problem. They had just broken into a tire store and stolen the tires. There were moments as I waited for the other officers when I thought, *What did I get myself into?*

Once I was off probation, I was assigned the Van Nuys Jail for three months. That was just the way it was. You were assigned to the jail, Parking and Intersection Control, or Communications. As soon as my three months were just about up, I went to see the guy in charge of transfers. I wanted to go somewhere that was more exciting. They sent me to Wilshire Division.

Wilshire Station was on Pico Boulevard. It was an old station set down in a hole. There was a hill behind the station with houses looking down at you on one side and the old Sears and Roebuck on the other side. I always thought you'd have a tough time trying to defend the place. The roll call room was down in the basement, and there were certain places you didn't want to sit because the sewer pipes were exposed above you and the pipes leaked. I had a lot of fun at Wilshire, and some pain too.

It was about three o'clock in the morning, and my probationer and I received a radio call to assist the Fire Department with traffic control on Exposition near Crenshaw Boulevard. They were fighting a big building fire, and about a dozen engine companies were there. We set a flare pattern to block the street and divert traffic. At one point, we were replenishing the flares when I heard a pursuit up in the north end of Wilshire Division on our car radio. The driver's door was wide open, and I leaned in to turn up the radio so we could hear the pursuit. This was long before handheld radios. The next thing I remember was hearing glass breaking, and then I woke up in the street in a lot of pain.

Wilshire Division police station, circa 1936

A drunk driver had driven through the flare pattern. My partner, who was laying out additional flares, jumped up onto the curb to avoid being hit. The drunk driver swerved and skirted the police car on the driver's side and just wiped me right off! It took the driver's door of the police car and bent it back into the front fender. His car carried me about twenty feet or so before he stopped. The impact ripped my gun off, and it was up the street another ten feet. I had a three-inch Smith and Wesson revolver in my back pocket, and it was even further up the street.

My partner put out a help call. I remember waking up momentarily, seeing a lot of people around, and being placed on a board by the paramedics. I then lapsed into unconsciousness. In the ambulance, I was in and out of consciousness and still didn't know what happened. Later the next day, I was told what happened to me.

The drunk was probably doing about thirty miles per hour. The glass I heard breaking was the headlight on his car hitting me on my right side at the hip. My pelvis was fractured in multiple places. My right knee had torn cartilage and ligaments. I had internal bleeding, a concussion, and numerous abrasions and lacerations to my face, my head, and my body. The drunk driver was arrested for attempted murder, but it was later reduced to drunk driving.

*Lieutenants Bob Smitson, left, and Patrick McKinley: "Lieutenant
Smitson took care of everything."*

Our watch lieutenant, Bob Smitson, was working that night. He
drove all the way out to my house, explained to my wife that I had been
seriously injured, and drove her to the hospital. According to my wife,
he wanted to leave some police officers to babysit our kids, but we had a
daughter that was fifteen years old and she took care of that. He not only
drove my wife to the hospital, but also drove her back home. Lieutenant
Smitson took care of everything. He was a wonderful man, and it was
great to work for him.

I was in the hospital for a month, did five months of rehabilitation,
and was back to work six months from the day of the incident. When I
came back, I had a limp, so I couldn't run very well. During my
recovery, the doctors told me I should consider taking a medical
pension. I told them, "No way!" I only had three years on the job, and I
wasn't going to do that. I worked out pretty hard and made it back. Just
recently, I was presented with a new award for the Department, the
Purple Heart, for what happened to me that night.

When I first got to Wilshire, my two partners were Mike Kriha and
Ed McDonald, both good partners. The three of us were assigned to a
car on morning watch. One night I was off, and Mike and Ed were

working together. Around midnight they received a radio call of a suspicious package at an accounting business on Western Avenue. The accountant and his wife had been out to dinner, returned to the business, and found the package on the doorstep. They took it inside, didn't open it, and called the police

Mike and Ed decided to open it. They unwrapped the paper, and it was a metal box with a key taped to it. They used the key, and as they opened the box, it exploded. One lost his left hand, and one lost his right hand. The explosion shattered windows in the office and started a fire. By the grace of God, Mike and Ed survived and continued their careers. Mike had a hook for a hand, and Ed had a prosthetic hand. The package was left by a laundromat businessman who had a dispute with the accountant. He was arrested and booked for attempted murder.

I was working with Lloyd Parry and around two o'clock in the morning we saw a car going southbound on Crenshaw Boulevard. We followed this car and saw a whole lot of activity in the back seat. The driver wasn't staying in the lanes properly. I turned on the red lights and tried to stop them, but immediately they took off, and we went in pursuit. We chased them almost all the way down to Jefferson Boulevard.

The suspects pulled into a parking lot behind a fast food place. We were right on their tail, and as soon as they stopped, the doors flew open. The driver took off running back across the street. I went in a limping foot pursuit of him, but I kept up with him. He ran across Crenshaw and into the parking lot of a big market. He reached an eight-foot cinder block wall, but he couldn't get over the wall.

That's when I got him. I handcuffed him and brought him back to the car, and Lloyd caught the passenger. There was a girl in the back seat screaming. She and her boyfriend were hitchhiking up in Hollywood. These guys picked them up, robbed the boyfriend, kicked him out of the car, and kidnapped her. She was being raped in the back seat when we first saw them on Crenshaw. Both suspects were convicted of rape and robbery.

On morning watch one night, my partner and I saw a car in a residential area pull away from the curb with its lights out. We followed him and ran the license number. It came back stolen. I turned the red lights on, and he took off. We went in pursuit and finally caught him pretty close to Wilshire station.

As we were taking him into custody, he said, "What did you arrest me for?"

"For a stolen car."

"How did you know it was stolen?"

"We ran it on the radio, and it came back stolen."

"It couldn't have been. I just stole it."

He stole a stolen car! It had already been stolen and dumped.

Do you remember Judge Noel Cannon? She was a Superior Court judge downtown. She was a little bit different from most judges, somewhat eccentric. Her judge's chambers were painted pink. I remember being in her court a couple times, and she would have a little dog on her lap during the proceedings. One time a mother was on the stand testifying about her son, and she was crying. During the mother's testimony, Judge Cannon said, "Wait a minute! I want a five-minute recess." She got up and left the courtroom because her dog had to go outside.

I was in roll call one night, and I got a note with instructions to go to Judge Cannon's chambers the next morning. In Judge Cannon's chambers, I sat down, and she handed me an envelope. In the envelope were thirty-two one-dollar bills.

I said, "Judge, what's this for?"

"Remember that kid you testified against here six months ago?"

We had arrested this kid, and during the booking process, he started to fight. He bit me in the chest and ripped my uniform shirt. He left teeth marks in my chest and a v-shaped hole in my shirt. The kid was convicted, and part of his sentencing was he had to pay for my shirt. For several months, he would come back to court with one-dollar bills and give them to Judge Cannon. When the amount reached thirty-two dollars, the cost of a uniform shirt back then, she sent me the note to collect the money. I had already bought a shirt and forgotten all about it.

We received an ambulance shooting call at a bar one night down on Washington Boulevard. I was working with a probationer. The victim had been shot in the mouth. As we're trying to find out what happened, the victim spat out the bullet. He refused to tell us who shot him. He even refused to be treated by the paramedics. I finally got him to tell me who he was drinking with, and it turned out to be his girlfriend.

We went to her apartment, made the arrest, and recovered the gun. He and his girlfriend had a fight in the bar, she shot him right in the mouth, and the bullet took out one of his teeth, but stayed inside his mouth. The gun was a little .25 automatic, and the bullet was a real light load. He was one tough guy. He literally spat the bullet out.

After several years at Wilshire, I transferred to Van Nuys Division to be closer to home. I was not at Van Nuys very long when I was told by a sergeant to report to Rampart Division the next day. I went to Rampart, and there were nine other policemen there along with a sergeant and Commander Frank Beeson. Commander Beeson was in charge of the Vice units for the Department. Beeson talked about a massage parlor problem in the city, primarily prostitution occurring in the parlors. He said, "We're going to crack down on it. We're going to form a task force, and you guys are the task force."

I was thinking, *Wait a minute! I'm not very good at vice.* I had only worked vice on loan in Wilshire a few times. I tried working some prostitutes, and they pretty much laughed at me because I couldn't talk the talk. Yet there I was being told I'm part of this task force. I explained to them that I was not the kind of guy that could go in and talk to these people. They made me the administrative officer.

The rest of the guys worked the parlors and made out affidavits on the violations they saw, and I would present it all to the city attorney for civil abatements. We closed down twelve massage parlors in four months. At the end of the task force, I went back to Van Nuys and later became part of a new unit, the Valley Field Investigative Unit.

The Valley Field Investigative Unit generally worked morning watch hours, handled all death investigations, and was first investigative responders to officer-involved-shooting scenes in the Valley divisions. I did that for a couple of years, and after a while, I got tired of dealing with death reports. The one thing that really bothered me was when I had to deal with the death of an infant, generally from SIDS. I had a lot of them, and each one was sad.

One day I received a death investigation at a motel on Sepulveda Boulevard in Van Nuys. At the motel, a guy was lying in bed naked, deader than a doornail. The Fire Department was there and said it looked like a heart attack. I asked, "How did you get the call?" They told me the caller was a girl who told them there was a dead man in this motel room. I completed the death report, and the coroner came and took the body

I went to the dead guy's house and informed his wife that he had passed away. I explained that her husband apparently had a heart attack. Fortunately, she had her neighbor visiting with her. She was crying and wailing, and her neighbor was consoling her. At one point, she stopped crying and asked, "Where's his car?" I told her it was parked behind a motel. I had not yet told her where he had died. Then I could see things starting to click in her brain. She says next, "That rotten son of a bitch."

He was a college professor and supposed to be teaching a class. Instead, he was having an affair in the motel with some girl, and he had a heart attack right in the middle of it. I'm sure if he had not died and his wife had found out about it, she would have killed him anyways. She was really mad.

At one time, I held the largest cocaine seizure in the Valley. It was all of eleven ounces, if you can believe that. I was working the Narcotics Unit out of Van Nuys Division, when I arrested a woman from Central America. She was a real devious woman involved in cocaine. I did a search warrant on her house and recovered the eleven ounces of cocaine in a fake shaving foam can in the refrigerator.

Right away, she started giving me information on other suspects, and people she sold to including some people that worked at the Board of Education. This was way out of my league, so I turned her over to Administrative Narcotics. Unfortunately, she was a manipulative woman, and the officer she was providing information to was later caught with cocaine. Whatever happened to her, I don't know. It was just sad to see an officer taken down that way.

The Narcotics Unit was a good detail, but management decided that all of the divisional narcotic units would become part of Administrative Narcotics. The sergeants and detectives went to Narcotics, and I went back to patrol with the other policemen.

At roll call one night, the sergeant mentioned that the captain was concerned about traffic citation production. Apparently, it was not where the captain wanted it to be, especially on morning watch. The sergeant said that during the night he was going to meet us individually in the field and look at our ticket books. Well, I was a training officer, and I always had my probationer write the tickets as part of their training. When I heard the sergeant say this, I thought, *I don't think I have a ticket book.* After roll call, I went to my locker, and fortunately, I found a ticket book underneath all my stuff.

During the watch, we met with the sergeant in the field. He was thumbing through my ticket book and saw that my last ticket was dated October fifteenth, and it was now the twenty-first. He handed my ticket book back to me and said, "Ticket last week, that's pretty good." I thought, *What is he talking about?* After he left, I looked at the ticket book, and the ticket he looked at was from October fifteenth three years prior! But the sergeant was happy, and I even received a commendation at one point for writing tickets on morning watch.

I don't remember what year we were issued the Monadnock batons, but I didn't like it. I remember one incident when we received a radio call about a family dispute. My partner was a probationary female officer. This guy and girl both in their mid-twenties were living together. When we got there, we saw a coffee table out on the lawn. It was a heavy piece of furniture that he had just picked up and thrown through the living room window. I was trying to get them separated and the girl to go outside so she could talk to my partner.

The guy did not want that to happen, and he came after me. We started fighting, and I took my Monadnock baton and hit him in his knees to take his feet out from under him. Well, he was stout, and that didn't work. He charged me again, and as I swung the baton, he ducked, and I hit him on the side of his head. He went down like a ton of bricks. I had one handcuff on him, and he came to and started fighting again. I was holding onto one handcuff because I didn't want to let loose of it.

My partner was by the girl, and the girl was now screaming. I had to tell my partner to radio for help. She stood there unsure of what to do. I was a little disappointed with my partner's actions at the time, and we talked about it later. Eventually, we got the guy handcuffed and in custody. It took twenty-three stitches to sew up his head.

Dick Postma

I realized then that the Monadnock baton was a lethal tool. This occurred right after the use-of-force policy had changed and the chokehold was only available to you as a last resort. I remember telling the sergeants after this incident that this was not working. I said the Monadnock was going to get somebody put in jail. The Rodney King incident later proved my point. King was hit multiple times with the baton, and the officers were criminally charged with excessive force.

Previously, if you had to, you used the chokehold, rendered the suspect unconscious momentarily, handcuffed him, and it was all over. Now you pull out your Monadnock, and you start beating on him. To me that was the wrong way to go. I don't know what the policy is nowadays.

For the rest of my time on the job, I stayed in patrol. I had a great time. I would recommend the job to anybody, and I have. I don't think there is another job like it. I could not do a job where you go in every day and do the same thing, day in and day out. I did a short stint in detectives and worked the Investigative Field Unit and Narcotics, and that broke up my twenty-two years on the job. But detectives came in every day and had another pile of paperwork waiting for them. I couldn't handle that. I was glad I didn't make detective for that reason. The action was on the street, and that was good for me.

Joseph "Joe" Getherall

Birthplace: Boston, Massachusetts
Career: 1968–1996
Rank at Retirement: Detective III
Divisions: Hollenbeck, Public Disorder Intelligence, Special Investigation
  Section, Robbery-Homicide

I took my medical exam to come on the Department at Central Receiving Hospital. As the doctor placed my chest X-ray on the view box, a nurse came into the room and requested his presence outside. When he left, I looked at the X-ray, and it clearly showed thirty pieces of shrapnel in my back from wounds suffered three separate times in Vietnam. I took the X-ray down and put it back in the envelope.

The doctor came back in and said, "Now, where were we?"

"We just looked at my X-ray, and everything looked fine."

He gave me the okay, and off I went!

Growing up in South Boston, I lived in the Old Harbor Housing Projects, was a member of a gang, and dropped out of high school. The Marine Corps saved me and after I got out, I had two options as an Italian: I could be a hit man or a cop. I took the option with the most likely longer life span. I was married, and my wife was pregnant. The starting pay for the Department was $677 a month. That was a lot of money in 1968.

On day one at the Academy, I was the first one there, and I waited on the steps leading up to our classroom. As I was sitting there, a guy was walking toward me, and as he got closer, I thought I recognized him. He must have had the same thought because as he approached his eyes got bigger and bigger. It was Len Page! Len and I were both wounded in Vietnam and hospitalized at the same hospital.

Joe Getherall

In the hospital, when a guy was not in his bed in the morning, everyone figured he died during the night. I was medevacked to Japan during the night for special medical treatment and was gone when Len woke up. He had thought I died.

He walked up to me and said, "Are you Getherall?" You could tell he was shocked. We both would be part of the color guard at our graduation.

Hollenbeck was my first division. One of my training officers was Ernie Valenzuela. He was a great training officer and a firm believer that you should treat people like they treat you. I drove us into the Aliso Village projects one night, and as we were about to leave the projects, we saw a gang member put up his hand and give us the finger. He flipped us off!

Joe Getherall, front row, center, Len Page, on left, next to Getherall: Academy class, 1968

Ernie said, "Stop the car."

I stopped the car, and Ernie jumped out. He went over to this gang member and had a very forceful talk with him. Ernie told him, "Every time you see an officer I want you to stand at attention and salute, you understand?"

"Yes, sir."

A few days later, we drove in there again. The gang member saw us, popped to attention, and saluted.

Morning watch took some getting used to, and I was working a second job at the time. One night I was working with Tom Russi, and we got a report call. I was in the front seat completing the report, and the victim was in the back seat. The next thing I remembered was that we were on our way back to the station. Tom told me I fell asleep. When I looked at the report, there was a pencil line drawn downward across the report that I had made as I was falling asleep.

Tom and I saw smoke one night and found a house on fire. We ran inside and were able to get two people out of the house. They told us there was a baby inside. As we were about to run back in, the house exploded. After the Fire Department put out the fire, we went back in and saw the baby still lying in the crib. The baby was the same age as my daughter. That image had a lasting effect on me.

I was working with an officer one night who I had not worked with before and who had about two years on me. There was a call of a robbery in progress at a market on Whittier Boulevard. Once there, I went to a corner window of the market, looked in, and saw it was going down. There were two guys with guns. My partner was behind our police car, which was parked a ways back. I was by myself. Right then both suspects came out of the market. I confronted them, and they stopped, gave up, and put their guns down.

After we finished booking the suspects, I said to my partner, "You left me alone."

"I was by the radio."

We did not have handheld radios in those days. I never worked with him again.

Later I became a training officer. I was working with a probationer, and we were in pursuit of a stolen vehicle suspect. The pursuit took us on the Pasadena Freeway. My partner was driving too fast. I told him to slow down several times. He did not slow down, and just as we reached a sharp curve, I could tell he was losing control of the car. I reached over and turned the engine off.

As we coasted to the shoulder, the other police cars passed us and continued the pursuit. The probationer understood why I did what I did and was receptive to my criticism. But he ended up not making it. It was not because of me; he just didn't have it. He had no street sense and no confidence, so he didn't make it.

While I was at Hollenbeck, I became a member of SWAT for a little over a year. This was before SWAT became a part of Metropolitan Division. We worked SWAT in addition to our regular assignments. I missed the biggest operation though: the raid on the Black Panther Party headquarters at Forty-First Street and Central. I was on vacation out of the country, and when I got back and found out about it, I was very upset. You know, when you are a young officer, you want to be involved in stuff like that. Unfortunately, I never was involved in anything in SWAT. The Black Panther raid would have been my only operation.

Joe Getherall   *Hollenbeck Division police station*

Someone told me about an opening working undercover in Public Disorder and Intelligence Division. I applied and was accepted. I worked undercover in a very radical and violent Maoist group. My job was to monitor and let my handlers know about the group's activities. They were involved in demonstrations, and I was even arrested at one. I was jailed at Parker Center, and fortunately, I was not recognized by anyone. The way I looked, not even my brother would have recognized me. I looked like a real radical with a long beard. I ended up being released along with a few others.

I worked undercover for a little over a year. Was there a moment I thought I had been found out? Yes. Twice I was challenged, but both times I went right back in their face. They became more scared of me and thought I was more radical than they were.

When our first daughter was a couple of years old, my wife became pregnant again. I decided it was time to get out from being undercover. I was then assigned to PDID Detectives working with Larry De Losh. Larry was a great detective and taught me everything I know about how to be a detective.

At the time, everyone was looking for Patty Hearst. Patty Hearst, daughter of Randolph Hearst, a newspaper publisher, was abducted by the Symbionese Liberation Army, a radical left-wing group. Over time, she eventually supported their cause and participated in their illegal activities.

Joe Getherall, PDID

Our unit followed an alleged friend of Patty's to see if he would make contact with her. He was a member of the Weathermen, a revolutionary group that bombed government buildings. We followed him for several days, including down into Mexico past Ensenada to a place called La Bufadora, where a blowhole, a marine geyser, was a tourist attraction on the beach. It was a winding road down to the beach. A couple of our guys followed him down on foot to see if he made contact with anyone, while the rest of us stayed up off the road. We were there overnight.

During the night as we were sleeping in our cars, all of a sudden there was a blood-curdling scream from one of the female officers in the unit. It was a warm night, and she had left her window down and laid her head against the door. A burro came along and started licking her face. She woke up to the face of this burro and screamed. It was pretty hilarious.

Patty Hearst was not there. The guy never hooked up with her, and we dropped the surveillance a few days later.

Larry had classmates and other guys he had worked with who were all working SIS, Special Investigation Section. SIS did surveillance of criminals. There was an opening, and Larry encouraged me to apply. Unbeknownst to me, Larry made a call on my behalf to Danny Bowser, the lieutenant in charge of the unit. I did not think I had a shot because the guys in SIS all had fifteen to twenty years on the job and I only had eight. But I was taken into the unit, primarily based on my military background, my work on the Department, and Larry's recommendation.

A couple of days after I started at SIS, I was working my first case, a stick-up guy hitting markets. It was Jack Giroud's case from Robbery-Homicide Division, and I was in charge of the surveillance part of it. We were sitting on the suspect's house when a kid in an old yellow and black Opal backed up the driveway. The suspect came out of the house, followed by his wife, and loaded up in the car. The kid drove off with the suspect, as the wife yelled, "Have a good one, honey."

They drove to Sylmar where the suspect got out of the car and went into a liquor store. A few minutes later, he came running out and got into the Opal. We confirmed there was a robbery and went in pursuit. The older suspect started shooting at us. The suspects turned a corner and drove into a church parking lot. There was a field behind the church, and the suspects hit a wire fence and started spinning. My partner hit the brakes, and we stopped next to the suspects' car.

I was now facing the shooting suspect, passenger to passenger. I got out, my shotgun ready with a round chambered and aimed at the suspect as he was getting out of the car. He started to come down on me with his shotgun, and I let my first round and my second round go. One round hit him, and he went down. The other round hit his shotgun causing it to misfire. The guy also had a handgun. The suspect died, and the kid gave up. They were responsible for a number of robberies, and the kid went to jail.

We worked the Freeway Killer, William Bonin. Bonin and three other guys would pick up young boys, have sex with them, torture them, and then kill them primarily by strangulation. It was a Robbery-Homicide case, and once Bonin was identified, we followed him. One night Bonin was driving his van and exited the freeway at Santa Monica Boulevard in Hollywood. He drove past a young kid hitchhiking. He turned around, came back to the kid, and picked him up.

They pulled into a vacant lot at Normandie and Santa Monica, a little field behind what appeared to be a torn-down store. They stopped, and Bonin and the kid stayed inside and went to the back of the van. Jerry Brooks walked up to the van and started listening. All of a sudden, Jerry heard the kid moaning, and he signaled to us.

Luckily, the door was unlocked. Bonin was sodomizing the kid, and he had a knife ready to do him. He was going to kill him. We saved the kid's life. We took Bonin into custody. He was a twice-paroled sex-offender. He was convicted of fourteen murders and later executed.

These two brothers were big-time robbers. I mean really serious robbers. We followed the two brothers and a third suspect, and watched them stop near a flower business. Two of them walked into the flower store and robbed it. They came out, got in their car, and left.

Dennis Krueger was right behind the suspects as they turned onto a side street. The suspects stopped, and Dennis stopped behind them. As Dennis was getting out of his car, the suspects shot, blowing out the windshield of Dennis' car. We saw Dennis go down.

Thinking he was hit, I ran up to him, grabbed him by his collar, and pulled him back. Dennis suffered glass fragments in his eyes. I had my shotgun in hand and saw one of the suspects rise up in their car with his gun, and I let go of a round, hitting him. During the ensuing gun battle, one brother and the third suspect were killed. The second brother was severely wounded and later was convicted and sent to prison. The three were responsible for over sixty robberies. It was Ralph Waddy and Jimmy Grayson's case from Robbery-Homicide.

Two weeks later, we were working Mexican Mafia bank robbers. There were four males and a female driver in a Cadillac. We followed them to a bank where they parked in a big parking lot behind the bank. The four males got out of the car all dressed in black. The female stayed in the car.

The robbery went down, and they started to come out a side entrance of the bank. They immediately saw a black-and-white police car driving on the street in front of the bank and went back inside. The officer in the black and white was unaware of the bank robbery. A few minutes later, the suspects ran out the front entrance of the bank and split up. Two suspects were taken down by other guys in the unit.

The other two suspects ran into a beauty salon. Bob Harris and I were at the back door of the salon, and Mike Sirk was off to our side covering the door. Bob pulled the back door open, and one of the armed suspects was right there. The suspect appeared startled when he saw Mike and pointed his gun. *Boom!* The suspect went down wounded. As we entered the salon, employees and customers all pointed to a supply room, indicating to us the position of the other suspect. Upon seeing us, he raised his gun. Bob let a round off. It first hit the floor and then the suspect, killing him.

At federal court, the remaining four suspects pled guilty. Judge Manny Real went right down the line, saying to each one of them, "Twenty years, twenty years, twenty years, twenty years."

Robby Welborn, a detective working Robbery at University Division, was investigating a series of robberies and asked for our assistance. The robberies were of fast food places, donut shops and gas stations. I believe he had a snitch telling him who was committing the robberies, but we needed to corroborate it.

The first night, we followed the suspects to a gas station. There were four people in the car. They went in and robbed the gas station, and we saw it going down. They came out and drove down the street.

Curt Hagele tried to block them. They shot at Curt, and he fired back. They drove down to Santa Barbara Avenue, made a right turn, and then drove into a market parking lot. When we got there, one suspect sitting in the back seat pushed the seat forward and got out. He turned toward me and capped a round. I was about a hundred and fifty feet away.

I fired twice and he went down. It was a one-in-a-million shot. We took him and two other suspects into custody. The fourth suspect was dead. Curt's shotgun round hit the suspect and wounded the driver in the hand. They had committed twelve robberies.

In 1980, we lost Curt when he was shot during our surveillance of two robbery suspects. After robbing a bank, the main suspect fired at other detectives as he ran up a sidewalk that paralleled the parking structure he was trying to get to. I went into the bank to verify the robbery.

Curt was chasing the suspect, and the sidewalk elevated in a few steps. Curt could not be readily seen and was accidently shot in a crossfire just before the suspect was killed. I came out of the bank, ran to Curt, and he looked at me like he was asking what happened. I held him in my arms until the paramedics took him to the hospital where he died. I worked with Curt in SIS for four years. We called him Prince Valiant. He was one of the best street cops I had ever worked with.

Why did I leave SIS? Again, I did it for my family. I was coaching my kids in sports, and I needed steady hours. I went to Robbery-Homicide and worked the bank squad. My old partners, Larry De Losh from PDID and Dave Warren from SIS, were there.

The year I went to the bank squad, there were 863 bank robberies in the city. In the city! Eight hundred and sixty-three bank robberies! Incredible. That was why Los Angeles was known as the bank robbery capital of the world.

Joe Getherall and Larry De Losh

One group of robbers was known as the "West Hills Bandits." West Hills is part of the San Fernando Valley. Two families who lived in a house in West Hills had converted their basement into a shooting range. They had an unbelievable amount of weapons, over a hundred guns, including some automatic weapons. I think they robbed thirteen banks, including the robbery with the largest amount of money ever taken up to that point in Los Angeles, $430,000. These guys were good. Larry and I had the case. The FBI caught two of them after they committed a robbery and that ended the robberies.

Another case I had was a guy who robbed twenty banks. He never used a gun, only a note. He was caught, and when I was interviewing him, I could tell he was not a street-type guy. He had never been arrested, never had a traffic ticket, not even a parking ticket. Nothing. He was clean.

I wondered what was going on, why the robberies? He told me that one night he was with some people and got tipsy when they got him drinking. After he became drunk, they gave him cocaine. From then on, he was hooked on cocaine, and the money from the robberies supported his addiction. Over time he lost his house, his family, everything. He was crying by the end of my interview. The guy was a good guy. I went to court and got him probation and no jail time with the stipulations, that he makes restitution and he gets cleaned up. He did both, and he still calls me to this day and thanks me for saving his life.

My last day of work was on May 31, 1996. The guys in the office took me out to breakfast to celebrate. During our meal, all of a sudden everyone's pager went off. We did not have cell phones then. A bank in the west end of the San Fernando Valley was being robbed. We got there, and the suspects were gone. Two suspects took close to a million dollars. The two suspects, Larry Phillips and Emil Matasareanu, a year later committed the now-infamous North Hollywood bank shooting in February 1997. Both died during that robbery.

Tina, Joey, and Joe Getherall

Do I miss the job? Not even a little bit. That's because I still get together with retired partners once a week for breakfast. It's also hard for me to miss the job with my strong family connection to the Department. My daughter Tina served twenty-one years and retired as a detective. Her husband is a sergeant on the job. My son Joey is currently assigned to the K-9 Bomb Unit. My other daughter, Anna, did not come on the job, but she is married to a pilot at Air Support. Now that is a true LAPD family!

Kenneth "Ken" Welty

Birthplace: Riverside, California
Career: 1969–1998
Rank at Retirement: Lieutenant II
Divisions: University, Traffic Enforcement, South Traffic, Southwest,
    Internal Affairs, Hollywood, Wilshire, Planning and Research,
    Narcotics, Operations Central Bureau CRASH, Bunco-Forgery

It was in the tenth grade that I decided I wanted to be a cop. In college, I majored in police science. Three of my instructors were retired LAPD: Griff McKay, Bob Calhoun, and Maurice Thomas. I became good friends with Griff. His son Randy and I are still best of friends.

I applied to both LAPD and the Los Angeles Sheriff's Department. Although I wanted LAPD, the sheriffs called first, and I entered their Academy. While in the Sheriff's Academy, I was given a note to call LAPD. When I did, I was told I had a place in their next Academy class, so I switched. I didn't really want to work the jail for five years, and that was where you went when you graduated with the sheriffs.

The very first day at the Academy after roll was taken, we were told we had to move our cars. Everybody moved their cars, but two guys never came back. On the first day! That stayed with me. I couldn't believe it.

During our time at the Academy, our class attended the funerals of Robert Cote and Jerry Maddox, two policemen killed on duty. Cote's death was tragic and did not have to happen. He responded to a robbery in progress radio call at a department store in Hollywood.

Ken Welty

Cote entered the store, and at some point, he and the suspect confronted each other. The suspect shot Cote in the femoral artery. He was taken by ambulance to Central Receiving Hospital, the protocol at the time, even though he was literally within two blocks of several other hospitals. He bled to death. The policy changed because of Cote's death.

Several weeks later, Jerry Maddox was killed by a sixteen-year-old juvenile who ran from him. When Maddox caught up with him, the juvenile disarmed and shot Maddox with Maddox's own gun.

Two policemen, two funerals, all while I was in the Academy, and I still wanted to be a policeman. When you're young and stupid, you don't think anything is going to happen to you. Over the course of my career, fifty-eight LAPD officers died in the line of duty, and I knew a number of them.

On my ride-along, I went to Harbor Division. We made an arrest on Beacon Street, and I contracted hepatitis from an arrestee after a bloody fight. I wound up in the hospital in intensive care for several days. I lost two to three weeks of training, and I was placed in the class behind mine to make up for the missed weeks. I didn't want to graduate with that class because I didn't go through the Academy with them.

Ironically, the graduation ceremony for my original class was not held until after they had a month in the field, so both classes were part of the same graduation. However, I marched with my new class and was listed on their program. Looking back, believe me; I was happy enough just to graduate. When I graduated, I was sent to University Division. A few months later, the name of the division changed to Southwest Division.

Roger Ferguson and I were working together one day when Communications broadcasted that a citizen was reporting that an officer needed help on Florence Avenue near Western. A citizen had seen a guy who he thought was a plainclothes policeman shooting at another guy. Turned out it was a businessman who had been robbed at gunpoint. As the suspect fled, the businessman grabbed his own gun and started shooting. The armed suspect ran several blocks. We responded and saw the suspect run into a house on West Seventieth Street.

Motor officer Chuck Behrle got to the house just as we did. Chuck and I ran into the house after the suspect and caught him. Our tactics were awful. You wouldn't do that now, and we should not have then.

But you chase guys to put them in jail. The businessman later wrote a letter to Chief Ed Davis that was published in the Department's monthly magazine, *Los Angeles Police Beat*. He called us "damn fools" for rushing into the house, but also praised us for our bravery.

nitro pills. These didn't help him. In less than a minute his eyes rolled, he slumped down and passed out.

Since I am crippled with arthritis and only 5 feet and he a 6 footer, he was hard to handle. We were in front of a gasoline station and I started to scream for help. I was trying to hold him up, not knowing whether he was alive or dead. No one came as I screamed but just as I was trying everything I could, a car stopped and two gentlemen came to my rescue.

They started to call an ambulance, but my husband came out of it and said he wanted to go home which was right around the corner. They drove us home and just as they helped him walk to the lobby, he passed out again and they insisted on calling the City Ambulance and he was taken to the Hollywood Receiving. He got wonderful care from the drivers and the hospital but it was only then did I find out that these men were of the Internal Affairs Division of the L. A. Police. Their names are Sgt. Albert C. Miller on loan to IAD from Foothill Division and Sgt. Harold L. Justice, IAD.

If it weren't for them, again I say I believed my husband wouldn't be here today and I don't know how I could have handled it. So God bless you for having such wonderful men and God bless them for being there at the right time and all the kindness they gave him. They should receive a medal for a good deed.

From two very grateful people.

Mr. and Mrs. S. Axelrod

"Damn Fools"

Dear Chief Davis:

You have two damn fools working for you — **Motorcycle Officer Behrle,** 112271, and **Ken Welty,** 15159.

I was robbed recently at my office and the thug shot at me but missed, after he robbed me. I was in a police car cruising the area for the thug when a call came through that there was a suspect at 1725 W. 70th; the car I was in raced to the address, and just as we arrived this damn fool Behrle leaped off his bike and the other damn fool Welty jumped off of his and they both ran to the front door of the house and barged right in and caught the armed thug in the bedroom with his gun and my money.

Chief Davis, doesn't that brave and courageous fool Behrle know that he is supposed to write traffic citations and not bolt head-on into a house after a robbery suspect he knows is armed and had just shot at a hold-up victim?

And Welty, he doesn't have any more sense than Behrle because he was right at Behrle's side as they stormed into the house after the thug.

I sincerely praise these two men for their fearless bravery and their courageous conduct. I wouldn't be a policeman working out of Southwest Division for any amount of money — your requirements for courage are too high. I still get chills six weeks after the robbery when I think how those two officers stormed into that house without a moment of hesitation.

If I ever hear anyone call one of our Los Angeles police officers a "pig," I will be in jail myself for assault.

Sincerely,
Frank Z. Yates

"Non-Irritating"

Dear Sir:

I was called on in my hotel room at the Los Angeles Hilton by Officer Joe E. Chandler, No. 14817. The reason for this call was a burglary report I had made.

I am writing to inform you that I think Officer Chandler is one of the most courteous and finest police officers that I have ever talked to. Naturally, at the time he called I was upset because of the fact my credit cards and a considerable amount of money had been stolen. Officer Chandler was overly courteous, and to make a simple statement, was **non-irritating** to a man who was already irritated.

Since this burglary report was made, I have learned from several people that the Los Angeles Police Department is one of the most efficient in the United States. You can rest assured that I believe the reason for this is that you have men like Joe Chandler on your force.

Respectfully,
C. W. Ennis, Jr.

University Division police station

When you're out in the field, it's imperative you know where you are. I didn't know one night, and it could have been really bad. Barry Staggs and I were working together, and we came across this big party on Forty-Eighth Street. A couple of guys from the party were out in the middle of the street, so we stopped just to let them know to get out of the street.

One thing led to another, and they came at us. Several guys attacked Barry on his side of the car, and a couple guys came at me punching and hitting. I grabbed the mic as I was trying to hold them off and put out a help call, but I put out the wrong street. The street I gave was blocks from where we actually were. Fortunately, one of the units responding accidently found us. We didn't get hurt, and those guys went to jail.

Ernie Woods and I were working one night on morning watch when a Seventy-Seventh unit put out a shots fired help call on Manchester and Denver Avenue. Ernie and I jumped on the freeway, and when we got there, Milburn Bolton and Don Brown were handcuffing the second of two suspects. They had just shot it out with two Black Panthers. The first suspect was lying on the street with gun in hand and a bullet in his head. The suspects' car was on Denver facing northbound just south of Manchester. The officers' car was in a parking lot on the west side of Denver facing the suspects' car.

Bolton and Brown were following these guys on Manchester in a plain vehicle, but in uniform, when the suspects made the officers. The suspects made a U-turn and continued back on Manchester. At Denver, they made a left turn and then immediately made another U-turn back toward the officers. The officers backed up into a parking lot on the southwest corner and took cover away from their car, leaving their headlights on. The suspects, now driving back northbound, stopped, exited their car, and started shooting at the police car, apparently thinking the officers were still there. The officers returned fire, killing the driver and wounding the passenger. It was a hellacious shootout. Prior to their contact with Brown and Bolton, the suspects, using the same tactics, killed an officer in New Jersey and an officer in New York.

In April '70, I was just about to get off probation. I was getting dressed for work when an officer came into the locker room and said, Earl Riddick had been killed trying to arrest a bank robber. Earl was my training officer at the time. He was on a day off.

At roll call, we were all told what happened. Earl went to the Security Pacific Bank on Western Avenue to cash his paycheck. Unbeknownst to him, the bank was being robbed by Charles Henry Mack. On his way out of the bank, Mack shot and killed the security guard. When Earl tried to take him into custody, Mack shot Earl. As Mack was leaving the parking lot in a car he had stolen earlier in the day, Earl fired two rounds that hit the back window of the car Mack was driving. Earl died in the bank parking lot.

When Mack drove out onto Western Avenue, he nearly collided with motor officer Chuck Teague. Neither Teague nor his partner knew of the robbery, but they saw the bullet holes in the rear window of Mack's car and gave chase. Mack was ultimately killed by two detectives while taking cover behind a boat blocks away from the bank.

Earl was one of the calmest, low-profile guys I had ever worked with. One time Earl and I got a radio call of a burglary investigation in the Leimert Park area, an upscale part of the division. We walked in the front door, and this black female said, "I want that nigger out of my house." I looked around wondering who she was talking about. She was talking about Earl. It surprised me. Earl very calmly told her we were there to take her report. We took the report and talked about it afterwards. Earl said that was just the way it was.

I stood as part of the honor guard over Earl's casket at the viewing and served as a pallbearer along with Phil Calamia, P.J. Jones, and three other officers. There are a few things that I wish wouldn't have happened during my career, Earl's death being one of them.

One night Dave Dalton and I got a radio call where a pizza delivery guy was robbed at gunpoint. The suspects ordered a pizza over the telephone and gave an address where the pizza was to be delivered. The address was a vacant house, and the pizza delivery guy was met with a gun. As we were on our way to the call, a description of the suspects was broadcasted. We caught one of the suspects walking in the area, but not the other one.

In court as the victim was testifying, the prosecutor asked him, "Look around the court. Do you see the person that robbed you that night?"

The purpose of the question was to determine if the victim could identify the defendant as the person who committed the crime. The victim looked around the court and said, "Yeah. The guy in the back of the courtroom in the blue shirt!"

Everybody looked to the back of the court—the second suspect had come to court to see how his buddy was doing.

The judge said to him, "Don't go anywhere."

There were police all over the court, and he was quickly handcuffed and taken away. The victim also identified the defendant that we caught.

In roll call one night, the sergeants read off an application notice for anyone interested in applying for motors. I thought it would be a nice change, even though I had never ridden a motorcycle before. Three of us from Southwest went to motor school: Bruce Wallace, Bob McGratten, and me. Bruce and I were partners at the time, and we were roommates. We both passed motor school, and Bob decided it wasn't for him.

Ken Welty

After our break-in period of working with a seasoned motor officer, Bruce and I teamed up. One day we were riding eastbound on Santa Barbara Avenue just past Normandie when we heard gunshots. We saw a woman come out of an apartment building shooting at a guy running from her, and then she went back into her apartment. Bob Hill, a detective on his way to court, saw and heard the same thing we did. The three of us stopped, kicked in her apartment door, took her into custody, and found the gun. The guy she was chasing was her husband, and he was not hit by any of the shots. It was a family dispute. She went to jail. She was so focused on him that she didn't see us when she started shooting.

We worked late one night, and when we got home, we pulled our motorcycles into the garage. Bruce was on my left, and as I put my kickstand down, I started to get off the bike. Well, my kickstand didn't go down all the way, and I fell over onto Bruce who was still on his bike, and Bruce fell over. I was pinned underneath my bike, and Bruce was pinned under his. Here were two of LAPD's finest trapped in an open garage. Bruce was cussing me out, and I was laughing. No matter how we tried, we could not free ourselves from under the bikes.

Bruce suggested calling it in on the radio, but just as quickly, we vetoed that suggestion for fear of embarrassment. Now mind you, this is three thirty or so in the morning. The neighbors heard us and came to our rescue. They helped get my motorcycle off me, and then we helped Bruce up. Bruce stayed on motors for thirty-some years and retired as a motor sergeant.

Bruce was working by himself one day in Harbor Division while I was in court. He saw a guy jaywalk in front of traffic. Bruce stopped the guy to cite him for the jaywalking, and just as Bruce was getting off his motorcycle the guy tossed something underneath a parked car. Bruce thought the guy was acting strange, so he handcuffed him. Right then Bruce heard police sirens and watched the arrival of several black-and-white police units pulling up to the Bank of America across the street from where he was standing.

One of the officers came over to Bruce and told him the bank had just been robbed. Bruce looked under the car and found a bag of money. Thank God, the guy didn't have a gun. Bruce didn't know about the robbery silent alarm radio call because we operated on a different radio frequency and the call was on the Harbor Division radio frequency. There was a big write-up in the local newspaper about Bruce catching the bank robber, and the bank even bought him dinner!

Bruce Wallace

When I was on motors, Ken Walters, a young officer at Southwest, was killed in an on-duty traffic accident. I had been one of his training officers before I went to motors. He was a tall, good-looking kid and former Marine. The night he was killed, he was the passenger. A car pulled in front of him and his partner. They swerved to avoid the car and skidded into a cement lamp standard on Ken's side of the car. I went to the boneyard where they kept the black and whites that had been in traffic accidents to see the car. There was blood all over it. Ken's loss bothered me. He was a good officer and would have had a good career. His life was gone much too quick.

Jeff Watkins and I were working the Newton Division area one night, and at end of watch, I got on the Harbor Freeway to go home. Just as I got on the freeway, I heard a broadcast of an armed robbery with a description of a suspect and vehicle. There was a Newton black-and-white police car in front of me on the freeway, and I saw the described car from the broadcast in front of them. They saw the car too and flipped on their red lights. The suspect pulled over to the shoulder of the freeway near the Slauson Avenue exit and stopped. The Newton unit stopped behind him, and I stopped behind the Newton unit.

As I was getting off my bike, I saw both officers and the suspect outside of their cars. Then I heard gunshots and saw one of the Newton officers fall down the freeway embankment. Thinking the officer had been shot, I ran over to the top of the embankment where I saw the suspect running down and climbing over a chain link fence at the bottom. I fired at him, but missed. I put out an officer needs help shots fired call. Ernie Wood and J.J. Thompson from Southwest Division caught the fleeing suspect.

The officer that went down the embankment had fallen, but had not been shot. The shooting I heard initially was the driver officer shooting at the suspect. Jeff was heading home on Slauson Avenue and had heard me put out the help call over the radio. He turned around and hauled back to my location, but it was over by then.

About a week later, I had my first and only crash on the bike. A car pulled out right in front of me, and I broadsided it. I remember flipping over the car and landing against a wrought iron fence. I was fortunate not to hit and bounce off the car. That had happened to Bill Valdez, who was in my motor class. Similar type accident, but he hit the car with his body, broke everything you can break, and had to medically pension off the job.

As it was, I broke my thumb, tore ligaments, had numerous abrasions, and there was a big chunk out of my helmet. My motorcycle was totaled. I had just gotten a hand-me-down bike from a motorcycle drill team member. It was a beautiful Harley Davidson. I was very excited to get the bike because newer motor cops usually got the older pieces of junk. It took a lot of seniority to get a new motorcycle, and that wasn't going to happen in my short motor career.

I was off for a couple of months to recover. When I came back, I rode for a while, but I was too scared of another accident and I knew it. I went to Southwest Detectives until I made sergeant.

When I promoted to sergeant, I stayed at Southwest Division assigned to morning watch. I had not been a sergeant too long when I was driving southbound on Crenshaw and saw a car stopped in the middle of the street. As I got closer, I saw a guy outside of the car with a knife. He then got in the car and made a U-turn to go northbound on Crenshaw. There was a second guy still standing in the street. I drove up to the guy in the street, and he told me the other guy had just stabbed him and stole his car. I requested an ambulance for him and, because his injury wasn't life threatening, turned around and went after the suspect.

By this time, other units were with me. We stopped the suspect and took him into custody. A lieutenant from the station came out to the scene and chewed me out for doing police work. My response to him was, "I'm in a black-and-white police car, and I'm in uniform. Am I supposed to ignore it?" He didn't really answer. I was yelled at for doing a good deed.

Another sergeant and I were having coffee one day when a unit put out an assistance call regarding a mentally ill person with a butcher knife off Adams Boulevard. We responded, and at the scene was a Los Angeles County Psychiatric Emergency Team, along with the unit that had requested assistance. The PET team was there at the apartment of a mentally ill man to evaluate him. At one point, the man grabbed a butcher knife and chased them out of his apartment. They called the police, and two officers responded. The man's mother also came to the location and provided a key to the apartment. Getting no response from the man, the officers tried the door and could feel pressure on the door from inside. The man was intentionally holding the door shut. Fearing that he was a danger to himself, they requested additional units.

Richard Taft, one of the officers at the scene, came up with a game plan. It was decided that we would force the door open and knock the man back. An officer with one arm wrapped with a sheet for protection was tasked with taking the knife from the suspect. We had an ambulance standing by in the event of an injury.

The officers unlocked the door, and the man kept applying pressure. They forced the door open, and the man fell back with the knife in one hand. The officer tasked with taking the knife away hit the man on his arm with a baton, causing him to drop the knife. No one got hurt. The suspect was taken into custody and to the hospital for evaluation. I wrote Taft and the other officers a commendation for their outstanding effort.

When a supervisor position opened up in West Bureau Vice, I applied and got the job. At the time, the Vice units from Hollywood, Wilshire, Pacific and West Los Angeles were combined into one unit, West Bureau Vice. However, the concept proved ineffective, and each Vice unit returned to their respective divisions. I went to Hollywood.

One of our methods to fight the serious street prostitution in Hollywood was to have undercover female police officers on the street in the area of high prostitution activity. The intent was to target the customers of prostitutes. One night a guy pulled up to our undercover female officer and offered her money for sex. We arrested him, and upon searching him, we found a large butcher knife taped to his leg underneath his pants.

The Hillside Strangler had not been caught yet, so we called Robbery-Homicide Division. He was not their suspect. However, after we had arrested him and he was taken from the scene, two SIS detectives approached us and told us they had been following him. He was apparently a prolific burglar. Once we booked him, he bailed out, and SIS resumed their surveillance.

In '79, I made lieutenant and went to Wilshire Division. One night when I was driving into work with Charlie Duke, we heard over the radio an announcement that David Kubly had been killed. David was an officer at Wilshire on the night watch. Charlie and I got to the station, suited up, and responded to the perimeter that had been set to catch

David's killer. The perimeter was in Southwest Division. Gary Reichling, the lieutenant for the Wilshire night watch, was in charge. There were cops all over the place. We were out there until daylight, and it had started around eleven o'clock the night before. We had officers from several divisions stationed on the perimeter and conducting searches.

When morning came, the captain from Southwest told Gary that he needed to shut down the perimeter. To his credit, Gary stood up to the captain and said he was not closing down the search until the suspect was caught. Not too long after that, a woman called and said she found blood on a shed in her backyard. Officers responded and found the suspect hiding in her shed with the gun that he had used to shoot David and money that he had taken in a robbery.

David was working a report car by himself, saw a car speeding down Crenshaw Boulevard, and gave chase. At Twenty-Eighth Street, the car tried to make a left turn and crashed into a business on the corner. David overshot the suspect's car when he stopped. The suspect came out of his car and shot David as he was getting out of his police car. The suspect had just committed a robbery in Hollywood. David died at the hospital.

Eventually, I took a job in Narcotics Division, working the Field Enforcement Section. One of my detectives at Narcotics was Norm Eckles. Norm and I worked patrol together at Southwest Division. Norm was an outstanding detective and dope cop. On one morning, Norm and others from the unit were going to serve a search warrant at a ground-floor apartment of a two-story apartment building. I was home with the flu when I got a call advising me that Norm, Lovie Nettles, and Jim Tomas had been shot during the service of the search warrant and were at Daniel Freeman Hospital. I raced to the hospital. Lovie and Jim had minor wounds from bullet fragments, but Norm took a round under the armpit and was paralyzed.

While Lovie and Jim were prying the steel-screen security door, the suspect inside fired several rounds in a sweeping motion through the door and adjacent wall over to the front living room window covered with drapes. Norm was standing near the window. One round came through the window and hit him. Ken Wilkinson was standing right next to Norm, watched him fall to the ground, grabbed him, and upon kicking in the door of an adjacent apartment pulled him into the apartment out of the line of fire. There was a hell of an exchange of gunfire between the detectives and the suspect until the suspect ran out of ammo. The detectives entered and took him into custody.

Norm was medically pensioned off the job and died five years later as a result of his injury. During those five years, although paralyzed, Norm used his police background to the fullest, providing narcotics enforcement training to law enforcement agencies. The suspect could have been charged with murder if Norm had died within three years and a day of the date he was shot. Because it was beyond the three years, the suspect could not be charged with murder. He did go to prison for other charges.

I left Narcotics and went to Operations Central Bureau CRASH as the officer-in-charge. CRASH, Community Resources Against Street Hoodlums, was responsible for enforcement efforts against gang-related crime. Central Bureau was comprised of Central, Rampart, Hollenbeck, Newton, and Northeast Divisions. We had sixty-three gang-related homicides in the two years I was there.

One homicide in particular stands out because of the age of one suspect. He was fourteen years old. He and several other gang members committed some armed robberies in the Hollywood area one night. At one point, they were driving on Beverly Boulevard and stopped at a traffic light. While they were stopped, the fourteen-year-old took a shotgun, shot, and killed the passenger in the car next to them.

They were caught later that evening and brought back to the CRASH office. I listened to this fourteen-year-old, and he was very cavalier about it. To him, killing the guy in the car was like brushing his teeth, no big deal. Cold and callous—it was stunning.

Before I got to the unit, one of the sergeants, Larry Ariaz, had been in an officer-involved shooting. I was tasked with presenting the facts of the shooting to the shooting review board. To prepare for it, I did a walk-through with Larry. He and another sergeant, Danny Torres, were riding together on Alvarado when they saw a car with two people pull out of a gas station at a high rate of speed. Thinking that a robbery may have just occurred, they followed the car for several blocks.

At one point, the car made a turn onto Union Street. The sergeants were a little ways behind them. When the sergeants made the same turn, they were hit on the passenger door of their car with a shotgun blast from one of the suspects now standing on the sidewalk. He then ran down the street to where the other suspect had stopped the car. The sergeants were not hit, and both of them got out of their car. The suspect running down the street with the shotgun stopped to reload. Larry fired a shot, hit the suspect in the jaw, and dropped him like a deer. However, the suspect got up and continued to run. The other suspect drove off, leaving the first suspect who was then caught. The suspects had committed a robbery at the gas station. We measured Larry's shot, and it was 167 feet. That was a hell of a shot. It was a good shooting.

After a while, I was tired of being called out in the middle of the night on gang homicides, so I went back to Narcotics Division, working the Major Violators Section. When I got there, Operation Pisces was already in progress. We had an undercover officer posing as a source for the Colombian drug cartels to launder their drug money. It was attacking the drug problem from a different angle. Instead of following the drugs, we followed the money and that led us to the drugs. It was a very successful operation. We indicted over two hundred people and recovered thousands of pounds of cocaine and several millions of dollars in cash.

The effort was not without at least one setback. We arrested one dealer from Colombia. His father ran a big Colombian cartel and set his son up in the drug business in Los Angeles. The son was selling cocaine and laundering the money from the drug sales. He was eventually arrested and booked into the Los Angeles County Jail.

With the help of an insider, probably bribed, an unauthorized release message for the son was sent via computer to the jail. The son was transferred to the inmate reception release area and, from there, made his way out of the facility. His escape was not known for six days. This was in '87, and as far as I know, there is still a warrant in the system for his arrest.

When the Rodney King riots occurred in '92, I was still working Narcotics Division. The day the riots started, I was home watching on television when the verdicts for the four officers were announced. The officers were found not guilty of excessive force against King, the impetus for the riots.

Ken Welty with seized narcotics and money

During the riots, I was working with one of my detectives, Rich Ginelli. He was driving, and we were in the Newton Division area. We went by a closed business, and I saw someone moving around inside. I told Rich, and we asked for Newton units to meet us on a possible burglary in progress. It took them a little bit to get there.

We did a cursory inspection of the outside, and there was no evidence of forced entry. There was a dog inside the business. One of the officers asked me, "Lieutenant, are you sure you saw someone inside? It could have been the dog." We had the owner of the business meet us, and he opened the place up. Lo and behold, there was a stack of computers, and the owner told us the computers were not stacked like that when he closed the business.

I looked at the officer who had questioned what I saw and said, "Do you think the dog stacked up these computers?" He looked a little sheepish. Unfortunately, the suspect was gone.

On February 8, 1986, on my way to visit a friend with the Escondido Police Department, there was an announcement on the radio that Arleigh McCree and Ron Ball had been killed while defusing a pipe bomb on a call out. Arleigh and Ron were part of the Department's bomb squad, and I was friends with Arleigh. I had to pull off the road to think about what I had just heard. Both, especially Arleigh, were bigger than life on the Department and very highly respected bomb technicians.

A year to the day of their deaths, we did a narcotics search warrant at a house and found a kilo of cocaine and a large number of handguns and rifles. Gary Bitteroff and I were searching in the garage when Gary came across a clothes hamper. At the bottom of the hamper, he found two pipe bombs. I told everyone to stop what they were doing and to evacuate. We called the bomb squad. That date and those circumstances were not lost on the bomb squad or us. Everyone had Arleigh and Ron in their thoughts. The pipe bombs were removed, we continued the search, and we all went home safe.

Bunco-Forgery was the last stop of my career. We handled major fraud cases, including ones involving political corruption. The detectives I had working for me were some of the best in the Department, and I felt fortunate to have spent my last five years there.

On my last day on the job, after I had decided to retire, I said my goodbyes and waited until I was the last one in the office. After almost thirty years, walking out the door for the last time was very difficult. One day you're a policeman, and the next you're back to being a civilian. No more going from an adrenaline rush and then back to a normal routine. The job was extremely fulfilling, and I have great memories of my time as a policeman.

Donald "Donnie" Simpson

Birthplace: Detroit, Michigan
Career: 1970–1986
Rank at Retirement: Police Officer III
Divisions: Wilshire

I always liked guns. I had an uncle who worked at Mattel Toys, and whenever they came out with a new toy gun, I got it. As I grew older, the guns went from toy to real.

Before I went in the Marine Corps, I worked at a restaurant in Inglewood. One night a guy tried to rob the waitress who was leaving the restaurant to make a bank deposit. He whipped out his little .22 revolver, and I whipped out my .38. I held him at gunpoint until the police came and got him. Another night some guy broke into the coin box of the phone booth outside the restaurant, and I held him until the police arrived. The Inglewood Police Department got to know me pretty well.

At the time of the '65 Watts riots, I was living with my grandparents on Fifty-Fourth Street and Fourth Avenue—in the middle of the riots. On one of the nights, I was driving home in my Austin Healy convertible when a carload of bad guys in a '55 Chevy got right on top of me. I started driving side streets. They're chasing me, and one of them fired a round at me. I stopped near my grandmother's house, grabbed my twelve-gauge shotgun I had in the car, and cranked off a round at them, hitting their car. They left. Two officers from LAPD showed up. I told them what had happened, and they told me to be more careful and left.

Near the end of my tour with the Marine Corps, I learned that a local college near Camp Pendleton had a mini police academy. The Marine Corps had an early-out program, so I went to the mini police academy and subsequently applied to the LAPD.

Part of the hiring process for LAPD was taking a physical examination. The doctor measured my height and said, "You are five foot seven and three-quarters of an inch." The height requirement at the time was five feet eight inches.

I told him, "No. I'm five foot eight."

The doctor stuck me in the butt with some kind of probe he had in his hand, and I jumped. He said, "Okay, five foot eight." Later on the job when I told that story, I was given the nickname "Three-quarters."

The funny thing at the Academy was I had trouble qualifying, and I had shot expert rifle and pistol in the Marine Corps. Turned out the grips on my revolver were too small and had a sharp edge. I developed a blister between my thumb and forefinger, so every time I fired the gun it was like being stabbed with a needle. I could not get qualified. I was told if I didn't qualify, I would not graduate. I showed my blister to John Hurst, one of the shooting instructors, and he wrapped the grips with duct tape. He said, "Now try it." That made the difference, and I finally qualified.

Donnie Simpson

For two weeks, our class went out in the field. I went to Venice Division along with three of my classmates, Dave Leaton, Harry Winston, and a guy with the last name Parker. The four of us were assigned to traffic control at the Manchester Shopping Center. The sergeant dropped us off and said, "Just walk around," and with emphasis said, "and don't do anything." We wouldn't have known what to do anyway.

He put Dave and me on one side of the street, and the other two on the other side. No car, no radio, no nothing. We were just out there. At one point, Dave and I were flagged down by some people who said a guy was acting crazy inside this store and messing with the store clerks. We went in, and he saw us and took off. We tackled him, and as we were wrestling with him, a bunch of pills fell out of his clothing. We hooked him up and took him outside. The big question was, *Now what are we going to do with him?* We decided to walk him the five blocks to where the sergeant was going to pick us up. When the sergeant came, we told him what happened. We eventually booked the guy for sales of narcotics.

The next day the sergeant took us back to the Manchester Shopping Center and again told us, "Don't do anything." Dave and I switched sides of the street with the other two. We were standing in front of a Bank of America, and all of a sudden, we heard a loud gunshot from behind the bank. We ran to the back of the bank, and in the parking lot, a woman was sitting inside a '56 Ford Thunderbird screaming. We saw a guy running between the cars with a gun in his hand.

We knelt down and as we drew our guns, two guys dressed in suits on the other side of the parking lot started shooting at him. They hit the guy, and he went down. The shooters were detectives from Venice Division, and this guy had tried to rob the lady while she was in the car. When she started screaming, he got so excited that he fired a round into the floorboard of her car. That caught the attention of the detectives who happened to be in the area. They radioed for help, and the world showed up, including our sergeant. We were put on the desk for the last two days!

The next week, our class was assigned to work traffic units. I was working with a traffic officer when a help call was broadcasted at Adams and Crenshaw Boulevard. We responded, and when we arrived, we saw eight policemen behind a wall at a gas station next to a motel. We ran to their position, and they're shooting at a barricaded suspect in the motel. They asked if we had any ammo because they had just about shot everything they had. I told them I had a hundred rounds of ammo in my bag in the car, and they told me to go get it. I did and gave it to them. You could hear rounds being fired on both sides of the motel. My partner said, "There are enough policemen here, and with you still in the Academy maybe we should leave."

When my class returned to the Academy, we had a share day to tell about our experiences in the field. Before they started, a commendation was read off for the four of us on our arrest of the narcotics suspect in Venice Division. When it was time for me to tell of my experiences, I didn't know any better and I said I was at two shootings.

The instructors all looked at each other, told the class to take a break, and said, "Simpson. You stay here." They grilled me about what had happened. I told them about the shooting at the bank and about the barricaded suspect at the motel. They asked if I had shot in either situation, and I said no. They were relieved and actually got a kick out of the stories.

Once I graduated, for whatever reason, I did not work the Jail, Communications, or Parking and Intersection Control like my classmates. That was good because I didn't want to go to any of those places anyway. I was assigned to Wilshire Division, where I stayed for the rest of my time on the job.

Then it started. I was working a report car by myself, and I received a call of a burglary investigation at a gas station. The gas station was closed, and I was waiting for the owner. All of a sudden, I saw somebody inside the gas station office trying to break into the cash register. I ran to my car, got on the radio, and called for a backup on a burglary suspect.

When the units got there, they searched the gas station, but they could not find the suspect. "Are you sure you saw somebody in there?"

"Yeah, he was trying to break into the register."

"Well, he's not here now."

They left, and as I was taking the report from the owner, we both heard something from above us in the storage space, when a stack of tires fell over. The burglar was hiding in the stack of tires! It was high enough that nobody looked over and inside. I ordered him down, handcuffed him, and then requested a unit for transportation of the burglary suspect. A couple of the units returned and said, "We searched it." I told them where he had been hiding, and they couldn't believe it.

Rick Gillette and I were working one night, when a father holding a three-year-old child flagged us down. The father was hysterical and saying his child was not breathing. We were getting ready to call for an ambulance when we checked the child and realized he was still breathing, but his breathing was very shallow. There was not enough time to wait for an ambulance, so I got in the back seat with him, and we rolled red lights and siren to the hospital.

On the way, the child did stop breathing, and I gave him mouth-to-mouth resuscitation. At Central Receiving Hospital, the medical staff was waiting for us. The child was placed on a gurney and rushed inside. After a short while, the nurse came out to us with the good news that the child would be all right, but the doctor thought the child had spinal meningitis.

I said, "What?"

"You're going to need some shots."

I was given four shots, two in each butt cheek, with a quart of white stuff. It hurt like heck. I didn't get spinal meningitis.

We came down from PM watch roll call one night, and Ken Fromel, the front desk officer, called me over. He had been trying to give this forgery call to somebody, and the minute you mention forgery nobody wants it.

Ken said, "Donnie, come here. I got a call for you."

"What call?"

"A forgery at The Broadway on Wilshire Boulevard."

I initially told him no because that meant you had to go downtown, have the arrestee do handwriting exemplars and a bunch of other stuff.

"No, no, we don't have him yet. But I found out the suspects tried to use a credit card that had been taken in a robbery in Ventura at a liquor store. These guys got in a shootout with the Ventura County Sheriffs, but they got away. The sheriffs felt with the number of rounds these guys fired, they had to have had two guns each. The car they were in was also taken in the robbery, and it was still parked in The Broadway parking lot. So these guys are real bad guys."

"Okay, we'll take that one."

My regular partner, Dave Balleweg, was off, so I was working with Billy Rice for the first time. I asked Billy if he carried a backup gun. He said he did, but there had been a report of a prowler in his neighborhood the previous night so he left his backup gun with his wife. I always carried a backup gun, but I also kept a four-inch revolver in the glove box of the police car. I told him to use that as his backup gun.

We talked to the security guard at The Broadway, and he said they had tried to stall the two suspects, but the suspects got hinky and left. He told us they still had to be around because, when they ran over to their car, they saw him looking at them, so they took off on foot. We requested an unmarked unit to sit on the suspects' car in case the suspects returned. We looked around for about an hour, but we could not find them. The watch commander then told us to return to our assigned area on the east side of Wilshire Division. The unmarked unit remained at The Broadway watching the suspects' car.

Billy and I were driving east on Wilshire Boulevard when we saw a guy fitting the description of one of the suspects walking on the sidewalk eastbound on the south side of the street. As we went by him, we could see he was sweating profusely. It was about seven o'clock at night, and it was not that hot. We passed him, and at the next street, Muirfield Road, we made a right turn heading south. We assumed he would think we were going around the block.

As I got to the end of the block, I did a U-turn and headed back north on Muirfield. I stopped the car on the wrong side of the street next to the curb just south of Wilshire. There was a big hedge bordering the sidewalk, and it continued around the corner. It was about seven feet tall and blocked our view of him as well as his view of us. I told Billy that once he cleared the hedge, he'll be in the open and we can make the stop.

We were sitting there waiting with the engine running. He didn't show. We thought maybe he had crossed Wilshire. Just as I started to move the car forward, he cleared the hedge. His shirt was now open, and he was holding the grip of a four-inch Ruger .357 Magnum stuck in the waistband of his pants. I could see it plain as day. We both yelled, "Gun!"

I hit the brake, threw the car in park, drew my gun, and kicked open the door as he was pulling his gun and taking aim at me. I fired two quick rounds through the open window of my door, and then I bailed out onto the grass parkway and fired another round. That round hit the grass in front of me and made a big divot.

I rose to one knee and fired three more rounds. The suspect was still pointing his gun at me. I thought, *I couldn't have missed him.* Then my gun went *click click.* It was empty. I hit the grass, rolled, dropped my revolver, and drew my backup gun. I came up to shoot, and he was not there. I looked between my arms and underneath my gun, and I saw him lying on the sidewalk face down with one hand under him. I ran around the back of the police car to Billy's side. Billy had not used his own service revolver, but fired with the gun I had let him use. I ran into the first lane of traffic, waving for the cars to stop as I was holding my gun on the suspect.

Billy came up onto the sidewalk, and I said, "You cover, and I'll search. If he moves, I'll bail out of the way, and he's yours." I searched him and did not find another gun. He was dead. I hit him with five of my six shots. The first shot went through his heart. He was dead at that moment and didn't know it. The coroner said my second shot went through his shoulder striking the nerve that went to his trigger finger. He tried to shoot, but the finger could not press the trigger. He never got a round off.

We put out a help call because there was still a second suspect that was unaccounted for. As we're waiting for help to arrive, a brown Plymouth came sliding up. A guy got out and said, "Do you need help?" At first, I thought he was a detective, but he was Boris Yaro, a photographer for the Los Angeles Times. He had been sitting across the street in his car. When the shooting started, he began to take pictures. The shooting made the front pages of several newspapers across the country the next day.

About twenty-five minutes later, the second suspect returned to their car parked in The Broadway parking lot. Freddy Miller and his partner were waiting in the plain unit. They took him into custody, and he was booked at Wilshire Station. The second suspect was convicted and sent to prison.

Donnie Simpson, right, and Billy Rice: "You cover, and I'll search. If he moves, I'll bail out of the way, and he's yours."

Dave Balleweg and I received a call of a disturbance on Wilton Avenue at Fifteenth Street one night. The woman pointed to a house and told us a crazy guy was holding her sister at gunpoint and he wouldn't let her go. It was the sister's boyfriend, and she had been there a couple of days. I went up onto the front porch, and Dave stayed at the bottom of the steps off to the side. I banged on the door. No response, so I banged on the door again. The door opened a little bit, and a girl was standing there. She looked scared.

"Everything okay?"

"Yes."

I took my index finger, kept it close to my chest, and simulated a gun. She looked at me and nodded her head as if to say yes. I said out loud, "We got a call here about some kind of disturbance." And as I said to her, "But seeing how everything is okay," I put out my hand as if to shake her hand. She put her hand down near mine, and I hit the door with my shoulder, pulled her out, and yelled, "Gun!"

We went flying off the porch. The suspect was behind the door and had a shotgun pointed at her head the whole time. He retreated as soon as I pulled her out. We eventually entered the house and found him hiding in the back. We took him into custody and recovered two guns.

You know me, I never do anything; things just come to me. One night Ron Ponzi and I received a missing child investigation, and we were driving around the area looking for a fourteen-year-old girl.

As we're coming down Western Avenue, we stopped for a red traffic light at Oakwood Street. I'm driving. All of a sudden, we heard a gunshot to our left at a drive-thru fast food restaurant. A guy climbs out one of the service windows with a gun in his hand. Then a second suspect comes partially out of a second service window, but he can't get out. I'm now out of the car, the first suspect turned toward me, and I fired a round. He spun, dropped the gun, and ran behind the restaurant. I went after him, while Ron took the second suspect who was stuck in the window into custody. There was a dirt field behind the restaurant and a burned-out house. I'm thinking I'm never going to find him in there, and I'm by myself. I put out a broadcast that a robbery had just occurred and gave a description of the suspect who fled.

About an hour later, a Hollywood unit picked up our suspect. He was wounded in the side from the round that I had fired. What happened was he saw our black-and-white police car, got excited and cranked off a round accidentally. Had he not done that, when the traffic light changed we would have continued right on down the street, unaware of the robbery.

I was working with Jimmy Barnett one night, and there was a crime broadcast of a hijacked semi-truck in West LA Division. Another semi-truck driver had witnessed the hijacking and was following the hijacked truck. They were last reported traveling eastbound on the Santa Monica Freeway in our direction. Jimmy and I figured the suspects had to get off the freeway somewhere, so maybe we would get lucky.

We were driving on Washington Boulevard parallel to the freeway, and at Redondo Boulevard, we heard the blast of a semi-truck horn. There was a semi-truck approaching the intersection, and as it crossed the intersection, we could see the driver looking at us and pointing down Redondo at another semi-truck. We figured he was the witness trucker. We pulled up next to him, and as I pointed to the semi-truck in front of us, I simulated a gun. He looked at me and said, "Yes."

Jim Barnett

The suspects turned a corner, stopped, and bailed out of the truck. The passenger ran toward an alley. I focused on him and saw him pull a blue steel two-inch revolver out of his jacket pocket. I yelled to Jimmy, "Gun!" We followed him into the alley, and as the suspect turned, he pointed the gun back at me. He was about fifteen yards in front of me, and I let loose with a round from my shotgun. The round hit him, and he went tumbling into some brush. The suspect got up and ran to a fence. He lifted his gun hand again, and I cranked off another round. He went to the ground. I approached him and said, "Are you hit?" His only response was to curse at me.

Jimmy then set up the search for the driver suspect who ran to the next street over. The searching officers heard dogs barking, looked over a fence, and observed the suspect hiding in a doghouse. The suspect was armed, but he was also taken into custody.

A search was made of the alley, and we could not find the first suspect's gun. After a while, Lieutenant Tom Cornwell put his arm around me and said, "Donnie, are you sure he had a gun?"

I said, "I'm telling you, he had a gun, a large, blue-frame two-inch."

Lieutenant Cornwell called downtown and had two light trucks brought out, and the whole alley was bathed in light. All of the yards were searched, and the gun was found on the other side of the fence from where I had shot the suspect. Some of the pellets from the shotgun round had hit him in the hand between the thumb and index finger, which made the gun go flying. With the recoil of the shotgun, I didn't see the gun go over the fence. The gun was a Hollywood stolen. The semi-truck was hijacked for the load of office furniture inside. The hostage was handcuffed and still inside the truck. Both suspects pled guilty and got prison time.

Jimmy and I responded to a robbery silent alarm at a pharmacy on the corner of Pico Boulevard and Western Avenue one day. We parked up the street a little and approached the front door on foot. I peeked inside and did not see anybody. I told Jimmy, "No clerk. No pharmacists." When I peeked again, I saw this guy come from the pharmacy area and walk behind the counter over to the cash register. I leaned back so he would not see me, and then we heard banging sounds. I looked again, and I saw him hitting the cash register with a handgun, a German Luger. I told Jimmy to get us backup.

Jimmy ran over to the car and requested a backup on a robbery in progress with an armed suspect. He was told there were no units available. What we didn't know was the suspect's car was parked in the alley to the rear of the pharmacy. At that moment, a motor officer who did not hear our backup request was writing a citation on the car for illegally parking in the alley. Meanwhile, people were gathering across the street watching us.

I peeked again and saw that the guy could not get the cash register open. He started yelling back toward the pharmacy area, asking how to get the register open. He gave up on the register, went back to the pharmacy area, and started filling a shopping bag with pill bottles from the shelves. Jimmy came back and told me he didn't know if any backup was coming. I said, "It doesn't matter. It looks like he's getting ready to come out."

The suspect started toward the front door. He had one arm under the bag filled with drugs, and his other arm around it. I wondered, *Does he have the gun in the hand under the bag or in the hand around the bag?* I had my shotgun, and I whispered to Jimmy that we would take him right at the door. The suspect opened the door and stepped out. Like a rifle with a bayonet, I stuck the shotgun right into his stomach and said, "If you move, I'm going to blow you in half!"

He froze.

"Drop the bag."

He dropped the bag, and the pills went everywhere. The German Luger had been sitting on top of the drugs, and it slid onto the sidewalk. As we hooked him up, all the people across the street started clapping. They must have thought we were making a movie. The motor cop in the alley had finished writing his ticket and then saw us. He had no clue there had been a robbery. The pharmacist and his employees were in the back of the store tied up with duct tape.

There was a time at Wilshire Division when the officer who had the most recovered stolen cars would receive a voucher for a free dinner at one of the big restaurants on Wilshire Boulevard. I won the voucher, and when Captain Joe De Ladurantey presented it to me, he asked, "Are you going to take me to dinner?"

I said jokingly, "I'd like to take the chief."

"Okay."

Two days later Captain De Ladurantey called me into his office and said, "I talked to the chief yesterday, and he said he would love to go to lunch with you."

"Okay. Here's the deal. I want that day off because I'm going to order a martini."

"You got it."

A date was set, and on that day, Chief Daryl Gates showed up with his driver. We sat down for lunch, and the first thing I did was order a Beefeater Martini. Chief Gates and his driver ordered iced teas. At one point during our conversation, I said, "You really don't have a clue on what is going on in the street because sergeants want to be lieutenants, lieutenants want to be captains, captains want to be commanders, and commanders or above want to take your job. So everybody gets rosy whenever you ask about what is happening in a division. Every so often, you should attend a night or morning watch division roll call and talk to the officers. A lot of the guys will be afraid and not talk to you, but there are some like me who will tell you what's going on."

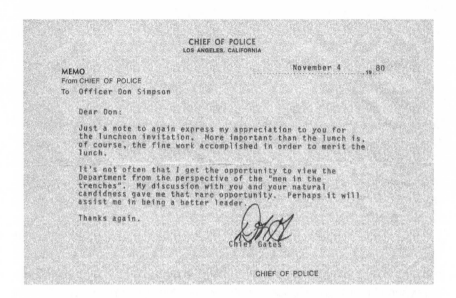

A few days later, Chief Gates came to our roll call and talked with the officers. I was there, and he said, "I already talked to Simpson." A couple of guys spoke up, and it was a good exchange with Chief Gates. It was my understanding that from then on he picked a division every couple of weeks and attended a roll call.

I later received a "Blue Note" from Chief Gates thanking me for my candor. At a retirement dinner sometime later, I spoke with Chief Gates. He told me his visits to the roll calls were an eye-opener for him. He said he heard things that he had no clue were happening. I said, "Yeah, well, I told you."

One night near end of watch, Richard Rinker and I were driving on La Cienega Boulevard when there was a radio call of shots fired in West Los Angeles Division on the nineteen hundred block of Holt Street. La Cienega is the border between Wilshire and West L.A. Divisions, and Holt is several streets west of La Cienega. We were right there. We responded and were the first unit to arrive. The location was an apartment building. We could see that the sliding glass door of one of the upstairs apartments was broken out.

A fence ran between the apartment building with the broken glass and the adjacent apartment building. I told Rich, "Give me a couple of minutes to get behind that fence." It allowed me a view of the stairwell leading up to the apartment.

Rich stayed at the front of the building. I walked behind the chest-level fence to the area of the stairwell and saw a guy coming down the stairs. He was holding an armload of leather and fur coats. Then I saw that he was holding a six-inch revolver in one hand. Using the cover of the block wall fence, I yelled, "Police. Drop the gun!"

He lifted his hand and fired a round at me. It missed, and I fired at him. My first shot missed him, and the second shot hit him. He fell down onto the stairs and dropped the coats. He started moving back up the stairwell in a crab-like fashion with the gun still in his hand. I fired again and hit him in the leg as he moved up the stairs.

An officer from West L.A. came around the corner, and he too fired up the stairwell at the suspect. The suspect stopped moving, but he was still holding the gun. A dope deal had gone sideways when the suspect I shot and two other suspects brought guns instead of money. Eight people were tied up in the apartment. The second suspect jumped out the window of the second-story apartment when he heard gunfire. He was caught a block away trying to walk on two broken ankles. The third suspect took his shirt off, put tape over his mouth, loosely tied his hands, and tried to pose as a hostage. As soon as we took the tape off, the others pointed him out as a suspect. The stack of coats belonged to the hostages. All three suspects went to jail.

The bullet the first suspect fired at me missed me by inches. It put a hole in a plant leaf right next to my head and then blew up a teakettle in the apartment behind me.

Carson Pierce and I were working together when we arrested this big guy for fighting with his girlfriend. He fought with us until we got him into custody, and then he fought with us again when we were booking him. He suffered some injuries from all the fighting and we were told to take him downtown and book him in at the jail at Parker Center because they had a medical dispensary.

I told him, "We have to book you downtown. If you don't fight with us anymore, we will stop at Tommy's Burgers on the way there and get you a chili burger."

"You would do that?"

"Yes. But if we have to fight you again, you're not getting one."

"Deal."

Tommy's Burgers: "He couldn't believe it."

We stopped at Tommy's and ordered three chiliburgers. We handcuffed him in front, and he ate his chiliburger. He couldn't believe it. We finished our burgers, and we booked him downtown. No more fights.

About three months later, I was walking by the holding tank at Wilshire Station, and I heard, "Officer Simpson." Our guy was in the holding tank with some other arrestees. He said, "I told these guys if you're arrested by Simpson, don't fight with him, and he'll get you a Tommy's burger. I told them you had promised me a Tommy's burger, and you came through."

Of course, the watch commander, Sergeant Kip Meyerhoff, heard part of the conversation and asked me what it was about. I told him the story. When I got to the part about buying the suspect a burger, he said, "Okay, okay, I don't want to hear anymore."

By this time in my career, I had had knee surgeries on both knees and surgery on my wrist after a PCP suspect bit it and would not let go. That incident happened the first day we were not allowed to use the chokehold. Earlier that day, the PCP suspect had set fire to an apartment building. Firemen on the scene observed the suspect drinking a can of paint, and the paint was all over his lips and beard. He was high on PCP and naked. The Fire Department called for the police. The guy was taken into custody and placed in the padded cell at Wilshire Station.

As I was coming down from roll call, Sergeant Meyerhoff told me, "I need you and your partner to go book a guy downtown."

"Okay, where is he?"

"He's in the padded cell."

I thought, *This is not going to be good.* We looked through the window of the padded cell, and the guy was standing there with white particles in his beard. The particles were part of the padding on the cell walls. He had eaten about one square foot of it, and the pad was several inches thick. He ate it. It was gone. You could see his teeth marks in the edges of the padding. I was thinking, *You've got to be kidding me.*

We opened the door, and I told him, "We've got to take you downtown to the doctor. But to ride in the car you have to have handcuffs on. I want you to turn around so we can handcuff you."

He refused to turn. Normally when a suspect continued to refuse to turn, your partner would go around the suspect and place a chokehold on him to put him out, so we could cuff him. Nobody gets hurt. We couldn't use a chokehold anymore, so I reached up with my left hand to push on his shoulder to turn him. He bit into my wrist, clamping down hard and would not let go. I put my right hand up under his throat and slammed him against the padded cell. I was yelling, "He's got my wrist!"

Other officers showed up, and we slammed him onto the ground. He had bitten into my wrist like a Pitbull. I hit him as hard as I could and actually broke his jaw, and that was fortunate because I was then able to pull his unhinged jaw down and release my wrist. We handcuffed him, wrapped him in a blanket, and put him in the car. I later went to the hospital and was treated for the bite. It hurt, but I continued working.

A few days later, my partner and I were having dinner at a restaurant. The waitress handed me my plate, and as I reached up to take it from her, it felt like a needle was stuck in my wrist. I dropped the plate. I saw a doctor and eventually had to have surgery to repair the damage. It took three months for it to stop hurting.

I worked the evening watch for most of my career, but one time they put me on morning watch. I got off work one morning about six thirty and was driving my '74 Volvo. I left the station, which was a half block east of La Brea, made a left turn onto La Brea, and parked at the curb at a liquor store. I wanted to buy cigarettes and some sodas to keep me awake for my trip home. The liquor store was not open yet. Just ahead of me, across the driveway that led to the back of the liquor store, was a '69 Plymouth parked with three guys in it. The owner of the liquor store arrived and went to the door to unlock it. The left rear door of the Plymouth opened and out stepped this monstrous three-hundred-pound guy wearing a poncho. I could readily see two inches of shotgun barrel sticking out below it.

The guy confronted the owner at gunpoint, and I was sitting there thinking, *This ain't good.* I pulled back into traffic, drove ahead about fifty yards, and made a U-turn. I came back and parked across the street, wondering what I was going to do. I had an AR-15 in my trunk, and I thought I could drop him with two or three shots, get the driver real quick, and then drop the front passenger if he bails and has a gun. But I thought, *No, if I do that, the Department is going to get mad at me.* It was change of watch, and I knew there would be a lot of policemen in the parking lot, so I drove back to the station, and I yelled that a robbery was going down at the liquor store. I then drove back out of the station with police cars following me.

The driver of the suspects' car had made a mistake. He had parked right behind another parked car. I pulled up behind his car, blocked it in, and bailed out with gun in hand. Three black and whites came screeching to a stop. All three suspects were in the car. We got them all out and recovered the shotgun and one other gun. All three were high on cocaine. The big guy with the poncho had committed a robbery. The driver was a parole officer, and the other two were his parolees who were recently released from prison. In the last twenty-four hours, the three had committed eighteen robberies all over the city. That arrest worked out really good. I received a commendation for showing great restraint and not initiating a gun battle.

Near the end of my career, I worked a Z-car, a crime suppression unit that did not receive radio calls. Carson Pierce and Bruce Barber were my partners. In one eleven-month period, we were credited with one hundred and twelve arrests. Seventy-six of those suspects were armed and dangerous, and ten of them were arrested for murder. We had twenty-two vehicle pursuits, and we recovered sixty-eight stolen cars and fifty-six guns. The suspects were good for one or two crimes a week. If you take them out of circulation, your crime is going to drop. I had two shootings during those eleven months. If you arrest that many people with guns, something is going to happen sooner or later. That was right before my last rating period in '85.

During my career, I found that when fighting a suspect, you fight them until they stop. Once it's over, it's over. After that, if you treated them with respect and did not bad-mouth them, you didn't have any trouble. There was one suspect we had a fight with, and because he was so big we beat him bad. Once we got him controlled, it was over. Later that night, he said that we were the nicest policemen he was ever arrested by and that once the fight was over we treated him good.

He told me, "You be a man, and I be a man, and we both work every day."

"The problem is my work is being a policeman, and your work is as a criminal. That's not good. You've got to change your ways. I'm sure I'm going to see you again, and that's when I got to go to work."

Carson Pierce

Donnie Simpson

I truly believe my approach was why I only had one personnel complaint during my career, and that complaint was not sustained, meaning there was no evidence to prove or disprove the complaint.

On the way to the Academy for a training day, I started coughing up blood. It was determined that all of the anti-inflammation medication I took for all my injuries had caused a hole in my esophagus. I received a medical pension.

I wanted to be a street cop, and that was it. Had I stayed longer with the number of shootings I had, I might have pushed my luck. I do miss catching bad guys though and working with great partners like Dave, Jimmy, and Carson, and for great supervisors like Kip Meyerhoff. There was never a day I did not want to go to work, and a lot of times I did not want to get off work. I found a home in Wilshire. There was no place I could have done the work I did any better than there.

Jerry Stokes

Birthplace: Austin, Texas
Career: 1970–1999
Rank at Retirement: Sergeant II
Divisions: Wilshire, Training, Southeast, Seventy-Seventh, Foothill

One night my wife and I went to a movie in downtown Los Angeles. When we left, I was pulled over for speeding. The officers were talking to me, and once they found out I had been in the Marine Corps, they wanted to know if I was interested in being a cop. I hadn't thought about it, but I took down the information they gave me. And yes, they still gave me a ticket.

At the time, I was working at the Graybar Electric Company. My co-worker Paul Barron knew I had been in the military and asked me to teach him how to march. He wanted to learn because he was going into the Police Academy. On our breaks, I showed him how to march and how to do exercises that he would probably be doing at the Academy. Soon after, Paul left the company and went on the LAPD.

I received a phone call one day at Graybar. I wondered who was calling me. It was an LAPD recruiter. He told me that Paul Barron had highly recommended me to be a police officer. The recruiter asked if I was interested. I was.

In March 1970, I entered the Academy. Because of my military background, I was appointed a squad leader. I was also one of the more decent runners in the class. This one time we were running, and Gil Strap, the instructor, told me and a couple of other runners, "Go back and pick up the stragglers."

Jerry Stokes receiving diploma from Chief Ed Davis, 1970

We did as we were told and encouraged the slower guys to catch up with the class. Afterward in the locker room, one of the other squad leaders told me that a couple of the runners who had fallen behind were a little upset with me. They said that I pushed them in the back as I was trying to help them, and they told this squad leader that they were going to do something about it if it happened again. I told him, "If they can't run any faster than they were running today, it's not a fear." Nothing ever came of it.

On our month out in the field, I was assigned to West Los Angeles Division. I worked patrol with Paul Montgomery, another black officer. One day we got a burglary report radio call. We responded to the residence where an elderly white woman lived by herself. When she came to the door, she was very polite, but said that she wanted other police officers, meaning white officers. As a young officer, I was taken aback by her comment.

Paul was a veteran officer and calmly said, "Ma'am, we have just one type. We all wear blue."

"I'm sorry, but I just don't want you coming into my house."

Paul Montgomery, second from left

Paul, seeing a nice swing and chairs on the porch, said, "Would you feel comfortable taking the report out here on the porch?"

"Yes."

She came out onto the porch, and Paul had me take the report. I completed the report, and she signed it. Then we thanked her and went on our way.

Paul didn't get upset and call for a sergeant to say we were disrespected. He was very professional, and I remembered that for the rest of my career. That experience taught me you can't let how you feel personally get involved, because we were there to provide a service. I commended Paul for the way he handled the situation.

Upon graduation, I went to Wilshire Division. My very first day I was working with Mack Andrews. We received a burglary suspect there now radio call. As we rolled up to the location, several other units also arrived. One of the other officers told me, "Rook, you go to the side of the building and stand by the window in case he tries to jump out."

I did as I was told and watched the window. Everybody else went to the front. I think they were just trying to get me out of the way, because it was my first day. Then I heard all this banging on the door from within the building. All of a sudden, the window raised up, and this guy came flying out the window. I drew my gun and started giving him commands, "Get on the ground," and all the other Academy stuff.

He hesitated for a moment. I told him again to get on the ground. He then went down. As I put my weapon away to approach and handcuff the suspect, the other officers came around the corner and handcuffed him. Everybody was saying, "Hey, the rook did a good job!"

The only complaint I received was from the officer who sent me to the side of the building. He said I should have whacked the suspect across the knees with my baton when the suspect hesitated. I think he was trying to save a little face. Mack told me I did everything I was supposed to do. He said, "You don't want to draw your baton when you have your gun in your hand." From that point on, I guess I had a little credibility because they found out I could handle myself.

At the time, each station had officers posted as security due to various groups like the Black Panthers who advocated violence against the police. I had security duty, and I was posted outside in front of the station on an extremely cold night.

A gentleman approached me and said, "Hello, officer. How are you doing?"

I said, "Good, sir."

He asked me to direct him to detectives. I told him they were on the upper floor and showed him the staircase inside the station. In the old Wilshire Station, you could hear people walking up and down the staircase even from outside. I heard him go up, and a few minutes later, he came back down with his son.

I guess the son got in trouble along with some of his buddies. When the father came down the stairs with his son, you could clearly hear his displeasure.

Once they were outside, the father looked at me and said, "You sure look cold."

"Yes, sir. I am."

He took off his mittens, gave them to me, and walked away. They lived up in the northern part of the division. I did see the kid several times while I was on patrol, but I never saw him again in the station.

Al Mack and Willie Myers were my primary training officers. Both had over twenty years on the job, and both were great coppers, truly legends as they say. They always talked about the folks who could de-escalate a situation. Long before we started naming those types of skills, Al was the guy. He handled things well, and he knew everybody. He taught me that you need to know the people in your assigned area and pay attention to things.

One day we were in roll call, and the description of an armed suspect was given for a robbery that had occurred the night before. When we got in the police car to start our watch, Al told me that the description sounded like, for the sake of the story, Jim Jones on Third Street. Al was driving, and we drove to the neighborhood where the person he was thinking of lived.

As we drove slowly down this street, Al pointed to an apartment building and said, "He lives right there." We came back around the block, and as we started down the street again, he saw the guy walk out of an apartment and head down the street. Apparently, the suspect saw the police car the first time we drove down the street and thought we were gone.

With his hand discreetly on his revolver, Al pulled up to the guy and said, "Hey, Jim. Tell me what happened last night."

"What do you mean, Mack?"

"They tell me you robbed somebody."

"That wasn't no robbery, Mack. He owed me that money."

"We'll have to take you down and get it squared away."

Al told me to handcuff the guy. I did, and we took him to the station.

Al just had that type of instinct to know how to handle situations by knowing the people in his neighborhood. He was very respected. We made all kinds of arrests and didn't have any problems.

Al had twenty-five years on at that time, and he drove, if I remember right, a '49 Chevy to work that he bought after he came on the job. He used to park it in front of the station, and the command staff would complain because it took up a parking spot. They would tell him to move it, and he would say, "Okay, boss." The next day it would be right back in the same parking spot! Al Mack was quite a character.

Willie Myers was about six four and an outdoor type. He was always telling me, "Kid, those hamburgers are going to kill you." He would bring venison and that type of thing for code seven, our mealtime. He was a health guy even back then. On morning watch, I would freeze because he always wanted the car windows down. A lot of officers smoked, but not Willie. He had twenty-two years on the job. When I became a sergeant, it amazed me that we had training officers with three years on when I had the opportunity to train with two very experienced officers.

Probationers did not drive with Willie. One night, however, he said, "Okay, kid, you're going to drive."

During the evening, we got an assault call. The victim was to be transported to the hospital by ambulance. Willie said, "Follow the ambulance, stay about a car length behind, but don't turn on our red lights and siren."

Willie had me chasing this ambulance, and I stayed with it. At one intersection, a car from the opposite direction came through it behind the ambulance and in front of us. I hit the brakes and our hats and briefcases flew all over the place, but we didn't hit anything.

Willie said, "Well, maybe that was some bad advice."

"Yeah, you're probably right."

We made it to the hospital.

The Department had a program called PAL, Police Athletic League, where each division sponsored athletic teams for kids. I was still on probation when I was asked by the captain, who knew I had played basketball in college, to coach a kids' team that was being formed as part of PAL. I accepted his offer, and we had a team of ten- to twelve-year-old kids from the local neighborhood.

The games were played in the Van Nuys Division area. My wife and I would take the ten kids, along with our three young sons, in the station B-wagon. We even went on the freeway to get there! The kids had a lot of fun, and we came in second in the league. That led me to first play on the Department basketball team and later coach both the Department men's and women's teams for ten years. We played in the Police Olympics and even won some championships.

I stayed at Wilshire for about four years, long enough to be there when we moved from the old station on Pico Boulevard to the new station about a block away on Venice Boulevard. I worked the old station on the very last night before the move. Most of the furnishings were already gone. I was in the station with an arrestee when morning watch was in roll call down in the basement. I didn't see it, but I immediately heard that three officers streaked the morning watch roll call. They weren't completely naked—they had something over their heads to disguise themselves. Why they did it, I don't know. Perhaps to commemorate the very last watch to work the old station. Someone told me who they were. It was the usual station pranksters.

Arthur Sewell and I were working together one night when we got a radio call of a robbery in progress at a liquor store on Adams at Rimpau. We pulled up to the rear of the store, but were still on the street. As we got out of the car, we saw this guy come around the corner running with a gun in his hand. Using a parked car for cover, I yelled for him to drop his weapon. He stopped, started to hold up his weapon as if he was going to point it at us, then dropped it to the ground.

He was a teenager. The weapon was a replica of an old western-style revolver, and there had been no robbery. We received a commendation for not shooting him, for showing restraint. I was asked why I didn't shoot. I said I never felt threatened by him even though I could clearly see he had a gun.

Had I been a younger cop without a lot of experience, it might have turned out differently. If we had shot, I believe it would have been a good shooting, but it would have been a tragic situation. The initial call was made by someone who had seen the kid in the liquor store with the gun and thought he was robbing the place. We arrested the kid.

Jimmy Darr was a sergeant at Wilshire and a good one. He told me one day, "Stokes, you need to apply for something." He was talking about me getting some more experience. I thought about what he said. Although I was now a training officer, I was getting a little tired of patrol. I put in applications to the Academy as a physical training and self-defense instructor, for a spot in Vice, and for Metro Division.

The Academy called first, and I decided to go for that. One day a week for three weeks, I had to instruct a class. The folks at the Academy wanted to see me in a teaching environment before giving me a job. The staff would show me a particular technique, for example, with the baton. I would practice it, and then I would present the technique to a recruit class the same day. The staff observed me so they could watch how I responded under pressure.

Sergeant Jim Darr

I later found out that none of the other instructors had to do that when they had applied. I thought that was a little unfair. I talked to Jimmy about it and said I was thinking about not taking the job.

He said, "That's not how you want to handle it. They have never had a black instructor assigned to that unit. They're going to test you. They want to make sure they got the right guy. You need to do it."

After my talk with Jimmy, I felt good about going there. I took the job, and I was the first black physical training instructor in the history of the Department. Working the Academy would become a major part of my career and one of the best jobs I've ever had, and I met some of the best people that I have ever known. I'm very grateful to Jimmy for that.

The Unisex Program started in late 1973, and I came up to the Academy in 1974. Prior to 1973, women could not work the field as police officers. They held the rank of policewomen and could only work juvenile, jail or administrative positions. In '73, all that changed. Women could be certified as police officers the same as men.

Jerry Stokes, first row standing, far right: first class as physical training and self-defense instructor, 1974

We lost some women at first because they could not meet the minimum standards. As a result, a separate program was initiated for women to prepare them before they came to the Academy. Karen Fleming and I ran the Academy-sponsored program using the facilities at East Los Angeles College. We taught after hours. To make sure the women understood what they were getting into; we treated them as they would be treated at the Academy. We yelled at them, made them do push-ups, everything we could think of, so they would not be shocked. It also gave them an opportunity to find out if that was what they really wanted to do. That program was extremely helpful and is still in existence today.

I was at the Academy one day when I got two calls, first from Robbery-Homicide Division and then from my wife. My wife worked new accounts at a bank on Adams at Crenshaw. There had been a robbery, and two of the suspects were killed by Metro Division officers staked out in the bank.

My wife was ready to go to lunch when a man approached her about opening an account. She directed him on what to do, and at some point, he showed her a gun and demanded that she collect money from the tellers. She did as she was told, collected the money, and handed it to the suspect. As he was turning to leave, she made a prearranged signal with Metro officers. Upon seeing my wife's signal, the officers confronted the suspect, and a shooting ensued. The officers shot the suspect and then shot a second suspect outside the bank. Two other suspects escaped. My wife witnessed the killing of the first suspect. Needless to say, not too long after that, her career as a banker ended.

Captain Bob Smitson, who was a lieutenant at Wilshire when I was there, offered me a Vice spot at Southeast, a brand new division. I accepted his offer. I had been at the Academy for a couple of years by then and was ready for a change. I would eventually work two tours in Vice during my career, first as an officer at Southeast and later as a sergeant in charge of the Vice Unit at Seventy-Seventh Division.

While a sergeant at Seventy-Seventh Vice, a bookmaker tried to bribe me. He was also running prostitutes, and we had arrested him several times. One day he called me at the station and asked to meet with me. He wanted to set up an arrangement that would be, quote, beneficial to us both. I told the captain, and we contacted Administrative Vice Division.

I wore a wire, and I met the bookmaker in a golf course parking lot outside of the division. He was by himself. I forget how much money was discussed, but he made an offer in exchange for me letting him know when we were coming to arrest him. What he wanted to do was, when he got the notification, he would put somebody without an arrest record in his position. We would get credit for an arrest and the bookmaker would not go to jail. Back then, bookmaking was a misdemeanor, and once you were arrested twice for bookmaking, it became a felony. We took him down right there in the parking lot, and he was booked for bribery.

While at Southeast, I left Vice and became a senior lead officer, the first black senior lead at Southeast Division. I worked that for a while, and then I took a position in Southeast Detectives working juvenile sex crimes. There was one big case. A mother had reported that a janitor at her daughter's school had inappropriately touched her daughter and other students. I met with the mother and her seven-year-old daughter, Camille, the sharpest young lady I had ever met. Camille told me that the janitor at her school had touched her and seven other female students. We eventually arrested the janitor, and the case went to court. The prosecuting attorney did not think Camille was going to be a good witness because of her age. In court, she was asked to point out on a large diagram of the school what the janitor did and where it took place.

Camille stood up there with a ruler and said, "This classroom right here. This is what I saw." Then she described what occurred. "And in this classroom over here, this is where he had so-and-so sit on his lap." And she pointed specifically where each allegation of sexual activity occurred and described it. I mean, it just totally impressed everyone. The janitor was convicted, and he did some prison time.

Camille did an outstanding job. I helped prepare her to testify at court, but even I was astounded by her ability to tell what had happened. Her mother brought her to the station a couple of times after the trial to thank me for my investigative effort. I've often wondered whatever happened to Camille as she grew up.

One day Frank Whitman, a sergeant at the Academy, asked me to come back and work the Academy. There was a feeling that the classes were becoming too undisciplined. I had enjoyed the Academy my first time, so I went back, not as a physical training instructor, but actually in charge of a class. I was a drill instructor. Roger Fox, Patty Fogerson, and I were each in charge of our own recruit class.

Although I was a drill instructor, I often ran with the classes. Kent Carter and I were leading a class on a run one day, and we could hear police sirens as we were coming up a hill. A Northeast Division unit was in pursuit. The car they were pursuing came around a corner, and the driver had to slow down because we were right in front of him.

Kent and I were yelling to the class to get out of the way, but the suspect hit one of the female recruits, and she landed on the hood of his car. A male recruit was also hit, but not as bad. Kent tried to reach in through the driver's window to grab the car keys, but the suspect took off. He was later caught and arrested.

I went with the female recruit to the hospital. Fortunately, she only sustained some cuts and bruises. The suspect slowing was the only thing that saved her. For a minute there, it could have been something really bad.

Patty Fogerson

I handled all the classes for the graduation ceremony because of my marching background in the military. A graduating class would march in formation to begin the ceremony. When it came time for Patty's first class to graduate, she wanted to handle her class's marching, but she didn't know how. She asked me, and I agreed to teach her. We met several mornings on the field before anyone got there. It was just the two of us. I worked with her to teach her how to call the cadence. She got it. When it came time for her class to graduate, she was scared to death, but she made it through and did a good job.

When I promoted to sergeant, I was sent to Seventy-Seventh Division. By this time, the police cars were equipped with computers, and my only exposure to computers was in a classroom setting at the Academy. The first night I was looking at this computer, and I was lost. I saw one of the kids that I had put through the Academy and said, "Give me a cheat sheet on how to use this computer."

"Sure, Sarge." He wrote some brief instructions on how to use it.

I was driving around, and the computer kept making a dinging sound. Sometime during the night, I asked another officer what the sounds were, and he said the sounds were letting me know that there were messages for me. He then showed me how to retrieve the messages. All of them were from people congratulating me on making sergeant and welcoming me to the division.

On Christmas Eve that same year, I was working morning watch. I was driving down Imperial Highway at about three o'clock in the morning. I momentarily caught a reflection of headlights in my rearview mirror, but then refocused back to the road in front of me. All of a sudden, my car was slammed from behind. The impact knocked the glasses I was wearing onto the floor. I immediately pulled over, put my glasses back on, and watched the car that hit me go around me and speed off. There was a lone male in the car, and the car was smoking from traffic accident damage.

I advised Communications that I was in pursuit of a hit-and-run driver. I pursued this car for about a mile and a half. At one point, his car gave out, and he came to a stop. I ordered him out of the car and to the ground. He complied as other officers got there and handcuffed him.

The guy was a drunk driver, and I was the last car he had hit after he struck several other cars on his way home. He was a young guy and had just come from the Christmas party where he worked. At the station, everyone was asking me if I was hurt and shouldn't I go to the hospital. I told them I was fine, that it was Christmas morning and I had young kids at home. I was stiff for a little while, but other than that, I didn't have any major issues from the accident.

Not too long after that, the Rodney King incident went down. Rodney King and two others were arrested by officers from Foothill Division at the end of a pursuit by the California Highway Patrol in the early morning of March 3, 1991. King alleged the officers used excessive force when they took him into custody. The arrest was captured on videotape and became a national incident. Because of the racial aspect involved—King was black, and the officers were white—the Department made a change in the command staff at Foothill. Paul Jefferson became the patrol captain. He called and asked me to transfer to Foothill. I accepted his request and went to morning watch.

All of the officers on morning watch were also transfers from other divisions. Even though they were experienced officers, invariably I would get a request to meet them at whatever radio call or incident they were handling. They would tell me what they had, I would ask how they wanted to handle it, and I generally agreed with what they wanted to do.

So much focus was put on the division that the officers just wanted to have a supervisor present at the call. The atmosphere was such that no one wanted to be second-guessed on how they handled things.

I was at Foothill less than a year when Paul transferred to Seventy-Seventh Division and asked me to be his adjutant. I agreed and followed him to Seventy-Seventh. In response to the not-guilty verdict in the trial of the officers involved in the Rodney King arrest, riots broke out in '92, starting in Seventy-Seventh. The initial spark was an agitated and hostile crowd that confronted responding officers at the intersection of Florence and Normandie in Seventy-Seventh Division.

At one point, the officers were ordered by the watch commander to leave the intersection. When the officers left, the crowd gained some level of confidence to destroy property and assault people. We didn't agree with the decision for the officers to leave. The officers should have been allowed to do their jobs and make some arrests if necessary. By the time you let people build up animosities, it becomes a different situation. That night and the next day there were things we would have liked to have done, but there were other folks higher up on the command staff making the decisions.

Paul and I drove through the neighborhoods at one point during the riots. Normally, when the kids saw two black officers, they would wave. But this time there was nothing in terms of friendliness. It was not a pleasant situation, but the officers during the riots handled themselves in a dignified manner and did as good a job as they could do under the circumstances.

I spent the last part of my career back at the Academy. After I had been there for a while, I figured I wasn't going to make lieutenant or go back out into the field and start over, so I thought about retiring. I had a satisfying career. It took care of my family and me financially. I worked about every job on the Department that I wanted to work.

The retirement counselor told me the difference between staying until thirty years and leaving at twenty-nine was about fifty dollars. He said if I thought I could make up the fifty dollars by retiring now, then I should do it. I told him I had some plastic bottles at home I could recycle for the money, and I retired.

Assistant Watch Commanders J.J. May, Terry Tatreau, and Jerry Stokes

Being an instructor at the Academy provided me with the skills to teach police work at a college level. I started teaching part-time at Fullerton College Police Academy while with the Department, and once I retired, I taught full-time. I just recently retired from that as well.

Rick Faulkner

Rick Faulkner

Birthplace: Longview, Washington
Career: 1970–2002
Rank at Retirement: Sergeant II
Divisions: Southwest, Seventy-Seventh, Communications, Southeast,
  Hollenbeck

What inspired me to be a policeman? I idolized and looked up to my uncle who was a Washington State Trooper. So toward the end of my tour in the Marine Corps, I applied to various police departments, including the Los Angeles Police Department. But when I saw the LAPD Academy with a setting that looked so much like Washington, where I was from, I said, "This is where I want to go." I entered the Academy on November 30, 1970.

I did well at the Academy because I was in good physical shape. I had been a boxer my last two years in the Marine Corps, and I made it to the Eleventh Naval District Boxing Championships and the military West Coast Boxing Championships. I even fought four times at the Grand Olympic Auditorium in downtown Los Angeles.

Part of our physical training was running the hill across the street from the Academy. The hill is no longer there, and the area is now part of the parking lot for Dodger Stadium. One day our instructor, Bob Smitson, said, "Hit the hill!" Well, our class got smart, and we ran to the base of the hill and slapped it. For that, he made us run up and down the hill four times. We weren't so smart after that.

Rick Faulkner, middle row, fifth from left: Academy class 1970

Upon graduation, I was sent to Southwest Division. My first night I worked with Barry Solon. We received a residential burglary in progress radio call at a house behind a business, and we were close to it. We drove into the back parking lot of the business, and I saw the suspect putting a TV into the trunk of a car. I yelled, "There he is!"

Barry yelled, "Well, go get him!"

So I bailed out of the car, the guy saw me and jumped over a wall. As I reached the wall, I remembered from the Academy, "Never go over a wall or around a corner quick." So I hesitated for a minute, and when I looked over the wall, I didn't see him. I jumped the wall and continued to look for him.

Somebody in an upstairs apartment yelled to me, "He ran out to the street!" I pointed my gun at this guy because he startled me, and then Barry came between a garage and the apartment building into the area where I was, and then I pointed my gun at Barry. Other units caught the suspect about a block away.

Barry asked me, "Is that the guy?"

"I'm not sure."

Rick Faulkner receiving diploma from Chief Ed Davis, 1970

The suspect was hot and sweaty and had scratch marks from going over the wall. Fortunately, the guy admitted he was burglarizing the residence, and we booked him. That was my first experience out in the field, my first real experience.

One of the first major traffic accidents I investigated involved a guy who was drunk driving. He hit a fire hydrant, went up onto the front yard of a house, and then hit a chain-link fence. One of the rails from the fence went through the windshield, struck this guy right on his chest and pinned him to the driver's seat. The guy was lucky; the rail did not impale him, and he wasn't really hurt. He insisted he wasn't the driver. He was sitting in the driver's seat with this pole sticking him right in the chest. There was nobody else in the car! We booked him for drunk driving.

In the early '70s, each station had officers posted outside for station security because of all the threats against policemen by various anti-war groups. One night, stationed at the back entrance on La Salle Avenue as part of the station security, I smelled smoke coming from nearby. I notified the watch commander, and then I located a house on fire near the station. When no one answered, I kicked the door in and found a man who was unconscious in the heavily smoke-filled room. It was a kitchen fire, and there was smoke going through the attic. When other officers arrived, we got him outside where he recovered. The Fire Department responded and put out the fire. I was commended for my actions.

In February 1973, at roll call one night, we received information about a young male wanted for robbery and attempted murder by Venice Division. He was driving a Chevy Impala, blue with a white top, and the car had Texas license plates. He carried a nine shot .22 caliber revolver. He was also wanted for the attempted murder of two Texas police officers. Bob McGratten and I were working together, and we were stopped at a traffic light westbound on Adams at Western. A car drove northbound through the intersection that matched the description given in roll call.

Bob said, "Isn't that the car that was read off in roll call?"

I saw the Texas plate and said, "That's it!"

Bob broadcasted that we were following the suspect. When the suspect was nearing the freeway on-ramp, we decided to light him up even though no other unit was with us yet; we didn't want him to get on the freeway. I turned on the red lights, and he immediately pulled over next to a gas station. We could see only one person in the car. I exited the car and screamed for him to turn off the car engine and throw the keys out the window of the driver's door. As I was doing that, I took my attention from him and to Bob who had moved away from the police car and taken a cover position in the gas station. Bob had the shotgun with him.

As I directed my attention back to the suspect, I heard a loud bang. Bob had fired a round, hitting the passenger door of the suspect's car. He believed the suspect had raised a gun and was going to fire at me. I fired three shots, two rounds going through the back window and one round into the left rear fender that then hit the left rear tire. The car took off, and we were in pursuit!

We pursued the suspect up to Washington Boulevard in Wilshire Division and then eastbound to Normandie Avenue. We chased the suspect southbound on Normandie and then eastbound on Twenty-Third Street.

The suspect pulled his car partially onto the private driveway of a house and bailed out, running and shooting at us. He looked like a scared rat, trying to decide which way to go. He went up onto the porch of the house as I ran to the back of his car. He came off the porch and ran in front of his car and over to a mattress leaning up against a garage. He fired several rounds at me, and I fired three at him as he tried to take cover under the mattress. My rounds hit him in the chest, and one, I was later told, went through his heart. One of his rounds hit my left arm, rendering my arm useless, although I didn't know I was hit as I fired my rounds. I then felt blood and realized I was shot in the arm.

The suspect came out from the mattress shooting, and I dove to the ground behind his car to reload. Although my left arm and shoulder were numb, I managed to crawl over to the driver's side of the car away from the side of the car where I last saw the suspect. Lying on my back, I tried to reload with one hand, cradling my gun in my chest area.

Suspect vehicle: "Lying on my back, I tried to reload with one hand..."

Rick Faulkner and Bob McGratten police vehicle

Bob engaged the suspect and put him down. I heard sirens and then police cars screeching as they braked. A sergeant ran up to me, and I told him I was hit. One of the officers applied pressure on my arm to stop the bleeding, which saved my arm. The suspect had fired eight rounds, and there was still one round in the gun. He was made on seven robberies and five counts of attempted murder in Los Angeles, and he was a federal fugitive from Texas where he had pulled a gun on two Texas officers serving a search warrant on his house.

The round severed the artery in my arm. I was lucky: the orthopedic surgeon had just come back from Vietnam and was used to doing surgeries on gunshot wounds. Besides the severed artery, my elbow was shattered, and the bone above the elbow was like sawdust. I was off for nine months, came back to light duty on the desk for a couple of months, and then went back into the field. I received the Medal of Valor because I continued to engage the suspect after I was critically wounded.

l-r Gerald "Blackie" Sawyer's wife and son, Joseph Lang, Ronald Quick, William Whyte, and Rick Faulkner: 1974 Medal of Valor recipients recognized at Dodger Stadium (Sawyer posthumously awarded)

I believe in that month, February 1973, more police officers were killed nationwide than at any other time and that 1973 was the peak year for officer firearms-related deaths, even to this day. There were five officers shot, not killed, in Los Angeles alone around the month of February: Steve Nielsen and me from Southwest, Ed Obendrauf from Harbor Division, and Rich Beardslee and Jack Rand from Wilshire.

I had responded to Beardslee and Rand's help call. They made a vehicle traffic stop of three guys and a gal. They ordered the guys out of the car, and they complied. When the officers ordered the female out, one of the guys lunged at Rich, and the fight was on. At some point, one of the guys yelled at the gal to shoot the officers. She had a gun and fired, hitting Rich in the chest. Rich tried to shoot her, but the guy he was fighting with was holding on to the barrel of his gun. The gal shot Rich again, this time in the stomach. Jack made the help call while fighting with one of the other guys, and then he was shot in the stomach too.

All the suspects fled when both officers went down. When we arrived, other units were already there. Both officers survived. Because Rich and Jack had identifying information from the suspects during the initial stop, the suspects were later caught. This shooting was one week prior to my shooting.

I had an opportunity to work Scientific Investigation Division as a fingerprint specialist for the Hillside Strangler Task Force and the Skid Row Slasher investigation. I taught myself to take prints because there was a kid who was ripping my assigned area with burglaries. He committed multiple burglaries, and I couldn't catch him. I knew who he was, and I stopped him from time to time, but I could not get the evidence to tie him to the burglaries. Finally, I learned how to do latent prints, and I made him on fingerprints on a couple of burglaries. He was convicted and served two years in CYA, the California Youth Authority, a prison for juveniles.

About two years after his conviction, I was in court, and one of this kid's buddies was there as a victim of a crime. I asked him about the kid, and he said, "Well, you've been looking at him all day."

"What are you talking about?"

This kid had been sitting in the back of the court, and I didn't recognize him because he was buffed up and grown up. When I left the court, walking through the parking structure, he saw my car and kidded, "Hey, Faulkner. I've got your license number. I'm going to burgle your house." He was laughing, and I just laughed back.

A week later, I got a call that he had been killed. He was in a shooting and was shot with a shotgun, the shotgun round putting a hole in his chest the size of a basketball. The shooter was caught. His mom called me at the station and said, "Officer Faulkner, I just wanted to thank you."

"Thank me?"

"I want to thank you for all you tried to do for my son."

She was thanking me because for several months I tried to catch this kid, I tried to talk to him, to get him out of the crime that he was doing. She knew that I was never trying to put a case on him. I could never make him on a burglary until I made him on fingerprints. He would never incriminate himself. She felt that I had tried everything I possibly could to stop him at a young age. But the more he got away with, the more he did.

One day on my way back from a print investigation, I was on the freeway in the Hollenbeck area when I saw a male running along the side between the freeway fence and a row of apartment buildings. He was carrying a gun. I put out a call over the radio. It turned out he just shot and killed a Los Angeles Sheriff's Deputy. The sheriffs were serving a search warrant on a house, and this guy was in the house, but escaped. The deputy chased him, and the suspect either shot the deputy or disarmed and shot the deputy with the deputy's own gun. The air unit showed up, and a perimeter was set. I drove back to that area and told them what I saw. The suspect escaped that day, but was found a month later in Mexico and arrested for murder.

In 1975, I became involved in the church. Everyone thought it was because of being shot several years earlier, but it was because my family was breaking up. I almost got a divorce three times. I was always coming home from drinking, and my wife was going out with the girls partying all the time. At some point, she became involved in the church and found the peace that she was looking for. I saw such a change in her, I thought, *Well, that's what I want.*

Once I became a Christian, I had to prove to others and myself that I could still be a policeman. A sergeant told me once he didn't believe a Christian could wear a badge and carry a gun. I told myself if I have to take some action requiring me to shoot at someone, our shooting policy is that we shoot to stop, not to kill. If it takes one bullet to stop him, I've done my job. If it takes fifteen bullets to stop him, I've done my job. So it never bothered me. I was good with that.

I didn't become a Department chaplain, but I did have officers that knew or heard that I was in the faith and wanted to sit down and talk with me. I was the assistant watch commander at Hollenbeck, and a retired detective came into the station one night causing a ruckus, being loud and boisterous. He had been retired for about two years. I grabbed this guy and said, "Let's go into the locker room." We sat down in the locker room, and he was four sheets to the wind.

As we talked, I realized that this detective was contemplating suicide. When he was working, he had been involved in many things.

Once he retired, those activities went away, and he became a despondent alcoholic. He felt like he was losing everything, and he didn't think there was any hope left. His presence in the station that night was, I believe, a plea for help. I talked to him for a long time and then initiated efforts through Department resources to help him.

About a year later, I saw him at a retirement party for another officer. He told me, "I want you to know you saved my life." He successfully participated in an alcohol rehabilitation program and regained a sense of self-worth.

When I became a Christian, I was in the middle of my Vice tour. When I first went to Vice, I was a drinker, smoker, and carouser. That fit in with some of the environments you encountered when conducting vice investigations. After my conversion with Christ, I no longer smoked or drank. When we worked the bars, I'd order a beer and then when they weren't looking, I'd pour my beer into a plant or something right behind me, or my partner would finish his beer and then we'd switch glasses, so I was able to work.

After a while though, it became readily apparent that a Vice assignment was not in my best interest or in the best interest of the unit. I spoke with my lieutenant, Gary Reichling, and he agreed, so I left the unit. He was very supportive.

The last five years of my career, I was an assistant watch commander at Hollenbeck Division. Once I retired, I obtained my ministerial license and became a chaplain in the prisons. I also started a chemical dependency program in Orange County and became involved in an international Christian Intervention Program.

Previously, I did some work in the prisons while I was a policeman. In fact, I remember one day long before I retired, I was visiting a guy in Chino prison as part of my ministry. I had been talking to this guy for about two years. He said to me, "You can't just do this. You've got to have some other job. What do you do for a living?"

Rick Faulkner

"I'm a cop."

"You're a what?"

"A cop."

"Do you know why I'm here?"

"No. It wasn't important to ask."

"I'm here because I assaulted a cop!"

After that, we had an understanding and became good friends.

I'm now doing the same thing as I did on the job, but I'm on the other side of the fence. Now I'm trying to get people out of jail or prison and keep them out. I hope that I can give them alternatives to turn to, rather than the insanity of doing the same thing over and over and winding up in a jail cell.

Timothy "Tim" Anderson

Birthplace: San Francisco, California
Career: 1971–2000
Rank at Retirement: Sergeant II
Divisions: Northeast, Office of the Chief of Police, Seventy-Seventh,
    Southwest, Metropolitan, Hollywood, Operations West Bureau CRASH,
    Anti-Terrorist, Training, Wilshire

While attending college in Northern California and majoring in criminology, I worked for a 911 ambulance service as a medic for the fire department, and, as part of my law enforcement degree requirement, as a reserve police officer with the local police department.

Following my graduation, I completed four years of military service, and after returning from Vietnam in December of 1970, I returned to my job at the ambulance service.

One Sunday morning while on duty at the fire station, a firefighter laid a newspaper down on the desk and pointed to a recruitment ad for a Los Angeles Police Department out-of-town recruiting program. He knew that my ultimate goal was to become a police officer and thought I might be interested. I had already applied to another agency, but at that point had not received an acceptance call or letter. I had never been to Los Angeles, and my only familiarity with the Los Angeles area was from watching the television show *Adam 12*.

The next day I called the recruiter listed in the advertisement. I was so impressed with him that I made an appointment to start the hiring process. In October of '71, I entered the Academy. In the first week, right out of the blue, I was yanked out of class and told to report to the PT staff office. I knocked on the door, and a very loud, gruff voice told me to enter. I entered and stood at attention as four instructors interrogated me.

Tim Anderson, far right holding class flag, Art Ruditsky, two officers left of Tim Anderson: Academy class, 1971

They were saying things like, "You were a military officer, so we are very concerned that you are not going to be able to take orders!" "We want you to know right up front you're not going to be in a position of leadership in your Academy class. Do you understand that?"

This little confrontation lasted for about ten minutes before I was dismissed. It turned out they did the same thing to Art Ruditsky, one of my classmates. We both had been captains in the military and were the only two in the class who had been military officers.

Although I was moved to squad leader when my first squad leader was relieved, Art was never considered for a position of leadership or increased responsibility. That was an interesting decision on the part of the staff as Art finished number one in the class and I finished number three.

Upon graduation, I went to Northeast Division where one of my training officers was John Sack. John was a senior lead and an outstanding training officer. One night about two o'clock in the morning, John was driving, and we were checking out a new construction site at San Fernando Road and Fletcher Drive. We were on a dirt surface with almost no ambient light when suddenly the front end of our car went straight into a ditch, putting us in almost a vertical position. Fortunately, we were seat-belted in as the car was literally resting on its front end. We called for a tow truck and managed to crawl out of the car.

Back at the station, the investigating sergeant asked me what I was doing at the time we went into the ditch. I said, and it's the absolute truth, "I was writing in my log." He looked at me with raised eyebrows in a questioning manner. At that point in my career, I had no idea a passenger officer's standard answer to jokingly cover themselves was, "I was writing in my log."

When I was finally off probation, George Padilla and I were assigned as regular partners. On May 17, 1974, we responded to a radio call of a naked man on the roof of the Northeast YMCA on Eagle Rock Boulevard. It was a single-story building, and, sure enough, when we arrived there was a stark naked white guy running back and forth on the roof yelling incoherently at the top of his lungs. It was broad daylight, and a crowd was gathering. While George and I stood there looking up and trying to figure out what we were going to do, the YMCA manager stepped out of the building and motioned for us to come inside. He said to me, "You guys got to see this!"

Just as I approached the manager to ask what the problem was, I heard this blood-curdling scream from behind me. I turned around, and the gentleman on the roof had jumped off the roof and landed on George! Poor George was on the ground wrestling with this naked man. Believe me, it was quite a sight. I ran over to George, and together we were able to handcuff him. As a side note, George was a second-degree black belt in Tae Kwon Do at the time of this incident, and before we took another step, he made me promise I would not tell another soul of this embarrassing predicament. Of course, I promised him I wouldn't, until now!

We walked the guy into the YMCA to see what the manager had wanted, and he pointed to the office television. It was the day of the SWAT shootout with the SLA, the Symbionese Liberation Army. The SLA was a radical group involved in murders, robberies, and bombings. Six of the SLA died when the house they were barricaded in burned.

George later transferred to Community Relations at the Office of the Chief of Police and called me to be his partner. I joined him there, and our job was to act as liaison officers with groups such as the American Indian Movement and the Jewish Defense League. While there, I attended a training day in Rampart Division where Sergeant Ron McCarthy from SWAT gave a presentation on the SLA shootout. I was mesmerized! Right then, I decided Metro, and specifically SWAT, was where I wanted to go. But to get there, I needed more patrol time. I immediately told my sergeant that I was going back to patrol. He looked at me dumbfounded and said, "Nobody leaves the Chief's Office unless they promote." Well, I did.

I transferred to Seventy-Seventh Division, where they paired me with another officer who was also new to the division. On one of our first days working together, we were driving slowly down a main street when a Los Angeles Sheriff's unit pulled alongside us. The passenger deputy looked at me and said, "What are you doing in Firestone?"

"We're not in Firestone. We're in Seventy-Seventh."

"No, you're not. You're in Firestone."

I looked at my partner, and he checked the map. He said, "We're not in Seventy-Seventh."

We thanked the deputy for his assistance and snuck back to Seventy-Seventh. I worked there for several more months before transferring to Southwest Division as a training officer.

My probationer and I were driving southbound on Estrella Avenue in a residential area late one night when we saw two males running out of a house. They saw us, turned, and ran back down the driveway of the house. We drove to the next block, which was Bonzallo Avenue, and saw them come over the backyard fence. Upon seeing us, one of them turned around and went back toward the fence. The other continued running westbound across Bonzallo. We made the decision to allow this suspect to go and focused on the suspect who doubled back.

I was driving that night, but when the first suspect doubled back, I stopped the vehicle and told my partner to drive our unit around the block and establish a perimeter. I then chased our suspect on foot as he went back over the backyard block wall. When I got to the wall, I moved several feet to my left and took a quick peak over the top of the wall. The suspect was crouched down at the base of the wall in an apparent attempt to physically engage me when I followed him. I drew down on him, climbed over the wall, took him into custody, and walked him to the police car.

Other units arrived, but the second suspect was gone. We knocked on the door of the house they ran out of and spoke with the two elderly women who lived there. Both stated they had just been raped and robbed. The other suspect was eventually caught several days later, and both were convicted and sent to prison.

To apply for Metropolitan Division, an applicant had to be the rank of a training officer and have a minimum of five years in patrol. I had about three and a half years on the Department and just over two and a half years in patrol when I decided to give it a shot. With my military, police, and fire department backgrounds, I was hoping I might get a waiver. After finishing my morning watch shift, I put on a coat and tie and went to the Georgia Street Station where Metro Division was located. I presented myself to the front desk officer and told him I wanted to submit an application for the division.

Sergeant Bob Steele, who was on light-duty status from an injury he had suffered working SWAT, came out to meet me. I had no idea he was the senior SWAT sergeant. Very nice guy, I found out, but hard nose and a physical stud. He displayed little interest in me, and there was no chitchat. I followed him to his desk where he pointed to a chair and told me to sit down. He said, "There are a certain number of qualifiers we have to get over before we go any further. What's your rank?"

"PIII."

"How many years on the job?"

I took a deep breath and said, "Almost three and a half."

Suddenly, it was like somebody had kicked him in the groin. He looked at me and said, "Almost three and a half! Do you know you have to have a minimum of five years on the Department in uniform before you can apply for Metro?"

"Yes, sir. But I think I have some qualifications that might get that waived."

"You're kidding me."

"No, sir, I'm not. I want to fill out an application."

Georgia Street police station

"Do you know where I file applications with less than five years on the job?"

"No, sir."

He pointed to the trashcan next to his desk.

As I was starting to sweat, I wondered, *What was I thinking*? He pulled out an application and handed it to me.

As I stood up and started to leave, he said, "Where are you going?"

"I'm going home to fill out my application."

"No, you're not. You're going to sit right here and fill it out now."

After I completed the application, he read it over. He said, "You do have more qualifications than the normal guy coming in. Stay here. I'll be right back."

He walked into the captain's office and was in there maybe five minutes. When he returned, he said, "The captain has given you a waiver. We'll call you when we're interested. Now, get out of here."

There were three of us that went to Metro at the same time. As the junior officer among the three, I spent my first month on station security. As it turned out, the Department cancelled the station security detail the following month. This made me the last officer to ever stand station security at Georgia Street.

The majority of the next five months I spent on the Skid Row Slasher detail. There had been several murders of transients in the downtown, Hollywood, and Wilshire areas, where the suspect slashed the throat of his victims with a knife. It was wintertime, and it was cold and miserable. Even in the rain, we were out there on stakeout. Those were long nights, but nothing happened. The Skid Row Slasher, Vaughn Greenwood, was eventually caught and convicted.

After six months, I was transferred to SWAT where I spent the next five and a half years. My partner was Jimmy Dahl, a team leader. We had a general rule that whichever team leader got to a call-up first, he handled the call. One day while we were in training, a barricaded suspect situation developed in Southwest Division. Jimmy wanted to get there first so he could be in charge. But while we were en route, we were directed to pick up the SWAT truck at Georgia Street Station. Although the truck had emergency equipment on it, it was slow and cumbersome. We called it the "Rambling Wreck from Georgia Tech."

Tim Anderson, left, Jimmy Dahl: Metro Division inspection, 1975

Because we had to go to the station, Jimmy was going to be delayed. He dropped me off, then drove furiously to get to the call-up first. I drove the truck, which obviously made me the last guy on the scene.

When I got there, I saw Jimmy looking a little depressed. I asked him, "What's our assignment?"

"We don't have one. We're the only two without an assignment."

So now, we're both depressed. All of a sudden, Sergeant Mike Hillmann stepped out the front door of the building where the barricaded suspect was and motioned Jimmy to come to him. Jimmy said to me, "Looks like you're the only guy without an assignment. I got one!"

Now I'm even more depressed. Jimmy hurried over to Mike, who handed him an electrical cord for a floodlight and said, "Plug this in when I tell you!"

I looked over at Jimmy and said, "Okay, big man, how'd that work out for you?"

We both laughed.

Very early one morning, I got a call and was advised that an officer had been shot while investigating a silent robbery alarm at a fast food restaurant in Devonshire Division. A suspect, armed with a handgun, tied up two employees before the restaurant was opened. When the manager arrived, the suspect forced her to open the money safe, which activated a silent robbery alarm.

Patrol officers Zlatko Sintic and Andrew Cordova responded to the call. The officers pulled into a parking lot behind the restaurant. Cordova moved to check out a trash bin area as Sintic went to the employees' back door, which was ajar. The suspect heard the officers and confronted Sintic at the door. He fired a round at Sintic striking Sintic in his elbow as Sintic fired a round. Sintic's round missed the suspect, and he was unable to fire again. His arm incapacitated, Sintic turned to seek cover as the suspect fired again, striking Sintic in his left side. As Sintic reached the corner of the building, the suspect fired once more, striking Sintic in the back and causing him to collapse in the parking lot.

Cordova, unable to shoot initially because Sintic was in his line of fire, fired at the suspect forcing him back into the building. Officer Larry Mudget pulled Sintic out of the line of fire, and transported him to the hospital. Unfortunately, Sintic's injuries were so severe he did not survive.

When I arrived, Sintic had been rescued and was en route to the hospital. Once a plan was formulated, Sergeant Mike Hillmann moved an entry team into the rear of the building in an attempt to establish communication with the suspect, who was now in the basement with the manager as a hostage. Mike negotiated the release of the hostage, but the suspect refused to surrender and ultimately took his own life.

I was assigned to cover a side door, which, other than the rear door, was the only other option for the suspect to exit the building. My guidance was that if the suspect attempted to exit through this door, I would prevent him from running into the parking lot. This was my very first call-up and my baptism into SWAT.

Metro Division then developed a hostage negotiation program where all primary negotiators would be SWAT officers. I was fortunate enough to be selected as one of the first operators to go through the training and had the opportunity to act as the primary negotiator on a number of incidents.

One of the incidents was in San Pedro, where a disgruntled employee took a taxi company manager as a hostage and threatened to kill her if his demands were not met. I think it is fair to say that most SWAT officers would rather work the tactical side of an operation as opposed to being a negotiator. However, on this particular incident, my number came up. I was the primary negotiator and was able to assist in concluding the incident with the hostage being rescued and the suspect being taken into custody without incident.

It was an interesting event because I was able to set up in the same building where the hostage was barricaded and actually observe the takedown as it occurred. After he was in custody and walked out of the building to a police cruiser, I was able to listen to him scream and holler about how I had lied to him. This gave me a completely new perspective on how effective a negotiator could be, and I looked forward to the next opportunity I would have to work the position.

One of the more tragic events I remember was when Jimmy and I responded to a robbery in progress/barricaded hostage situation at Ralph's Market at Third Street and Vermont on New Year's Day 1981. When we got there, we were advised that an armed robbery suspect had taken the manager hostage and was barricaded in the manager's office. This office was on the second floor of the building with multiple windows that overlooked the main part of the store. Once deployed, I was responsible for covering the office windows.

This was a particularly hard situation for us because there was only one approach, a stairwell, to the office where the suspect and hostage were located. And harder yet, the suspect had the intercom system on, and we had to hold our positions while listening to the store manager begging for his life.

One of the suspect's demands was that we provide him a helicopter to fly him out of the area. The demand was agreed to, and a helicopter was landed in the parking lot directly in front of the store. Our plan, of course, was that if he actually selected this option, he would not make it to the helicopter.

Unfortunately, while our negotiator was doing his best to resolve the situation, we heard two shots over the intercom. When there was no immediate response from the suspect or hostage, our entry team executed a crisis entry and forced their way through the office door, which the suspect had locked and barricaded. When the team breached the door, they found the hostage and suspect dead. For some unknown reason, the suspect simply decided to execute the hostage and kill himself. Needless to say, we were all devastated by this outcome. But after our incident debrief, we had to pack up our gear, return to the street and finish our shift.

When I first went to SWAT, Ron McCarthy was one of my sergeants. Ron was a great guy, but he often came up with some of the strangest ideas. One day he told us, he had an idea that for our next physical fitness test we were going to run through Death Valley. Some of us were stunned, while others said, "No, we're not."

And he said, "Yes, we are!"

On March 21, 1979, we paired up to run individual legs of six miles across the 116.3 miles of Death Valley. We started the run at Scotty's Castle at midnight on a freezing night, and finished sixteen hours and forty-five minutes later in blistering heat. Our feat was recognized as a world record by the Guinness Book of World Records, and we were happy it was over.

Tim Anderson, front row, fourth from right, Ron McCarthy, front row, third from left: Metro Division Death Valley Team, 1979

Tim Anderson, Death Valley

Los Angeles County Sheriff's Department Special Enforcement Bureau, which was that department's SWAT Team, asked us if we planned to run it the following year. Coupled with a few derogatory comments about our team, the gauntlet was laid down. Although SEB ran a very strong race, we persevered and won! After four or five years in Death Valley, the race became so big that we had to leave the park and find a new course. Thus began the Baker to Vegas Relay, which today draws over 200 teams.

When I promoted to sergeant, I called Captain Pat McKinley, the commanding officer of Seventy-Seventh Division, and asked him if I could come to his division. Pat was my first SWAT lieutenant, and he made that happen. Department policy at the time was that new sergeants spend one year in their first division of assignment and then they are transferred to a second division. At the end of my probation at Seventy-Seventh, as a supervisor, I was on the transfer list to Hollywood Division. On my last day, however, I opened my locker and discovered that everything but my uniform, boots, and equipment belt had been taken out. Whoever raided my locker left me one uniform shirt and one pair of pants. As I was trying to figure out what was going on, I saw that my sergeant's stripes had been painted with red lipstick and that my uniform shirt reeked of perfume. I thought, *Okay, if they went to this much trouble, I'll wear it like it's nobody's business. We'll see who flinches first.*

Since I was the watch commander for the shift, it was my duty to conduct roll call and read off assignments. Prior to roll call, however, I walked around the station conducting my perfunctory watch commander duties. Not one officer asked me why I smelled like perfume or why my sergeant stripes were red.

As I entered roll call, I noticed that there was a small group of senior officers, all of them miscreants, sitting in the back row with wicked smiles on their faces. Then detectives and civilians began entering the back of the room. Suddenly, and without warning, in walked a male dancer dressed in a red and green outfit blowing a kazoo. He walked right up to me, put his hand on my arm, and said,

"My, you have big muscles. Welcome to Hollywood, Sergeant Anderson!"

"Welcome to Hollywood, Sergeant Anderson!"

I later found out that my fellow officers hired this "gentleman" to welcome me to Hollywood Division. Trays of food were then brought into the room, and the rest of roll call was spent holding a going-away party. It also turned out that several officers had made prior arrangements for me to take the night off to go to dinner with them. It was quite a send-off! The following day I was transferred to Hollywood Division.

One Saturday night in Hollywood while working morning watch, I was assigned a ride-along who was interested in becoming a police officer. Around one o'clock in the morning, while eating a hamburger over the hood of the police car, a burglary in progress, any unit to handle radio call was broadcast to all Hollywood units. While the dispatcher was waiting for a unit to pick the call up, it was upgraded to an attempt murder in progress. I was about six blocks away from the call, and when no units acknowledged the call, I showed myself responding.

As I approached the location on Cherokee Avenue, I observed a crowd of about fifteen people standing in the street in front of the residence when a male in his thirties ran out of a small city park just north of the location. He was signaling me that he wanted to talk. He told me that a man had been standing in front of the house, just south of the park, yelling to an occupant inside that he was going to kill her. The man was holding a very large knife and was waving it back and forth. He said the man then walked down the driveway and was now trying to break into the back door of the residence.

I told my ride-along he needed to get out of my vehicle and find a place of safety. I approached the residence on foot. I could clearly hear the suspect trying to break into the back door, while he was also yelling at the occupant inside. It was very clear to me that I had only two choices: take the suspect down before he was able to gain entry, or follow him into the residence and try to stop him from killing the occupant. The choice was clear. At this point, no other Hollywood units had acknowledged they were responding, so I advised Communications of my situation and requested assistance.

Prior to moving down the driveway towards the rear of the residence, I noticed that there was a large amount of construction material in the driveway and that a detached garage sat about thirty feet to the rear of the house and at the end of the driveway. There was a little ambient light from a single light fixture on the front of the garage. There was a wooden fence between the house and the garage, which I assumed the suspect had climbed over, separating me from him and the back porch of the house.

I moved down the driveway and saw the suspect at the back door. I identified myself as a police officer and ordered him to stop what he was doing and show me his hands. He looked directly at me over the top of the fence. After hesitating for a few seconds, he was suddenly standing in front of me with a very large knife in his hand.

This sudden move surprised me because I thought he would have to climb back over the fence to get to me. What I did not see, or anticipate, was that he had torn several wooden slats out of the fence and the opening was hidden by a stack of construction materials. He then looked directly at me and said that he was going to kill me.

I backed up several steps and ordered him to drop the knife, but he began aggressively moving towards me, continuing to tell me he was going to kill me. I fired one round that struck him in his chest and knocked him to the ground as if someone had swept his feet out from under him. It was not until I had finished handcuffing him that my first backup unit arrived.

Although the suspect was critically injured, he did survive. He knew the lady inside the residence, and they had had a dispute. When I went to court on his preliminary hearing, he pled guilty to trying to kill me. My ride-along did become a police officer, and the last time I talked to him, he was a sergeant on a local police department.

Mike Hillmann, one of the new lieutenants assigned to Anti-Terrorist Division, formerly Organized Crime and Intelligence Division, called me to see if I might be interested in working for him for the 1984 Olympics. I had worked for Mike in SWAT and he's one of those types of individuals you don't say no to. He's just outstanding in every way. So for the Olympics, I was assigned to the Anti-Terrorist Operations Center with the FBI at their office in West Los Angeles.

Following the Olympics, I transferred back to Hollywood patrol night watch. One evening I was directed to meet four detectives from a local police department who were in Hollywood to serve an arrest warrant on two contract murder suspects who lived in an apartment in our division.

I met the four detectives, who were wearing raid jackets, in a parking lot on Hollywood Boulevard. After confirming their identity, reading the warrant, and reviewing their plan, I requested a two-man patrol unit to accompany us, just in case things did not go as planned and we had to assist. The address was on the second floor of a very nice 1940's apartment house just off Hollywood Boulevard.

As many plans do, everything runs smoothly until it doesn't. The plan was that if the suspects complied with the detectives and allowed them to enter the apartment, they would be taken into custody and everything would be over. If the suspects refused to comply and allow entry, they would be contacted by telephone. If they still refused to comply, we would turn it into a barricaded suspect situation, and LAPD would take over.

When one of the suspects opened the door, the first detective identified himself, and the suspect immediately tried to slam the door shut. A second detective, who was the size of a Sherman tank, pushed the first detective aside and rammed the door, forcing his way into the apartment. As he entered the apartment, the door shut and locked behind him.

While I was trying to digest this turn of events, the gunfight started. The detective was armed with a .357 Magnum revolver, and both suspects were armed with .45 caliber automatic pistols. They were all firing! Things were not going as planned.

I had to assume that the officer inside the apartment was most likely down and wounded. But to force open the door in the middle of a gunfight was not smart.

We did not have handheld radios, and finding an apartment door unlocked, I used a telephone to request help. At one point, the detective inside yelled through the wall that he was not wounded, that he had shut himself inside a bedroom, and that he was out of ammunition. He told us both suspects were wounded, but still armed. We then forced our way into the apartment and took both suspects into custody. Both suspects sustained severe gunshot wounds and were almost totally incapacitated.

As my officers were clearing the rest of the apartment, I heard a loud scream from one of the officers in the bathroom. Assuming the worst, I quickly moved to his position and was stopped in my tracks when I observed a very large boa constrictor snake that was so large, it almost filled the bathtub. It just laid there looking at us, wondering why we were intruding on him. I quietly told the officer to back out and close the door, and we would deal with the snake later.

In the hallway closet, I noticed a bullet hole. It looked like it went through and into an adjacent apartment. Hoping that no one was injured in that apartment, I knocked on the door. A young man let me into his apartment, and we observed that a bullet had come through the wall of his bedroom and lodged in the opposite wall. Right below the hole was the young man's bed. He had been asleep in his bed when the shooting began. If his head had been on a pillow, he would have taken the round right in his head. This time, luck was on our side.

Before I left the apartment, I remembered the snake. I asked the young man if he knew the two men next door and if he knew they had a snake. He said that he did and that he played with their snake all of the time. He even called the snake by name. I explained to him that we were taking both of his friends to the hospital for medical treatment and asked if he would mind taking care of the snake. He said that he would be more than happy to. With that, I escorted him to the bathroom where he enthusiastically picked up the snake from the bathtub and walked back to his apartment. Problem solved. The outside agency handled the officer-involved-shooting investigation, and I covered the incident with a sergeant's log entry. It was just another night in Hollywood!

From Hollywood, I worked Southwest Division, the Academy, and Wilshire Division, before I ultimately went back to Metro Division as a supervisor with the K-9 Unit.

One of the more memorable incidents I handled while assigned to K-9 occurred while I was working the evening shift. Shortly after starting our shift, I received a call from a West Los Angeles Detective supervisor requesting our assistance. He was working a multi-agency task force that was targeting a robbery suspect who had committed multiple takeover supermarket robberies since his release from jail thirty days prior. He told me they had received information that the suspect was going to hit another market that evening. They had him under surveillance and were going to attempt to take him into custody once he committed the robbery.

Unfortunately, later that evening, they lost him during the surveillance, and he hit a different market from the one their informant provided. I was re-contacted by the detective who said they were going to stake out the suspect's residence on Fourth Avenue on the off chance he might return there. He asked me if we could continue to stand by, and I told him we would.

Several hours later, there was an officer-involved shooting in progress on Fourth Avenue. We responded, and when we got there, the lead detective explained that a team observed the suspect park in front of his residence. He exited his car carrying a bag in one hand, which turned out to be the money stolen in the robbery from that evening, and a handgun in the other hand. When they attempted to take him into custody, the suspect began firing at them. A running gun battle ensued. The suspect escaped, and the detectives set a perimeter and requested help in searching for him. I divided my K-9 units into two search teams.

Since I was short one K-9 officer, I assumed the position of rear guard on the second team. My team consisted of Doug Roller with his dog, Keno, Adam Bercovici, and Kevin McClure.

After we had been searching for about thirty minutes, Keno alerted to the suspect's scent at the back of a residence across Fifth Avenue. The residence was burned out. As we entered the backyard, I was watching the residence as the rear guard, while Keno moved to a large stand of ivy on the back fence that stretched the full length of the back yard. All of a sudden, the suspect fired multiple rounds from within the ivy at almost point blank range. We could not physically see him because he was hidden in the thick ivy.

Doug and Adam engaged him, both firing multiple rounds where they saw muzzle flashes. The suspect stopped firing. Doug yelled for the suspect to surrender. Rather than surrender, he fired more rounds. We engaged him again until he stopped firing. There were no more shots coming from the ivy. Amazingly, he missed every one of us. Kevin and I crawled into the ivy, located his hiding spot, and it was immediately evident that he was dead.

On the first day of the Rodney King riots in '92, my first assignment out of the command post was for my strike team to escort the Los Angeles Fire Department to a multiple-structure fire at Slauson Avenue and Crenshaw Boulevard. When we arrived, we found that an entire shopping center was on fire, except for a market that had been saved by the sprinkler system. The market had been looted.

We protected fire units for about two hours, until the fires had burnt themselves out and it was safe to secure the scene. Prior to advising the command post that my strike team was available for reassignment, I directed several of my units to search the inside of the market to see if there were still any looters inside. They found five looting suspects hiding inside.

When they brought them out, one looked at me and told one of the officers he knew me and wanted to talk. As I followed the officer to the suspect's location, I could hear him shouting, "Colonel Anderson, Colonel Anderson, you have to help me!" I immediately recognized the suspect as an ex-Marine who had been assigned to one of the battalions I had commanded in the Marine Corps Reserve. It was interesting that he was asking for my help because his performance was so substandard that I had him administratively discharged from the Corps several years earlier.

This individual went on to explain that he had lent his car to a friend prior to the start of the riots and that this friend had contacted him and told him he had left it in the parking lot of the market. When I pointed out that the car was full of food from the market and that he was hiding in the market when my officers found him, he just gave me a blank stare. You should have heard him scream when I told my team to book him. Sometimes you just gotta love being a cop!

On the morning of January 17, 1994, at about 4:30 a.m., I had just returned home from assisting SWAT with a call-out in downtown Los Angeles when an earthquake hit. It hit my house like a freight train. After checking my house for damage and confirming that my gas line did not rupture, I turned everything over to my wife and two young daughters and headed for the Metro Division assembly point at the Academy. Since all of my K-9 units were still on the freeways headed home, they immediately turned around, and we were the first to meet there. Once assembled, I advised our Metro dispatcher I had formed a strike team and was headed to the San Fernando Valley, the epicenter of the earthquake.

We reached the Valley just as the sun was coming up. The devastation we observed was right out of a war movie. Electricity was out, water mains were broken, portions of buildings were collapsed and others were on fire.

Our primary mission was to establish a law enforcement presence in an attempt to maintain order. Fortunately, it was a weekend, and almost everyone was at home in bed. We observed no looting or illegal activity and made no arrests.

After we had been in the Valley for several hours, we were approaching a major intersection when a building in front of us suddenly exploded, blowing debris across the roadway directly in front of my vehicle. The building that exploded appeared to be a restaurant, and we had no way of knowing if it had been occupied.

Tim Anderson, front, second from left: K-9 Unit, 1998

We immediately notified the Fire Department. John Hall took half of our team and ran around to the rear of the structure in an attempt to find the shut-off valve for the gas line. I took the other half to check the inside of the building. The whole front of the building was missing, portions of it were on fire, and the smoke was too heavy to see through. Two or three of us got on our hands and knees and crawled into the restaurant looking for survivors, while a couple other officers tried to extinguish the fire with handheld fire extinguishers we carried in our cars.

We were fortunate that the restaurant had not been occupied at the time of the explosion. The Fire Department arrived just as we were loading up to continue our patrol. They apologized for taking so long to get to us, but explained that there were simply not enough assets to handle all of the calls for service.

Three or four hours after this incident, we received a call to respond to an apartment complex to assist the Fire Department in searching for survivors of a damaged building. When we arrived, we were briefed that the complex was a three-story building that had pancaked into a two-story building and that there were multiple fatalities.

We formed three K-9 search teams and worked the building for the next several hours. Although we found a number of bodies, we did not find any survivors. In all, sixteen residents died. They were all on the first floor.

Jack Schonely with Gundo, Linda Travis, and Tim Anderson: "...we did not find any survivors."

Fifty-seven people died in the earthquake, and more than 8,700 were injured. Property damage was estimated to be between $20 and $25 billion, and the economic lost around $50 billion, making it one of the costliest natural disasters in U.S. history.

On February 28, 1997, I had gone to sleep at 5:00 a.m. after finishing my regular K-9 shift. At approximately 9:30 a.m., my pager activated, indicating I was to call the Metro dispatcher as quickly as possible. When I called, the desk officer directed me to respond to the Bank of America at Laurel Canyon Boulevard and Archwood Street in North Hollywood, where a robbery was in progress with shots being fired by multiple suspects. He added that there were hostages in the bank and officers were down. He then hung up the phone.

When I turned on my police radio, it sounded like World War III had started. It only took me fifteen minutes to get to the bank. Tom Runyun, our SWAT lieutenant, brought me up to speed on what had happened. He also told me that a citizen had reported seeing a third suspect who she believed had entered a single-family residence several blocks from the bank. The information she provided was considered solid enough that a team of SWAT officers had been sent to the location. Tom directed me to meet them and provide whatever assistance they needed. I spent the next several hours at the location, but we determined that if a suspect had been there, he fled prior to our arrival.

As the morning progressed, both suspects, Lawrence Phillips and Emil Matasareanu, were dead, Phillips self-inflicted and Matasareanu died in a hellacious shootout with Metro officers Donnie Anderson, Rick Massa, and Steve Gomez. The hostages in the bank were rescued, and twelve wounded LAPD officers were transported to local hospitals. Again, there was information on an outstanding third suspect. The information seemed reliable enough that a search of the surrounding area was conducted.

The area we were directed to search covered approximately twenty-eight square blocks. Search responsibilities were assigned to Metro Division with combined SWAT and K-9 teams conducting the initial search, and other Metro officers would follow-up with a detailed search. We were also assisted by the Los Angeles County Sheriff's Department

Special Enforcement Bureau SWAT team. We concluded our search near midnight without finding any evidence of a third suspect.

For approximately ten years, I was a part of the Department's Underwater Dive Unit. Although most of our work was pure drudgery while diving under limited to no visibility conditions, one dive operation stands out in my memory. Although the City of Los Angeles has over five hundred miles of shoreline, which includes lakes and oceanfront property, this dive was in the city of Redondo Beach.

The dive took place just north of the Redondo Beach Pier where a floating restaurant boat had previously been anchored. A medical doctor residing in Los Angeles committed a murder by shooting his victim with a handgun. Following the murder, he and a friend drove to Redondo Beach where he threw the murder weapon into the bay near the restaurant boat.

LAPD homicide detectives located the suspect's friend who had witnessed him dispose of the murder weapon. The homicide detectives asked the dive unit to try to recover it. The only problem was it had been over two years since the doctor had thrown the weapon into the bay, and during that period, the restaurant boat had been sunk by a large storm that had devastated the Redondo Beach area. On top of that, the boat had been salvaged and moved out of the bay, limiting our chance of finding the weapon to almost zero.

Not to be daunted, however, we put a plan together to conduct a detailed grid search of the area to see what we could find. Halfway through the second day of our search, I had just finished my dive and was standing on the shore when a diver surfaced giving a thumbs up, indicating he had just found a handgun. Since the gun had been in salt water for so long, we had to put it into a special container and transport it to the lab still in salt water. It fit the description of the handgun provided by the detectives.

We held our breath for the next several weeks until the case detective called and told us that it had been confirmed as the murder weapon and that a solid link between the doctor and the weapon had been established. The doctor was found guilty of the murder and went to prison. More kudos for the dive unit.

Tim Anderson, back row, third from right: LAPD Underwater Dive Unit, 1989

During the Rodney King riots, after spending the first night in the field, I went home to quickly shower and shave and then return to the command post. As I was shaving, my wife looked at me and asked, "How do you do it? They are calling not only the police officers terrible names, but even the fire fighters, and shooting at anybody and everybody." I replied, "Because there are good people living down there!"

That is what police officers do every day: They fight the fight for those who can't stand up for themselves. This is a great profession. It is a calling. And it was a privilege to work with the finest men and women who are the Los Angeles Police Department. I would have had it no other way.

Enoch "Mac" McClain

Birthplace: New Orleans, Louisiana
Career: 1971–2002
Rank at Retirement: Detective III
Divisions: Newton, Metropolitan, Robbery-Homicide, Seventy-Seventh,
    Organized Crime Intelligence

It was originally my intent to have a career in the Marine Corps. After one tour in Vietnam, I received orders to return, but my brother was already serving in Vietnam as a Marine, and if you had a brother serving over there, you were exempt from going. I became an instructor teaching tactics and ambushes to the guys going to Vietnam. I liked instructing and asked to go to drill instructor's school. They told me I could go, but first I had to go back to Vietnam because they needed sergeants. My brother was already home, and I only had nine months left of my second enlistment, so I said, "No."

A government program called Project Transition provided training for a job outside of the Marine Corps so you could make a living. I had been in the military police, so when I looked down the Project Transition list of civilian jobs and saw law enforcement, I thought that maybe I'd try that.

The training was at a local college and was essentially a police academy. The instructors were from various police departments, including the Los Angeles Police Department. On the weekends, we would visit different police agencies, and on one weekend, we went to Los Angeles. While at the Los Angeles Police Academy, they gave our class the opportunity to take the written entrance exam. Only two of us passed, and we were given an oral interview right then and there! I was the only one who passed the oral interview.

Mac McClain receiving diploma from Chief Ed Davis, 1971

After having completed the training at the college, I received a phone call from the Marine Corps advising me that LAPD had scheduled me for their January class.

The Academy was a change for me. In the Marine Corps, I had been the one doing the screaming and yelling at people. Now I had somebody yelling and screaming at me. That took some adjustment, but I managed to get through it.

While on probation at Newton Division, I worked with Dennis Mahle, a young policeman too, and a good one. One day we received a radio call of a robbery that had just occurred at a liquor store. The name of the suspect, Elbert, was also broadcast over the radio. Dennis looked at me and said, "I know Elbert. I arrested him for burglary." We talked to the owner of the liquor store, and he said Elbert robbed him of some liquor.

Elbert lived in an apartment above the liquor store. We went and knocked on Elbert's door. He opened it and had two women in his bed, and all three were naked. Dennis said, "You're under arrest for robbery." Elbert started whining as he was putting on his clothes. Stalling, he pretended he couldn't find his shoes. Dennis said, "Elbert, you have had enough time to find your shoes. You can go without them." We handcuffed Elbert, placed him in the back seat of the police car, and took him to the station.

I was driving, and Dennis was in the back seat with Elbert. We arrived at the station, and I advised Communications that we were out to the station. The dispatcher didn't acknowledge. I said it again. I was sitting in the car with one foot out, waiting for Communications to acknowledge. Dennis said, "I'm going to take Elbert inside and put him in the holding cell."

While walking Elbert through the parking lot, Dennis realized he had forgotten his notebook. He came back to the car and left Elbert standing at the back of the car. Dennis opened the front passenger door, reached in, and grabbed his notebook. As he stood up, I heard him yell, "Dammit, he's gone!" I thought he was kidding. We looked under every car in the station parking lot, but we could not find him.

Dennis said, "We're going to have to report this."

"Yeah, I know."

We told the watch commander, and he broadcast a description of Elbert, "No shoes, handcuffed, last seen running...." A lady called the station and said she had been offered ten dollars to cut handcuffs off a man with no shoes. One police unit parked around the corner from Elbert's apartment and waited. Sure enough, Elbert came running. He ran from the thirteen hundred block of South Central Avenue down to Fortieth Street where he lived. He had to have been running in record time, but we got him.

After the internal investigation, Dennis and I received four relinquished days off, which meant we worked four days without compensation. When the captain was advising us of our punishment, Dennis told him that it was his fault and that I should not take any days. The captain said that it didn't work that way, that we were both responsible. I had been worried that I was going to lose my job, so four days sounded good to me.

Art Zorrilla and I were handling a call when we heard "Officer needs help, shots fired." We were reasonably close, so we flipped the car around and got there quick. We saw two plainclothes police cars and a black-and-white police car stopped behind another car. The plainclothes detectives were in a shootout with three suspects who were

Newton Division police station (rebuilt 1965)

still in their car. One uniformed officer, Dennis Kalpakoff, wounded and bleeding, was lying down underneath the rear bumper of the suspects' car. His partner, Lonney Maxwell, and two detectives were shooting at the suspects' car to protect detectives Donald Beasley and Ed Brimer as they dragged Dennis to safety. The shooting stopped just after we arrived.

The three suspects were all Black Panthers. The detectives and the black-and-white unit followed them from a Black Panthers meeting where, it was learned later, the meeting was to discuss plans to kill a police officer. The detectives wanted Dennis and Lonney to stop the car so that they could identify the three suspects. The shooting started when Dennis was approaching the driver's side of the car and one of the suspects shot him in the arm and leg. Dennis' arm was pretty messed up, and he never worked as an officer again due to his injuries.

There had to be sixty to seventy bullet holes in the suspects' car. I kept thinking the suspects had to be dead when the shooting stopped. Two other officers and I made the initial approach to the car. Two of the suspects were in the front seat, and the third one was in the back. There was blood everywhere. All three were shot multiple times, but they survived. I was still on probation, but the situation was not shocking to me. I was in a firefight in Vietnam where twenty people were killed in a matter of minutes, so I was able to function even though I was new to police work.

Initially, the detectives got a bad hat for what happened when a rumor spread that they had not told Dennis and Lonney that the suspects were Black Panthers. I was with Dennis at the hospital, and I heard him say that the detectives told them that they believed the suspects were Black Panthers and that they were possibly armed. So whenever I heard someone say otherwise, I would try to correct him. Don and Ed ultimately received the Medal of Valor for their actions. Lonney should have been recognized for his actions as well. The suspects were later convicted and sent to prison.

One night I was working with Tim Moss, and we were driving on Long Beach Boulevard. It was one o'clock in the morning, and we were the only car on the road. Tim was driving when we saw car headlights coming from the opposite direction. As the car came closer, something told me we needed to stop that car.

I told Tim, "We got to stop that car."

"What?"

"We got to stop that car."

"I thought we were going to get off on time."

The car passed us as we were arguing, and finally Tim said, "Okay, Mac. You better be right about this."

Long Beach Boulevard had railroad tracks running down the center of the street, so we had to drive to the next place we could make a U-turn. We made the U-turn and went seventy miles an hour to catch the car. We hit the red lights, and the car pulled over and stopped. Suddenly, the back passenger door of the car opened, and a partially nude woman came running out. She ran up to me crying and yelling, "Thank you, God. Thank you, Jesus." She was hanging on to me. I didn't know what had happened, but I knew it wasn't anything good.

We got the four suspects out of the car and handcuffed them. We found out she was a nurse who had gotten off work at Los Angeles County Hospital and was waiting for a bus to go home. These guys pulled up and asked her if she wanted a ride. She told them no. One of them got out of the car, pulled a knife, and forced her into the car. She said that in the car they were discussing where to take her as they were stripping her of her clothes. The driver saw our police car and said, "Here come the pigs."

The others told the driver not to do anything that would give us a reason to stop them, so he slowed the car down. She said she started praying that we would turn around and stop them. She told me she never prayed that hard in her life. They sped up once it looked like we were going to continue away from them. To this day, I don't know what it was that told me we needed to stop that car. We arrested them for kidnapping and assault. I will always remember her saying, "I'm so thankful to be alive."

Tim Moss was my favorite partner at Newton. He had been a Marine and was like a brother. We still talk to each other periodically.

One night a sergeant got a hold of Tim and me and asked us to meet him at this house. At the house, he said, "There's a lady here, and she's crazy. She's been beating up on members of her family, but she's calm now. The family will take her to the hospital psych ward. I want you to follow them." I questioned him on the family transporting her, but the sergeant was insistent.

Tim Moss

We followed the family. The lady was in the back, seated between two family members. As we entered onto the freeway, all of a sudden, there were brake lights and the rear passenger door opened. The lady jumped out of the car holding a clump of hair. We found out later she pulled it from her mother's head as she leapt from the car.

We were on an overpass, and the lady started running toward the railing. Tim stopped our car as I jumped out and ran up to her. She was trying to go over the railing, but she was too big and had trouble getting her leg over. Had she jumped, she would have landed in traffic below. I grabbed her, and she was pulling me with her as she continued to try and go over the railing. Fortunately, Tim reached us, and we managed to take her to the ground and handcuff her. Once she calmed down, we put her in our car and took her to the psych ward.

When we walked her into the psych ward, I told the female Los Angeles Sheriff's Deputy that the lady had been violent and warned her not to take the handcuffs off her. The female deputy looked at her male partner, who told me to take off her handcuffs. I tried to warn them again, "I really don't want to take the cuffs off because I've seen how she acts." But the male deputy insisted.

There were two secure doors with a pass way in between. I placed the lady in the pass way, took off her handcuffs, and then stepped back. The door closed between us, and then the inner door opened. The male deputy approached her, and she hit him in the face and knocked him out cold. I mean cold. The alarm bells went off. Tim and I were yelling to the female deputy to let us in, and she pressed the button that opened the door. The door opened, and we entered and helped get the lady handcuffed again. The male deputy was lying on the ground, his face all red and his nose bleeding. I said, "I told you she was dangerous."

Back at the station Tim and I told the sergeant what had happened, including her almost taking me over the rail and onto the freeway. When confronted with his order to let the family drive this woman to the hospital, he said, "I never told you any such thing." We were stunned.

Pat McKinley was one of the watch commanders at Newton. A lieutenant position opened at Metropolitan Division, and Pat got the job. Before he left Newton, he told me I should apply to Metro. I did and made it. When I first applied, other black officers told me that I should not go to Metro that, in their opinion, black officers did not last there. I even had some white officers tell me that out of concern for me. I told them all that as a nineteen-year-old I led a squad of Marines in Vietnam. If I could do that, then I could sure as heck work Metro.

At my oral interview for Metro, I had sergeants sitting across from me with ribbons and medals all over their chests. One asked me, "What makes you think you're good enough to be one of us?"

That kind of angered me, but I very calmly said, "I've seen everybody that you have in this division, and I don't think you have anybody any better than I am." Just like that.

The sergeants started chuckling, and one of them stood up, reached across the table, shook my hand, and said, "Welcome to Metro."

I was treated great during my time at Metro. I loved the division, and I loved the guys that I worked with there. I'm still friends today with some of the officers that I worked with at Metro.

This next story doesn't end up in a shooting, but it sure could have. Frank Risca and I were driving down the street one day, and a guy flagged us down. He said there was a guy up in his apartment that had a gun and was threatening to kill people. As we got out of our car, he pointed to an upstairs apartment and shouted, "There he is!"

The guy came out of the apartment and walked down the exterior stairs to the ground level. We saw that he was holding a gun in his hand next to his right pants pocket. He was unsteady and obviously had been drinking or was on drugs. We ordered him to drop the gun. He did not comply with our command and kept the gun pointed downward at his side. We continued to order him to drop the gun, but he would not comply.

I told Frank that I would try to get to the side of him. I went behind the police car and then over to a hedge near where the guy was standing. I crawled behind the hedge, and when I came to the end of the hedge, I could see the side of him. He had not moved and was still facing Frank. My intent was to knock him down. I was not going to shoot unless necessary.

Frank kept talking to him, and I told myself, *Okay, here goes.* I quickly went at him and using my forearm, I hit the suspect on his side, and he went down hard. I grabbed the gun, and we handcuffed him. We searched him, and he had a second gun in his waistband. Even though there was danger, I honestly thought I could take him out. That was one time, though, things could have turned ugly.

Pat McKinley became the SWAT lieutenant and asked me to apply. I did and became an element member in SWAT. When I first came to SWAT, there were no hostage negotiators yet. The strategy was we told the suspects three times to come out or we were coming in. If they did not come out, we threw in tear gas, kicked the door open, grabbed them, and brought them out. Most of the time they voluntarily came out.

One of the first incidents I responded to as part of SWAT was a hostage situation in Wilshire Division. A burglar broke into a house not realizing that there were three people inside. At one point, the three became aware of the burglar, and one escaped out the back. The burglar found the other two and held them hostage. The one who escaped called the police.

Mac McClain, second row from bottom, fifth from left; Patrick McKinley, left side holding flag: Metro Division SWAT

Mac McClain, left: SWAT call-out

The police got there quick and surrounded the house. SWAT was called, and we responded. We told the burglar to come out or we were coming in. No response. We did this two more times to no response, so we shot tear gas into the house. Still no response. I was prone out in the front yard with a shotgun, covering the entry team as they approached the front door, but the house caught fire from the tear gas.

Smoke was going everywhere. The Fire Department responded, but they had a policy not to put themselves in danger with a barricaded suspect. So five SWAT officers grabbed the fire hose and ran to the house to fight the fire. But policemen are not firemen. The hose reached its limit before the officers reached the house, and all five fell down. It was hard not to laugh.

Eventually, the fire forced the burglar and both hostages to come out with their hands up. The burglar was taken into custody and arrested with no shots fired. The firemen were able to enter and put the fire out, but the house had burned enough that later it had to be rebuilt.

I'm not sure what the genesis of it was, but at some point after that incident, somebody came up with the idea of hostage negotiators. The first three guys they approached to receive the training were me, Vick

Pettric, and Mike Hillmann. I didn't want to do it because I wanted to be part of the entry team, one of the guys going in the door.

The one incident as a hostage negotiator that stands out was at a hotel. When I got there, the suspect was holding his girlfriend hostage in the bathroom of their hotel room.

The suspect and his girlfriend had a fight, and the police were called. The responding officers knocked on the room door and identified themselves, and the suspect fired a round at them. He then grabbed the girl and locked himself and her in the bathroom.

After being briefed, I laid down on the floor outside the bathroom door and started talking to him through the door. I told him who I was and why I was there. He was not talking. I kept talking and still nothing. At times, the girlfriend would respond to me. At one point, I asked her what he was doing. She said, "He's sitting on the floor asleep."

"Why don't you just open the door and walk out."

"He's leaning his back up against the door so I can't walk out."

The girl was responding to everything I asked her, but when the suspect was awake, he would not say anything, and I was getting a little frustrated. After about three hours, the detectives told me that the suspect's background check showed that he had two kids. I used that information and said to him, "What would your kids think, knowing their father was sitting here holding a poor helpless woman hostage in a bathroom in Los Angeles?"

Gosh, what did I say that for? I was hoping that mentioning his kids would bring him out, but instead he went ballistic. After all these hours of not saying a word, he started yelling and cussing me out, hollering that he was going to kill me.

"Don't you bring my kids into this, McClain. You're going to be the first guy I kill when I come out this door."

There was a SWAT guy to either side of me, and I looked up at them and said, "You guys have a round chambered, right?" I had my handgun, but I was lying on the floor at a disadvantage. They assured me they had me covered.

The suspect settled back against the door and went back to sleep again. I could hear him snoring. I thought if I had to be up, then he had to be up, so I asked for a stick. Somebody handed me a broomstick, and I started beating on the door with it, saying, "Wake up! You're not going to go to sleep on me." He woke up and called me and everybody else a bunch of names and then went back to sleep.

Several more hours passed, and finally the decision was made to get him out of there. We pumped gas into the bathroom, and then we forced the door open. When the door opened, the suspect was standing there holding his girlfriend in front of him with a gun to her head. He was tall, and she was about the height of his chest. They were both wet and naked. He started screaming, "I'm a thoroughbred! You can't kill me! I'm a thoroughbred!" He then slammed the door shut.

Seeing them wet, we understood why the gas had no effect. He had previously filled the bathtub with water, and they both climbed in to avoid the effects of the gas. We forced the door open again. He was in the same position, and the shot was taken. He fell into the bathtub, as an officer grabbed the girlfriend and pulled her out. The paramedics tried to save his life, but he died. I was on that floor for a good fifteen hours.

One night Bobby Jakues, a former Marine like me, and I had just finished eating and were driving down a street, when we saw a guy standing in front of a liquor store who appeared to be selling narcotics. I slowed down as we approached the liquor store, and then I saw white lights in my rearview mirror. Right then, a drunk driver slammed his car into us from behind at about seventy miles per hour.

It dislodged the front seat, and the gas pedal became stuck causing the car to take off. The car went about a block and up over a curb onto a sidewalk before Bobby was able to reach over and turn the ignition off. The car that hit us then hit a telephone pole, and two of the four people inside the car died.

We were in the same emergency room with the people from the other car, and the doctors were working on all of us. Later, an officer I knew told me that he was in roll call at Venice Division on the night it happened and a sergeant came in and announced that I had died in the crash. Metro went to my house to tell my wife I was hurt, but she wouldn't let them in. She thought if they were at the door that meant they were there to tell her I was dead. I was off work for nine months because of the injuries.

When I came back, I went on loan to Robbery-Homicide Division, working the Southside Slayer Task Force. Detective John St. John was the lead investigator, and some other Metro guys and I followed up on about four thousand clues. Ultimately, a suspect was arrested, convicted of two of the murders, and sent to prison where he died.

The suspect slept in an abandoned car behind his mother's house because she wouldn't let him stay in the house. He had brought a prostitute to the car and at some point, strangled and killed her. After he killed her, he got his brother to help him carry the body into the alley. He didn't tell his brother that he had killed her; he just said she had a heart attack and died. A neighbor was looking out her window and saw the suspect and his brother carrying something heavy. She recognized the brother, became suspicious, and called the police. The police responded and found the dead girl's body in the alley.

The suspect was also convicted of the murder of another girl found in the alley near his home that had occurred two months earlier. After he was captured, the murder of prostitutes stopped. However, within the last two years, I believe someone else has since been identified as being responsible for the other prostitute murders.

While at Robbery-Homicide, I became friends with Detective Tom Lange, also a former Marine. He asked me one day if I would like to help him with a murder case he had that was several years old and unsolved. It involved porno star John Holmes and the killing of four people. It was dubbed the "Wonderland Murders" because the murders occurred on Wonderland Drive.

Then we received information that a witness who was in jail for robbery had knowledge of the murders. Tom and I interviewed the witness at the Hall of Justice. According to the witness, Holmes was buying dope from Eddie Nash, a nightclub owner and dope dealer. Holmes became friends with some thieves and small-time dope dealers who considered themselves a gang. Holmes told them about Nash and that Nash had a lot of dope, money, and guns. The gang talked Holmes into setting up a robbery of Nash at his house. Holmes' role was to go to Nash's house, buy some dope, and leave the door unlocked when he left.

The witness said the gang entered the house, tied up Nash and his bodyguard and then took the money and dope. After the gang left, Nash and the bodyguard freed themselves. They decided not to report it to the police, but to try to get the money and dope back on their own. They figured Holmes had set them up, and two days later the bodyguard found Holmes and brought him back to Nash.

Holmes was forced to identify the gang and agreed to set the gang up for retaliation. Nash gave Holmes money to buy dope from the gang. He did, waited until they were asleep, and then left, leaving a door unlocked. The bodyguard and some other suspects entered the three-story home and used metal pipes to beat four victims to death. Another victim was left for dead with her head crushed in.

Our witness said he was present at Nash's house when the suspects returned with money and dope. He identified the bodyguard as one of the suspects.

Holmes' fingerprint was found at the murder scene, and he was originally charged with four counts of murder. His attorney successfully argued that Holmes was a victim, and he was acquitted.

Our witness testified against Nash and the bodyguard, but the trial ended in a hung jury. There was a second trial, and both were acquitted. It was later determined that Nash had bribed the holdout juror in the first trial. Nash pled guilty to bribery as well as drug trafficking and money laundering. He went to prison and just recently died. The bodyguard died in 1995.

I also worked another of Tom's old cases, the murder of an actor who was gunned down in the driveway of his home. Although he had a history of being a forger and counterfeiter, he was killed over a woman. The actor's screenwriting partner introduced his beautiful, six-foot-tall girlfriend to him.

One day the partner went to the actor's house and saw his girlfriend's car parked there. He did not go in, but returned home, telephoned the actor, and accused him of dating his girlfriend. The actor told him she was a grown woman and can do what she wants. The girlfriend was living with the partner, and when she returned home, all of her stuff was out in the street. She told me what happened, and we used her as a witness.

The partner tried to hire two guys to kill the actor, but they refused to do it. They told him they would take a baseball bat and break his knees, but they would not murder him over a woman. The partner then hired another guy who subcontracted the hit to two other guys. Those two laid in wait and killed the actor in the driveway of his home.

We learned about the three suspects through the first two guys that the partner tried to hire. We sought the public's help in finding them and put the case on the television show *America's Most Wanted*. The OJ Simpson case occurred about that time, and Tom became one of its lead detectives, so I had the case by myself.

One morning I received a call from the Ventura County Sheriff's Department. "Detective McClain, are you looking for a guy named Rosenberg?"

"Yes."

"We have him."

He was arrested at a hotel, where he was visiting a friend. The friend's car horn went off in the parking lot, and the police were called. They encountered Rosenberg, who gave a phony name. The police demanded identification, and Rosenberg had multiple identifications in various names, including one in his real name.

I went to Ventura, and in Rosenberg's duffle bag, I found a yellow piece of paper with an address on it. The address was to a hotel in the state of Washington. I contacted law enforcement in Washington, and officers arrived at the hotel just as the other two suspects were leaving in a car. They were arrested.

Rosenberg had cancer and was essentially on his deathbed. He testified against the partner, and the other two suspects in exchange for not going to prison, although he was convicted. The two suspects were also convicted and sent to prison. Rosenberg has since died. We tried the case against the partner three times, and it was a hung jury each time. He walked free. That was a shocker. He has also since died.

When I promoted to detective, I left Robbery-Homicide and went to Seventy-Seventh Division, working Autos. It drove me crazy. There were eight detectives and one car, and there were not enough desks for everyone. I had to wait for one of the other detectives to be on a day off to use a desk.

Then a lieutenant that I had worked for at Metro called me and asked if I would like to go to OCID, Organized Crime and Intelligence Division.

I said, "Sign me up!"

Tim Moss and Mac McClain

And that's where I finished my career. Why did I retire? There's an old song, "I'd Rather Leave While I'm in Love." I did not want to spend thirty years on the Police Department and become bitter.

At my retirement party, Chief Bernard Parks and several deputy chiefs, along with the mayor and two city councilmen from the town I was living in all attended. As I was listening to them and my old partner Tim Moss speak about me, I remember sitting there reflecting back on my life. I grew up in a small town in the south with less than five hundred people. I actually went to a one-room school that had a wood fireplace and an outdoor toilet. Each of the grades, first through the fifth, had their own row of desks. Our teacher would teach the first row then give them something to keep them busy, go on to the second row, then the third, fourth, and fifth. That's where I came from. Now to have these people praising me was very humbling.

Frank Galvan

Birthplace: San Antonio, Texas
Career: 1973–2001
Rank at Retirement: Detective II
Divisions: Venice/Pacific, Rampart, Juvenile, Narcotics, Internal Affairs

While I was in college, I worked the night shift for the Southern California Gas Company. I had worked my way up the ranks to the position of serviceman—and that was as far as I was ever going to get for the next thirty years. Jim Reeves, an LAPD officer who worked Wilshire Division, was my sister's friend, and we used to go camping. Jim talked to me about the Police Department. I thought about what he said and applied. I guess you could say Jim talked me into coming on the job.

The Academy wasn't easy. We were the first class that had "Modular Training." Each recruit sat at their own cubicle with a television set and watched videos of various aspects of police work. I hated it. It was the worst thing, especially after physical training. I was tired, and it wasn't hard to start nodding off watching a video. We also had some live instruction, and I got more from having an instructor in class than from watching a video.

There was a field with a hill across the street from the Academy, dubbed "Billy Goat Hill." Our physical training instructors, Bill Arnado, Rex Shields, Terry Speer, and Bob Jarvis, would have us run up and down that hill until our legs gave out. And this was after we had done our other exercises and self-defense training. There were a few mornings as I left my house for the Academy I threw up just thinking about the PT that we would have to do that day. But those instructors made us tough and weeded out the weak.

Frank Galvan receiving diploma from Chief Ed Davis, 1973

I worked the old Wilshire Station on my ride-alongs. On my first ride-along, they let me clear the shotgun before we went out in the field. At the same time, I was clearing it, I was told about the policeman that was checking the shotgun and had a round go off right into the carport ceiling, and then when the officer was showing the sergeant how it happened, he accidently fired a second round. I looked up, and, sure enough, there were buckshot holes in the ceiling.

Out of the Academy, I went to Venice Division. While I was there, the division name changed from Venice to Pacific, and we moved to a new station. The best thing that happened to me at Venice was working with Bart Carlson on the beach car. Bart taught me about narcotics. There were a lot of marijuana and heroin users and sellers at the beach, and we made a lot of arrests. That was instrumental because I later would work Narcotics for a good part of my career.

Bart Carlson   *Venice Division police station*

One day a purse snatch call came out, and as luck would have it, the suspect ran right in front of us with purse in hand. We were in the Oakwood section of the division, and I was driving. The suspect ran into a dead-end alley. He turned and ran right back at us as we drove into the alley. As the suspect ran by, Bart bailed out and went in foot pursuit. There was no room to turn around, so I put the car in reverse and floored it to catch up with Bart.

The next thing I heard was a loud crash on the passenger side of the car. I didn't realize Bart had left the passenger door open and the door hit a cement meter stanchion. The door was barely hanging on. Bart caught the guy and put him in the back seat. We took the door off the hinges, put it in the trunk, and drove back to the station with no front passenger door. On the way to the station, a citizen looking at where the door should have been asked us what happened. We joked that the air conditioner stopped working!

It was good working Venice, and I didn't want to leave, but I was wheeled to Jail Division downtown in Parker Center. I wasn't there too long when I met Wally Matsura and Ron Aguilar from Rampart Division. They talked me into putting in a transfer for Rampart when my time was up at Jail Division. I did and was fortunate to go there.

Frank Galvan, second from left, with fellow Rampart officers and Chief Gates

Rampart was a great place to work, a tight division with great camaraderie. The word "brotherhood" is a fitting description. We did a lot of things together outside of work, like hunting, fishing, and water skiing, both family and non-family trips. I would be at Rampart for the next ten years.

Mark Espinoza and I were working one night when we got a radio call that a dead body had been found on Alvarado Boulevard. When we got there, we found a nude female on the side of a hill, and she appeared to have been strangled. She was Kimberly Diane Martin, one of the victims of the Hillside Strangler. We protected the crime scene and called for detectives. Eventually, the suspects, Kenneth Bianchi and his cousin Angelo Buono, were captured, but not until after they had killed eleven females, including Martin.

I was working with Mark when we encountered our first PCP suspect. We received a radio call to a store on the north side of Sunset at Silver Lake Boulevard. The call was about a guy breaking the store's windows. When we got there, a guy buck-ass naked and bleeding was doing karate chops to his reflection in what remained of the storefront window.

We tried to talk to him, but he was incoherent. We figured we'd better take this guy into custody before he hurt himself further or damaged more property. That was our mistake. The minute we tried to grab him we felt his strength right away. Mark and I were pretty big guys, but he knocked me down onto the sidewalk. I got up and was trying to grab him, while Mark started sticking him with the baton—we had the straight sticks in those days—but that wasn't very effective. We both backed up to the car to get to the radio, and the suspect came at us.

I put out a help call, and we started battling him again. He tossed me over the hood of the police car as Mark was still trying to stick him. Mark broke one of the guy's legs and one of his arms with the baton, but that didn't stop the guy.

More officers finally got there, and by sheer numbers, we were able to take this guy down and handcuff him. PCP was new to us, even the handling of it. I recall officers putting PCP-laced cigarettes recovered from arrestees into their uniform shirt pocket. As the Department learned more about it, safety standards were implemented in the handling of PCP and better tactics were developed to deal with a suspect under the influence of it.

This incident was a week before a Rampart sergeant shot a guy who was naked and under the influence of PCP. The sergeant responded to a call of a naked man climbing a traffic signpost on Hyperion Street. During their confrontation, the suspect knocked the sergeant's baton out of his hand, and he, in fear of his life, shot and killed the suspect. It was a controversial shooting.

Soon after I got to Rampart, I was chosen to work the Special Problems Unit. The unit focused on specific crime problems in the division. One year a series of rapes of females was occurring in an area of mostly apartment buildings. Most of the victims were walking home from work late at night and were usually holding something in their hands like a bag of groceries. The suspect would grab them, take them between two buildings, and rape them. I believe there were ten to fifteen rapes.

Frank Galvan, third from left: Special Problems Unit, rape operation

Officers Kathy Jackson and Beverly Brink and Policewoman Shirley McCollum posed as lone females and walked the areas where the rapes were occurring with us as covering officers. For the first couple of nights, nothing happened. Then one night a suspect came out from between a couple of buildings and grabbed one of the female officers. We were on him like gangbusters and took the guy down. It was the rapist, and he was convicted and sent to prison.

Rick Salazar and I responded one night to a motor officer's request for crowd control where a traffic accident had occurred at Eighth and Irolo Street. We helped disperse the crowd and asked the motor officer if he needed anything else. He told us there was a witness standing on the east side of Irolo, a half block north of Eighth Street, and asked if we could get the witness' information.

We walked up the street and contacted the witness, a young female about sixteen years of age. Rick was on one side of her and I was on the other as we stood on the sidewalk. We were taking her information when all of a sudden we heard shots being fired. One of the rounds struck the girl, and I saw blood coming out of her chest. Rick and I went right down between a car and the curb with the girl in hand to shield her. Rick applied pressure on her chest to stop the bleeding.

I put out a help call and told Rick I was going to get the car so we could get this girl to medical help. I crawled back to the police car using parked cars as cover. I reached the car, and some other officers were there in response to the help call. I took out the back seat of our car, and we draped our armor vests on the windows. I climbed into the back seat area, and another officer drove. I told him, "Start driving and I'll tell you when to stop."

We got to where Rick and the girl were. Rick threw her on top of me, he jumped on top of her, and we took off. We did not hear any more shots other than the initial ones, about eight to ten shots. A round punctured the girl's lung, but she recovered. We never did find out who fired the shots.

Rick and I responded to a call of a woman screaming for help in a drug rehab place at Olympic and Westmoreland. When we got there, we could hear a woman screaming for help from an upper floor. The building manager told us it was the girlfriend of a guy that lived upstairs. We knocked on the door, and a woman shouted from inside, "Help me. He's got a knife!"

Just as we were going to kick the door, a guy opened it, and he had a knife in his hand. We could see his girlfriend, and she had blood all over her. We later learned he had stabbed her about twenty times. He quickly closed the door, and Rick kicked it open. We had just been issued the small tear gas containers, and I sprayed him right in his face with the gas. He went down, but that was the dumbest thing I could ever have done because we all gasped for air and the girlfriend started yelling that the gas burned in her stab wounds. It just permeated the room. We took the guy into custody and got both of them out of there. The boyfriend was booked for attempted murder. I never used the gas again.

In '85, Rick went to work Rampart Detectives, and I left for Juvenile Division. I worked with two detectives, Vivian Gomez and Vicki Calagna. Vivian and Vicki had a lot of influence on me. I knew how to conduct investigations, but not as well as those two. I took what they taught me, along with what I learned from our detective supervisor, Rich Parker, and by the time I left Juvenile Division I thought I was doing good police work.

Child abuse cases are tough because you usually have a kid that loves his mother and father even though they've been beaten or sexually abused by those parents. I handled maybe fifty homicide cases from my learning stages to when I became an expert in child abuse investigations.

The worst child abuse case I worked was a Hollenbeck case of a missing child. The little girl was four years old and was left one day in the care of the mother's boyfriend. The boyfriend believed in Satan and had various representations of Satan throughout the house. He called the police and said that the girl was missing and that he thought the gardener took her. At one point during the investigation, we thought he was lying.

He kept denying it, but as the night went on, he finally broke down and said, "Well, I hurt her."

"Tell me where she's at. Maybe I can get her some help."

He took us up into a canyon of the San Gabriel Mountains and directed me to a heavily wooded area off a fire road. I was in the brush in my coat and tie searching around and there was nothing.

"Quit bullshitting me. Tell me where she's at."

He then takes us another quarter mile up the hill and says, "I think she's in there." He pointed to another area with brush.

I was on my hands and knees, using my hand to sweep back and forth over the ground, and then I touched her toes. They were very cold. I moved the leaves that he had put over her. She was dead. He had beaten her, shaved her head, and sodomized her. Raped her. She had severe trauma in her vaginal area. There were numerous hematomas about her head, and her eyes were blackened. It was bad.

He had put her in a gym bag, rode up into the San Gabriel Mountains area on his motorcycle, and threw her into a dry reservoir. Then he left, but changed his mind, thinking she might be found, and came back to the reservoir. He grabbed her and took her up to the spot where I found her, and he buried her in a shallow grave. It was the coroner's conclusion that she was alive at the time he buried her. Captain Martin Pomeroy elected to stay with me through the night until daylight, when it was safe for the coroner to come to the scene. His presence was very comforting, and I'll never forget that.

At court, the boyfriend was found guilty, but before sentencing, the mother of the dead girl asked the judge if he would marry her and the defendant before he went to prison. That really angered me. This man killed her daughter. You could tell what kind of a mother she would have been. She had another child, a boy a little older, and we took him away from her.

That case has really affected me all these years. I still think about it. I still dream about it. There were other cases, but none as severe. I kept the homicide pictures for the longest time. I don't know why I wouldn't let go, but finally I ended up burning them.

My hat is off to all the men and women who work child abuse cases. Homicides are one thing. Two people going at it, one kills the other—you become calloused. When it comes to a baby or a child, especially if you are a family man, it can affect you tremendously. It took a toll on me as far as my health. Vicki used to check everyone's blood pressure every now and then, and I kept telling her no. Finally, I gave in. She took my blood pressure, and it was out of this world. Rich sent me over to Central Receiving Hospital, and I was diagnosed with high stress. I was told to get a less stressful job, so I went to Narcotics Division. Less stressful, yeah right! I worked the Major Violators Section and had dope cases that took me throughout the United States.

I was working with DEA, the Drug Enforcement Agency, on a case where the suspect had fled, leaving behind ten kilos of cocaine and his driver's license. We recovered the cocaine and booked it. A year later, the suspect was arrested, and the case went to court. During the hearing, the judge directed me to bring the cocaine to court. I went to Property Division, and when they brought me the package, I could tell right away something was wrong. It was not sealed the same way as I had sealed it, and it felt a whole lot lighter. We opened it up right there in the property room, and most of the cocaine was gone.

I immediately called my supervisor who in turn notified Internal Affairs Division. The investigation determined that an officer had checked out the package through fraudulent means and stole the cocaine. He was arrested and sent to jail. His arrest led to the now-infamous Rampart scandal. To try to get a reduced sentence, he told of corruption within the Department, most of which I think was made up.

While at Narcotics Division, I also worked the narcotics buy team with Rick Salazar, my longtime partner from Rampart. For the buy team, we had officers assigned to us that worked undercover posing as buyers of narcotics

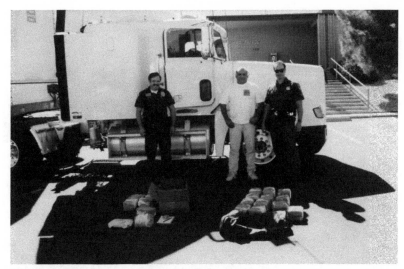

Frank Galvan, center: narcotics seizure

Officer safety was our biggest priority. We couldn't stress officer safety enough. We didn't want another Blackie Sawyer situation. Blackie was working undercover and was killed by dope dealers that tried to rip him off during an operation. His death happened when I was in the Academy. Our class was the "Blackie Sawyer" class. We told the officers the way we wanted them to do it, and if they weren't going to do it that way, then don't do it at all.

We had one officer that was going to make a buy in front of a dope dealer's house. The officer was electronically wired so we could hear any conversation. He went face-to-face with the dealer in front of the house, and then the dealer invited him into the house. Sure as all get out, our officer went into the house when we had specifically told him not to go inside. We could hear the conversation, and things weren't going right.

The officer was pushing it a little too much, and the dealer was getting suspicious. The dealer brought out some dope and wanted the officer to use some with him. I told Rick, "Let's call this." He agreed, and we went in there like gangbusters. There were six suspects in the house. We took everybody down and recovered dope and guns. Fortunately, it all worked out, and yes, we had a long talk with the officer. We all went home safe that night.

Frank Galvan and Mike Neel: Narcotics Division inspection, 1998

One of the big cases I worked on was Operation Green Ice. We learned to follow the money from a prior narcotics investigation called Operation Pisces. Pisces was part of a joint task force with the FBI and the DEA where an LAPD officer posed as a finance facilitator laundering money obtained from drug sales for some drug cartels, mostly Colombian. I worked surveillance for Operation Green Ice. We focused on another cartel from Colombia. The operation went worldwide, and, ultimately, over a hundred suspects were convicted, including mafia from Italy.

After working Narcotics, I worked the Surveillance Unit at Internal Affairs for a while, and then it was time to retire. I retired after twenty-eight years on the Department and then went to work for the Department of Justice for five years doing narcotics investigations. I still remain friends with a bunch of guys from the job, most of whom I met from my days at Rampart. Like I said earlier, brotherhood.

My time on the job went by too fast, and I miss it. If I could go back in time and do it over, I would. Well, maybe not so much the Academy physical training part.

John Puis

Birthplace: Paris, France
Career: 1974–1994
Rank at Retirement: Police Officer III + I
Divisions: Northeast, Communications, Newton, Metropolitan

Where do I start? I was born in Paris, France. There were no jobs in France for my dad, so we immigrated to the United States via Canada, ultimately settling in Los Angeles. We were not here long before we moved back to France. When my father died, my mom decided to raise my sister and me in the United States. We relocated to Los Angeles.

I developed a real love for mechanical drawing in high school. After a tour in the Navy, I went to a local college to further my interest in drawing. While there, I met some classmates whose parents were involved in search and rescue with the Los Angeles County Sheriff's Department. I took a real interest and became a reserve deputy and member of the Search and Rescue Team.

Law enforcement looked interesting, so I put in several applications, including with the Sheriffs and LAPD. LAPD called first and asked if I could take the test. I did, finished the hiring process, and entered the Academy in March 1974.

Our first day we were lined up, and Officer Perkins—we never knew his first name—was our drill instructor. I was thin at the time, and he came up to me, grabbed my jacket sleeve, and said, "Do you have an arm in that sleeve, mister?" A number of us were former military, so we were not intimidated. However, a few quit that first day. In fact, they quit within the first three hours.

John Puis, middle row standing, seventh from right: Academy class, 1974

While in the Academy, recruits would go on ride-alongs in the divisions to get first-hand exposure to police work. I went to Northeast Division for my ride-alongs. In roll call, the watch commander was giving out information on suspects. I was sitting in the front row writing down everything that he was saying. I was assigned to work with these two officers who had no interest in me whatsoever; they wanted me to just sit in the back seat of the police car and be quiet. As we were driving, I was looking for suspects, when I saw one of the cars described in roll call going in the opposite direction.

I said, "Sir, excuse me, sir."

They kept talking and ignoring me.

I raised my voice a little more, "Sir?"

"Yeah, kid, what do you want?"

"Well, you know that blue car they mentioned in roll call that was wanted for robbery?"

"Yeah. What about it?"

"It just made a left turn at the last intersection."

"What!"

We made a quick U-turn, and when we got back to the intersection, we could still see the wanted car two blocks away. We caught up to it and made the arrest. The two officers thought I was pretty good after that and even called the Academy. I was given a commendation for a good observation. I thought that was pretty cool.

Some of us finished our Academy training early, and at first, they didn't know what to do with us. We were sent to divisions, and I went back to Northeast. Northeast didn't want to put me in patrol because I hadn't graduated yet, so I was assigned to work with an old-time homicide detective whose partner was on vacation. Of course, I didn't know anything about anything; I was just carrying his books. He decided he wanted to see if the new kid could handle it, so he took me to the morgue to watch the autopsies. He thought for sure I would throw up, but I didn't. Actually, I thought it was interesting.

At graduation, they announced the valedictorian, and my name was called. I was shocked. I had no clue. I did well in everything, but was not number one in anything. I was asked to make some comments, and I had to think of something off the top of my head.

John Puis recognized as class valedictorian by Chief Ed Davis and Police Commissioner Marianna Pfaelzer

I returned to Northeast after graduation. One night I was working with Scott Curry, when Kirk Harper and Jim Van Pelt put out an officer down, officer needs help call. They had encountered a violent suspect who knocked Kirk down a hill, disarmed and shot Jim, and then went looking for Kirk. Unable to see him, the suspect fled with Jim's gun.

Jim had already been taken to the hospital when we got to the scene. When I heard he had been shot, I was like, *Whoa, there really are bad people that want to kill policemen.* Jim survived, but he was really messed up from the gunshot wounds and eventually medically pensioned off the job. It was my second week out of the Academy—that was a wakeup call for me. I helped with the search, but the suspect, Raymond George, was gone. He was caught several months later and convicted of several murders and the attempted murder of Jim.

After several months, Lieutenant Gary Reichling told me I was going to work a one-man car. I didn't think I was ready to work a one-man car, but the lieutenant told me that my training officers said I could handle it and reassured me I would be all right.

It was Sunday in my second week in a one-man car on day watch, and it was raining pretty good. I saw a beat-up lowrider car with four gang members in it. I ran the license plate, and Communications said the system was down. I was following the car, and Communications updated that the system was slow. You can only follow somebody so long, so I turned off. Not a minute later, Communications told me the car was a stolen vehicle.

I made a U-turn and looked down all the side streets for this car, when I saw it parked halfway down an alley with the four guys standing next to it. I drove down the alley, put out a backup request, and jumped out of my car. I yelled for them to put their hands up, and they complied. Communications asked me my specific location, but I wasn't exactly sure. "I'm south of Isabel and two blocks west of Loosmore." Those were the last streets I had looked at before the alley. After a minute or so, I could hear the engine roar of police cars. I knew the cavalry was on its way! All four were arrested.

From Northeast, I went to Communications where Sergeant Endel Jurman was my supervisor. We had a good rapport because we both liked working on cars. Ten years earlier, Jurman was shot the night detectives Robert Endler and Charles Monaghan were killed at the Sears department store next to Wilshire Station. The security at Sears had detained a suspected forger and his girlfriend and had called the detectives. Jurman, although off-duty, walked with Endler and Monaghan over to Sears. As the three entered the Sears security office, the suspected forger, Leaman Russell Smith, took out a revolver and shot all three. Only Jurman survived. Smith escaped, but he was caught several days later in Chicago and sentenced to life in prison.

Terry Speer told us in the Academy about the Sears shooting, along with other shootings, in his officer survival class. He really emphasized the will to survive. Now I was working for a survivor of one of the shootings Terry talked about, and I was impressed.

When I left Communications, I went to Newton Division. I had about three years on, and I thought I knew everything. Boy was I wrong! It was a shock when I got to Newton. The level of violence was beyond comprehension—shootings and cuttings every night. I was not prepared for that.

One of the most memorable violent incidents for me in Newton started out as a radio call of a family dispute. The call was upgraded to an assault in progress and then a few minutes later to a murder in progress. It wasn't our call, but we were just a couple of blocks away. We drove to the apartment building, and there was a crowd in front. People in the crowd told us it was upstairs.

We ran upstairs, looked down the hallway, and saw Timmy Russell who worked Newton Vice. Timmy had responded just ahead of us and was now looking through an open door into an apartment, his gun pointing into the room. He didn't say anything, but motioned to us to come to him. We looked in the apartment, and there was blood everywhere, pools of blood on the floor and blood on the walls.

Across the room on the floor was an overweight girl in her late teens lying on her back, breasts exposed. A big butcher knife was stuck in one of her breasts. A man was sitting on her, and there was another butcher knife a couple of feet in front of him lying in a pool of blood. The man was looking at us, but he had that thousand-yard stare. He started to windmill his fists like he thought someone was approaching him, but he didn't go for either knife so we couldn't shoot him.

My partner, Ken Yerkes, holstered his gun, knocked the guy over, and we handcuffed him. The guy was on PCP. He had got into a fight with his girlfriend and then got atop her and stabbed her repeatedly. He had plunged the knife into her face, her eyes, her throat, everywhere. She was stabbed ninety-five times. He also stabbed himself in his legs. Her mother tried to stop him by hitting him repeatedly with an iron frying pan, but to no avail. Both knives were at least fourteen inches in length. We went to court, and he was convicted. What surprised us was he looked like nothing had happened to him physically, even though he had been clobbered with a frying pan.

Ken and I were partners for a long time, both at Newton and later at Metro Division. The interesting part is the parallels between his life and mine. We were born twelve days apart. We were both industrial arts majors in high school. We both joined the military at the same time; he was in the Marine Corps, and I was in the Navy. Our boot camps were separated by a six-foot block wall. We were in Vietnam at the same time, although Ken lived in the mud, ate C-rations, and earned the Purple Heart medal for two wounds in action.

Ken Yerkes

When we joined the Police Department, we both lived in the same city, a few blocks apart. We even worked Northeast at the same time, but we didn't know each other. I was at Newton first, and I remember the sergeant saying, "Hey, you're going to get a new partner. Ken Yerkes is coming to Newton." We teamed up, worked a car together, and were partners for a long time.

After about five years on the job, some go through what I call the five-year syndrome, when you think you know everything and then you make mistakes. I believe it is one of the most dangerous times in an officer's career. One night Ken and I got a radio call to see a woman about a violent, mentally ill male on Thirty-Fifth Street just west of Hooper Avenue. We got there, and a couple other units showed up along with Sergeant Joe Van Fleet. The woman told us that her brother had a history of mental illness. Earlier that day the brother argued with their mom, and when she refused to give him the keys to the family car, he choked her.

The sister arranged for him to be admitted to a hospital, but she wanted our help in getting him there. She told us that he was in the back of the house and that he did not have any weapons. Six of us walked down the driveway while Sergeant Van Fleet stayed with the sister. There was a screened porch and no lights on in the house. The only light was from a streetlight behind us that reflected on the porch screening, which made it difficult to see into the porch area.

We called out the brother's name and said we would like to talk to him. He was on the porch right at the back door to the house, and he told us to go away several times. One of the officers said, "He's naked, and he's got something, maybe a broom." Apparently he also said, "Or a rifle." Some of us didn't hear that part. The brother then scooted into the house and partially closed the back door.

I went in first. I was ready to push open the back door, when it slammed in my face. Now I was upset, twice this guy had rebuffed us. I pushed the door open and entered into a small kitchen. I immediately heard a door to my right slam shut. Now I was really pissed and going to get this guy. And that's what I mean by the five-year syndrome. I let this guy push some buttons, and I should not have done that.

I had to close the back door to access the door that just slammed shut. Everyone else stayed on the porch. I stood off to one side of the closed door and tried to kick the door, but it didn't open. I repositioned myself a few inches to get a little better angle. I kicked the door again, and it flew open. The brother was standing there with a .22 caliber rifle at a shoulder position, and he fired at me.

The round went through the joint of my right shoulder, and the pain was just unbelievable. It felt like somebody had hit me with a baseball bat as hard as they could. The impact spun me around, and I wondered, *What the hell just happened?*

My gun that was in my right hand and my flashlight dropped to the floor. I found the gun, but had to put it in my left hand because I couldn't use my right hand after he shot me. The door closed again, and I thought the guy was still in the room. I saw a stove and wanted to get behind it and take a barricade position. I told Ken and the other officers not to come in. If they entered, they would cross the threshold of the room the brother was in and be in his line of fire. I said, "I'm shot. I'm okay. Don't come in." I was convinced the brother was still in the room.

As I took a step toward the stove area, I was shot again, but not from the room. Unbeknownst to me, there was another door in the room that led to the living room, and from the living room, there was a hallway leading back to the kitchen. He had gone into the living room, saw my silhouette cast by the streetlight, and fired again. I was hit in the neck and dropped like a sack of potatoes.

I was down on the floor and only had a slight pain in my back, but I couldn't move my right arm or use my legs. I touched my legs, and it was like touching a foreign object. There was no response. I was paralyzed. Doctors later told me that the second round hit bone, went downward, and lodged against my spine causing a spinal cord concussion. It didn't feel as bad as the first shot because I think my body had already gone into a defensive survival mode.

I put my gun on my chest using my left hand, figuring I'd better have it in case this guy tried to finish me off. I told Ken I was coming out. Using my left hand, I tried to push myself closer to the back door. I barely moved an inch. I was getting weak, but I never lost consciousness.

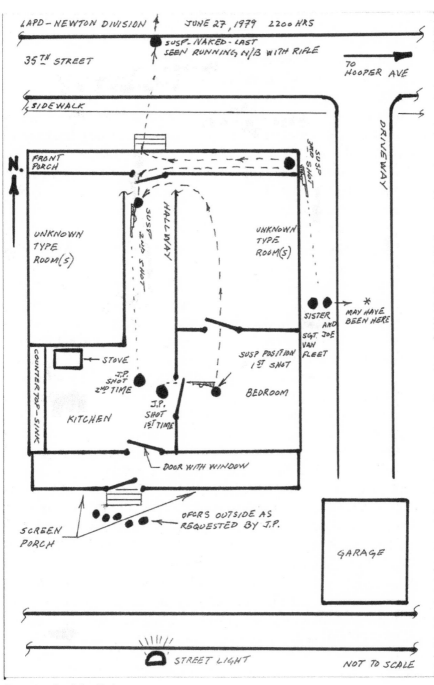

Drawing by John Puis

Ken and the others made entry. After the brother had fired at me the second time, he ran out the front door and fired a shot at Sergeant Van Fleet and the sister, missing both. Then he ran to a football field at a nearby high school. SWAT was called and they searched the grounds. Bobby Avina and Raul Galindo were searching the bleachers on the football field when they saw a rifle pointed at them from under a bleacher seat. Although they couldn't see the brother, they fired and hit both him and the rifle. He was alive and taken into custody.

I was taken to the hospital. The first bullet was a through-and-through, and the second bullet lodged against my spine. It is still there to this day. The doctor said taking it out might have caused further damage. I felt some tingling in my toes after about twenty-four hours. As the days went by, I eventually could get out of bed and walk on my own.

I was in the hospital for five days and then went home and did my own therapy. At first I walked, then jogged, and finally ran. I love to run, and eventually I did get back to distance running. I was off the job for two months. I was able to return to running the law enforcement Death Valley Relay, which later became the Baker to Vegas Relay, every year for the rest of my career, although I never fully recovered. For the longest time, you could put a hot poker or an ice cube against my leg and I couldn't tell the difference. Nerves are that way, I guess. Today I'm better.

Nothing happened to the brother. He claimed insanity, the court went along with it, and he was not prosecuted for shooting a policeman. Instead, he was sent to a mental hospital. Years later, I got a letter from the City Attorney's office because the brother was going to be released from the mental hospital. According to a psychiatrist, this guy was cured. They asked me how I felt about it, and I told them I didn't care.

While I was in the hospital, Ken gave me his Vietnam Purple Heart medal. I still have it to this day. Ken blamed himself that I got shot. I told him neither he nor the other officers did anything wrong, but he carried that guilt for a long time. I was awarded the Medal of Valor for my actions protecting the other officers, but I felt I screwed up by letting this guy push my buttons.

Terry Speer, right: "He told us even if we were hit, we do not give up."

I do give a tremendous amount of credit to Terry Speer for instilling in me the will to survive. He told us that even if we are hit, we do not give up. I may have had only one hand, but I wasn't going to give up.

When I was working with Harold Bowman at Northeast while on probation, we booked a suspect one night at the Parker Center Jail. There were two officers ahead of us booking an arrestee. These officers looked sharp, like they had just gone to an inspection. I asked Harold about them, and he said they were officers assigned to Metro Division. I was impressed. After Ken and I were training officers at Newton for a few years, we applied and were both accepted to Metro.

When you first get to Metro, you're like a boot all over again. You're a nobody. It didn't matter if you had ten years on; you're the third man in the car, meaning you're working with two guys who are regular partners with each other. Again, I didn't know as much as I thought I did.

One night I was working with Mike D'Amato in Seventy-Seventh Division. It was about two o'clock in the morning, and Mike said, "Did you see that?"

"What?"

"That."

I was looking, and there was nobody around.

He said, "See those two guys by the phone booth? One just handed a bindle of dope to the other guy and then took money from him."

I was looking a block, two blocks ahead, didn't see anyone, and was starting to feel like an idiot. We didn't swoop on them because if they saw us they'd be in the wind. We crept up real slow, and at the last minute, we jumped out of the car. Sure enough, he was right. One had a bindle, and the other had the money. Mike and all the officers at Metro had a power of observation that was just unbelievable. I was impressed, and, of course, years later I was doing the same thing.

Eventually, Ken and I became regular partners again. One night we were working Newton area near the Pueblos Housing Project. We stopped a car for a traffic violation, and it was a gang member from Long Beach.

I asked, "What are you doing in this part of town?"

"I got some friends up here."

"You don't mind if I stand real close to you?"

"No. Why?"

"Well, the gang members around here have a habit of shooting at us. If I stand real close to you, maybe they won't shoot."

He started laughing.

A few seconds later, we saw the muzzle flash of a shot, and a bullet went right past us. We all hit the ground. We were right next to railroad tracks with rocks on both sides of the tracks. I still have a scar on my hand from hitting the rocks when I went down. The bullet came from between two buildings in the housing project. We put out a help call, but the shooter had disappeared into the projects.

I said, "See what I mean?"

"They do shoot at you around here!"

We made a believer out of him, and he was very glad to get out of there.

One night Ken and I were driving by a Mexican bar on a corner when we saw a guy leaning into a double-parked car. He was having a conversation with the four people in the car. We were in a plain car, but in uniform. Ken honked the horn for them to move. The guy outside the car looked back at us and then continued his conversation. I guess he didn't recognize our car as a police car. Ken honked again, and they ignored us.

We turned on the red light with a quick beep from the siren to get their attention. The guy outside the car immediately walked away and disappeared into the bar. The car drove on, but we kept the red light on because we were going to cite the driver for double parking. They drove down the street, and then they took off, pedal to the metal. They went onto the freeway, and we did one hundred miles per hour in pursuit. After several miles, they exited the freeway, but they were going too fast and lost control of the car at the bottom of the off-ramp. We saw them throw guns out of the car just before it stopped. All four doors opened, and they took off running.

Ken went after the two from the driver's side, and I chased the two from the passenger side. I caught one and hit him as hard as I could. He went down. I thought I had knocked him out. Then I chased the other guy and caught him, but when I came back with him, the first guy was gone. I think Ken caught both of the suspects he chased.

Other units showed up, and we found three guns. All four guys were with the Mexican Mafia. They were getting orders from the guy they were talking to at the bar to kill someone. We prevented a hit from taking place, at least for that night. We went from a simple double parking violation to stopping a homicide!

How many officers can say they actually saw or observed a drive-by shooting? Not too many I think. We actually saw it. We saw the muzzle flashes coming out of the car. Ken and I were driving near San Pedro and 112th Street late one night. We were ready to turn onto 112th Street when we saw a car with the headlights out driving real slow in our direction about a half a block from us. All of a sudden, we saw muzzle flashes coming out of the car and a rapid set of shots. I mean long muzzle flashes. This was not a handgun; this was a rifle. The shots were aimed at someone or something outside the passenger side of the car.

The car took off toward us going very fast. I backed up a little to avoid being hit, and the car went right by us. We immediately got behind them. They turned their headlights on, and then as they tried to make a turn, they lost control of the car. It spun around and came to a stop facing us. We were headlight to headlight.

Ken and I were both out of the car screaming, "Let me see your hands! Let me see your hands!" The driver put his hands on the steering wheel and did not move. The passenger slowly leaned down toward the driver, then came back up and opened the passenger door. He came out with nothing in his hands. He started walking backwards, and then he was off to the races. I couldn't go after him because we had not cleared the car for other suspects. Once we knew there were no other suspects in the car, Ken took the driver into custody. There was an AK rifle on the front floorboard.

I could still see the suspect that took off, and I ran after him. I was catching up to him, but then he went over a couple walls, and I didn't hear anything. I thought that he might be hiding and he might be armed. I told myself no one knows where I am, and Ken is by himself. I needed to go back, and I did.

These guys shot five people, causing serious wounds but no deaths. A gang unit arrived and took control of the crime scene, and Ken and I took the suspect and the rifle to the station. One of the gang officers had his book with photos of various gang members. He got a description of the shooter from the victims, found the photo of the guy he believed it to be in his book, and showed it to each victim.

"Is this the guy?"

Everyone said, "Yeah, that's him."

Guess what? It wasn't him. At the station, I printed the gun for fingerprints. The prints were of an ex-con who had been paroled several months earlier. He had been in prison for shootings and robberies. A warrant was obtained for his arrest, and he was eventually caught. However, the district attorney would not file a case on him because the witnesses had identified someone else. He said there was no way to win the case because of the initial identification issue. It really upset us that this gang officer blew the case. Fortunately, the ex-con violated his parole, and he went back to prison for possession of a rifle.

Metro did special details in addition to crime suppression. Our platoon was sent to Southwest Division at five o'clock one morning to look for a suspect who had separately kidnapped three girls, eight to ten years old, on their way to school. He either lured them or forced them into his car, where he then raped them. We had a description of the suspect and his car, but no license plate number.

Ken and I went to our assigned school and started cruising about five miles per hour. Down one street, we saw a car that was a pretty good match, and we detained the driver. I saw a rip in the headliner over the back seat that matched one of the descriptors provided by a victim who had focused on that rip as she was being raped. We thought this had to be him, or it was an incredible coincidence.

We contacted the Metro office and had them contact the detectives. The detectives said to do a field interview card on the suspect and to release him. Ken and I looked at each other in disbelief. I immediately requested a Metro supervisor to meet us. Sergeant Dave Welts responded, and after looking at the car, he agreed with us and said, "I'll handle it."

Dave went to Southwest Station and was back in twenty minutes with a detective and a detective trainee. The detective had the same attitude at the scene, to do a field interview card and release him, but the trainee disagreed with him and prevailed. The victims identified both our suspect and the car. I was very proud of that arrest.

We were involved in this one shooting. I say "we," but I was in the car and didn't get any rounds off, only Ken did. We were working crime suppression in Seventy-Seventh. We were a couple blocks west of Figueroa on Eighty-Seventh Street, approaching a four-way stop. Ken was driving. Just as we came to the stop, a newer model Ford Mustang convertible came to a stop from the opposite direction. The two guys inside both looked like gangsters. They looked at us, and then they punched it. They burned rubber as they took off, and the chase was on.

The driver threw on the brakes at Figueroa to avoid cross traffic, and he stalled the engine. The passenger door opened, and the passenger got out and ran southbound. The driver got the engine going and started to drive northbound. Ken followed the guy running southbound.

"Ken, what are you doing? The car is going the other way!"

"Yeah, but the guy that's running has a gun in his hand."

I didn't see the gun. Like Mike D'Amato, Ken had incredible vision. At Eighty-Seventh Street, the guy turned the corner and ran eastbound. At the next corner, he turned to run northbound, pointed his gun at us, and fired a shot. Ken had his left hand on the steering wheel. He pulled his Beretta out with his right hand and held it across his chest. When the guy shot at us, Ken stepped on the emergency brake on the car because he didn't have hands to put the car in park. Ken returned fire, first from a sitting position through the open car window and then continuously as he bailed out to a standing position.

I had to get out of the car to get in a position to shoot, and I took a barricade position at the front of the car. The guy went down just as I came up on target. Ken hit him five times. I had broadcast the direction the Mustang went during the chase. Mike Damanakes and Lenny Munoz found it parked behind an apartment building several blocks from where we had last seen it. The driver was in the wind, but he was caught three weeks later. The two were recent parolees and had taken the Mustang in a robbery in Inglewood ten minutes prior to our first seeing them.

On the night of the first day of the '92 riots, our platoon was tasked with protecting firemen responding to a major supermarket fire at 114th Street and Central. We left the command post, and on the way we passed numerous businesses where looting was in progress. The scene was beyond belief. The looters were laughing while they stole everything they could. More than likely, they would then throw a Molotov cocktail to burn the business down. We saw this, but there was nothing we could do other than notify Communications. Our immediate mission was to protect the firemen on the two fire trucks en route to the fire.

At the scene of the fire, Jim Moody and I were positioned to the northeast of the fire, next to an alley. As we were standing there, I heard gunshots coming from the housing project southeast of us. We heard all of this gunfire, like from an AK rifle, but we couldn't see the projects from where we were. I told Jim I was going to see if I could pinpoint where the gunfire was coming from. He agreed, but said that I should make it quick.

I walked down the alley to a backyard that gave access to Alvaro Street, the first street east of us. On the south side of the house was a walkway bordered by an eight-foot wall. A church parking lot was on the other side of the wall. On top of the wall was a short wrought iron fence. Over the wall, I would have a visual of the projects and the intersection of 114th and Alvaro. The rest of the wall around the parking lot was four feet high with the same wrought iron fence on top. I went back to Jim and told him I found a spot.

We both returned to the spot and found a shopping cart to stand on. I put the shopping cart on its end and was able to see over the wall. I wasn't there two minutes when I saw two guys walking between two housing units of the projects. One was holding an AK rifle and took a kneeling position at the corner of one of the housing units, put the AK at his shoulder, and started firing non-stop in the direction of Central Avenue. I knew that other officers and firemen were on Central and believed that this guy was targeting them.

I was a counter-sniper by this time in my career, and I took this guy on. I started firing at him with my rifle. As I was firing, I saw sparks across the church parking lot. I realized some of my rounds were hitting the wrought iron fencing on top of the four-foot wall surrounding the parking lot. I kept shooting, and finally he stopped shooting. I was so focused on the guy with the AK that I didn't realize the other guy had left. The guy with the AK got up and started walking back into the projects, when all of a sudden he fell. He stayed down for a few seconds, got back up, continued walking, and disappeared into the shadows behind one of the project buildings. I thought perhaps I had hit him.

Thinking others in the projects had to have seen me shoot, I ducked down behind the wall. Nothing happened. I raised my head and took a quick look, and I saw a different guy come out with an AK. He fired from a hip position in the direction of Central. At first, he shot in a general direction, and then he started fanning his shots to include where I was standing. As he was doing that, I was shooting at him. He wasn't going down, and I started to question if my rounds were getting through the iron fencing. The guy turned, and he too disappeared into the shadows. I ducked down again and put in a fresh magazine. I heard more gunshots and took a quick peek after the shooting seemed to stop, but I didn't see anything. I was scanning, but I saw nothing. I heard more shooting farther away, but I couldn't see who was doing the shooting.

Jim had been monitoring the radio and told me that we were pulling out. "What do you mean we're pulling out? It's a war zone out here. Why are we pulling out?" I thought that was crazy. Turned out the other officers in the platoon and the firemen on Central were pinned down by the gunfire coming from the projects. They were able to return fire, but at one point, the decision was made for us to leave. I think the command post felt that staying at the location was too risky.

To this day, I disagree with the decision. I feel we should have gone after anyone responsible for shooting at police and firemen. I received a second Medal of Valor for my actions. It was said that I neutralized some of the threat by shooting two of the suspects who had pinned the officers down. With the amount of gunfire, it was absolutely amazing that no officer or fireman was hit.

When I reflect back on my time on the job, I consider myself a lousy officer compared to some of the guys I worked with. They were superb officers, and I learned so much from them. Ken was truly a great partner. We worked together for so long that we reached a point where he knew what I was going to do and I knew what he was going to do. We were a perfect team.

John Puis, back row, second from left: Medal of Valor ceremony, 1993

John Puis

I couldn't wait to get to work, especially when we had a good arrest the day before. I loved being in foot or vehicle pursuits. I drove like a maniac. Ken used to call me a "freeway terrorist" because I drove so hard. And when a suspect I was chasing would give up and stop running, I used to get mad and say, "Hey, keep running. I'm having fun."

But everything changed after the '92 riots. It became harder, I believe, for officers with the hanging threat of being called a racist or being unfairly hit with an accusation of excessive force. It was a good time for me to retire. I thank God for being an American and for the opportunity to have been a police officer.

Jay Moberly

Birthplace: Los Angeles, California
Career: 1975–2010
Rank at Retirement: Detective III
Divisions: Hollywood, Communications, Wilshire, Metropolitan, Van
 Nuys, Central, Robbery-Homicide

For as long as I can remember, I had wanted to be a policeman. My cousin J.J. Thompson joined the Police Department in '63. He was always Jimmy to me, but everybody on the Department knew him as J.J. I was nine years old when I went to his Academy graduation. In the Watts riots in '65, I remember him getting his uniform all torn up, and I think he might have even gotten a bullet graze through his uniform shirt. I was fascinated by what he did. Whenever we'd have family functions, I was all over him asking him to tell me police stories.

When I turned eighteen years of age, Jimmy told me about the student worker program and helped me get hired as a student worker for the Department. The student worker program fit the bill, and I thought the program was outstanding. You had to carry a full load in college, and you could only work twenty hours per week. It was a good job because it gave me insight into how the police worked.

In September of '75, I entered the Academy as a policeman. Jimmy was thrilled that I went on the Department, and he attended my Academy graduation.

Years later when I was working K-9, we had just finished a search for some robbery suspects in Devonshire Division. Jimmy was an assistant watch commander at Devonshire, and we talked when the search was over. I was a little boy when he came on the job, and now I was talking to him policeman to policeman. It was kind of surreal to me.

Jay Moberly with cousin J.J. Thompson: Academy graduation, 1976

At the Academy, I had no confidence in my pistol shooting ability. I thought I'd be disqualified based on my inability to shoot a pistol, even though I'd been a hunter since I was a kid. Shotgun and rifle I was okay with, but a pistol that was different. I had an unrealistic view that policemen could shoot the gun out of a guy's hand, that I had to be an expert pistol shot. As it turned out, despite my initial deficiencies with the pistol, I finished first overall in my class, and that gave me a good burst of confidence.

My first assignment was morning watch at Hollywood Division. The morning watch was a tight group. To say they were cliquish is an understatement. To walk in there and have to prove yourself wasn't easy, especially when you had a lot of military veterans at the time. I had no military experience to speak of. I was in the Air National Guard, but that paled in comparison to Marines that had been in Vietnam.

One of my first training officers was Frank Valdez. The first time I saw Frank was when he walked into roll call. He looked like he was mad at the world. His nickname was Grumpy. He was a good training officer. He taught me a lot and didn't put me in any bad situations.

Hollywood Division police station

The first night I worked with Frank, we got a call to go pick up a forgery suspect at the Holiday Inn. The suspect was in his mid-twenties and the classic Hollywood street hustler. He had gotten into some sort of fracas with the hotel security, and he had a cut lip. Many officers would prefer not to deal with a forgery arrest due to the investigation complexity, but not Frank. He was anxious to teach me about all police work.

On the way to the station, I was trying to fill out a field interview card, and the suspect wouldn't tell me his name or anything. At the station, we put him in the holding tank and went upstairs to Detectives. Frank started to write the arrest report, when the watch commander, Lieutenant Phil Sadlier, came upstairs. He wanted to know whose arrestee was in the holding tank because he was kicking the door. Frank told me to bring the suspect upstairs. I got the suspect, and as we walked by a water fountain, he said his first words, "Can I get a drink of water?"

"Sure."

I pushed the button down for him, and he got a drink of water and washed the blood from his lip. He straightened up, told me his name, and said, "I'll talk to you and nobody else but you. I've got a stolen car sitting behind the Holiday Inn." Then he rattled off the license plate number. I was still new, but who can rattle off the license plate of their own car let alone a stolen car?

I'm in long sleeves and had a butch haircut; I obviously look like a new policeman. I said, "Look at me, man. I'm so new I don't even know where to start."

"I'm only talking to you, so you do with it what you want."

We went upstairs, and I told Frank what the guy had said. Like a good training officer, Frank didn't get too excited. He said, "Go advise him of his rights and get a statement from him."

In the meantime, Frank sent a unit to the Holiday Inn to verify this guy was being truthful. Sure enough, the car was there. I read the suspect his rights, and he started rattling off the crimes he had committed from the Canadian border down to San Diego. He had dates and times and license plate numbers of stolen cars.

I had to stop him. I said, "You are so far over my head I can't keep up with you. Look, my partner's a smoker, and he'll let you smoke. He's a nice guy and will treat you right. You need to let him come in here. I'll stay with you." Frank came in and took the statement. I was impressed. We called in detectives, and it was a big thing. This guy was good for a lot of crimes.

Frank Valdez: "He was anxious to teach me about all police work."

Ike Williams

After probation, I wheeled out of Hollywood to Communications Division. For six months, I would answer a couple hundred phone calls a day. Would I do it again? No, thanks! At Hollywood, I was starting to feel like I knew something about being a cop, and then they put me in purgatory.

From Communications, I transferred to Wilshire Division and shortly thereafter worked the Wilshire Special Problems Unit, a crime suppression detail. My partner was Ike Williams. We were partners for about six months, and Ike and I became pretty close.

One night about ten o'clock, we were in the northeast part of the division in a plain car, but wearing our uniforms. We saw three guys walking on a sidewalk. It didn't matter if they were black, white, or green, Ike would stop anyone who looked like they didn't belong.

When we got out of the car, I heard something metal hit the sidewalk. The suspects had stocking masks and female jewelry in their pockets, and one had blood on his shoes. These guys just looked evil, absolutely evil. I was wondering if the metal sound I heard was a key for a nearby car. I looked around and found a door key. There were only apartment buildings around us. Bud Jablonski and Doug Tantee, part of our unit, met us, and I told Ike, "I'll take a quick look around."

I walked back up the street and turned the corner, and there in front of an apartment building was an ambulance with its lights flashing. The attendants were putting a female into the ambulance, and they had her head all wrapped up. She was in dire straits. The attendants said that she was stabbed in the eye with a knife and in danger of dying.

Ike and I went up to her apartment, and there was a huge puddle of blood and a knife with an eight-inch bent blade lying in the blood. The three guys we stopped had forced their way into this girl's apartment, stabbed her in the eye, and took her jewelry. The knife was plunged into her eye so deep that the suspect actually bent the blade trying to force it deeper. She survived, and later in her testimony in court, she told how she tried to play dead. She also testified that she heard one suspect say, "Kill that bitch," and from another, "She's already dead." How she was able to do that I'll never know.

The lead suspect was on parole from the California Youth Authority for killing a man in front of the man's ten-year-old son. By this time, I'd been involved in a lot of arrests, but this was one of the first times I really questioned the system. I could not understand how somebody like that could be out roving the streets.

This girl came from Texas with aspirations of being a model or an actress. She rented an apartment in what she thought was a decent area, but the female manager of the apartment complex set this girl up. The manager gave one of the thugs a building key. The three guys knocked on the girl's door, she opened it, and they entered.

I'll never forget seeing her in court. She wore a plastic bubble over the eye that had been stabbed. My heart went out for that poor girl. That case was a huge deal for me and a blazing example of what kind of animals are walking around out there. It fortified my desire and my will to fight evil. Fighting evil was why I wanted to be a policeman.

David Kulby's death also had a big impact on me—I remember it like it happened yesterday. Like David, I was a young policeman with about two and a half years on. We were in Wilshire Station when Sergeant Kip Meyerhoff announced over the loudspeaker that David was in a vehicle pursuit southbound on Crenshaw Boulevard. David was working by himself. Ed McKeon and I, along with our supervisor, Mark Mooring, flew out of the station to respond. As we responded, we heard "shots fired, officer down" over the radio, but the radio was broken up and hard to hear.

When we arrived, David looked dead to me. I will never forget the impact of what I saw, and, unfortunately, later on in my career, I saw too much of it. David wasn't dead at the scene; he passed later that night. It was all so senseless because the suspect was an ex-con from Texas. He had committed a robbery in Hollywood and was speeding down Crenshaw when David saw him. Why wasn't he still in prison? The suspect was caught the next morning hiding in a shed in the backyard of a house.

In '79, Mark Mooring and Donn Yarnall submitted a proposal for a Department K-9 Unit. Mark liked my work ethic and knew I trained my own hunting dogs. He asked if I would be interested if the proposal was accepted. I loved working with dogs and told him yes. Several months later Mark called me and said the K-9 Unit was approved. They had authorization for two more handlers, and he asked John Lopata and me to be in the program.

My first dog was Elka, a female shepherd. She was a little dog that looked like a coyote. John's dog, Rooster, looked like a bear. Officers in the field would look at Rooster and then look at Elka, and I could sense they were looking at me and thinking, *What are you going to do with that little thing?*

Jay Moberly, Elka, Donn Yarnall, Popeye, Mark Mooring, Blue, 1981

Elka was a good dog. When I first went to look at her, she wouldn't even let me in the house. I had to sweet talk her, and by the time our initial meet was over, she was good with me. She was about one and a half years old at the time, and I ended up having her for almost fifteen years. She outlived them all. When I had to put her down, it was not a lot different than losing a child or a family member. She would have laid down her life for me without even thinking about it. She was with me twenty-four hours a day for four years of her life when she was in service. Elka was a fantastic dog and a great home protector.

However, she could be moody. Some nights she wasn't on her best game, but on others, she did exceptional stuff. I remember searching the train yards in Central Division for a robbery suspect one night on morning watch. It was foggy, colder than hell, and the wind was blowing. We were walking along, when she put her nose up and started running. She ran a couple hundred yards and then made a beeline to a railroad car. There was our guy wedged up between the axle and the undercarriage with only a small patch of his jeans showing. We would never have found that guy without a dog.

My first shooting was on Mother's Day, and my wife was home pregnant with our first daughter. I had Elka in the back seat, and I was driving on Pacific Coast Highway. The K-9 Unit was still working out of West L.A. Division. It was around nine o'clock at night; it hadn't been dark all that long. All of a sudden, a car with college-age kids stopped next to me. They were in a full-blown panic and yelling, "There's a black guy with a knife down the street trying to kill a white guy."

Then another car stopped, and I was told the same story. I put out a broadcast that citizens advised a possible assault was in progress at Will Roger's State Beach. There was a mile or more of parking lots along the beach, and as I was looking in the parking lots, I saw a big guy holding a long two-by-four, waving at me frantically. He said, "This guy tried to kill me, he tried to kill my girlfriend, and he's in the parking lot. He's crazy."

I pulled into the parking lot, and I saw a black male holding a knife down by his side. The guy was mumbling to himself and prancing around in a circle. I put out an assistance call, and I lit him up in my headlights. His eyeballs were dancing around, and I immediately thought PCP. He seemed focused on a car parked to my left with several females inside and a group of people standing behind it.

I got out of my car, shined my flashlight on him, and told him to drop the knife. He was about thirty feet away and now focused on me instead of the car, which was what I wanted. I was in a remote location, and at this point, all I could do was hold my ground, wait for the cavalry, and hope he holds his ground.

Meanwhile, Elka was in the back of the car going insane. She wanted to come out and do her thing, but that was a suicide mission. I wasn't letting her out on a guy with a knife—that's just nuts. That's not what the dogs are there for.

The suspect became considerably more heated up; more agitated, and then all of a sudden charged toward the civilian car yelling, "I'm going to cut one of these motherfuckers."

I fired a round, and it paralyzed him instantly. Then I put out a help call. Just before I fired, an incident I was involved in as a training officer at Wilshire went through my head. We responded to a help call at Pico and La Cienega where an officer had just shot and killed a PCP suspect who earlier had thrashed a liquor store and armed himself with a knife. He then ran into the street, climbed up onto a car stopped at the intersection, and jumped up and down on the roof of the car. The female driver quickly rolled up her window and locked the door. The suspect broke the glass of one window and stabbed the girl in the face. Officer Amos Lauder engaged the suspect who then started chasing Amos around the car with a knife. Amos shot and killed the guy. I thought about that when I was in the standoff with this guy. The people inside the car think they're in a safety zone, and I know they're in a death trap.

The incident at the beach started when the guy with the two-by-four and his girlfriend got a flat tire. As the guy retrieved items from the trunk, the suspect came out of nowhere saying, "I'm going to kill you." The suspect chased the guy, as the guy tried to back away. The college kids saw this and then stopped me. The suspect then went after the guy's girlfriend, who had gone to a payphone to call the police. He put a knife to her throat and dragged her out into the parking lot. The boyfriend and a truck driver were about to try to save her when they saw me. She managed to escape from the suspect.

The shooting was deemed out of policy. By the look on your face, I see you're just as perplexed by that decision as I was and a lot of people were. The shooting review board thought my actions were precipitous, that I should have done all kinds of different things. Suggestions included: Why didn't I use Elka? Why didn't I take on the guy with my baton? I somehow should have disarmed the suspect prior to him charging the group.

Lieutenant Chuck Higbie who was in charge of the officer-involved-shooting investigation team said to me, "I've got to remain neutral in these things, but you got screwed big time." Higbie said he took a chair and threw it clear across the room and stormed out.

Chuck Higbie was the lead investigator on four of my five shootings. He was a man that gave so much of himself because he loved cops so much. He gave you a fighting chance, gave you every benefit of the doubt, believed in what you did and would go to the mat for you. Chuck was a huge influence on me, no doubt. I revered the guy. He gave me his Sam Browne equipment belt when he retired.

l to r: Chuck Higbie, Eddie Garcia, George Haines, Patrick McKinley, Bob Smitson (all retired LAPD)

I received an official reprimand, which didn't make sense to me because they were essentially saying I got a paper penalty for killing a man I shouldn't have killed. I appealed the decision, and for three days, civilian witnesses came in and testified to what they saw. I still lost the appeal.

I don't believe it was personal, just politics. I was bitter for a long time because I didn't understand nor did I accept their decision. Did it really hurt me in the long run? No. Temporarily, it was bad news. All the people that testified came and thanked me. In the big scheme of things, that was all I needed.

While still battling the Department on my first shooting, I was involved in a second one. A couple of bandits were running around the San Fernando Valley robbing folks about four o'clock in the morning. Phil Wagner and his probationer, Bob Kraus, Jr., spotted the bandits in a 7-Eleven parking lot on Balboa at Sherman Way. One suspect was an ex-con and gave up right away, no fighting. The younger suspect got out of the car and ran. He slipped through an opening in a fence behind the store into a dirt field covered with thigh-high mustard plants.

Bob, who would later work SIS and whose father had been on the job, went after the suspect. As Bob started onto the field, all of a sudden *boom boom boom!* He was being fired on. Bob didn't see any muzzle flash; he only heard the gunshots with the bullets landing near him when he went to the ground for cover.

Mike Long and I responded. When we got there, Mike and I decided his dog, Duke, was a much better dog for this situation than Elka. We were going to clear the field, but we needed to get Bob out of there first. He was dug in, afraid if he stood up he would be fired on. We convinced him that we had him covered, and he came out of the field.

Mike and I started the search with Duke. Behind the field was a row of apartment housing with a wall separating it from the field. We had to clear the field first to get to the wall, and I remember never having been so fearful in my life. The mustard plants were so thick I couldn't see my feet, and the suspect could be anywhere. It was just the two of us; Mike was handling the dog, and I was the shotgun guy. I thought, *If I see a muzzle flash, I'm pulling the trigger because that may be our only chance.*

We cleared the field and were working our way up the block with a pretty stiff breeze at our backs. Duke walked past a car in a driveway, and then I saw the suspect under the car. The second I saw him the dog alerted on him. I yelled to Mike, "The suspect's under the car!"

We were scrambling for cover. The dog circled the car, trying to figure out a way to get under it. The suspect was trying to decide what he was going to do and when he was going to do it. He had his gun in his hand. I told him three or four times to stop moving his hands and to drop the gun. He said, "Get that dog out of here!"

I knew what was coming and yelled at Mike, "Get your dog! Get your dog!"

The suspect raised his gun, and I fired.

About six months later, I was in the station, and the desk officer said, "Hey, Jay, you've got a phone call."

I picked up the phone and said, "Officer Moberly. Can I help you?"

A female voice said, "Is this Officer Moberly?"

"Yes."

"This is the sister of the man you killed, and you're going to die."

She hung up the phone. There was an investigation, but she denied making the call. Nothing ever happened, but I had police protection at my house for several days for fear of something happening to my family.

When Elka developed hip dysplasia, she worked no longer, than we had to until I could get another dog. I grabbed Erko when he became available, and we worked together for six years. I've seen some great police dogs, but none could top Erko's desire to hunt.

One of Erko's most amazing searches was in Rampart Division. Erko engaged the suspect, and they're battling. The suspect got away, climbed onto a wooden fence, and then up onto an overhanging garage roof. Erko got half of his body onto the fence and then propelled himself up onto the roof. Once on the roof, Erko re-engaged the suspect, who pushed Erko off the roof. Erko fell onto a pile of bicycles between the fence and the garage. I looked down at him from the other side of the fence, but now I was in the heat of a battle with the suspect. I figured Erko was probably dead.

We managed to pull the suspect off the roof, and he was still fighting. Next thing I know, Erko found his way back into the yard and was back in the fight, and we were able to take the suspect into custody. Erko just amazed me all the time. Fortunately, he only had a few bruises; it didn't slow him down at all.

One time there was a two- to three-week period where a string of banks on Ventura Boulevard were being robbed by guys wearing different kinds of masks. One day a witness saw the suspects' car as it was leaving a bank they had just robbed and called the police. An officer spotted the car, and the chase was on! It ended in the hills overlooking the San Fernando Valley.

The suspects bailed out of the car and ran into the hills. The officers found masks in the car, so they knew they were the bank robbery suspects. I was called out, along with two other K-9 units, to conduct a search. It was summertime, and it was hot. This was rattlesnake country big time, just wide-open territory. I even told the air unit to pick a landing spot in case a handler or a dog was bitten. We could not establish an effective perimeter because there were no boundaries. We searched and searched—and nothing.

Then Erko picked up a foxtail thorn in his ear, which can kill a dog. I radioed the sergeant and told him Erko was hurting and we were on our way back. We were walking along the edge of a gully, and when I say gully, I don't mean the kind you can step across—it was big and deep. You'd have to hike down one side and then back up the other to cross. Erko was out ahead of me a little bit, his head came straight up, and he picked up his pace. His tail flagged, and all of the sudden he took off.

You have to remember that we're not following ground tracks. The dog is working off the scent that comes off the body. To a properly trained dog's nose, the fear scent a person pumps out when they're in fight or flight syndrome is overpowering. Humans can't smell it. We went for several hundred feet along the top of this embankment, and we were off to the races. We were not walking; we're running.

I didn't want to stop Erko; I knew he was on the right track. He zipped down to the bottom of the gully and into some trees where he found the two suspects, and the fight was on. One suspect tried to kick Erko in the face to get him to back off, which made him fight harder. Then they pepper sprayed him, but that didn't affect him. We took them into custody, and one suspect still had on his mask. Without a good dog, those guys might still be robbing banks today. Erko was hurt; he had blood in his ear from trying to shake out the thorn and was on his way back to the car when he found both suspects. That was classic Erko.

One night John Hall and I were called to Southwest Division after officers had pursued four gangsters who shot at them during the initial stop and again during the pursuit. The pursuit ended in an area full of alleys and multiple-story apartment buildings. The suspects crashed their car and ran. One suspect exchanged gunfire with the officers as he ran across the street and then down an alley. John and I were tasked with finding him.

In this area, the odds of finding a suspect were against you because some residents would let the crooks come in and hide. I thought it was an exercise in futility because by now these guys were probably in somebody's house. I had no confidence that we would find them.

John had his dog, Chaz, and I had Erko. John will tell you as quickly as I will; Erko was the better dog for this type of scenario. As a dog handler, you have to know your dog's pluses and minuses because you go into the worst of the worst and you need a dog that really wants to battle. It wasn't five seconds after I unleashed Erko that he goes into a full-blown alert. Even at that point, I didn't think he found him, probably just a cat or a rat. Erko went into a carport stacked two deep with cars. Behind the deepest car in the carport, I heard Erko growling. I went prone to the ground, and John did the same to my right. I heard John yell, "Gun!"

I saw the gun in the suspect's hand pointed at us, and we both fired. Once we were convinced the suspect was neutralized, I went to get Erko out of there. John had the suspect covered, and I had to go over the top of John to get to my dog. I grabbed Erko, and as I went back over John, Erko grabbed John by the butt and latched on.

Oh, John has never mentioned that to you. He forgot that part, did he? He's got the scars to prove it, trust me. Erko put a big love bite on him. Erko had just been in a fight and had heard gunshots—it was a reflex type of thing. It was another one those situations where a less capable and driven dog might have just walked past that guy, and then we ultimately would have had our backs to the suspect. Who knows what could have happened then.

Eventually, Donn Yarnall left the unit, and I became the head trainer. Then things changed. The Department initiated a find-and-bark policy, which is difficult to rely on in tactical situations. Before, our policy was to find the suspect and go from there; the suspect will dictate what happens. A dog will bite if a suspect is aggressive or tries to get away; it won't bite a passive suspect. I just couldn't go with the new policy.

We also reduced the number of searches we were involved in. We went from being out in the field and backing up officers to staying on the training field and waiting for the big one. A handler recently told me they're lucky if they do one hundred searches in a year. In a year, we had done over two thousand searches. The mindset became: The less you do, the less you get in trouble, the less you may be sued. I was sued multiple times in municipal, state, and federal courts, all involving dog-bite situations. I never lost a lawsuit.

Another change for the unit was that the Department wanted supervisors to just be supervisors, so they no longer handled dogs. There may be some logic in that, but it started to cause a problem. We took direction from sergeants with no concept of what it took to handle a dog.

It just wasn't fun to go to work anymore. I don't blame the Department; that's just the way things evolved primarily from a civil liability standpoint. A team of civil lawyers had a database on all of the dog handlers. They knew us better than we knew ourselves. They knew our dogs' names, their bite ratios, all this stuff. All the changes actually did me a favor because I would have never taken the sergeant's test otherwise. I ultimately decided to promote to sergeant because I didn't necessarily agree with the changes taking place within the K-9 Unit. Probably even more of a factor though was that Erko was still active when he died in his sleep next to my bed. My spirit for K-9 operations died with this incredible dog.

I made sergeant and was assigned to Van Nuys Division. I had one bad day as a sergeant, and that was my very first one. Near end of watch, I was walking around wondering where my people were and realized how I was now responsible for others. I had come from a place where I was responsible for just my dog and me. I came home and told my wife I thought I made the biggest mistake.

Jay Moberly and Erko

On the way to work the second day, I told myself, *You're a sergeant of police now. You get to make decisions. That's why they're paying you.* That day I got in some stuff in the field requiring me to make some decisions, and from that day on, it was fun and I loved it. I loved every day of it.

When it came time to be wheeled, I was sent to Central Division. On morning watch, I realized there was no one on the downtown streets but cops and criminals. What really spiked my interest was the number of junkies walking around, heroin addicts by the dozens, it seemed.

One night I was around Seventh and Main, and it looked like a junkie convention in front of this hotel. I started talking to the younger cops and asked them, "Do we not book hypes anymore?"

"Nope, nobody books them anymore."

To them a hype arrest was only a misdemeanor and not worth their time. I tried to impress on the officers that when you're looking at a hype, you're looking at a one-man crime wave. If a hype has a hundred-dollar-a-day dope habit and no job, how do you think he's supporting that habit? Nobody was really too interested to be honest with you.

In fact, one night a couple young officers wrote a guy a traffic ticket at Seventh and Maple—a long-haired white male who looked like he belonged down on the beach, but was clearly a hype. I watched their contact with him. The guy was loaded. They wrote him a ticket and let him go. He just walked down the street. I was amazed they let him go. I stopped the guy, and we had a conversation. His name was Peter. I arrested him for being under the influence of heroin.

About a month later, I was in line for a cup of coffee at a coffee shop at Seventh and Maple, and I heard this raspy voice behind me say, "Hey, Moberly."

I turned around, and it was Peter.

"You remember me?"

"Yeah, I remember you."

"Can you talk?"

"Sure."

We went off into the shadows, and then he said, "Do you know who Jimmy Lee Smith is?"

"Yeah, of course I know who Jimmy Lee Smith is."

In 1963, Smith and Gregory Powell kidnapped Officers Ian Campbell and Karl Hettinger out of Hollywood Division, drove them to Bakersfield, and killed Campbell. Smith and Powell were caught and sent to prison. Smith was later paroled.

"Do you want him?"

"Of course I do. Where's he at?"

Peter told me that Smith hung out around Ninth and San Pedro with a longhaired American Indian and that both were junkies. Peter thought the other guy was also wanted.

I went to the area with another unit, and there was Mr. Smith, the infamous Onion Field Killer himself. Both guys were loaded, and the other guy did have a felony warrant for robbery. We arrested them both, and I booked Smith for being under the influence. Smith went back to jail for a hundred-plus days. Smith was later released and arrested again. He went back to prison, where he eventually died. No one should forget that God-awful thing he did that night in '63.

I started arresting hypes every now and then, and I would do everything myself. One night I was writing the arrest report on a hype when our new patrol captain, Dave Smith, asked if he could ride with me. You didn't tell a captain no, so we went out in the field.

I said, "Captain, there's really not a lot going on out here. Do you want to ride around all night and do nothing, or would you like to go talk to some folks?"

"You do whatever you do. I'm just sitting here."

So we went out and talked to a couple hypes. I was always amazed by a hype's story about where they came from and how they got to be on the street. I remember one who had been an electrical contractor and lived in a big house with a wife and kids. He tried heroin, and the next thing he's living in the bushes at Third and Flower with rats chewing on his clothes. He became one of my better informants for who was dealing dope and where. After we talked to a few folks, Captain Smith made a comment to me that it seemed like I knew everybody out there.

Soon thereafter, Captain Smith formed a ten-man Hype Task Force with me as the supervisor. This was one of the most incredible periods of my career. We were golden. We booked a hundred to a hundred and fifty hypes a month. We decreased property crimes by forty-two percent or some incredible thing like that. The unit was very successful.

At the time, Al Gonzalez was in charge of Central Division Homicide Unit, and he offered me a spot in Homicide. I turned him down, and he offered again about six months later. I turned him down a second time. When he offered a third time, I thought, *I have twenty-one years on the job, and this might not be a bad time.*

In twenty-one years, I never had a daytime job. I worked off-hours my whole career. Now that would change. I went home and talked to the family. I told my seven-year-old daughter that I could be home at night with her and on the weekends. She started crying. That was enough for me, that was all I needed to make the decision. I accepted and went to Central Homicide.

In Homicide, I had a great partner, Cliff Shepard. Cliff was an experienced detective who I had known for a long time. Our first case was a classic Skid Row case. A guy was robbed for a pack of cigarettes. The suspect pushed the guy down, and the guy got injured and went to the hospital. He developed peritonitis and died never having left the hospital. The coroner labeled it a homicide.

The robbery report was all of eight lines. The suspect was described only as a black male. The robbery occurred at Fifth and Main, and the person who called the police was never identified. Cliff and I went to the hotels at Fifth and Main and started knocking on doors and talking to folks. It was eight months after the robbery—who's still going to be in any of these rickety hotels?

We played the tape-recorded phone call of the unknown person who reported the robbery for a security guy at one of the hotels. He listened to the voice and said, "That's Ina."

"You're sure?"

"Yeah, that's her voice."

Cliff Shepard, far left: "...a great partner."

We went to her room, and there was a great view of where the robbery happened. She told us she recognized the guy that did the crime and knew him only by his initials: L.D.

Cliff was a wizard with the computer. I knew a lot of folks on the street, but Cliff knew the computer. We identified the suspect, and he was in custody for a robbery in Chicago. We took a trip to Chicago and extradited the suspect back to L.A. Once here, the suspect admitted to the robbery and got a couple of years in prison.

The kind of witnesses you have working murders on Skid Row are down-and-out folk, and they are the toughest witnesses. First of all, good luck finding them. And if you find them, you have to establish a rapport with them so they'll want to help you. If you talk right, they can be great witnesses. My way of thinking is if you can take a homicide on Skid Row to its very end and be successful, then you can probably do it about anywhere. It was fun because it was challenging.

A year later, I got an offer to work Robbery-Homicide Division. I was assigned to a task force investigating the SLA, the Symbionese Liberation Army, a left-wing revolutionary group involved in bank robberies, murder, and the kidnapping of Patty Hearst, daughter of William Randolph Hearst, the newspaper mogul.

In 1974, six SLA members were in a shootout with SWAT, and all six died when the house they were in burned down. In retaliation, Kathleen Soliah and other SLA members placed pipe bombs underneath two parked police cars, one in a parking lot of a restaurant in Hollywood and the other at Hollenbeck Station.

John Hall, my partner later in K-9, and J.J. Bryant were finishing dinner in Hollywood, when they rushed out to respond to a robbery in progress radio call. J.J. was driving, and the way he jerked the car backing out of the restaurant parking spot created a gap between the contact pins of the pipe bomb underneath their car. One-sixteenth of an inch prevented the bomb from detonating. If the bomb had gone off, the officers and restaurant patrons would have died or been seriously injured.

Unaware of the bomb underneath their car, John and J.J. left the location. Citizens found it and notified the police. The Department initiated a check of all other police vehicles and found the second bomb. The Hollenbeck police car the second bomb was found under was often used to transport kids assigned to the Explorer Program. The subsequent investigation tied the bombs to the SLA.

I had heard about John Hall while I was a probationer at Hollywood, and it was obvious he was a division legend as a street cop. Just off probation, I got to work with John one night. My partner had called in sick, and John came up to me and said we were working together. It was like meeting Mickey Mantle. I was excited and a little bit fearful at the same time. I didn't want to let him down. After five minutes in the car, he was treating me like we're old buddies. He asked, "What do you want to do?" He made me comfortable so that I could learn from him. That made an impression on me, and later as a training officer, I would pattern myself after John.

Then John and I worked K-9 together for a long time. I started my career working with this legendary guy who I didn't even know on a personal basis, and the guy today is my best friend. Now twenty-three years later, I'm assigned to the task force investigating the bomb placed under John's car by the SLA.

John Hall: "It was like meeting Mickey Mantle."

The SLA Task Force was formed because of the effort of three young and energetic detectives from Criminal Conspiracy Section: Dave Reyes, Mike Fanning, and Ray Morales. While dusting off old warrant packages, they came across the name Kathleen Soliah with an outstanding arrest warrant for the attempted murder of a police officer. The initial investigative effort in '75 identified Soliah and others with placing the pipe bombs, as well as other crimes, but she fled and had been living on the lam for over twenty years.

They located Soliah living in Minnesota under the alias Sara Jane Olson. She was extradited back to Los Angeles. In order to prosecute her, we had to track down witnesses to the crimes she committed. My job was to track down witnesses to a bank robbery in Carmichael, California, where she and others killed bank customer Myrna Lee Opsahl, a forty-two-year-old housewife. We ultimately went to court in Sacramento, and Soliah pled guilty to her crimes, including placing the pipe bomb under John's car.

My biggest case at Robbery-Homicide was a quadruple homicide. I was at home when the phone rang. My lieutenant directed me and my partner, Vic Pietrantoni, to respond to a homicide in the Hollywood Hills. It was about six in the morning, a big crowd was there, and detectives were all over the place. The Fire Department had responded to a fire at the house and found four bodies inside. Was it a robbery? Was the house ransacked? How do you tell? The fire had demolished the place, and there was water everywhere. A crime scene like that is a nightmare for homicide detectives. How do you tell what's what? At the start, it was a complete whodunit.

It was a brutal scene, unlike anything I had ever seen before in my life. One of the victims was a sixteen-year-old girl, a dark-haired version of my own daughter, who was about the same age. The girl was bound with her hands behind her back, duct tape around her mouth, with her ankles tied together with zip ties. She was burnt so badly that part of one arm and part of one leg were burnt off. The family was killed in a way that I wouldn't wish on anything or anybody. Even a rattlesnake should get a more dignified death than that, and I'm not very fond of rattlesnakes.

The victims were this sixteen-year-old girl, her eighteen-year-old brother, their mother, and their grandmother. The father had come home from out of town around eleven-thirty the prior night to find his house on fire. He called the Fire Department and then attempted to save his family, but the fire was too intense. At first, we thought he may be our guy, but we couldn't figure out the motive.

The father owned a hotel. The hotel was very nice, a hotel where you would take your wife and daughter. However, next door was another hotel that you wouldn't be seen at with a two-dollar prostitute. It was a dive.

There was a shed-like structure sitting on an easement between both properties, and it had been the subject of a dispute between the father and the two owners of the other hotel. Both hotels wanted to expand into this easement. Initially, we didn't get too excited about the dispute, but as the case progressed, it was the only thing we had.

Turned out, it was all we needed because the dispute was the cause for the murders. They occurred six days before a hearing that would have probably been decided in favor of the father. The owners and a third person committed the murders. The third person testified against the owners because of the torture the two owners inflicted on the victims. All three went to prison.

When I retired, it wasn't because I was tired of being a policeman, that's for sure. I never got tired of that; I always loved it. I was always very proud of my job, and I was treated very well by the Department. I just thought I didn't fit anymore. I wasn't a tech guy, and things were getting so high-tech that I had to go to some of the younger detectives to help me. Nowadays, if you're not tech savvy as a detective, you're really behind the power curve because the crooks are all tech savvy. I was way behind on the tech stuff, and I was not motivated to get up to speed.

I miss the people; I really do. I believe that police officers are the purest people on the planet. One of the things I have to say, almost shamefully admit, is that I disconnected from the Police Department after retiring. Not on purpose, it just happened. Whenever I run into guys I used to work with, it's always fun to chat with them. It's amazing how a conversation refreshes your memory on things.

The one common interest we all shared was fighting evil. I liked learning how to find it and what to do with it. I like to dig. A policeman was all I ever wanted to be, and I wasn't disappointed.

Jay Moberly and Elka: "A policeman was all I ever wanted to be and I wasn't disappointed."

Frankie Yan

Frankie Yan

Birthplace: Hong Kong
Career: 1976–2003
Rank at Retirement: Sergeant II
Divisions: Southwest, Central, Rampart, Seventy-Seventh, Narcotics,
   Internal Affairs

While I was in college studying to be a criminologist, I worked at
Johnny's Liquor Store in Chinatown, where I grew up. I had
known Johnny since I was a kid. When I was eighteen, I started working
for him, stocking his store after closing time. I worked a couple of hours
every night. Once in a while, some policemen from Central Division
would come by the store. Johnny loved the police and had a great
relationship with them.

I would listen to their stories, and they encouraged me to become a
police officer. Once I graduated from college, I looked into being a cop,
but there was a hiring freeze, so I did odd jobs to keep myself busy.
When the freeze lifted, there was an advertisement that the Department
was accepting applications at Roosevelt High School. I slept overnight
on the sidewalk, waiting in line to put in my application.

Later, Officer Cliff Wong from the Recruitment Section contacted
me and helped me through the hiring process. Cliff was one of the first,
if not the first, Chinese officer on the Department. We became good
friends, and I still see him today.

When I came on in '76, there were only a few other Chinese officers
on the job. One of them, Arthur Soo Hoo, was in the Academy class
ahead of me, and we had known each other since we were kids. In '83,
Arthur and William Wong were killed when another car broadsided
their police car. There were three guys in the other car. Two were
arrested, and the driver fled the scene. He was caught almost twenty

years later living in Northern California. Arthur's death was a big shock to me. He was raised in Chinatown, and he died in Chinatown.

In the Academy, we went on ride-alongs, and mine were in Central Division. On the first ride-along, you rode as the third officer in the car. Then on your next one, you rode as the second officer in the car, and you handled the radio. On my second ride-along, I worked with Ken Small. I didn't want to mess up on the radio, so I kept telling myself what I had to say when I cleared us for radio calls. I memorized it and felt ready.

I grabbed the mic and said, "One Adam Eleven, show us clear, ready to handle radio calls." Kenny looked at me and said, "Why don't you try that again, and this time turn the radio on!"

On probation, I was sent to Southwest Division. On my first day, I had to wait several hours for my training officer, Al Pesanti, to get out of court. Not too exciting. Al was a great training officer. He was a hard charger, and I learned a lot from him, essentially how to do police work that made a difference.

Southwest Division police station (formerly University Division)

Al Pesanti

His favorite thing was a VIN switch on cars. A suspect would switch the visible vehicle identification number on the dashboard of a car that was not stolen onto a stolen car to hide the fact the car was stolen. We stopped a '66 Chevy one day that had a VIN switch. We arrested the driver and took the car to the station.

At the station, we put the car up on the hoist, and using a mirror, Al showed me the hidden number on the car frame. The hidden number was an additional identifier of the car. He said, "Okay, kid, read that number off to me." I did, and we were able to confirm the car was stolen.

One time Al and I had a victim whose wallet was stolen or lost. Someone had it and demanded a reward from the victim for the return of the wallet. We formulated a plan on how to get the wallet back. Keith Jackson was going to pose as the victim driving the victim's car. Al and I were going to hide in the trunk of the car. Keith was going to make contact with the suspect, honk the horn as a signal, and then Al and I would jump out of the trunk and arrest the suspect.

Al and I were in the trunk in uniform, and I was holding the trunk lid down with my hand. We got there, Keith had a quick conversation with the suspect, and then he honked the horn. Al kicked the trunk lid open before I could clear my fingers from the latch. That made a cut across my knuckles, and they started bleeding like crazy. We jumped out of the trunk and went in foot pursuit, and I caught the guy. When we took him into custody, the suspect started freaking out when he saw blood all over him.

Over and over, he was yelling, "You didn't have to shoot me!"

I told him, "That's my blood on you."

He really thought we had shot him. We got the wallet.

My first commendation was for my tactics in saving the life of a sergeant. We responded to a family dispute. When we got there, a sergeant was fighting with a female, trying to subdue her on the sidewalk. As my partner went to assist the sergeant, I took a position between the house and the sergeant. The sister of the girl fighting came out of the house with a barely visible paring knife in her right fist and walked toward her sister. The way she held the knife was in a position to stab. and I believed she intended to harm the sergeant.

I pulled my revolver out as I was telling her to drop the knife. She refused and kept coming. As I was making up my mind on whether to shoot or not, another officer hit her on the arm with his baton, which caused her to drop the knife.

My supervisor, Gary Thomas, who everyone called Bumper, told me afterwards, "Son, you just made probation." I had two months on. The sergeant who was in the fight also thanked me and said I may have saved his life. It made me realize how dangerous the job could be.

When I finished my probation, I remained at Southwest for a few months. One night I was working with Mike Apodaca. We got a radio call of a family dispute, possible cutting, on Adams Boulevard. It was an apartment building, and a lady met us when we arrived. She told us there was a couple in the upstairs apartment that had been recently married. She heard them fighting, went to investigate, and saw blood on the wife.

Mike and I went to the apartment, and the front door was ajar. We announced our presence, but no answer. We entered and saw no one, but the bedroom door was partially closed. We pushed the bedroom door open, and there was the husband sitting on the bed with a knife to his wife's throat as she sat on his lap. He looked at us and said, "I'm going to kill her." She had one hand on his arm with the knife trying to keep him from cutting her throat.

Mike and I drew our guns and used the doorframe to brace ourselves. Mike was telling the husband to drop the knife. The husband was yelling over and over that he was going to kill her, and then he started shaking uncontrollably. He really looked like he was going to lose it, really go off. Just as I was thinking, *Do I need to shoot this guy?—pop!* Mike let off a round.

The guy fell like a sack of potatoes. As he did, the knife fell into his wife's hand. She stood up on the bed hysterically screaming and hollering while holding the knife. I yelled at her to drop the knife. She calmed down somewhat and did drop it. Mike's shot hit the husband right between his eyes and nose. The bullet ricocheted downward, and when he fell to the floor, the bullet came right out of his mouth. He survived and even walked into court for the preliminary hearing. That was our 158-grain bullet for you. He pled guilty to assault with a deadly weapon.

When my turn came to be wheeled, I went to Central Division. At first, I walked a footbeat in Skid Row and drove the B-wagon. Eventually, I worked my old neighborhood in Chinatown. I knew all the gang members because I grew up with a lot of them. Just after I started working Chinatown, somebody shot the windows out of my dad's parked car with a shotgun. It was a message of intimidation by the Chinese gangs who believed I might use my position as a police officer to unfairly go after them. We never found out who did the actual shooting, but I came to an understanding with the gangsters. They knew if they screwed up, I would do my job, as I would with any other person. Straight-up police work: either I had the evidence to arrest them, or I didn't. There were no further problems.

A Chinese fireman was going to get married and had a bachelor party at a strip club in Chinatown. When the party was over, the fireman and his brother came out to the parking lot where they tangled with some gang members and a fight ensued. One gang member was losing his fight and shot the fireman's brother, killing him. The gang members fled. I wasn't working that night, but the homicide detectives came to me and gave me a description of the shooter. I kept a little book with pictures and pertinent information on the Chinese gang members. Once I was given the description, I said this is his name and here is his information. They then centered the homicide investigation on him.

Chinatown

A few days later, I was working with Candy Shimizu, a probationer, and we made a traffic stop at Alpine Avenue and Broadway. As we were finishing our stop, one of my informants walked by and told me the homicide suspect who killed the fireman's brother was around the corner. I ran around the corner, and the suspect was walking out of a restaurant. I grabbed him and took him into custody.

The suspect said, "What are you arresting me for?"

"For murder."

As I was walking him back, Candy, who did not know of the fireman's murder, asked me what I was arresting the guy for.

"Murder."

"Really?"

We took him to the station, and when we arrived, the detectives that were handling the case were walking out of the station to go home.

I said, "I have your murder suspect."

They both said, "Really?"

The suspect, the one I had identified, copped to the murder and went to prison. That arrest was possible because I knew the neighborhood and the people in the neighborhood.

My first suicide call in Central was a jumper. Rich Kansaki and I got a radio call of a naked man on Eighth at Hope Street. When we pulled up, we could see a naked man walking along the edge of a four-story parking structure. I turned my head for a moment to see if any pedestrians were coming and as I turned my head back and looked up, all I saw was a body falling. He landed maybe fifteen feet away from me in the street. This guy hitting the street is a sound I'll never, ever forget. I can hear it in my mind as we talk. We later found out he might have been under the influence of PCP.

After a couple of years at Central, I applied for a Vice spot at Rampart Division and got it. That job was probably the most fun I had in my career—and the most dangerous.

We had a gambling complaint one time in an alley at Twelfth Street and Arapahoe. Our game plan was to have George Azpeitia and Marvina Strong park a car in a position close enough to watch the gamblers and, as cover, act like they were lovers. My partner, Adam Gauba, Sergeant Sal Hoyos, and I would be in another car covering them. I was driving, Adam was in the front seat, and Sal was in the back seat. We were in an old two-door Plymouth Volare. It was nighttime.

On the way to the location, George and Marvina told us they were stopping for cigarettes. We told them we would meet them at the location. I made a right turn off Alvarado onto Twelfth. As we were driving on Twelfth, I looked in my rearview mirror and saw a car with its headlights on coming up behind us fast. I pulled over to the right and jammed on the brakes. We stopped real fast, and a red AMC Javelin went right by us as the passenger fired a shot at us. He missed, and the car abruptly stopped about fifty feet in front of us.

The driver and the passenger in the car bailed out and started shooting at us. Adam and I returned fire. All we were carrying were five-shot revolvers. Sal had his duty gun, a four-inch .38 revolver, but he couldn't get out of the back seat. These guys were unloading on us with nine-millimeter handguns. I shouted to Adam, "I'm empty." I was dropping the empty shells and reloading as I was putting out a help call.

Then Adam yelled he was empty and had no other ammo. I had more rounds in another loader, and I threw it over to him. The two suspects must have heard us yell we were out of ammo and started walking back toward us shooting.

Sal, who was stuck in the back seat, leaned over the top of the passenger front seat and out the side of the car and started firing at the suspects. Sal's added fire stopped them. They ran back to their car, got in, and drove off.

Sal could not get out because of a malfunctioning latch lock that would not let him move the front seat forward. Because of this incident, the seat latch locks were disabled in other two-door undercover cars, and all undercover officers were required to carry extra ammunition.

The suspects drove to the end of the block and turned southbound on the next street out of sight. We got back in our car and drove to the end of the block where the suspects had turned, and there they were, stopped in the middle of the street. Anticipating a second attack, I reversed our car away from them, but they then drove off. The suspect's car was found abandoned on Alvarado near where we had seen a group of Hispanic guys hanging out when we made our initial turn onto Twelfth.

Sal Hoyos: "Sal's added fire stopped them."

The detectives did a follow-up investigation and several days later arrested one of the suspects. I went to court, and he pled guilty to assault with a deadly weapon. A warrant was issued for the other suspect, and he was caught several years later. When he went to court, the judge released him on his own recognizance, and he fled. He disappeared and was never arrested again.

Apparently, the group of Hispanics we saw standing on Alvarado were drug dealers and had been ripped off by other drug dealers earlier that evening. The other drug dealers were driving a car similar to ours, and so two guys from the Hispanic group came after us thinking we were the guys that had ripped them off.

Amazingly, nobody was hit, but our car was hit several times, including one round that went right through the middle of the driver's side door. Fortunately, I had learned not to stand behind the door but to sit partially on the seat giving you more protection with the body of the car and the engine block.

When my tour at Vice was up, I stayed at Rampart and became a training officer. In the Academy when the instructors talked about tactics and gun retention, one of the many shootings they referred to was the Van Pelt shooting in Northeast Division. Jim Van Pelt and his partner confronted a prowler who knocked Jim's partner down a hill, took Jim's gun from him, and shot Jim four times. Jim survived.

The suspect, Raymond George, escaped with Jim's gun and later killed a state police officer guarding a state building. George was captured, convicted, and sent to prison. He was paroled in '83, although he was schizophrenic and required medication to keep under some type of control.

In '85, my partner and I received a radio call of a naked man in the street on Alvarado at Temple. When we got there, we saw a naked man lying in the street with a knife stuck in his eye. He was lying on his back and flopping his arms. We called for an ambulance, and when they got there, they put a bandage around his head to keep the knife from moving.

They transported him to Los Angeles County Hospital. At the hospital, as soon as he said his name, Raymond George, I recognized it right away. I didn't recognize his face because I did not know what George looked like, but once he said his name, I knew who he was. He was living near where we found him, and there were witnesses to him stabbing himself in the eye. He survived the self-inflicted stabbing, and I believe it did not affect his vision. We didn't ask him about shooting Van Pelt.

Rampart was primarily a Spanish-speaking community, so I took Spanish language courses at a local college. The main reason for learning Spanish was a radio call. My partner and I got a call to meet the paramedics, who were holding a rape suspect. We got to the location, and the people only spoke Spanish. The paramedics didn't speak Spanish, and neither did my partner nor I.

A girl about eighteen years of age was being treated by the paramedics for a bleeding vaginal injury, and there was blood on the bed. The guy they were holding was about the same age. We put him in handcuffs, and we weren't very gentlemanly with him trying to get him to tell us what happened. But he spoke only Spanish.

Finally, a Spanish-speaking officer got there, and he immediately found out what happened. The boy and girl were boyfriend and girlfriend, and it was their first time having sex. It was an embarrassing moment for both of them. He was embarrassed, and she was doubly embarrassed. We apologized to them, and they accepted our apology. Within a few days, I signed up for the Spanish language course.

After a couple of years as a detective trainee at Rampart Detectives, I promoted to sergeant and went to Seventy-Seventh Division. The first memory that comes to mind of my time at Seventy-Seventh is the death of Danny Pratt. Danny was working a crime suppression plainclothes detail when he and his partner, Veronica Delao, heard gunshots. They then saw a car that they believed had just committed a drive-by shooting and followed it.

At Crenshaw and Florence Avenue, Veronica, who was driving, pulled into a car wash on the corner, either to take cover or to keep their cover as officers. The suspects must have known they were being followed, made a U-turn, came back, and fired on Danny and Veronica. Both officers fired back. Danny was hit in the face with a round and went down. The suspects took off, but they eventually turned themselves in.

I was at a restaurant having dinner when the help call came out. I responded to the hospital where Danny was taken. The doctor told me there was nothing they could do for him; he had died instantly. I made the necessary notifications and secured the room within the emergency room where he was lying on a bed. There were curtains around him, and the lights were off.

I stayed with him until I was eventually relieved. I didn't want him to be alone. He had a very peaceful look on his face, as if he were sleeping. There was no hint of violence, no blood. As I offered my own few words to Danny, the peacefulness of the moment was shattered, as I got closer and saw the bullet hole in his upper lip. It was very traumatic to see him lying there, especially as I had just seen him an hour or two before at the station.

Danny was a tactically oriented officer. I guess it was one of those "wrong place, wrong time" kind of deals. The death of an officer becomes—I don't want to say a normal thing—but you know it can and will happen. You deal with it as best you can. Probably one of the hardest things to do is go to a copper's funeral. How to put that in words? I don't really know.

One night I was the first responder to a call of a family dispute, and I immediately saw two girls fighting on the front lawn. One was atop the other holding a knife in her hand and making motions as if she was stabbing the girl underneath her. It was a ten-inch knife. I drew my gun, and I was yelling at her to drop the knife.

The girl hesitated, then dropped the knife and stood up. It was readily apparent that she was pregnant. The girl on the ground was not injured. It turned out the girl with the knife was actually striking her with the palm of her hand and not the blade of the knife.

I was relieved and thought, *Boy, am I glad I waited that extra second.* I could see the newspaper headline if I had shot this girl: "Fourteen-year-old Pregnant Girl Shot by Policeman." I was there to protect, but I needed to be sure. That extra couple of seconds I waited eliminated what could have been a nightmare for the girl's family and me. The girls were arguing over something that didn't amount to much.

Eighteen months at Seventy-Seventh was long enough to know supervision was not for me. I was on the detective promotion list, but I knew I didn't want to be a detective and push paper. I had done that as a detective trainee. Rich Roupoli, who was also a sergeant at Seventy-Seventh and had previously worked Narcotics, suggested I go to

Narcotics Division. I thought that sounded good, so Rich called a friend of his, Cleon Jones, who was at Central Division Narcotics. I interviewed with him, and he said if I gave him an eighteen-month commitment, he would take me. I said, "You got it." I worked Narcotics in downtown Los Angeles and was right back on Skid Row again.

One day I was working with Jim "J.J." Warren looking for heroin dealers. At the time, some of the heroin dealers would package the heroin in balloons and keep the balloons in their mouths. When someone wanted to buy some heroin, the dealer would take one balloon out of his mouth and sell it to him. We were on Fifth just off San Pedro Street, when J.J. yelled to me, "The guy in the red shirt, he's holding!" That meant he had a balloon of heroin in his mouth.

I jumped out of the car and grabbed the guy in the red shirt. Back then you could use the bar arm control hold to keep the dealer from swallowing the balloons, so I got this guy in a bar arm, was holding him down, and he started to spit balloons out. I could see the balloons coming out. Right then J.J. ran by me yelling, "No! No! You got the wrong guy! It's the other guy in the red shirt!" J.J. grabbed another guy in a red shirt. It turned out both were holding balloons in their mouths, so both went to jail for possession of heroin!

When Cleon Jones retired, Clay Searle, who had been working the Narcotics Interdiction Team at the Los Angeles International Airport, took Cleon's place. Clay taught us how to profile drug dealers because that was what the Interdiction Team did at the airport.

We were working the downtown bus station and watched this kid be dropped off. He was about twenty years old and had a suitcase. It was a big suitcase, and he was basically dragging it. He bought a bus ticket with cash. As he was leaving the ticket counter, I started walking with him, just talking to him, using the technique Clay taught us. I identified who I was as we walked, and at one point, he gave us consent to search the suitcase. We found six one-gallon containers of PCP. He knew what was in the suitcase, and he said a guy paid him to take it on the bus back east. Six gallons of PCP on a bus filled with people!

It can be very dangerous working in an undercover capacity. On one operation, undercover officer Ruben Galvan posed as someone interested in buying a large amount of cocaine. A guy saying he was a drug dealer called Ruben, and a meet was set up at a gas station on

Vernon Avenue. I was part of the cover team. They met, and the dealer wanted to see Ruben's money. Ruben told them he wanted to see the dope first. This went back and forth. It was a standoff. Finally, they broke off, and the dealer and his friends left.

Once they left, Ruben let us know that they had guns and that he thought they were not dope dealers, but were there to rob him of his money. I was the first to pick up the suspect's car, and I followed them until we had everybody in place, including a black-and-white police car with uniformed officers to make the stop.

The stop was made, and as the passenger came out of the car, I could see a gun in the waistband of his pants. I pointed the shotgun at him and told him to get on the ground. He dropped to the ground, and we took him and the others into custody. They copped that their intent was to rob Ruben of his money if he had shown it. That's one of the dangers in being an undercover officer, especially when large amounts of money are involved.

Working a federal narcotics task force, we were given information that an eighteen-wheeler propane tanker truck had crossed the U.S./Mexico border carrying a large load of dope, primarily cocaine. Our squad drove to Cathedral City to intercept the truck and take over the surveillance. We picked up the surveillance and followed the truck to a warehouse in Fontana. After a couple of days watching the tanker, people started showing up in trucks and vans. This one guy showed up looking like a typical drug cartel guy, and everyone stood around him. Then the trucks and vans went into the warehouse, where the propane tanker truck was parked.

Mike Neel followed the first vehicle that came out, and the vehicle was stopped. It was filled with marijuana. We wrote a search warrant and seized the tanker truck. We opened it up, and all we saw was marijuana. The captain was initially upset that it was just marijuana and not cocaine because of the time and effort put into the investigation. We unloaded bales of marijuana equaling several tons. Finally, cleverly concealed in the back part of the propane compartment, we found one hundred kilos of cocaine. Somebody was going to do jail time. Everybody was happy, including the captain. It was worth the expense and effort.

Frank DeCeasare, Frankie Yan, and Ray Shorb inside tanker recovering narcotics, 1995

Narcotics recovered from tanker truck, 1995

Frankie Yan

When I came on the job, I took note upon hearing the death notices of retired police officers, how long they had lived after retirement. It seemed that officers who retired with twenty-five years of service lived ten years longer than officers who retired with thirty or more years of service. My mind was made up. I would retire at twenty-five years to enjoy the fruits of my employment.

However, at twenty-five years, I was working the Internal Affairs surveillance unit, and I was asked to stay longer to teach surveillance to new personnel. So I stayed an extra year.

To this day, as I look back at my career, I feel very fortunate because I did something I really loved doing. It wasn't something I did because I needed a job. If I had to do it over, I'd probably do the same thing. I'm lucky because I spent a big part of my life doing something I really enjoyed.

Terry Lopez

Birthplace: Maywood, California
Career: 1982–2002
Rank at Retirement: Detective II
Divisions: Seventy-Seventh, Communications, Operations West Bureau
    Major Crimes, Operation South Bureau CRASH, Southwest, Juvenile,
    Office of the Chief of Police

Shortly after graduating from the Police Academy, I began weight training and bodybuilding. My first major competition was the Miss Los Angeles contest. However, I withdrew when I learned that some of my competition was steroid-enhanced and that I had no chance of winning. Soon after, Larry Moore, the director of the LAPD Sports programs, asked me to enter the female division of the LAPD Toughest Cop Alive Competition also known as TCA. There were eight individual events: three-mile run, shot put, hundred-yard dash, hundred-meter swim, twenty-foot rope climb, bench press, pull-ups and obstacle course. Unlike bodybuilding, I wasn't going to be scored by some judge, so I entered, and I won!

Larry then told me about a national TCA competition in Washington, D.C., scheduled for three months later. I really trained hard, and I won. Four months later, I won the World Police Olympics TCA. Over the next eight years, I was the Department, state, national and international TCA champion. I loved the sport and was honored to be an ambassador for the LAPD. I was ultimately inducted into the LAPD Athletic Hall of Fame.

Prior to the Academy, though, I wasn't in good shape. I played softball and basketball in college, but I concentrated on my studies the last two years of school and allowed myself to fall out of shape. When I applied to the Department, I entered the Candidate Assistance Program, twelve weeks of instruction designed to help women with their strength training. At one point, Sergeant Greg Dossey, who was in charge of the program, called me in and told me that I wasn't keeping up and that I should resign. I told myself after that conversation that I'm not resigning from anything. I'll do what I have to do to get in shape.

I went home and started running every night, and I went to the gym and started lifting weights. The extra time and effort paid off. About five weeks later, I was the strongest one in the class. Sergeant Dossey even asked me to be the class cadet leader, and that made me extremely proud. More importantly, I was physically fit when I entered the Academy. In the Academy, we began with seventeen women and graduated four. I finished highest of the four women and eleventh overall in my class.

Terry Lopez: TCA competition, 1989

Upon graduating, I was assigned to Seventy-Seventh Division, and within the first six weeks, my training officer told me I wasn't going to make it. Then I was assigned to Ed Lindsey, the training officer tasked with salvaging or firing a probationer. Ed turned out to be the absolute best training officer. He was a hard worker, and his drive inspired me.

One night we responded to a rape in progress radio call, along with some other units. Eleven gang members had followed a woman home and forced their way into her house. As they were raping her, someone heard her screams and called the police. When we got there, the gang members ran in different directions. I chased one suspect, and another officer followed behind me. I saw the suspect go underneath a house, and I told the officer where the suspect was hiding. He shined his flashlight underneath the house and said, "He's not there."

We walked back to the original scene and I told Ed where I had seen the suspect hide. I told him that the officer with me said the suspect wasn't there, but I knew he was. Ed called for the K-9 unit. That was Ed. I was his partner, and he believed me. He trusted me. The K-9 unit arrived, and the dog was sent under the house and found the suspect. I made probation because of the confidence Ed had in me. Of course, even when you make probation, your learning does not stop.

Ed Lindsey, second from right: "He trusted me."

My partner Stan Lemelle and I received a radio call of a woman screaming inside a two-story apartment building. As soon as we got there, a male was walking down the stairs from the apartment, and when he saw us, he ran back up. I followed, and he closed the door as I reached the top. We heard a woman's cry inside, and Stan kicked in the door. The woman was down on the living room floor. The suspect ran to a back bedroom, but I kept after him as Stan grabbed another suspect who was hiding in the bathroom.

I entered the bedroom just as the suspect leaped from the two-story window. I immediately sensed someone else in the room. I looked to my left and saw a guy holding a shotgun pointed right at me. I stepped back and told him to drop it, and he did.

We found narcotics and over ten thousand dollars in cash. The woman was the girlfriend of one of the suspects, and they had been arguing. The suspect that jumped out of the window was never caught. I didn't ask the guy with the shotgun why he did not pull the trigger. But I believe he was only there to guard the narcotics and money, and there would be nothing left to guard since it all was about to be seized by the police. Seeing that shotgun pointed at me, however, left an indelible impression on me. He could have blown me away.

I was always a fast runner and usually ahead of my partners in a foot pursuit. Onetime, I was outside of a house while a search warrant was being served, when the suspect jumped out of the window on my side of the house and took off. I gave chase, along with some detectives. Not too long into the pursuit, I had outdistanced the detectives and soon left them behind. I chased the suspect for several blocks, until he hid behind some trashcans. I didn't want to confront him at that point because I was by myself and we didn't have any handheld radios for me to let other officers know where I was.

The air unit came overhead, and I attracted their attention. They directed a police car to my location, and we took the suspect into custody. Afterwards, some of the detectives chastised me for going off on my own. Lieutenant Ted Oglesby stood up for me and told them that I had handled myself well. He also chastised them for being out of shape. The detectives later apologized. I think they were more embarrassed than anything.

There was a robbery where a kid had his bicycle taken at knifepoint. We later saw the suspect, and I chased him into a parking lot where he had nowhere to run except back toward me. He was armed with a four-inch steak knife. I told him to drop the knife. He didn't comply.

A large, hostile crowd had gathered and was encouraging him to attack. My partner stayed between me and the crowd, watching them as I dealt with the suspect. Suddenly, the suspect came at me with the knife. By then, I held a black belt in judo, and knives were a common weapon we trained to deal with, so it was not a big deal to me. I drew my baton and struck him across his knees, he dropped to the ground, and I handcuffed him. We took the suspect to the station, and he wanted to make a complaint of excessive force against me.

Sergeant Mike Holshof interviewed him and said to him, "Okay, you want to make a complaint that a female officer took out your kneecaps. Is that right?"

After a moment of reflection, the suspect said, "Oh, no, I think she did the right thing!"

We booked him for robbery. Judo gave me a confidence level I think most police officers would not have. I most likely would have done things differently had the knife been a butcher knife or a machete.

I believe Maria Marquez and I were the first two female officers to work together at Seventy-Seventh. It wasn't easy doing police work as a female back then, and now there were two of us in the same car. One day we received a domestic violence radio call. Maria knocked on the door.

A woman answered, looked at us, and said, "You're two women. I want the real police." She slammed the door shut.

We knocked again.

She opened the door, and I said, "We are here to help you. No one else is coming. Are you refusing our help?"

She slammed the door again and we left.

Citizens were not accustomed to seeing two female officers together and there were some reservations at the station. At the time, there was a push from the Department for women to work together, but no one was really doing it. Maria and I worked together for about two months. We survived.

Terry Lopez, back row, second from right: LAPD Baker to Vegas Women's team with Chief Daryl Gates

On the transfer wheel, I was off to Communications. I wasn't there very long when our captain, Larry Binkley, transferred to the Operations West Bureau Major Crimes Unit. They needed female officers, and he asked me to apply. I did and worked the unit for about a year and a half.

There were two squads. One squad worked bank robberies, and the other focused on narcotic crimes. I was assigned to the narcotics squad, primarily doing surveillance. Initially, I worked undercover with a male officer, posing as his girlfriend doing street buys of narcotics. That didn't work out because I was told I was too polite. I didn't swear—it wasn't in my nature. I decided being an undercover officer doing drug buys was not my forte, so I worked the surveillance part of the operation.

The unit was eventually disbanded. I went back to Seventy-Seventh, and that was a blessing. I worked with John Thomas, primarily tasked with writing traffic citations. We worked together for two years. Like Ed Lindsey, John was a hard worker, and that suited me fine. We would write twenty, sometimes forty tickets a day, and even though our primary focus was traffic enforcement, we would have twenty felony arrests per month. It was the best time of my police career.

John Thomas: "It was the best time of my police career."

On one occasion with John, we were chasing a narcotics suspect, and the suspect climbed a fifteen-foot chain-link fence. I was right behind the suspect and climbed over the fence after him. I caught him, took him into custody, and started to walk him back. As we came back to the fence, there was John. He was up on the fence, and his pants were caught, which prevented him from getting over the fence. He came down slowly, but his pants were ripped. I mean ripped good. I couldn't stop laughing. Years later, at my retirement party, I told that story, and I had the pants to prove it! We didn't let John forget.

I spent five years as a gang officer at Operations South Bureau CRASH. The Department was just developing computer systems, and there was an interest in computerizing our gang intelligence files. We had over fifty thousand files, and I was tasked with coordinating the project. I had eleven people working for me for a year on an overtime basis. When the system was up and running, if a homicide detective was looking for a gang member based only on a tattoo for example, the search was quicker and more thorough. No more hand searches. That was a very rewarding effort.

When I made detective, I went back to Seventy-Seventh and teamed up with Debbie Eggar to work robberies. I had been working detectives for a while, when the '92 riots occurred and we were put back in uniform. There was a radio call of a guy at a laundromat with a gas can. As we got there, he was pouring gas all over this laundromat with the intent to burn it down. He saw us and ran. I chased and caught him. This guy was responsible for at least eight other burned-down buildings. This wasn't some looter covering his tracks—we actually got a good arsonist.

I was working with two other officers, and we were driving westbound on Manchester Boulevard passing Vermont Avenue. Mike Strawberry was driving, and I was in the back seat. All of a sudden, the back window blew out, and a bullet passed right by my ear. It continued by Mike and lodged in the steering post. Mike got us out of there as we put out a help call. The sniper was never found.

After the riots, Debbie went to Southwest, and I followed her a few months later so we could work together again. She was a great partner. When our lieutenant, Vern King, transferred to Juvenile Division, he called and asked if I would come work the Abuse Child unit. I was reluctant at first, but I went to the unit on a thirty-day loan.

My first homicide case was an eighteen-month-old boy named Clarence. I went to the coroner's office on a day when it was filled with about twenty gang members that had been killed that weekend. Just gang member after gang member. I got through all those bodies, and I saw this little baby on a gurney with a cracked skull. There were no witnesses to his death.

I grew up with an abusive father who abused my mother, my three brothers, and me. The day he was arrested, two policemen showed up, and I clearly remember seeing their shiny badges. I was eight years old. They were advocates for me. Looking at Clarence, I knew right then that I wanted to be an advocate, a voice for him and others like him. I told Lieutenant King I wanted the job, and I transferred the next month. This job would consume my life for the next five years.

The Lance Helms death was a major case. Lance was two and a half years old, and he was punched in the stomach hard enough to cause his death. Eve, the girlfriend of Lance's father, David, was charged with his murder. During the trial, she plea bargained to a count of child endangerment causing death and was sentenced to ten years in prison. Despite her plea, Eve had denied guilt throughout the trial.

Lance was in Eve's care, along with her own four-year-old son, when David came home late in the afternoon. David told Eve to go to a pawnbroker for him to redeem some items. When Eve returned, Lance's lips were blue, and he was slumped over. He died before the paramedics arrived.

The crux of the case was based on a time factor. Deputy Los Angeles County Medical Examiner James Ribe testified that Lance had died thirty minutes to an hour after he was beaten, which meant Lance was beaten while in Eve's care, before David got home.

Lance's grandmother Gail believed that her son, David, was responsible. David had a history of being abusive to her, his sister, and his first wife, specifically by punching them. Lance's mother was in jail, and David's sister had temporary custody prior to the Los Angeles Dependency Court returning Lance to David six months before Lance's death. Once back in David's custody, Gail and her daughter noted various new injuries to Lance. Due to the pressure Gail applied, the Department conducted an audit of the murder investigation. My partner, Steve Bernard, and I were tasked with doing the audit.

There were thirty-three specific injuries to Lance, including a broken rib, split liver, tear in the structure that anchors the intestines to the spine, bruised diaphragm, and severed mesenteric artery. My major was nursing in college, and I worked in a hospital pediatric ward. I knew that when a mesenteric artery is severed, it causes instant incapacitation. Lance would not be moving, talking, or asking for water, as David had testified at the trial.

I spent three days with Dr. Ribe going over each specific injury. Dr. Ribe ultimately changed his opinion on the time factor of Lance's death. He concluded that there was a narrower timeframe between the time of the injury and the time of death than what he testified to. His new conclusion meant that David, not Eve, was the person responsible for Lance's death.

Now how do I prove that Eve was not present during this new timeframe? I went to the pawnshop and retrieved the ticket that documented the transaction Eve conducted there. Based on the timestamp on the ticket, Eve was not home at the time of Lance's injury.

The original investigation had focused on the theory that because Lance's mother was due for release from prison, Eve was jealous enough to kill Lance. Dr. Ribe's first conclusion supported that theory, and the original investigative detective didn't look any further. Thus, there was no interest in a follow-up to the pawnshop or a more challenging analysis of the injuries.

I presented the new evidence to Deputy District Attorney Eleanor Hunter. Eleanor was instrumental in securing a warrant for David's arrest and prosecuting him at trial. Dr. Ribe's testimony was found to be credible by the jury. Based on his testimony, along with the testimony of other witnesses regarding David's history of violence, David was convicted of murder and sentenced twenty-five years to life in prison. Eve was released from prison.

Why didn't Eve say David was the person who killed Lance? David was a vicious guy, and Eve was afraid of him. She took a plea deal with prison time to get away from him. She was more afraid of David than of losing her freedom—an act of total desperation.

It was a victory for Gail and the memory of Lance that the truth came out. It was also a vindication of the effort we put in to get the right thing done. After the jury foreman announced the verdict, I went to the bathroom and cried. That's part of what I meant when I said this job was life consuming.

In pursuing this case, Gail testified before the California State Senate. As a result, the state's emphasis changed from family unification to squarely on the safety of the child when determining placement of a child. The California District Attorneys Association awarded Gail its Patricia Lewis Witness of the Year Award for a witness' extraordinary courage and personal sacrifice. She was very deserving.

When I retired from the Department, Eleanor Hunter, who had become a judge, and Gail came to my retirement dinner. It was a complete and very emotional surprise.

I can't tell you how many cases I handled in the Abuse Child unit that I carried mentally with me. We got a call out to a hospital one time where a woman came to the hospital with placenta in hand but no baby. She told us she had suffocated the baby and placed the baby in a trashcan. We found out which landfill the trash was delivered to, I got a search warrant, and we searched the landfill. We never found the baby. I came home smelling like a landfill and very disappointed. The mother was convicted of murder, and she went to prison.

There were nights my husband found me walking in my sleep, saying, "I got to save the baby. I got to save the baby." He would wake me up and try to calm me down so I could go back to sleep. It was a disturbing assignment, and that was the effect of the stress. I was ready to leave after five years.

I worked the Office of the Chief of Police my last three years and retired after twenty years on the Department. At my retirement dinner, my old partner John Thomas said, "The Department got their thirty years out of Terry in twenty." I'll always remember that because it was true. I was high energy, always working.

My mindset when I competed in the TCA competitions was that every event was always about survival. Winning and survival were the same thing. If I didn't win, mentally it was as if I got shot and killed. There was no second place. Just like the Lance Helms investigation, just like any foot pursuit or overcoming being told to resign, be it in the cadet program or on probation, I had to prevail. And that's what I did!

Terry Lopez

Linda Travis

Birthplace: Arcadia, California
Career: 1982–2015
Rank at Retirement: Police Officer III
Divisions: West Valley, Narcotics, Hollywood, Metropolitan

My dad was an officer with the Pasadena Police Department for thirty years. He retired as a sergeant in 1982, the same year I came on the LAPD. I always wanted to be a police officer or, if not that, a veterinarian. My dad loved Pasadena PD, but he said I would have more options with a bigger department and he encouraged me to apply to LAPD. He was very proud of me when I came on the Department, and he would always introduce me to his friends as a police officer. He was my biggest fan.

There were over a hundred in my Academy class, and the class was divided alphabetically into two groups. I don't remember how many graduated, but we lost a lot of people. One day at the end of class, a classmate was waiting in front of the Academy for his ride home and set his stuff down on the sidewalk as he waited. When his ride got there, he jumped in the car, and they drove off, leaving his stuff on the sidewalk, including his service weapon. He was fired.

About a month before the end of the Academy, I broke my ankle wrestling. I could still do the physical training, but I could not run. I had already done everything academically, but I still needed to pass the physical fitness test. Fortunately, by the time of the test, my cast was off my ankle, and I passed.

Linda Travis and father

Linda Travis and father at Academy graduation: "He was my biggest fan."

Right before we graduated, detectives from Juvenile Narcotics talked to three of my classmates and me about working undercover in the school narcotics buy program. Undercover officers posing as students were assigned to high schools to ferret out the kids selling drugs. Some of the Academy instructors told me it would be good for my career, so I volunteered. One of my classmates tried to impress the detectives at the interview with everything he knew about narcotics. That led to another background investigation, and he ultimately was fired.

When I graduated, there was a delay in working the school narcotics buy program, and I was sent to West Valley Division to work patrol. At West Valley, some of the old-timers would comment to me that women should not be on the job, but I'm telling you, they really treated me great.

The one thing that stands out to me while working patrol at West Valley was when a female shoplifter cussed me out. I was so young, the things she said embarrassed me—I'm sure my face was beet red. As I listened to her, I thought, *Was this how people were going to treat me?* That wouldn't bother me in the least now.

After a month and a half at West Valley, I went to the buy program. I bought a lot of narcotics from kids at my assigned school. I identified the kids I had bought narcotics from for round-up day, the day the dealers were arrested. Between the day I bought dope from this one kid and our round-up day, he had hit a guy over the head with a hammer and killed him. He was arrested for murder. We had to go to Juvenile Hall to arrest him for the narcotics charge.

I worked the buy program for about seven months, but I didn't like it—I felt it wasn't the type of police work I should be doing. Working West Valley patrol may have influenced my thinking. If I had to do it all over again, I would not have worked the program.

When I left Narcotics, I went to patrol in Hollywood Division. Feeling like a brand new probationer, I had a lot of catching up to do. Luckily, I got to work with some great officers like Hal Collier, Dale Hickerson, Chuck Stubeck, and Ted Severns. I told them to treat me like a probationer, and they did, which was exactly what I needed. I caught on pretty good, and I didn't do a bunch of dumb stuff, but I'm sure in the beginning my tactics could have been better.

Ted Severns

There was a SWAT shooting at a house in Hollywood one day, and I was assigned to guard the front of the residence. After hours and hours of being there, I really wanted to go in and look. Lieutenant Chuck Higbie was in charge of the scene and at one point came over to me and said, "You want to come in here, don't you?"

"Yes, sir."

I didn't ask him; he could tell. He let me go in and look at the scene. SWAT had shot the guy with a shotgun, and he was pretty torn up. It was the first dead body I saw on the job.

One night my partner and I got a radio call of a kidnapping up on Laurel Canyon Drive, where a four-year-old Asian girl had been taken from her home. Two days earlier, the suspect had posed as a real estate assessor, but was not let in by the housekeeper. The day we got the call, he had come back. The housekeeper was in another part of the house, and the little girl, who had seen him when he had posed as a real estate assessor, let him in. He enticed her to leave with him.

The mother was hysterical and didn't speak English very well. She had a strong accent. She kept screaming at us, "They took my baby! They took my baby!"

While we were trying to get her calmed down, the phone rang. She answered and screamed at me, "It's him! It's him!" Then she threw the phone at me. I took the phone and tried to act as if I were the mother so the suspect would not know the police were involved. I yelled at him, "Bring my baby back!" It turned out he was from the Middle East and had a heavy accent himself. That helped because he couldn't tell that my accent was awful. He hung up and called back several times. Detectives from Robbery Homicide came to the scene, and when the suspect called again, I talked to him with my phony accent. He wanted money and somehow knew these people had money. They had tens of thousands of dollars in cash, right there in the house. A meet was set up.

The detectives brought in a male Asian officer to act the part of a family member for the meet. The meet was to take place on Laurel Canyon by a payphone, and the deal was an exchange of money for the baby. At the payphone, the officer was told to drive to another location. As he left in his car, the suspect pulled up alongside him, shouting at the officer further instructions.

Covering officers moved in at that time, and the suspect fled. The officers chased him, and he subsequently crashed, including into a police car. His car was not disabled, and he then tried to run over the pursuing officers now on foot and was killed. The officers went to the suspect's van, but the little girl was not there. They had no idea where she was.

The detectives were frazzled because the baby was not in the van. Then they found some paperwork with an address in the van to a relative of the suspect, and he gave the officers the suspect's address. The detectives went to the address and found the little girl all by herself. She was fine, but crying. I was at the family's house for a long time that night. It was an overwhelming sense of relief for everyone when the little girl was found.

Eventually, I worked the Hollywood Special Problems Unit and later became a training officer. While I was working Hollywood, I was also a volunteer on the Department Volunteer Mounted Unit. We used our own horses, trailers, and equipment. When there was a big event, I was assigned to work the mounted unit for that day.

When the unit became full time, it was assigned to Metropolitan Division. This meant, along with the oral interview, we had to pass a physical fitness test, including push-ups, sit-ups, and a three-mile run. Although I was six months pregnant, I passed the fitness test—back then, I was in pretty good shape. There were a number of people that were unhappy about the change though. Some had twenty-five years or more on the job and had put a lot of time into the volunteer unit, but they couldn't pass the physical fitness test. To them, it did not seem fair.

For me, working the mounted unit was great. I rode horses most of my life so it was something I was accustomed to, and I had the chance to work with some really good people. I never got hurt, but I did have one very scary moment. We were working the Fiesta Broadway event downtown. While mounted on my horse, this guy with a small child in a stroller asked if they could pet my horse. They were nice and polite, and we weren't doing anything at the time, so I let them pet the horse.

Within a minute, my horse went backwards at what seemed like ninety miles an hour. His back legs hit a curb, and both he and I flipped backwards with him landing on me, cracking the back of my helmet. Luckily, I had my helmet on, or I would have cracked my skull.

Linda Travis,
Mounted Unit

What had happened was, when my horse lowered his head as he was being petted, the tie-down strap went into his mouth. It was probably too loose. When he picked his head up, the strap cinched tighter in his mouth, and he reacted by backing up. The first person to come to my aid was the guy with his son. Then a motor cop immediately saw what was wrong and cut the tie-down strap with his knife. Fortunately, neither my horse nor I got hurt.

The mounted unit occasionally did crime suppression. We worked downtown one day and watched this guy do a hand-to-hand sale of narcotics. When we went to arrest him and while we were still mounted, we put him between our horses and grabbed his jacket, which was how we were trained. This guy came right out of his jacket and took off running. We loped down the street after him, which wasn't a smart thing to do because horses can slip and fall on asphalt. Fortunately, for us, a security guard from a business grabbed him after about a block.

Linda Travis and President Ronald Reagan

When President Ronald Reagan's term as president finished, he and his wife, Nancy, became full-time residents at a ranch in Santa Barbara with a Secret Service protection detail permanently assigned to him. President Reagan was an avid horse rider, so the guys assigned to his protection detail needed to be riders as well. None of them knew how to ride, so we trained them how to ride a horse at our Department facility. As thanks for the training, they invited us to meet President Reagan at his ranch. I can remember when I met him my heart was really beating. He was as humble and nice as I had hoped he would be

Even though I loved horses and still have some today, riding horses was nothing new for me. I left the mounted unit and went to a crime suppression platoon for about two years, and then I got the job I wanted from day one, the K-9 Unit. But when I first got there, I wasn't sure if I had made the right decision. There was in-house fighting between the guys in the unit and the newer supervisors mostly over the fact the newer supervisors were not dog handlers. The guys felt the newer supervisors would not have a real understanding of dog handling as it relates to doing searches.

There was also dissension over a new policy implemented by the Police Commission pursuant to a lawsuit over dog bites. The Police Commission mandated that the dogs were to be trained to find and bark. The dog was now supposed to bark to let the handler know a suspect had been found.

The policy also established new criteria for fleeing suspects. The suspect had to pose an imminent danger. If the suspect was running with a gun or was like a serial rapist, I could send my dog after him. But if the suspect running was a thief or a burglar, I couldn't send my dog. That's one thing I wish would change. If that thief ran into a house and harmed someone in the house, is the Department liable because I didn't send my dog after him? Maybe. But that was the new policy.

My first dog was Jalk. He was a German shepherd, and he was a beautiful dog. I had him for about a year and a half, but we had to get rid of him. On one search, he was attacked by a cat. The cat jumped on Jalk and bloodied his face up pretty good. About a week later, Brian O'Hara and I were doing a search with Jalk, and another cat attacked him. He howled like somebody cut his leg off. Jalk was never the same. After the second attack, if he went into a yard and smelled a cat, he would get behind me. I think he was just scared. He was not the toughest dog in the world, but gosh, he found a lot of suspects.

I was still in training with the K-9 Unit when the '92 riots hit. We deployed to the bus station at Fifty-Fourth Street and Van Ness. Just as I pulled into the bus station, a burning Molotov cocktail was thrown over the wall and landed near my car. Thankfully, it didn't explode.

They didn't want us to arrest people at first, just protect the firemen. After a while though, a curfew was set, and we picked up and arrested quite a few people on the streets. I can remember seeing the city burning. People were destroying where they lived, and chaos was everywhere. It made no sense to me.

When the major earthquake hit the Los Angeles area in 1994, the K-9 Unit was called in to work. We worked as a team traveling around the Northridge area of the San Fernando Valley where the quake was centered. We were directed to an apartment complex where the Fire Department had responded. The three-story complex had collapsed, and the two top stories had completely crushed the first level. The building now appeared as a two-story. The Fire Department had entered the building to try to find any survivors and to mark locations of the numerous dead bodies. The firefighters asked if we could use our dogs to help with the search.

The Fire Department cut holes in what had been the ceiling of the first floor, so we could climb down with our dogs. I entered with Brian O'Hara and his dog. There were places I had to literally crawl on my stomach. I came across a bed in what had been a bedroom, and there were two bodies under a blanket. I pulled the blanket back, and it was an elderly couple, dead, but huddled together. I can still vividly visualize that couple.

We went as far as we could go safely, but we found no survivors. The dogs alerted several times, but each time it was a dead body. A dog will alert on a body whether living or deceased.

After the earthquake, Steve Groover and I became the handlers for the first search and rescue dogs for the Department. The search and rescue dogs did not bite, unlike the K-9 dogs, who are more aggressive. I did a couple of missing persons searches with them. However, there really wasn't a big request for them because we did not have any major disasters. They were unbelievable search dogs.

Linda Travis, Dave Carter, and K-9 Asso: "...we found no survivors."

At the same time I had a search and rescue dog, I still had K-9 search responsibilities. I used to carry two dogs in my car. One would sit in the front and one in the back. I had a brand new police car, and I left Maxx, a Malinois K-9, in the car while I did some practice searches with the other dog. When I came back and opened the front passenger door, I looked in and said, "What is that!" All over the front seat was foam from the headliner. Maxx had chewed the headliner. He was a good dog and had never done anything like that before. He was the first Malinois in the unit, and now all the dogs are Malinois. The dogs used to be Shepherds and Rottweilers.

Later, when I became the unit's trainer, I gave Maxx to another handler that needed a dog. If I had to do it again, I wouldn't have given Maxx away, but I was a new trainer, and I wanted to do good. My job was to take care of the other handlers. That handler ultimately promoted out, and Maxx trained two more handlers. He was just a great dog.

Linda Travis and Maxx

One night in '96, the California Highway Patrol went in high-speed pursuit of a suspect who managed to elude them and got to his house on Harvest Street in the San Fernando Valley. When the officers arrived, he opened the door and fired at the officers, hitting one in the stomach, wrist, and arm. Unbeknownst to the officers, the suspect then fled before a perimeter could be set. The officers thought he was still in the house. We responded to hold the perimeter until SWAT officers took our place.

Once released from the perimeter, I met up with our training sergeant, Donn Yarnall, at a gas station on the corner of Rinaldi and Blucher Avenue. I was talking with the clerk at the gas station, and he knew the suspect. The clerk told me that just before we got there the suspect had been there. He bought cigarettes and he seemed real nervous. The suspect then left the gas station, crossed Rinaldi, and walked up Blucher Street. This was the opposite side of Rinaldi from where the perimeter was set.

We told SWAT what the gas station clerk had said, and they decided to stay with the house. We set up two K-9 search teams and went in the direction the gas station clerk had indicated. Chris Warren was leading one search team on one side of the street, and I led a search team on the other side. As Chris' search team neared some tennis courts, they heard a gunshot coming from some bushes near the courts, and they fired, hitting the suspect multiple times and killing him. Turned out the shot the officers thought had been directed at them was the suspect shooting himself in the mouth. The coroner determined that the suspect would have died from his self-inflicted wound. He had been released from prison a month prior to this incident, and he had a history of confrontations with the police.

We were working the Hollywood area, when we heard a radio call come out, a domestic violence involving a hostage on the east side of Hollywood. The man's wife had a restraining order against him, and he had climbed through a window of her apartment next to an exterior staircase and, once inside, forcibly raped her. She managed to escape and called the police.

When we got there, he was still in the apartment. We heard him fire a couple of rounds through the ceiling. SWAT was responding, and to assist in their effort, several K-9 officers and I started to evacuate the apartment building. As we were waiting for the people to come out from this one apartment, we heard the suspect exit his apartment and come down the stairs. We were directly below him.

The guy came down a couple steps, and when he saw us, he pointed his handgun right in our faces. We fired, hitting him multiple times. There was blood everywhere. We thought he was dead, but he survived. He was convicted of the rape and other charges and was sent to prison.

While in prison, he sent crazy mail to each of us that had shot him: Gordy Olson, Brian O'Hara, Dave Stumbaugh, and me. He wrote in his letters that we conspired with his wife to put him away. He even drew a poster of the shooting scene. I called the prison and said, "This isn't legal mail." The prison officials put a stop to it.

In Southwest Division one night, other K-9 units and I were searching for three robbery suspects. I was with my dog, Dillon, a Belgian Malinois, in the rear yard of a residence, when he alerted and started barking in the corner area of this big, overgrown yard. I had a couple of patrol officers with me as part of the search team. I was focused on the corner that Dillon alerted to, when a second suspect came over the wall from an adjacent yard into the yard we were in. The patrol officers went after him.

At the same time, the suspect Dillon was alerting to darted out from behind the overgrown ivy and ran to the side of the residence. Dillon went after him, and just as the suspect was about to reach a door to the residence, Dillon engaged him. The suspect swung his arm and knocked Dillon into a large ceramic water fountain. Dillon momentarily had the wind knocked out of him. It stunned him; you could tell it hurt.

Then the guy came at me, but Dillon jumped at him and took him down to the ground where I could handcuff him. I was a bragging mother at that moment! The second suspect escaped the efforts of the two officers and jumped back over the wall only to run into another K-9 dog, and he was taken into custody. We did not find the third suspect.

There were people inside the house who witnessed what Dillon did, and they were extremely grateful the suspect didn't make it into their home. They turned out to be good witnesses.

Linda Travis and Dillon: "I was a bragging mother at that moment!"

That fountain was solid. To be hit that hard and still be able to fight was just remarkable. Dillon did above and beyond. Yeah, I am a bragging mother! Dillon is here at home with me now. He shouldn't be retired; he still acts likes he's two years old. He's nuts, in a good way.

I did thousands of searches over the years, but there is one I'm going to talk about right now. It was a domestic violence situation in the San Fernando Valley. A wife had escaped from the house and called the police. Patrol officers requested a K-9 Unit to search the area around the residence and inside the residence because they were not sure if the husband was still there. The wife told the officers that there were two old rifles packed away in the house. There was no weapon used in the domestic violence incident itself.

It was my search, and my search team was my fellow K-9 officers, Steve Jenkins, Dave Wade, and Josh Kniss. We cleared the area around the house, and we were ready to go inside, but there were a couple little dogs inside the house that were barking. I stood off to the side of the front door near the garage to keep control of Dillon, while Steve, Dave, and Josh approached the front door. The plan was to open the door, let the little dogs out, make another announcement of our presence, and then we would enter. If the husband responded and surrendered, that was good. If he said he was not coming out, we would back off and wait for SWAT.

As soon as Steve opened the door, three shots were fired from inside, and he was immediately hit in the jaw and chest with two rounds. Steve turned and walked toward me like you walked up onto my porch this morning and said, "I'm hit." I was looking at him like I'm looking at you, and I could not see anything on his face. I called for an ambulance, and as I got him out of there, Steve was talking and walking—he had it together. Then he took a turn for the worse, and he went downhill fast.

Fortunately, the paramedic unit that was at the initial call had made a decision not to leave when they were told K-9 was going to do a search. The paramedics could have left anytime they wanted, but decided to stay, so when I called for an ambulance, they were there within seconds to take him to the hospital. I strongly feel that by staying these paramedics saved Steve's life.

Linda Travis, Steve Jenkins, and Dave Wade: "It was the worst day of my life and the best day of my life."

SWAT came and dealt with the barricaded suspect the rest of the night. This guy held his mud for a long time. SWAT officers eventually entered and killed the suspect. Steve was in a coma for a few weeks and remained in the hospital for a couple of months. He has since come back to work and still works to this day. It was the worst day of my life and the best day of my life. The worst that Steve got shot and the best that he didn't die.

The North Hollywood Bank of America shootout was one of my longest searches. It went on for hours upon hours. Two suspects, Larry Phillips and Emil Matasareanu, died at the scene after engaging officers in a shootout. Multiple teams of K-9 and SWAT officers covered about one square mile of residences looking for a possible third suspect. It was later determined that the third suspect did not exist.

In 2005, a southbound Metrolink train struck an abandoned sports-utility vehicle, causing the train to derail and strike both a northbound Metrolink train and a stationary Union Pacific freight train on another track. The derailment was in Glendale near Los Feliz and San Fernando Road. Eleven people were killed. I was asked to use my dog, Princess, to search the train cars for survivors. Two of the cars were on their side, which made the search difficult; I kind of lost my equilibrium a little bit. The coroner had not come yet, so the dead bodies were still in there. We didn't find anybody alive.

I had a cadaver dog for a while: Darr, a Dutch shepherd. He was the first cadaver dog for the Department. Darr was trained to find dead bodies, tissue, or blood. I had a retired FBI agent friend who had cadaver dogs. She had a lot of resources for training, so I would train with her and that helped me out a lot. Darr was still a police dog, so he would bark whereas most cadaver dogs were trained to sit when making a find. But there was not a big call for a cadaver dog. I think the only thing Darr found were bloody t-shirts after a shooting. The suspect had thrown some t-shirts up onto a roof of a house. We were searching, when Darr alerted to something above him. I climbed up onto the roof of this house and saw the t-shirts. That was pretty impressive that Darr had made that find.

Jim Hagerty, Marko, Linda Travis, Darr, Gordon Olson, Rico

Working K-9 is a job that will humble you. When you're searching for a suspect, you have to reason that these guys could be hiding anywhere. I've seen guys squeeze out of air vents that I would never, ever think could hide a suspect. Sometimes a suspect had hidden in a place, but left before we found him. The dog alerted, but to what we called a dead scent, a residual scent from the suspect or the suspect may have left an item of clothing. You don't want that to happen. You try to discourage that, but sometimes it happens.

To learn your dog, you follow up with the suspect to find out if they had been hiding in the spot the dog alerted too. Sometimes they'll tell you; sometimes they won't. But you try to find out what you did wrong or what your dog did wrong, and believe me, ninety-nine percent of the time it was something an officer did wrong, not the dog. Either we didn't put our dog in the right spot, or the dog did something and we disregarded what the dog was telling us.

For about eight years, I was the unit trainer. That got old, and I decided to go back to searching. As a trainer, you did search, but infrequently because you always had somebody in training. The dogs were the easy part. Matching somebody with a dog was the challenge. You can be the greatest cop in the world, but that doesn't mean you would be a good dog handler. I also traveled across the state to assist other police departments' K-9 units. But my passion was searching, and it was the best move I ever made to go back to searching.

When I retired, I had thirty-two and a half years on the job. I'm not going to lie: when I retired, it was hard. I loved my job, I loved the guys I worked with, and I loved going on searches. I struggled a little bit, and I was a weirdo around home for a while. The decision was okay, but really doing it was something else. I would see the LAPD on television, and I would tell myself I should be there. But I wasn't getting any younger. I was feeling the aches and pains, and it was just time. Besides, I have three grandkids now.

Stanley "Stan" Sokolis

Birthplace: Inglewood, California
Career: 1984–2015
Rank at Retirement: Police Officer II
Divisions: Southwest, Central, Newton, Northeast, Scientific Investigation

While taking general classes in college, I worked security for an aerospace company, but I had not decided what I wanted to do for a career. That all changed when I attended a graduation at the Los Angeles Police Department Academy. After that, I said to myself, *I think I might be a police officer*. After I went on a ride-along with Hollywood Vice, that was it—I was inspired. I started taking criminal justice classes, and I applied to the Department. It took time, but I eventually was hired.

In the Academy, our class was dubbed the "Meet Weaver" class. Our shooting instructors, Larry Hutchins and John Helms, taught our class the Weaver shooting stance and compared the results to the class ahead of us who were taught the Isosceles shooting stance. We must have done pretty well because after that the Weaver stance was adopted.

Our class went on several ride-alongs, and mine was in Seventy-Seventh Division with Sandy Jo MacArthur, who recently retired as a deputy chief. Back then, she was a training officer and very "gung ho." She took control of things, and you could tell she was a hard worker. She made an impression on me. We rolled on a shooting that resulted in a murder. I stood by as she handled the crime scene until the detectives arrived. I had not seen a dead body before, and for a kid from the beach that was an eye-opener.

Stan Sokolis , third from left: Academy Inspection

Stan Sokolis, second row from top, fifth from left: Academy class, 1984

After graduation, I was sent to Southwest Division and worked with Trevor Asfall. We responded to a gang shooting homicide one day, and unlike my ride-along, it was my turn to handle a crime scene. The kid was about sixteen years old, and he was killed by a shot in the back. The next day Trevor let me go with the detectives to the autopsy. I was able to see the whole case from the street to the morgue. I was given a tour of the morgue, and there were six autopsies going on. As I watched, I told myself, *When I die, put a sign on my forehead, "Handle with care."*

Trevor and I received a child abuse call about an older brother molesting his younger brother. We entered the house and inside were a twelve-year-old, a seven-year-old, and their father. All of a sudden, Trevor grabbed the twelve-year-old by the throat and threw him on the ground. To see Trevor slam this twelve-year-old, I thought, *Oh my gosh. Why is he attacking this kid?* On our way there, Trevor had told me that we were going to be nice to the kid.

Unbeknownst to me, Trevor saw the twelve-year-old put a bunch of pills in his mouth and he C-clamped the kid to keep him from swallowing the pills. He was trying to commit suicide right in front of us and Trevor was trying to save his life. The kid knew why we were there. He was holding a washcloth with a knife hidden underneath, and it fell out when Trevor grabbed him.

The dad was shocked that his son tried to commit suicide. The mother and father lived separately and the older kid stayed with the father. Whenever the younger kid was dropped off at his father's, his older brother molested him. We took the twelve-year-old into custody and to the hospital.

Larry Tate was my training officer when I went to night watch. One night as we were pulling into the parking lot of a donut shop to get coffee, a car was coming out. The guys in the car looked at us with big eyes. Larry said, "Those guys are bad news." I was driving, and he told me to follow them.

We followed and stopped them. Larry told me to call them out. I stood behind the driver's door and ordered them out. The driver and the passenger appeared to be reaching under the front seat, and then both of them looked back at us. I ordered them out again, and *boom!* They took off. We jumped back into our car, and we're in pursuit through Southwest Division and then up into Wilshire Division. At one point during the pursuit, both the driver and passenger threw objects out of the car.

At one intersection, they almost T-boned another car, and the pursuit ended when they fishtailed and crashed into a parked Wilshire police car. The officers had been out of the car taking a report.

The bad guys got out of their car, but the Wilshire officers were right there with Larry and me, and the bad guys had nowhere to run. When we searched the car, we found a MAC-10, a Thompson submachine gun, and a .22 pistol, all accessible to them. We also found ski masks.

We backtracked to where we saw them throw out the objects. The objects had broken windows of two parked cars and landed inside of them. Both objects were handguns, and both parked cars turned out to be stolen vehicles. Larry and I both thought, *You've got to be kidding!*

The two suspects were members of the Black Guerilla Family. They were hit men and ex-cons. One guy did not talk, but the other one did. Apparently, they were going to do a hit on a dope dealer in Pasadena.

With their weapons, we were clearly outgunned. We only had .38 caliber revolvers. What if they had wanted to take us on? That was a shot of reality for me. It was probably one of the best arrests of my career.

On the transfer wheel, I went to Central Division. One night I was working with Hank Cousine. The burglar alarm went off at a toy store at Fifth and San Pedro. The alarm company told us that they could hear movement inside through their sensors. We had the place surrounded, and Joe Vita, a K-9 officer, arrived. He only needed one officer to go with him and his dog to search the business. Hank and I flipped a coin. Hank won the flip and accompanied Joe on the search.

Inside, the toy boxes were stacked very high. In some places, Hank had to climb onto boxes to ensure they did not miss the burglary suspect. One of the boxes gave way, and Hank fell, immediately drawing the dog's attention. The dog thought it was a bad guy and attacked Hank. Outside, we could hear screams and thought the dog got the burglar. When the screams subsided, Hank came out with dog bites to his thigh and arm. He was bleeding pretty good. I told Hank after he had been medically treated, "I'm glad you won that coin flip." There was no burglar inside.

B-wagon

I drove the B-wagon quite a bit, picking up drunks and taking them to the detox center. The B-wagon looked like an old Helms Bakery bread truck. We had no siren, but we did have emergency lights, and we used to do traffic stops. People knew we were the police, but they didn't think we made traffic stops in the B-wagon. Eventually, the B-wagon was replaced with a truck, and the people we picked up had their own individual seats and were strapped in like a ride at Disneyland. There were no individual seats in the old B-wagon, just open space.

Traffic Enforcement Week was a week where we specifically focused on traffic enforcement. I teamed up with two footbeat old-timers, Don Moody and Larry Soeltz. I wrote about twenty tickets, and I was feeling pretty good about it. When I met up with Don and Larry, they had written 178 tickets in one day. I thought, *How did they do that?*

During the same week, a citizen flagged me down to tell me that a baby had just fallen out of a window into an alley off Fifth Street between Broadway and Main. I drove into the alley, and the scene hit me hard. The baby boy was three years old. He had fallen from seven stories up and was lying on his stomach, still alive and crying. I could tell he was totally busted up, and his tongue was bit off. I called for an ambulance and gently massaged the baby's back while waiting for the paramedics to show up. It was heart wrenching to see.

We set up a crime scene once the paramedics and other units got there. It was determined to be an accident. The baby's family was staying in the old Frontier Hotel apartment building. The baby pushed on a window screen, and it gave way. The family did not even know that the baby was gone. I remember one officer saying, "That's life in the city." I thought, *Really?* That bugged me. I didn't say anything to the guy, but I thought, *That's not right.*

Frontier Hotel, left side of alley

U2, a rock band, did an impromptu concert on the rooftop of the Republic Liquor Store at Seventh and Main Street in '87. The concert was being filmed, and I worked crowd control. The crowd grew too big, and it was decided to shut the concert down. My partner went up with the sergeant to advise the band, while I stayed down on the street. The concert was for a music video, and at one point in the video, you can see my partner on the roof with the band. When I saw it, I thought, *Darn! I could have been in a U2 video.*

I was walking a footbeat on Main Street with Jesse Sanchez and John Degan, when we arrested a couple of guys for possession of rock cocaine.

We asked them, "Where'd you get this?"

"We got it at this pizza place."

The pizza place was on Spring Street. They told us the dealer kept the narcotics in the dough. We went to the restaurant, and we found packaged rock cocaine in the bin of flour used for making pizza dough. The guy working there told us it was the owner selling the cocaine. We found out where the owner lived and that he was on probation. We did a follow-up to his apartment, and when he opened the door, in plain view were numerous bags of cocaine, both rock and powder. That was a nice little pinch.

Jesse Sanchez with recovered cocaine.

One night in December '88, I had just got home from work, when I saw on the news that two police cars collided in Central Division. I found out right away that my classmate Eddie Gutierrez, along with two other officers, Dave Hofmeyer and Derrick Conner, had been killed. A fourth officer, Venson Drake, was the only survivor. It was his first night on the job, and he was the only one wearing a seat belt.

What happened was both units were responding to a backup request on stolen vehicle suspects at Wall Street and Winston. The two police cars collided right next to the police station at Wall Street and Fifth. Eddie and Derrick were going eastbound on Fifth, and Dave and Venson were responding from the back of the station. Eddie's car landed in a construction excavation trench. Dave's car hit a traffic light pole.

The accident was devastating for Central. It was especially hard because Eddie was one of my classmates. We all had nicknames at the Academy. Eddie's nickname was "Eddie Munster" from *The Munsters* television show because he looked like the actor. Eddie had fun with it. After the Academy, I had a chance to work with Eddie a couple of times.

I worked a few of the Los Angeles Lakers' basketball championship parades downtown. Usually at the end of the parade, the players would address the crowd on the grounds of City Hall. One year Kareem Abdul Jabbar and some of the other players were speaking to the crowd from a stage. I was in uniform near the stage, and an elderly gentleman walked up to me and said, "I'm Lew Alcindor Senior, and I need to get to the front."

He was claiming to be Kareem's dad. I looked at him, he was maybe five feet ten, and Kareem is over seven feet. I said to him, "Okay. Anybody could say that. Can I see some identification?" He pulled out his identification, and it was Kareem Abdul Jabbar's dad! Kareem had changed his name from Lew Alcindor when he converted to the Muslim faith. I said to Mr. Alcindor, "Here you go," and I escorted him right up to the stage.

I transferred to Newton Division because I wanted to get back to a busy division. I got a chance to work one of the first bicycle units for the Department. Because there were so many drive-by shootings in one part of Newton, they put us on mountain bikes. There were six of us, and I teamed up with Steve Razo. We eventually became partners in patrol.

Steve and I were stopped for a red traffic light on Broadway at Martin Luther King Boulevard one day when we saw a guy walk up to a black Chevy Suburban and break the driver's side window. He reached in through the broken window, unlocked the door, climbed in, and took off. We started broadcasting over the radio that we were following a stolen car as we were pedaling after this guy. He drove straight, and then made a quick right turn.

We were pedaling as fast as we could and wondering what happened to our chase car. The bike unit had a designated chase car for just such an occasion. On that day, our sergeant was the chase car. We chased this stolen vehicle for a few blocks, and we could still see the car when a patrol unit caught up to it. When the patrol unit got behind the car, the suspect stopped. He bailed out and ran, but was quickly caught. I identified him and he was booked for stealing the car. The sergeant gave us some flimsy excuse for why he was not there, and after that we didn't think too much of him. We went to court, the guy was convicted and sent to prison.

I was working day watch when the verdicts from the trial of the officers charged with excessive force on Rodney King were announced. The officers were found not guilty. At five o'clock, they let us go home. The next day riots were in full swing from the night before by people upset with the court decision. We were sent to the command post at Fifty-Fourth Street and Arlington Avenue. It was a little chaotic because it took a long time to get cars and equipment.

My squad was in two cars, four officers to a car. We were sent to the Southwest Division area the first night. We were out of the cars at one place, when all of a sudden we heard gunshots. There was a street sign next to us and the bullets were hitting the sign. We all dove for the bushes. We had no idea who fired the shots or from where. We stayed for a couple of minutes. The shooting seemed to have stopped, and we left the area. We figured that was a freebie for someone.

Los Angeles riots, 1992: "...it seemed like the whole street was on fire."

We were then put on escort duty for the Fire Department, and we responded with them wherever they went. We followed them down a major street on one response and it seemed like the whole street was on fire. I had never seen anything like that, a whole block burning. I was never in an actual war zone, but it felt like we were right in the middle of one. It looked like a gigantic firebomb had hit the place.

The following day several of us were assigned to be with the National Guard in Newton Division. We had a black-and-white police car and two National Guard Humvees. I rode in one of the Humvees. We drove around in a caravan with the black and white leading because the guardsmen did not know the area. We were driving west on Washington Boulevard at Naomi Avenue when we heard gunshots. A car was coming northbound on Naomi and then made a quick right headed eastbound on Washington.

I yelled, "Drive-by vehicle!"

We turned around, stopped the car, and took them into custody. We drove back to Naomi and searched the area where we first saw the car, and we found a dead body lying there. They killed this guy in a narcotics rip off. The guys we took into custody had narcotics, money, and a gun.

National Guard Humvee, Los Angeles riots, 1992: "I yelled, 'Drive-by vehicle!'"

After the riots, I was working with Curtis Woodle. One night we were driving near Jefferson High School. Curtis was driving. We saw a car a little ways in front of us, and all of a sudden, the car went over to the other side of the road and drove real slow by this guy on the sidewalk. The driver took off when we caught up to the car. We followed in pursuit to a cul-de-sac, and the car stopped. The driver got out and ran, and the passenger came out holding a shotgun. I had my gun out, ready to shoot this guy. He looked right at me, and he dropped the shotgun. We took him into custody.

He had a double-barrel shotgun with a round in each barrel, but both rounds were duds. They were trying to shoot the guy on the sidewalk, but the rounds did not go off although the primers had been struck by the firing pin. The passenger held the shotgun in front of the driver as the driver leaned back when he tried to fire the gun. We were far enough behind that they didn't know we were there. We did not find the driver, nor did we find the person they were trying to shoot.

There was a shots fired radio call one night at Twenty-Third Street and Naomi. Kelly Artz and I were working together, and we heard Sergeant Steve Richards over the radio say he was code six, which meant he just got there. We were the first unit there, and as we pulled up, we saw Sergeant Richards' police car, but not Sergeant Richards. Then we heard him put out a backup request over the radio.

I asked some people standing in front of the house, "Where did the police go?"

They pointed to the rear of the house. We ran through the house, there was a second house behind it, and a fence behind that bordered an alley. We heard shots coming from the alley, and we ran to a gate in the fence. We saw Sergeant Richards coming back towards us, dragging his leg. He had been shot in the leg.

We entered the alley and grabbed Sergeant Richards. We pulled him out of the line of fire and back into the yard for cover. Rounds were being fired, and you could see rounds hitting blankets hanging on a clothesline. We saw a person fall on the porch of the second house. He took a round in the stomach. Other officers arrived, but the shooting then stopped. The shooting came from the backyard of a house across the alley that had been having a party.

Sergeant Richards told us he had gone into the alley and asked some males if they heard shots. One turned on him and fired. Sergeant Richards fired a couple of shots back and hit the suspect in the face. A second suspect fired from behind a fence, hitting Sergeant Richards in the thigh. The wounded suspect was taken into custody, and the second suspect was later arrested. Kelly and I were awarded a Police Star for our actions.

After five years at Newton, I thought that it was time to move on, so I put in a transfer for Northeast Division. It didn't come right away and I forgot about it when I was offered a chance to work the juvenile car in Newton Detectives. Before I agreed, someone said, "Hey, Stan. You're going to Northeast."

"What are you talking about?"

"You're on the transfer."

I talked to the captain at Northeast, but they would not release me from the transfer.

At Northeast one night, there was a call requesting any unit with a beanbag shotgun to respond to the Olympic Auditorium in Central Division. A rave concert had gotten out of hand. The Fire Department had made a decision to close down the concert because they were beyond the legal occupant capacity for the building. I had recently been trained in the use of the beanbag shotgun, so I responded with my partner, Dave Krempa.

When we got there, we were placed on skirmish lines. As the people came out of the auditorium, they started throwing bottles, fire extinguishers, everything, and some were throwing things from a parking structure. Dave was hit with a full forty-ounce beer bottle. It knocked him out cold, and he ended up with nerve damage as a result. It was like a mini-riot of about three hundred people. It was crazy. There were even some who were trying to flip over a Greyhound-type bus!

After the beer bottle incident, we deployed the beanbag shotguns. I fired the beanbag shotgun into the crowd three times from probably twenty yards away. I was not sure if I hit anybody, but I could tell the sound alone scared the crowd. Things eventually subsided, and the people all left. They never did tip the bus over, but they tried and tried.

I was at Northeast a long time, maybe ten or eleven years. At one point, I participated in a Department-wide training exercise involving wrestling and self-defense. Unfortunately, I hurt my chest, neck, and shoulder and tore my rotator cuff. As a result, I was light-duty status for the rest of my career. There was a guy who I used to work with in the Firearms Section of the Scientific Investigation Division, and he told me there was an opening. I applied and got the job.

At Firearms, we test-fired all weapons that came into Department custody, matched weapons to shell casings from crime scenes, and assisted with officer-involved-shooting investigations, essentially everything involving firearms.

One day we responded to a major crime scene at Vernon and Vermont where a vehicle pursuit ended in a big shootout. Over three hundred rounds were fired by both the officers and suspects. One suspect was killed, and one survived. No officers were injured. Our job was to collect the shell casings and other evidence and determine the trajectory of the shots fired. I counted holes in the suspect's car and collected evidence from inside the car, even with the dead suspect still in it.

Stan Sokolis: "It was an eye-opener for a naïve kid from the beach."

I had a great career and some great partners, and I really enjoyed my time on the job. It was an eye-opener for a naïve kid from the beach. I was told once by an officer, "Don't ever get your name in the paper." If you did, it usually was not a good thing. I'm most proud of not getting my name in the newspaper. In my thirty years on the job, I only had two suspension days. I'm pretty happy about that too.

Tribute

Time takes its toll on us, and for some of us, our memory is greatly affected. Two former officers I spoke to, Melva Meyers and Daryl Sievers, each in their nineties, struggled to remember aspects of their careers, and unfortunately, for you and me, the memories were not forthcoming. I was deeply impressed, though, with their eloquence. They are both the product of an era when refinement in your manners was evident in how you acted and publicly presented yourself.

Melva came on the Department as a policewoman in 1948 and retired as a sergeant in 1968. She worked various assignments, but primarily Venice Division Detectives (Juvenile and Homicide)

Melva Meyers

Melva Meyers, far left: Academy, 1948

Melva Meyers and Margie Collins

Daryl came on the Department in 1947 and retired as a lieutenant in 1976. He worked Newton, University, and Metropolitan Divisions, among others. He was in charge of the honor detail for the funeral of Chief William H. Parker, as well as the honor details for the Chief of Police swearing-in ceremonies for Tom Reddin and Ed Davis.

Daryl Sievers

Lieutenant Sievers, far left: Chief Parker Funeral detail

Sergeant Sievers, front row, far right: Metropolitan Division

Photo Credits

Note: All photos, unless indicated below, were from the officers in the book or were considered public domain.

The following photos were courtesy of:

Appleton Family 31
Barnett Family 253
Bell, Gustie 89
Binstein Family 53
Brokus Family 13
California Fraternal Order
   of Police Journal 401
Carlson Family 332
Darr Family 270
Davis, B. Family 121
Davis, T. Family 43
Farrant Family 72
Fogerson, Patty 274
Gilmore Family 76
Hall, Lomie 137
Hall Family 380
Hoyos Family 392
Kinsey, Kay 136
Kraus Family 87
Leeds Family 28
Lim, Stacy 173
Lindsey Family 402
Los Angeles Public Library
Special Collections 2, 3,
   19, 39, 42, 48, 66, 73,
   75, 92, 102, 104, 110,
   128, 134, 135, 146, 163,
   167, 179, 182, 190, 207,
   219, 231, 258, 295, 317,
   332, 362, 386, 390, 434,
   437, 439, 440
Los Angeles Police
   Museum 158. 433
Los Angeles Times xiii,
   151, 251
Loust Family 12
Lukes, Nancy 80
Maier, Shelley 141
McKinley Family 208
Meyers Family 445
Montgomery Family 265
Moss Family 319
Neel Family 340
Pesanti Family 387
Pierce Family 261
Rieth, John 118
Rogers, Tom 63
Severns Family 271, 414
Sheppard Family 378
Sievers Family 11, 446

Full Academy Class Pictures
Lee, Harte, Drees, Pfost

Los Angeles Police Training Class 4-16-37

LOS ANGELES POLICE ACADEMY
CLASS OF MARCH 1941

LOS ANGELES POLICE ACADEMY
SEPT 11 1942

L.A.P.D. CADET CLASS 1-21-55

Los Angeles Police Department
Patrol Divisions Map

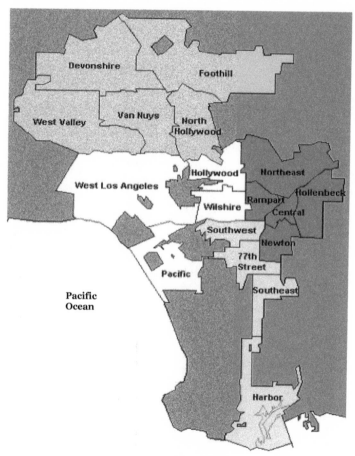

Note: Metropolitan Division deploys city-wide

CPSIA information can be obtained
at www.ICGtesting.com
Printed in the USA
FSHW04n0632260318
46150FS